Sexual Harassment of Working Women

Sexual Harassment of Working Women

A Case of Sex Discrimination

CATHARINE A. MacKINNON

Foreword by THOMAS I. EMERSON

NEW HAVEN AND LONDON, YALE UNIVERSITY PRESS

Designed by Thos. Whitridge and set in VIP Baskerville
type. Printed in the United States of America by The Murray
Printing Company, Westford, Massachusetts.

Library of Congress Cataloging in Publication Data

MacKinnon, Catharine A.

   Sexual harassment of working women.
   Includes index.
   1. Sex discrimination in employment—Law and
legislation—United States.   2. Sex discrimination
against—Law and legislation—United States.   I. Title.
KF3467.M3   344'.73'014   78-9645
ISBN 0-300-02298-0
ISBN 0-300-02299-9 pbk.

     3   4   5   6   7   8   9   10   11   12

Contents

Foreword

Sexual harassment of working women has been one of the most pervasive but carefully ignored features of our national life. As women's liberation makes progress, the facts are beginning to come into the open and the profound implications for our society are beginning to be understood. We have even reached a point where the law may start to do something about the problem. Up to the present time, however, no comprehensive treatment of the social and legal issues has been available.

Catharine MacKinnon's study of sexual harassment in the working place makes a unique contribution at several levels. First of all it provides a skillful analysis of the legal questions which are posed in the emerging effort to use the law to support women who seek to challenge the patterns and practices of sexual harassment. The questions are novel and in many respects complex. Is sexual harassment, when it occurs in connection with operations of government, a violation of the Equal Protection Clause of the Constitution? Is it a "discrimination" in employment because of "sex," forbidden by Title VII of the Civil Rights Act of 1964 and similar legislation? When a woman leaves her job because of sexual harassment, is she quitting for "personal" reasons or is she entitled to unemployment compensation? To what extent is an employer responsible for the actions of his employees who engage in sexual harassment?

The answers given by the courts thus far, in the few cases that have presented these issues, have been hesitant, inconsistent, and ill-informed. By setting the problem in the context of the inferior position of women in the labor market, by providing a full factual account of the nature and extent of sexual harassment, by showing how sexual harassment grows out of and reenforces the traditional social roles of men and women in our society, and by "fitting [this] experience to legal contours," MacKinnon makes a convincing case that sexual harassment does constitute unlawful discrimination within the meaning of the Equal Protection Clause and the relevant statutes. The legal foundations are thus established for a major effort to bring the force of law to bear upon an uncivilized practice that has long been silently sanctioned. How successful a litigation campaign might be is an open question. It could have a substantial impact upon the status of women in the United States.

Second, MacKinnon undertakes to give a new dimension to the Equal Protection Clause. In standard equal protection theory, when a law or official practice treats one category of persons differently from another, the courts examine the difference to determine whether there are adequate reasons for making the distinction. In the case of race classifications, the courts insist that the government demonstrate "compelling" reasons for any difference in treatment and, except for the Japanese detention during World War II, have never found such reasons to exist. In other types of cases the courts are satisfied if any "rational" reason or "substantial" reason can be found. The result has been that, in cases where a difference in treatment is based on sex, the courts have frequently held the different treatment justified. Moreover, in all types of cases, laws and regulations affirmatively designed to overcome the past effects of inequality have run into trouble on the ground that they themselves make invidious distinctions. The outcome has been that in many respects equal protection law, while it has prohibited substantial overt discrimination, has not succeeded in achieving actual equality between the groups involved.

MacKinnon argues that the focus in equal protection law should not be on the "differences," or whether the differences are "arbitrary" rather than "rational," but upon the basic issue of "inequality." In other words the courts should consider whether the treatment by the law results in systematic "disadvantagement" because of group status. Thus, in the area of sex discrimination, the "only question for litigation is whether the policy or practice in question integrally contributes to the maintenance of an underclass or a deprived position because of gender status."

Such an approach deserves serious consideration. It would force the courts to take into account the actual effect of claimed discriminatory laws and practices, rather than find distinctions rational because they reflected existing social conditions that in turn embodied the result of the very discrimination against which protection was sought. Furthermore, it would direct attention to the group nature of the problems of equality in our society. Under our system of law it is the individual who is entitled to relief, but ultimately the disparaties between citizens that the law seeks to eliminate through the Equal Protection Clause are "disadvantagements" as the member of a group. In addition, an "inequality" approach would more readily support the type of affirmative action that, as experience has shown by now, is essential to the achievement of real, as distinct from formal, equality.

There are problems with MacKinnon's view of the legal path to equality between the sexes. The concept of "inequality" or "disadvantagement" must be translated into more specific legal doctrine. And MacKinnon envisages, in part at least, the achievement of a dual system of rights, in which equality for women would not necessarily be measured by the prevailing standards of equality now imposed by the white male. But these may be only challenges to overcome, not necessarily flaws in her conceptual scheme.

On a third level MacKinnon offers us, or at least us males, important information about a dark side of our society, a sensitive insight into the plight of those on the receiving end of sexual harassment, and an eloquent statement of her vision of equality between the sexes. A Supreme Court which can decide that an employment disability plan covering every form of disability except pregnancy does not discriminate against women plainly has need of education on these matters. So do many others. MacKinnon's portrayal in depth of a pernicious social problem, and the light it throws upon the nature of our society, is not the least of the contributions made by this book.

One final word. Although the book is addressed in the first instance to a legal problem, it is not a book for lawyers alone. The law of sex discrimination is not so esoteric that, at least on the ultimate issues, it cannot be understood and appraised by lay persons. More important, in dealing with the legal questions MacKinnon necessarily moves into the economic, social, and political considerations that underlie the legal problem. It quickly becomes, therefore, a book for everyone.

THOMAS I. EMERSON

New Haven, Connecticut

Preface

Many social practices imposed upon women because we are women are not considered by the law to be based on our sex. The political argument around which this book revolves—although not the experiences that ground it—began with this realization. Sexual harassment has been not only legally allowed; it has been legally unthinkable. As I came to analyze it, sexual harassment also appeared neither incidental nor tangential to women's inequality, but a crucial expression of it, a central dynamic in it. Is its centrality to women's condition connected to its legal and social permissibility? In particular, is sex discrimination law as constructed, by inner logic as much as by outer limits, unable to grasp the true dimensions of women's inequality? Does sex discrimination doctrine embody a conception of sexuality, gender, and power that can even begin to touch their fused reality as women experience it? These remain my concerns.

The project began late in 1974. The argument was written by late spring 1975, and the draft circulated. At that point, no court had held that sexual harassment was sex discrimination; several had held that it was not. Since then, some courts have agreed with the analysis presented here. The feeling that the manuscript has been useful, perhaps even pivotal, in litigation establishing sexual harassment as a legal claim and term of art has supported me in the rewriting. These developments have, in turn, provoked changes in the presentation. The original argument of chapter 6, written before there were any precedents on point, relies upon basic principles and cases. Because basic argument is still important, it has been retained, with modifications reflecting the sharpening of some issues through subsequent litigation. I have also added a brief (Appendix B) to help readers professionally involved in this area of the law use the now favorable precedents.

This chronology partly explains the book's sometimes embattled tone. Moreover, we cannot assume the legal gains are durable until the Supreme Court has ruled favorably on the issue—and perhaps not even then. That legal gains will bring real changes in women's lives is even more problematic. A sense of this precludes relaxation and qualifies celebration when legal victories, as important as they can be, are won. It also underlines the social function that a book like this can have, if it is relentless in confronting the unconscious but acted upon conceptions of the powerful with their consequences to the less powerful.

This book aspires to be accessible to all who are interested in its subject. Some parts of the argument are complex, perhaps more so for those not theoretically inclined than for those not legally trained. To speak to both a legal and a general audience requires concessions to each, which requires mutual indulgence. Legal terms and cases are explained more fully than the specialist would require. The extended substantiation of the chapter 5 legal discussion appears as Appendix A. Women become "they." The "I" whose presence seems rather widely thought to undermine the appearance of authoritativeness in legal discourse is usually submerged.

I hope to bring to the law something of the reality of women's lives. The method and evidence chosen for this task deserve comment. To date, there are no "systematic" studies of sexual harassment in the social-scientific sense. So how do I know it exists? Chapter 3 presents evidence from women's observations on their own lives. Something worth knowing, uniquely appropriate to this investigation, and not adequately revealed in other ways can be found in such statements. What do women really feel? When an outrage has been so long repressed, there will be few social codifications for its expression. Depending upon who is asking them and how, victims may initially say (and believe) that they are not victims, so near is the denial to erasure. Women's consciousness erupts through fissures in the socially knowable. Personal statements direct from daily life, in which we say more than we know, may be the primary form in which such experiences exist in social space; at this point they may be their only accessible form. I therefore take immediate reflections on lived-through experience as data.

How valid and generalizable are such data? This issue is particularly important in the sex discrimination context. One woman can bring a legal complaint, but the group-based nature of the *claim* that one's treatment is based on sex requires that the complaint refer to a group-based *experience*. For this purpose, the admittedly selective and necessarily impressionistic evidence from personal life is more than anecdotal or illustrative. Individual experiences of sexual harassment are here seen to derive from a social context: the shared material experience of women as a group, with focus upon the world of work. The testimony of individual women, in this context, represents and substantiates a dimension of the social reality of women as a sex. To take this approach does not mean that the same things must happen (or feel the same) to each and every woman, or happen to each victim in the same way. It does mean that the factors that explain and comprise the experience of sexual harassment characterize all women's situation in one way or another, not only that of direct victims of the practice. It is this level of commonality that makes sexual harassment a women's experience, not merely an experience of a series of individuals who happen to be of the female sex. Ultimately, to me, this is also what makes sexual harassment sex discrimination.

I owe so much to so many. From my teachers—Leo Weinstein, Robert Dahl, and Tom Emerson—I learned more than I will ever know. Few women have been privileged to be supported and defended so they could do their own work. My mother and father have believed in me, cared about me, and worked for the conditions under which I could become the person I wanted to be. My office, friends, and colleagues provided a supportive and critical community and constant point of reference. Many of them responded in detail to earlier drafts. Tom Emerson, Barbara D. Underwood, Anne E. Simon, Kent Harvey, Jennifer Johnson, Seth Kreimer, Nancy Cott, Jack Getman, Karen Sauvigné, Jack Winkler, Gerald Torres, Andrea Dworkin, and Bob Lamm stand out. I did not always take your advice, but I always needed to hear it. Many students taught me, particularly Ann Olivarius, Abbe Smith, Linda Hoaglund, and Valerie Tebbetts. In addition to all their work on the notes, Anne E. Simon and Kent Harvey consulted daily on language and thoughts. They endured and contributed to dry runs of arguments. More, they lived with this project with humor and acerbic glimpses into the sanity all our lives might have without its presence in mine.

My clients shared their pain with me; their lives haunt these pages.

Lawyers and scholars sent me their papers; organizations contributed their files and materials.* The workers at the Yale Law Library, especially Jim Kennealy and Gene Coakley, satisfied far-reaching requests at all hours over a period of years. The Behavioral Science Publication Fund and the Yale University Press generously contributed to expenses. Those I worked with at the Yale Press, especially Marian Ash, wanted to bring out this book, saw its future, and gave it one. Laura Shafer typed the penultimate redraft carefully and beautifully. At times even more than I did, Linda Hoaglund concretely held this book together. Her strength, meticulousness, and dedication sustained me as she typed (over and over) the (ever to be) final version. And I owe more than I can say to Nancy Cott, who lent her vision of my task, her penetration of mind, and the grace of her style at a moment when it made all the difference.

All of you who have been excited about this book made it possible for me to write it. Now I want you to use it, criticize it, and move our work beyond it. Knowing how women feel (rightly, I think) about self-proclaimed authorities on our lives, I hope you will not trap me between these covers and what is made of them. Without women who trust me, I have nothing to say. Perhaps it is unnecessary to add that this book is not directed against any individual. But, given my method, had I not experienced the problem, I would feel I was the wrong person to write about it. Adrienne Rich has warned us against "denying that [our] wounds [come] from the same source as [our] power."†

This book is dedicated to all my sisters who fight back—each in her own way.

---

*Notable here was Working Women United Institute, 593 Park Avenue, New York, N.Y., 10021. The Institute provides resources for women who are sexually harassed, acts as a clearinghouse for information for lawyers and others, presents forums and workshops, and engages in research.

†Adrienne Rich, *The Dream of A Common Language, Poems 1974–1977* (New York: W. W. Norton, 1978), at 3.

1 *Introduction*

Intimate violation of women by men is sufficiently pervasive in American society[1] as to be nearly invisible. Contained by internalized and structural forms of power, it has been nearly inaudible. Conjoined with men's control over women's material survival, as in the home or on the job, or over women's learning and educational advancement in school, it has become institutionalized. Women employed in the paid labor force,[2] typically hired "as women," dependent upon their income and lacking job alternatives, are particularly vulnerable to intimate violation in the form of sexual abuse at work. In addition to being victims of the practice, working women have been subject to the social failure to recognize sexual harassment as an abuse at all. Tacitly, it has been both acceptable and taboo; acceptable for men to do, taboo for women to confront, even to themselves. But the systematic silence enforced by employment sanctions is beginning to be broken. The daily impact upon women's economic status and work opportunities, not to mention psychic health and self-esteem, is beginning to be explored, documented, and, increasingly, resisted.

Sexual harassment, most broadly defined, refers to the unwanted imposition of sexual requirements in the context of a relationship of unequal power. Central to the concept is the use of power derived from one social sphere to lever benefits or impose deprivations in another. The major dynamic is best expressed as the reciprocal enforcement of two inequalities. When one is sexual, the other material, the cumulative sanction is particularly potent. American society legitimizes male sexual dominance of women* and employer's control of workers, although both forms of dominance have limits and exceptions. Sexual harassment of women in employment is particularly

*Evidence for this conclusion is discussed in chapter 6, at 156–58 and 174–82.

clear when male superiors on the job coercively initiate unwanted sexual advances to women employees; sexual pressures by male co-workers and customers, when condoned or encouraged by employers, might also be included. Lack of reciprocal feeling on the woman's part may be expressed by rejection or show of disinclination. After this, the advances may be repeated or intensified; often employment retalia-tion ensues. The material coercion behind the advances may remain implicit in the employer's position to apply it. Or it may be explicitly communicated through, for example, firing for sexual non-compliance or retention conditioned upon continued sexual com-pliance.

Sexual harassment may occur as a single encounter or as a series of incidents at work. It may place a sexual condition upon employment opportunities at a clearly defined threshold, such as hiring, retention, or advancement; or it may occur as a pervasive or continuing condi-tion of the work environment. Extending along a continuum of sever-ity and unwantedness, and depending upon the employment circum-stances, examples include

verbal sexual suggestions or jokes, constant leering or ogling, brushing against your body "accidentally," a friendly pat, squeeze or pinch or arm against you, catching you alone for a quick kiss, the indecent proposition backed by the threat of losing your job, and forced sexual relations.[3]

Complex forms include the persistent innuendo and the continuing threat which is never consummated either sexually or economically. The most straightforward example is "put out or get out."

Typically, employers, husbands, judges, and the victims themselves have understood and dismissed such incidents as trivial, isolated, and "personal," or as universal "natural" or "biological" behaviors. This book interprets sexual harassment in the context of women's work and sex roles, in which women as a group are seen to occupy a struc-turally inferior as well as distinct place. Sexual harassment is argued to derive its meaning and detrimental impact upon women not from personality or biology, but from this *social* context. The defining di-mensions of this social context are employer-employee relations (gi-ven women's position in the labor force) and the relationship between the sexes in American society as a whole, of which sexual relations are one expression.

If sexual harassment is a product of social factors, it might be expected to be a common occurrence. Preliminary indications, although tentative, suggest that it is pervasive, affecting in some form perhaps as many as seven out of ten women at some time in their work lives.[4] Yet sexual harassment of women in employment has provided explicit grounds for legal action in only a handful of cases.[5] Why has so apparently massive a social problem surfaced so seldom within the legal system? The reasons are probably not limited to the lack of legitimized or sympathetic channels for complaint short of the courts, or to women's learned reticence, enforced through fear of reprisals, although these would seem deterrent enough. It is probably not because the problem has been adequately handled socially. That there has not been *even one* reported case until very recently implicates the receptivity of the legal system.

Applicable legal concepts, with the social relations they reify, have tended to turn women's differences from men at once into special virtues and special restraints. In effect, if not intent, the law has conceptualized women workers either in terms of their "humanity," which has meant characteristics women share with men, or in terms of their womanhood, which has meant their uniqueness. These two standards have been mutually exclusive. When women have been defined "as women" their human needs have often been ignored. An example is "protective" laws that, in shielding women's femininity from work stress, often excluded women from desperately needed jobs or job benefits.[6] Alternatively, when women have been analyzed as "human," their particular needs as women have often been ignored. An example is employment insurance plans that cover virtually every work disability (including many unique to men) except pregnancy.[7] In a long-ignored analysis that can be applied to the legal conceptualizations of women both "as human" and "as woman," the sociologist Georg Simmel observed:

Man's position of power does not only assure his relative superiority over the woman, but it assures that his standards become generalized as generically human standards that are to govern the behavior of men and women alike.... Almost all discussions of women deal only with what they are in relation to men in terms of real, ideal, or value criteria. Nobody asks what they are for themselves.[8]

On the whole, the legal doctrine of "sex discrimination" as interpreted by the courts has implicitly used such standards and criteria. In the analysis to follow, legal interpretations that give concrete meaning to the sex discrimination prohibition are reconsidered in their theoretical underpinnings, both for their potential in prohibiting sexual harassment and for their limitations, as the issue of sexual harassment reveals them.

The legal argument advanced by this book is that sexual harassment of women at work is sex discrimination in employment. The argument proceeds first by locating sexual harassment empirically in the context of women's work, showing that the structure of the work world women occupy makes them systematically vulnerable to this form of abuse. Sexual harassment is seen to be one dynamic which reinforces and expresses women's traditional and inferior role in the labor force. Next, reports of sexual harassment are analyzed, with a focus upon the dimensions of the experience as women undergo it. This is followed by an account of those few legal cases that have raised the problem of sexual harassment at work. Once the problem has been defined within its material context and as experienced, and the legal attempts to address it have been initially explored, the central legal question can be confronted: is sexual harassment sex discrimination?

Two distinct concepts of discrimination, which I term the "differences" approach and the "inequality" approach, emerge as approaches to answering this question.[9] These conceptions are not strictly legal doctrines in the sense that judges recognize them as alternative views on the meaning of discrimination. Rather, they are the result of an attempt to think systematically about the broader concepts that underlie the logic and results of the discrimination cases as a whole, with particular attention to discrimination law's most highly developed application: the cases on race. Applied to sex, the two approaches flow from two underlying visions of the reality of sex in American society. The first approach envisions the sexes as socially as well as biologically *different* from one another, but calls impermissible or "arbitrary" those distinctions or classifications that are found preconceived and/or inaccurate. The second approach understands the sexes to be not simply socially differentiated but socially *unequal*. In this broader view, all practices which subordinate women to men are prohibited. The differences approach, in its sensitivity to disparity and similarity, can be a useful corrective to sexism; both women and men can be damaged by sexism, although usually it is women who are.

The inequality approach, by contrast, sees women's situation as a structural problem of enforced inferiority that needs to be radically altered.

The view that discrimination consists in arbitrary differentiation dominates legal doctrine and scholarly thinking on the subject, reaching an epiphany in the Supreme Court's majority opinion in *Gilbert v. General Electric* (1977).[10] General Electric excluded only pregnancy and pregnancy-related disabilities from risks covered under an employee disability insurance plan. Had the case been approached with an awareness of the consequences of pregnancy and motherhood in the social inequality of the sexes, the Court would have found such a rule discriminatory. More narrowly, only women are excluded from insurance coverage against a detriment in employment due to temporary disability, creating unequal employment security on the basis of sex. Taking the differences approach, however, the Court thought that, although all pregnant persons are women, because pregnancy is unique (but not universal) to women, excluding it from coverage was not a distinction "based on sex," hence not discriminatory. Because women actually had *different* disabilities from men, it was not discriminatory to fail to insure them. By contrast, the result (although not every feature of the reasoning) in a 1978 case, *City of Los Angeles v. Manhart*,[11] illustrates the inequality approach. There, the Supreme Court found that requiring women to make larger contributions to their retirement plan was discriminatory, in spite of the proved sex difference that women on the average outlive men. A real difference between the sexes was not allowed to obscure or excuse socially unequal consequences.

Implicit in the distinction in approach are different conceptions of reasonable comparability: must women and men be able to be compared on the variable in question? Further, exactly what the variable in question is defined to be is decided by the approach which is taken. Under the differences approach, if the context is defined so that the sexes cannot be reasonably compared, discrimination cannot be seen to be sex-based. By contrast, the inequality approach comprehends that women and men may, due to sex or sexism, present noncomparabilities. In this view, lack of comparability is not a permissible basis for socially perpetuating women's disadvantages.

In terms of the social context discussed, and under the legal doctrines that context has produced, sexual harassment is argued in this book to be not simply abusive, humiliating, oppressive, and exploitative, but also to be sex discrimination in employment. Specifically, this is argued under Title VII of the Civil Rights Act of 1964, as amended, and the Equal Protection Clause of the Fourteenth Amendment. In relevant part, Title VII states:

a) It shall be an unlawful employment practice for an employer—
   1) to fail or refuse to hire or to discharge any individual, or otherwise to discriminate against any individual with respect to his compensation, terms, conditions, or privileges of employment because of such individual's . . . sex . . .; or
   2) to limit, segregate, or classify his employees or applicants for employment in any way which would deprive or tend to deprive any individual of employment opportunities or otherwise adversely affect his status as an employee, because of such individual's . . . sex.[12]

The Equal Protection Clause of the Fourteenth Amendment to the Constitution guarantees that no state shall "deny to any person within its jurisdiction the equal protection of the laws."[13] Sexual harassment is argued to be sex discrimination under these sections according to both the inequality approach, which is favored, and the differences approach, which is criticized.

Both arguments can be briefly stated. Under the inequality approach, sexual harassment is seen to disadvantage women as a gender, within the social context in which women's sexuality and material survival have been constructed and joined, to women's detriment. Under the differences approach, sexual harassment is sex discrimination *per se* because the practice differentially injures one gender-defined group in a sphere—sexuality in employment—in which the treatment of women and men can be compared. Sexuality is universal to women, but not unique to them. All women possess female sexuality, so the attribute in question is a gender characteristic. But men also possesss sexuality and could be sexually harassed. When they are not, and women are, unequal treatment by gender is shown. If only men are sexually harassed, that is also arbitrary treatment based on sex, hence sex discrimination. If both sexes are, under this argument the treatment would probably not be considered gender-based, hence not sex discriminatory. Thus, sexual harassment of working women is treatment impermissibly based on sex under both approaches.

Sexual harassment is also discrimination in employment. Current cases are analyzed in which courts have found sexual harassment "personal," "biological," "not a policy," and thus (implicitly) not employment discrimination as well as not based on sex. These objections are found uncompelling, mutually inconsistent, without weight in analogous areas of law, and ideologically sexist. Although some of the cases which rely on these formulations have been reversed on appeal, most of these assertions, which represent deep and broadly held social views on women's sexuality, have not been squarely controverted by the courts and continue to arise in litigation. The Supreme Court has yet to hear its first sexual harassment case.

Opposing sexual harassment of women at work through the legal system deserves evaluation from a social standpoint. Sexual harassment is addressed in this book in terms of employment, and women's employment status in terms of sexual harassment, not because work is the only place women are sexually harassed nor because sexual harassment is women's only problem on the job. Legally, women are not arguably entitled, for example, to a marriage free of sexual harassment any more than to one free of rape, nor are women legally guaranteed the freedom to walk down the street or into a court of law without sexual innuendo. In employment, the government promises more.

Work is critical to women's survival and independence. Sexual harassment exemplifies and promotes employment practices which disadvantage women in work (especially occupational segregation) and sexual practices which intimately degrade and objectify women. In this broader perspective, sexual harassment at work undercuts woman's potential for social equality in two interpenetrated ways: by using her employment position to coerce her sexually, while using her sexual position to coerce her economically. Legal recognition that sexual harassment is sex discrimination in employment would help women break the bond between material survival and sexual exploitation. It would support and legitimize women's economic equality and sexual self-determination at a point at which the two are linked.

2 Women's Work

Women work "as women." The American workplace and work force are divided according to gender. Compared with men, women's participation in the paid labor force[1] is characterized by horizontal segregation, vertical stratification, and income inequality.[2] Women tend to be employed in occupations that are considered "for women," to be men's subordinates on the job, and to be paid less than men both on the average and for the same work.

Sexual harassment on the job occurs in this material context and is directly related to it. Horizontal segregation means that most women perform the jobs they do because of their gender, with the element of sexuality pervasively implicit. Women who work at "men's jobs" are exceptions. By virtue of the segregation of most women into women's jobs, such women are residually defined as "tokens." So even women who are exceptional among their sex remain defined on the job according to gender, with sexuality a part of that definition. Vertical stratification means that women tend to be in low-ranking positions, dependent upon the approval and good will of male superordinates for hiring, retention, and advancement. Being at the mercy of male superiors adds direct economic clout to male sexual demands. Low pay is an index to the foregoing two dimensions. It also deprives women of material security and independence which could help make resistance to unreasonable job pressures practical.

This is not to suggest that sexual harassment alone explains these characteristics of women's position in the labor force. But very little is known about the day-to-day processes by which women's disadvantaged work status is attained.[3] This chapter takes the view that the sexual harassment of women can occur largely because women occupy inferior job positions and job roles; at the same time, sexual

9

harassment works to keep women in such positions. Sexual harass-
ent, then, uses and helps create women's structurally inferior status.

HORIZONTAL SEGREGATION

Most working women are employed in jobs which mostly women do:
this is horizontal segregation. In 1960, 47 percent of employed
women worked at occupations in which women comprised 80 percent
or more of the workers; only 2 percent of working women were
employed in occupations in which they represented less than 33 percent of the total workers at that job. Almost 90 percent of employed
men worked at jobs which had fewer than 33 percent women doing
them.[4] By 1970, the picture had changed little: 72.6 percent of all
employed women remained in occupations which were 45–100 percent female.[5] This segregation of women into certain types of jobs
characterizes occupational categories both as a whole and subdivided
by industry and firm. In 1974, 35 percent of working women had
clerical jobs, occupying 77 percent of those jobs; 43 percent of women
workers held service jobs, constituting 58 percent of all service workers.[6]

Women represent 98.5 percent of private household workers (paid)
and 41.7 percent of all sales workers. By contrast, women comprised
4.2 percent of craft and kindred workers, 18.6 percent of managers
and administrators and 15 percent of all farm workers.[7] Thirteen
percent were operatives (factory workers),* and 6.8 percent were sales
workers.[8] Taken together, this means that over 75 percent of working
women are employed in "women's jobs," that is, in job categories
noted for their sex-typing and in workplace settings characterized by
sex segregation. Women who work are typically secretaries, typists,
file clerks, receptionists, waitresses, nurses, bank tellers, telephone
operators, factory workers (especially as dressmakers and seam-
stresses), sales clerks in department stores or cashiers in supermarkets,
kindergarten or elementary school teachers, beauticians or cleaning
women.[9] This distribution of occupations by sex leaves everything

---

*Factory work is not generically women's work, unlike, for example, service or cleri-
cal work. But women who are employed as factory workers are overwhelmingly employed in sex-defined sectors or subsets of factory jobs, such as in small electronics
assembly, garment production, food packaging, and the like.

else—including both blue collar and high-status jobs—for men. In 1970, half of all women workers were employed in seventeen occupations of uniformly low status and pay, while half of all male workers were employed in sixty-three occupations which included a full range of pay and status.[10] In 1973, more than 40 percent of all women workers were employed in ten occupations, while the ten largest male occupations employed less than 20 percent of all working men.[11]

Women's jobs are usually "dull, repetitive, routine or dead-end."[12] So are many men's jobs. The difference is that women are almost universally restricted to a limited range of jobs at the bottom of the socioeconomic spectrum *because of their sex.* The remaining range of employment possibilities is open to men by comparison with other men (not, as a rule, by comparison with women) according to factors *other than sex,* race and class (or its proxy, education) being the most common. To grasp the precise interaction that keeps women defined by sex either in women's work or as token women and men doing everything that is considered either beyond women's capacities or sex-neutral would be to define a major dynamic of the socioeconomic system. But a single equivalence, at least, is clear: women's work is defined as inferior work, and inferior work tends to be defined as work for women.

Moreover, work that is considered inferior is often so defined on the basis of the same standards that define it as suitable for women: low interest or complexity, repetition and tediousness, little potential for self-direction, predominantly service-oriented, high contact with customers, involvement with children, and keeping things clean. These are tasks which men tend to shun unless there is no other job—or woman—around. Some of the most pointed documentation of the correlation of women's work with inferior work is revealed in explanations given for the shift in specific jobs from "men's jobs" to "women's jobs" between 1953 and 1961 in a large New Jersey county. Several typical explanations were:

"[Most] technological changes were of a type that would tend to increase the percent of women. For example, we have broken down the alignment of components and simplified [the] job and as the jobs called for less skill, they became women's work." "In assembly we have one job . . . which was formerly performed by men. We decided that the job was simple enough so that there was no point in continuing to recruit men for it. So we made it a woman's job. We couldn't redesign it; it was already too simple." "We feel that jobs requiring manual dexterity call for women. Also this work is particularly tedious and painstaking—definitely a woman's job."[13]

These observations are supported by studies which, taken together, suggest that as work becomes degraded by mechanization and routinization, it becomes defined as "women's work."[14] Given the qualities of jobs that make them considered women's work, it should be no surprise that many are easily replaced by machines.[15] At the same time, automation sometimes increases the available women's jobs by reducing to an unskilled operative level (for women) tasks that were formerly performed by a skilled worker (a man). This partly explains how women's labor force participation rate can increase while the overall unemployment rate, and the rate for women, also increases.

Another way of documenting the equivalence of women's work with inferior work is dynamically: the pay and status of whole occupations decline over time as women enter them. Clerical work,[16] primary and secondary education, and medicine in the Soviet Union are striking examples. As Andrea Dworkin synthesizes these trends, "when women enter any industry, job or profession in great numbers, the field itself becomes feminized, that is, it acquires the low status of the female."[17]

VERTICAL STRATIFICATION

Differentiation by sex holds as true within occupations as between them: this is vertical stratification. Women are generally men's subordinates on the job, with men in the position to do the hiring, firing, supervising, and promoting of women.

Only about 5 percent of all women workers occupy managerial or administrative jobs, accounting for only about 18 percent of all managers and administrators. As we have seen, women are overwhelmingly in positions that other people manage, supervise, or administer. Even in women's jobs, the managers are men.[18] A large percentage of professional women are teachers or health workers, yet they do not occupy the same proportion of the top positions in these fields.[19] The same is true in the federal civil service, where hierarchy is easy to observe. Compared with men, women are overwhelmingly concentrated in the lower-level civil service grades.[20]

Thus women work as men's workplace inferiors, either at inferior work or at inferior positions in the same work. Sex differentiation on the job need not be expressed in overt segregation, although often it is. Equally disadvantageous can be the gender-integrated situation where women do the same kinds of work as men but systematically occupy an inferior rung on the job ladder, dependent upon and vulnerable to male employers' or supervisors' approval for job security and career advancement. And at a certain point, especially when the prospects for upward mobility are limited, to do a lower-level version of the same job is to do a different job. Where the reason is sex, vertical and horizontal segregation tend to converge.

INCOME INEQUALITY

One particularly telling reflection of the foregoing two dimensions is women's income inequality with men. In 1974, women who worked full time earned 57¢ for every dollar earned by men. In 1976, the median earnings of year-round, full-time workers were only 60 percent of men's.[21] Computed by occupational group, adjusted for age and education, professional and technical women in 1974 made an average of 64 percent of the salaries of their male counterparts, woman nonfarm laborers, 72 percent. On the other end of the scale, female sales personnel made an average of 41 percent of the salary of salesmen. Broken down further, and stated differently, in 1974 the difference between women's and men's salaries was smallest for professional and technical workers and laborers, where women occupy the smallest proportion of the occupational category; the difference was highest in those jobs occupied mostly by women.[22]

This earnings differential was wider in 1974 than in most previous years, and the gap is increasing. In 1955, men's median earnings exceeded women's by an average of 56.4 percent, in 1974, by 74.8 percent.[23] Education does not proportionately improve women's status. In 1974, women with four years of college had lower salaries than men who had completed the eighth grade, and only 59 percent of the income of their male counterparts. This was a lower wage than was earned by fully employed men who did not complete elementary school.[24] Poor women tend to be substantially better educated than equally poor men.[25]

This means that the higher the job status, the more likely a woman is to be paid marginally closer to a man's wage-rate, and the less likely women are to occupy these positions at all, regardless of educational preparation. The more women there are in an occupation, the greater the likelihood that the few men in that profession will be paid dispro- portionately higher wages—and the lower-paid the job category as a whole tends to be when compared with jobs occupied mostly by men. Controlling for differences in education, skills, and experience (fac- tors which themselves could be created by discrimination), studies have found a remaining difference between men's and women's salaries of between 20 and 43 percent, a difference which can be explained only as discrimination.[26] In 1976 the Women's Bureau con- cluded, after discussing the possible contribution of many factors to wage differentials, including concentration in low-paying occupa- tions, working less overtime, differences in education, training and work experience, age, region, and degree of industrial concentration:

These differences between the earnings of men and women suggest that women are being paid less for doing the same job.... Studies have shown ... that even after adjusting for some of these and other factors ... much of the male-female earnings differential remains unexplained—representing a maximum measure of discrimination.[27]

A comparison of sex discrimination with race discrimination—a comparison which will be pursued throughout this discussion— completes the dismal statistical picture of women at work. The law has long based its efforts to alleviate discrimination upon the assumption that racial discrimination is the more critical and widespread and damaging social evil. Yet the President's Task Force on Women's Rights and Responsibilities concluded, "Sex bias takes a greater eco- nomic toll than racial bias."[28] Black women make less than white women, but white women make less, on the average, than black men. Since women's incomes are so low, it would follow that many women would be poor. Poor women outnumbered poor men by more than 4 million in 1975. Data for 1976 indicate that nearly two out of every three poor persons were women.[29] Black women are much more likely to be poor than white women, although poor white women outnumber their black counterparts by nearly two to one.[30] The con- clusion is unquestionable: women, as a definable social group, are disadvantaged in employment.

Nor can working women be ignored as economically unimportant because they are supported by a man. Women work because they need the money. Close to three quarters are either single (23 percent), divorced, widowed or separated (19 percent), or have husbands who earn less than $10,000 a year (29 percent).[31] Many working women are heads of households and the sole support of their families. They cannot typically afford to risk loss of work. In March 1974, approximately 12 percent of all families, or one out of eight, were headed by a woman.[32] In 1976, women headed 14 percent of all families.[33] Families headed by women also tend to be poor, further restricting women's job flexibility. While the labor force participation rate of women household heads is substantially higher (54 percent) than that of all women (45 percent), their income is lower than for families headed by men,[34] and their unemployment rate is higher (6.4 percent) than that for husbands in husband-wife families (2.7 percent).[35] As a result, in 1976, 48 percent of all poor families were headed by women. About one-third of all families headed by women were poor, more than five times the rate for male-headed families.[36]

Contributing to low pay, as well as to vulnerability to employer capriciousness and victimization, is working women's comparative lack of unionization. Unionized women's pay is closer to unionized men's than nonunionized women's pay is to nonunionized men's. But in the United States, women belong to unions far less often than men do, which is another way of saying that women's occupations tend to be less unionized than the rest of the labor force. In 1970, only 10.4 percent of all working women were unionized, compared with 27.8 percent of all working men. Among white collar workers, 7.4 percent of women were in unions, 12.5 percent of men; among blue collar workers, which includes relatively few women, 27.8 percent of women were unionized, compared with 42.1 percent of men. For factory operatives and like workers, 29 percent of women belonged to unions, while 46.2 percent of men did. The disparity is also impressive in service work, where an overwhelming majority of workers are women: in 1970, 5.7 percent of women service workers were unionized, compared with 20.1 percent of men. As with pay rates, the disparity in unionization is greatest in those jobs occupied mostly by women, and by most women.[37]

Taken together, these dimensions describe but do not explain sex segregation, one of the most tenacious rigidities of the labor market. It is clear that the current economic system requires some collection of individuals to occupy low-status, low-paying jobs; it is unclear whether there is any economically determinate reason why such persons must be biologically female. The fact that male employers often do not hire qualified women, even when they could pay them less than men, suggests that more than the profit motive is implicated.[38] Various reasons have been suggested for such unusual behavior by allegedly profit-maximizing businesses. One view is that money losses are overruled by psychological gains: "It feels so good to have women in their 'place.'"[39] Another view is that men *see* women as less profitable even when they are paid less: "Sex role stereotypes pervasive in our culture may lead employers to believe that women would be such inefficient workers in traditionally male jobs that they would not be worth hiring, even at low wages."[40]

Still another view is that capitalists as a whole "profit from discrimination and few if any individual capitalists lose money in the process, while many gain; . . . probably none see themselves as losing money from it."[41] The reason is the structure of monopoly in industry. The mostly highly monopolized industries, less affected by competition, can afford to sex-segregate jobs (that is, pay men more to do the work) because they pass on higher wages to consumers. The most competitive, less profitable industries almost universally employ exclusively female workers.[42] A contributing explanation might be that few men apply for women's jobs because they have options to these low-paying, dead-end positions, which, moreover, affront their manhood, while few women apply for men's jobs because they believe (with reason) they will not be hired. The employer may seldom be presented with two persons of different sexes for the same job, that is, with an opportunity to discriminate.[43] The contextual aspects of women's work that an examination of sexual harassment highlights may also contribute to explaining sex segregation. A defining element of women's jobs may be the subtle or blatant sexual prerogative afforded the (almost universally) male employer by having women employees perform certain jobs.

A good deal more has been written which documents the characteristics of women's work beyond its predominantly mindless, regimented, "service with a smile" segregation, coupled with low pay. Women can also expect to encounter discrimination in benefits, layoff policies that accentuate their status as a reserve labor pool, conflicts between workplace and home demands, and other frustrations, in-

dignities, and inequities. Sexual harassment may contribute to an undetermined extent to many aspects of women's employment experience, including absenteeism, turnover, productivity rates and work
motivation, job dissatisfaction, and unemployment. Whether or not
these rates differ by sex, the factors contributing to the women's rates
should be scrutinized. All these factors converge upon the central
characteristic of women's work, which is that it is just that: work defined according to their sex.

Segregation is more or less accepted as a dirty word when applied to
separation on the basis of race. (Imagine "black people's work" as a
classification.) But there seems to be a social sense that it is somehow
appropriate, or at least not without some just foundation, to divide
labor according to sex. The difference in the social attitudes involved
can be revealed by considering a hypothetical example: "How should
a court treat a school principal's decision, based solely on aesthetics, to
have black and white students sit on opposite sides of the stage at the
graduation ceremony?"[44] Professor Owen Fiss, discussing this example, has "little doubt" that this "unlikely" practice would violate equal
protection of the laws.[45]

But consider the everyday reality behind the statistics of women at
work: the linoleum and fluorescent undivided typing pool of thirty
women, typewriters clacking, ringed by a series of carpeted, wood-
paneled offices with closed doors, behind each of which sits one man.
Consider further a noisy shop floor full of whirring sewing machines
with a woman behind each one. Walking up and down behind the
women is a man, giving selective permission to go to the bathroom,
seeing who tries to talk to her neighbor, who is slowing the pace—
supervising.

Now reconsider the high school graduation, this time with the girls
on one side of the stage and the boys on the other, a common cere-
monial arrangement. Is this distinction between the sexes more de-
fensible as "aesthetic" than the distinction between differently colored
races? Would motive for separation be evaluated by different standards? Would any employer seriously defend race-based hiring on
the grounds that black skin "just looks better" in his white busboy
uniforms? But how many thousands of employers hire women for
their "aesthetic" appeal? To unpack these "aesthetics" further, are
those sex-exclusive hiring practices discriminatory in which male employers find women behind typewriters "prettier to look at" than

men? Directly to the point of our investigation, does this mean that being looked at (for a start) by the boss (male) is part of why many women are hired?

Sex-Defined Work

The feminization of whole sectors of the labor force is well documented.[46] Not recognized is that this gender-definition includes sexualization of the woman worker as a part of the job. Until it is changed, this makes sexual harassment systemically inevitable for the masses of women who must take the only jobs society opens to them. Women are secretaries (99 percent female), domestics (98 percent), nurses (98 percent), typists (97 percent), telephone operators (96 percent), child care workers (98 percent), and waitresses.[47] In such jobs a woman is employed as a woman. She is also, apparently, treated like a woman, with one aspect of this being the explicitly sexual. Specifically, if part of the reason the woman is hired is to be pleasing to a male boss, whose notion of a qualified worker merges with a sexist notion of the proper role of women, it is hardly surprising that sexual intimacy, forced when necessary, would be considered part of her duties and his privileges.

It is commonly observed that women's employment outside the home tends to monetize the roles and tasks women traditionally perform for men in the home. Concerning service work roles, overwhelmingly occupied by women, Talcott Parsons noted: "Within the occupational organization, they are analogous to the wife-mother role in the family."[48] Work relationships parallel traditional home relationships between husband and wife.

Women have jobs in which they are personal servants to individual men. The secretary is the standard example, although receptionists, nurses and research assistants all come into this category. The functions women perform are wife-like functions, such as ego-building, the housekeeping (tidying up, answering the phone, getting coffee), and the function of being a sex object.[49]

The secretary role is particularly clear. Thorstein Veblen's description of the role of wife converges with modern descriptions of the secretary and receptionist:

The servant or wife should not only perform certain offices and show a servile disposition, but it is quite as imperative that they should show an acquired facility in the tactics of subservience—a trained conformity to the canon of effectual and conspicuous subservience. Even today, *it is this aptitude and acquired skill in the formal manifestations of the servile relation that constitutes the chief element of utility in our highly paid servants, as well as one of the chief ornaments of the well-bred housewife.* . . . It is of course sufficiently plain, to anyone who cares to see, that our bearing toward menials and other pecuniarily dependent inferiors is the bearing of the superior member in a relationship.[50] (emphasis mine)

Compare a contemporary description of the secretary:

The private secretary must master all the small gestures that make her appear submissive, and yet "professional," and must present a classy image by careful behavior and a careful selection of clothing and make-up.[51]

A study of male managers' attitudes toward working women in 1971 found that the most important attitude of women toward men on the job was "deference."[52]

In a major study of workplace relations between the sexes, Rosabeth Kanter characterizes the major outlines of the secretary's job as patrimonial: based upon personal fealty, its tasks defined by individual whim, and lacking a rationalized task definition or clear criteria for advancement. She summarizes her analysis as follows:

When bosses make demands at their own discretion and arbitrarily; choose secretaries on grounds that enhance their own personal status rather than meeting organizational efficiency tests; expect personal service with limits negotiated privately; exact loyalty; and make the secretary a part of their private retinue, moving when they move—then the relationship has elements of patrimony.[53]

Agreeing with the "office wife" parallel, Kanter found that the secretary is valued by management, after her "initiative and enthusiasm," for her "ability to anticipate and take care of personal needs." She also observes, without elaborating, that "bosses had enormous personal latitude around secretaries."[54]

One need not be a secretary or hold a "woman's job" to be sexually defined on the job. Kanter describes the "seductress" stereotype as one of the few available images for the token woman in a male-defined occupation. Although this role is a perception, independent of the woman's actual behavior, "her perceived sexuality blotted out all other characteristics."[55] Other observers have come as close to recognizing sexual harassment without quite seeing it as such.

Is bringing coffee to your boss and chatting with him about his marital problems secretarial work or is it a personal favor? Is the fact that we have to worry
about our looks on the job a condition of work or is it the result of female
vanity?[56]

[The job includes a concern] not only with business work, but with her boss's
social appointments outside the office hours, and with his family (remember-
ing birthdays, covering up sexual affairs, booking vacations, etc.). She will also
serve as a "whipping boy"—someone a man can vent his anger and frustrations on, or demand a smile depending on his mood.[57]

Union organizers have long observed the private secretary's loyalty
as an obstacle to unionization. The context of sexual harassment, once
it is understood as such, becomes visible if the situation is scrutinized
with it consciously in mind:

Often, her boss or one of his colleagues keeps her further hooked into the
management frame of reference by insinuating that he actually might be
interested in her socially, as a girl friend or even as a wife. It doesn't matter if
he is already married.[58]

Or, more bluntly:

Male employers often use sex to control women and maintain their authority
at the work place. This divides the work force and makes it very difficult to
organize.[59]

The sexualization of women on the job is often seen as much more
an attitude or a feeling than a mode of behavior or an institutional
practice. Kanter, for example, reports that "several saleswomen at
[the company] felt, rightly or wrongly, that they were targets of the
sexual fantasies of male peers."[60] In describing male attitudes toward
secretaries as "substitute wives," Mary Kathleen Benet notes a pervasive sexualization but pursues it only as far as thoughts:

The first thing that comes to many a man's mind when he thinks about
secretaries is sex. . . . Men in offices speculate endlessly about the girls, comparing them, picking favorites, teasing them. In fact, most office men will tell
you that's why the girls are there. The sexual roles that women play in "real
life" have been transferred to the office . . . all this reflects the fact that
women are still thought of first as sexual beings, not as workers. No amount
of work on their part seems to dispel this assumption. No wonder, for it has
been embedded in our thinking.[61]

Yet one telephone company psychologist's advice to an "uppity" operator openly purveys the parallel of boss to husband as a standard for success:

"You should sell yourself," Mr. Beauflax smiled and said, "You should sell yourself, your work, your appearance, to the men. Some secretaries get ahead by dressing older and fixing their hair for their bosses." He said that clothes show if you're a "mature young lady" or not. "Some girls," he really said this, "please their bosses before their husbands."[62]

Accordingly, to enhance their graduates' employability, secretarial schools propose to make them into "a pretty package."[63] Why has it been so unthinkable, so carefully skirted, that such attitudes would be *acted upon,* that, to continue the metaphor, packages are meant to be unwrapped by the purchaser?

In these discussions of women's and men's workplace roles—in "the function of being a sex object," the "submissive gestures" required, "covering up sexual affairs," the injunction to "please their boss before their husbands," the "perceived sexuality," and the "enormous personal latitude" bosses have around their "pretty packages,"—sexuality remains subliminal. When gender—women and men—is discussed, sexuality per se is left to be inferred. Symmetrically, when sexuality is discussed, gender tends to be glossed over, as if sexuality means the same thing for women as it does for men. Such an assumption of gender symmetry underlies Herbert Marcuse's analysis of one expression of advanced industrial civilization, the freeing of sexual energy for its own frustration.

Without ceasing to be an instrument of labor, the body is allowed to exhibit its sexual features in the everyday work world and in work relations. . . . The sexy office and sales girls, the handsome, virile junior executive and floor worker are highly marketable commodities, and the possession of suitable mistresses . . . facilitates the career of even the less exalted ranks in the business community. . . . Sex is integrated into work and public relations and is thus made more susceptible to (controlled) satisfaction.[64]

By analyzing women's and men's participation in this dynamic as equal—if equally unfree—Marcuse diminishes the key fact underlying sexual harassment: women are required to market sexual attractiveness to men, who tend to hold the economic power and position to enforce their predilections. From a very different theoretical perspec-

tive, David Riesman makes a comparable observation and equaliza-
tion. As work becomes less interesting and demanding, "as job
mindlessness declines, sex permeates the daytime as well as the
playtime consciousness," so that sex becomes viewed as "a consump-
tion good" on the job.[65] Like Marcuse, Riesman misses the fact that
purported developments such as a "leisure mentality" do not fall
upon women and men equally. Rather, it is men who "consume"
women's sexuality on the job, and women who must accommodate
this fact as part of their *work*.

That the economic impact of sexuality differs by gender often becomes very clear to the women involved, even from the first job interview.

He then looked at my legs again and looked up and gave me a very big
paternalistic smile. "We usually don't hire married girls," he said. "We like to
have young, pretty and available girls around the office. You know," he
added, "it cheers things up a lot."[66]

The accumulation of observations such as these suggests that, for
women, "attractiveness"—meaning an ingratiating, flattering, and
deferential manner which projects potential sexual compliance—has
economic consequences. Whether or not the woman is ever overtly
harassed, the stage for sexual harassment is set. The impact upon
women's income of projected "desirability" is affirmed by women's
experience: "Waitresses are placed according to their racial and sexual 'desirability,' and where you are placed determines the amount of
money you can make."[67] As another woman obliquely put it, "Not
being attractive enough does have an economic effect. . . . You know
you can't get really well-paying jobs. If you ever go to the top floor of
an office building, you know the women look a certain way."[68] Stating
it directly, still another woman spoke of her succession of male
superiors treating her "not as a working person dependent on an
income, but as a woman, being measured against some sexual standard."[69]

In order to meet this standard, women are taught to telegraph
receptivity and to respond supportively to male sexual overtures, no
matter how they may feel about the man. It is this that makes a woman
"sexy" in the stereotypical sense. It is this that is often, in effect, a job
qualification, just as a deferential, flattering manner to whites was
once required of blacks of both sexes.[70] These observations suggest

that women tend to be economically valued according to men's perceptions of their potential to be sexually harassed. They are, in effect, required to "ask for it."

The point is not that employers prefer good-looking employees, men or women. The point is that it is the very qualities which men find sexually attractive in the women they harass that are the real qualifications for the jobs for which they hire them. Women know this. They know that the appearance an employer finds gratifying, that image which is much of what he is really paying her for, is, in substance, that "nice" provocativeness that she drops at her economic risk. It is this good-girl sexiness (in the case of black women, well-contained, bad-girl sexiness) that qualifies a woman for her job that leaves her open to sexual harassment at any time and to the accusation that she invited it. Ntozake Shange's lines mean as much for women in the workplace as in the street, where being "nice" is both a requirement for survival and a sexual invitation:

> nice is such a rip-off
> reglar beauty and a smile in the street
> is just a set-up[71]

3   *Sexual Harassment: The Experience*

Most women wish to choose whether, when, where, and with whom to have sexual relationships, as one important part of exercising control over their lives. Sexual harassment denies this choice in the process of denying the opportunity to study or work without being subjected to sexual exactions. Objection to sexual harassment at work is not a neopuritan moral protest against signs of attraction, displays of affection, compliments, flirtation, or touching on the job. Instead, women

are rattled and often angry about sex that is one-sided, unwelcome or comes with strings attached. When it's something a woman wants to turn off but can't (a co-worker or supervisor who refuses to stop) or when it's coming from someone with the economic power to hire or fire, help or hinder, reward or punish (an employer or client who mustn't be offended)—that's when [women] say it's a problem.[1]

Women who protest sexual harassment at work are resisting economically enforced sexual exploitation.

This chapter analyzes sexual harassment as women report experiencing it.[2] The analysis is necessarily preliminary and exploratory. These events have seldom been noticed, much less studied; they have almost never been studied *as* sexual harassment.[3] Although the available material is limited, it covers a considerably broader range of incidents than courts will (predictably) consider to be sex discrimination. Each incident or facet of the problem mentioned here will not have equal *legal* weight or go to the same legal issue; not every instance or aspect of undesired sexual attention on the job is necessarily part of the legal cause of action. Some dimensions of the problem seem to contra-indicate legal action or to require determinations that courts are ill suited to make. The broader contextual approach is taken to avoid prematurely making women's experience of sexual harassment into a case of sex discrimination, no more and no less. For it is, at times, both more and less.

I envision a two-way process of interaction between the relevant legal concepts and women's experience. The strictures of the concept of sex discrimination will ultimately constrain those aspects of women's oppression that will be legally recognized as discriminatory. At the same time, women's experiences, expressed in their own way, can push to expand that concept. Such an approach not only enriches the law. It begins to shape it so that what *really* happens to women, not some male vision of what happens to women, is at the core of the legal prohibition. Women's lived-through experience, in as whole and truthful a fashion as can be approximated at this point, should begin to provide the starting point and context out of which is constructed the narrower forms of abuse that will be made illegal on their behalf. Now that a few women have the tools to address the legal system on its own terms, the law can begin to address women's experience on women's own terms.[4]

Although the precise extent and contours of sexual harassment await further and more exacting investigation, preliminary research indicates that the problem is extremely widespread. Certainly it is more common than almost anyone thought. In the pioneering survey by Working Women United Institute,[5] out of a sample of 55 food service workers and 100 women who attended a meeting on sexual harassment, from five to seven of every ten women reported experiencing sexual harassment in some form at some time in their work lives. Ninety-two percent of the total sample thought it a serious problem. In a study of all women employed at the United Nations, 49 percent said that sexual pressure currently existed on their jobs.[6] During the first eight months of 1976, the Division of Human Rights of the State of New York received approximately 45 complaints from women alleging sexual harassment on the job.[7] Of 9,000 women who responded voluntarily to a questionnaire in *Redbook Magazine,* "How do you handle sex on the job?" nine out of ten reported experiences of sexual harassment. Of course, those who experience the problem may be most likely to respond. Nevertheless, before this survey, it would have been difficult to convince a person of ordinary skepticism that 8,100 American women existed who would report experiencing sexual harassment at work.

Using the *Redbook* questionnaire, a naval officer found 81 percent of a sample of women on a navy base and in a nearby town reported employment-related sexual harassment in some form.[8] These frequency figures must, of course, be cautiously regarded. But even extrapolating conservatively, given that nine out of ten American women work outside the home some time in their lives[9] and that in April 1974, 45 percent of American women sixteen and over, or 35 million women, were employed in the labor force,[10] it is clear that a lot of women are potentially affected. As the problem begins to appear structural rather than individual, *Redbook*'s conclusion that "the problem is not epidemic; it is pandemic—an everyday, everywhere occurrence"[11] does not seem incredible.

One need not show that sexual harassment is commonplace in order to argue that it is severe for those afflicted, or even that it is sex discrimination. However, if one shows that sexual harassment in employment systematically occurs between the persons and under the conditions that an analysis of it as discrimination suggests—that is, as a function of sex as gender—one undercuts the view that it occurs because of some unique chemistry between particular (or aberrant) individuals. That sexual harassment does occur to a large and diverse population of women supports an analysis that it occurs *because* of their group characteristic, that is, sex. Such a showing supports an analysis of the abuse as structural, and as such, worth legal attention as sex discrimination, not just as unfairness between two individuals, which might better be approached through private law.

If the problem is so common, one might ask why it has not been commonly analyzed or protested. Lack of public information, social awareness, and formal data probably reflects less its exceptionality than its specific pathology. Sexual subjects are generally sensitive and considered private; women feel embarrassed, demeaned, and intimidated by these incidents.[12] They feel afraid, despairing, utterly alone, and complicit. This is not the sort of experience one discusses readily. Even more to the point, sexual advances are often accompanied by threats of retaliation if exposed. Revealing these pressures enough to protest them thus risks the very employment consequences which sanctioned the advances in the first place.

It is not surprising either that women would not complain of an experience for which there has been no name. Until 1976,[13] lacking a term to express it, sexual harassment was literally unspeakable, which made a generalized, shared, and social definition of it inaccessible.

The unnamed should not be mistaken for the nonexistent. Silence often speaks of pain and degradation so thorough that the situation cannot be conceived as other than it is:

When the conception of change is beyond the limits of the possible, there are no words to articulate discontent, so it is sometimes held not to exist. This mistaken belief arises because we can only grasp silence in the moment in which it is breaking. The sound of silence breaking makes us understand what we could not hear before. But the fact we could not hear does not prove that no pain existed.[14]

As Adrienne Rich has said of this kind of silence, "Do not mistake it/for any kind of absence."[15] Until very recently issues analogous to sexual harassment, such as abortion, rape, and wife beating existed at the level of an open secret in public consciousness, supporting the (equally untrue) inference that these events were infrequent as well as shameful, and branding the victim with the stigma of deviance. In light of these factors, more worth explaining is the emergence of women's ability to break the silence.

Victimization by the practice of sexual harassment, so far as is currently known, occurs across the lines of age, marital status, physical appearance, race, class, occupation, pay range, and any other factor that distinguishes women from each other.[16] Frequency and type of incident may vary with specific vulnerabilities of the woman, or qualities of the job, employer, situation, or workplace, to an extent so far undetermined. To this point, the common denominator is that the perpetrators tend to be men, the victims women. Most of the perpetrators are employment superiors, although some are co-workers or clients. Of the 155 women in the Working Women United Institute sample, 40 percent were harassed by a male superior, 22 percent by a co-worker, 29 percent by a client, customer, or person who had no direct working relationship with them; 1 percent (N = 1) were harassed by a subordinate and 8 percent by "other."[17]

As to age and marital status, *Redbook* finds the most common story is of a woman in her twenties fending off a boss in his sixties, someone she would never choose as a sexual partner. The majority of women who responded to the survey, in which 92 percent reported incidents of sexual harassment, were in their twenties or thirties, and married. Adultery seems no deterrent. However, many women were single or formerly married and ranged in age from their teens to their sixties. In the Working Women United Institute speak-out, one woman mentioned an incident that occurred when she was working as a child model at age ten; another reported an experience at age 55.[18] The women in that sample ranged in age from 19 to 61. On further investigation, sexual harassment as a system may be found to affect women differentially by age, although it damages women regardless of age. That is, many older women may be excluded from jobs because they are considered unattractive sex objects, in order that younger women can be hired to be so treated. But many women preface their reports of sexual harassment with evaluations of their appearance such as, "I am fat and forty, but . . ."[19]

Sexual harassment takes both verbal and physical forms. In the Working Women United Institute sample, approximately a third of those who reported sexual harassment reported physical forms, nearly two-thirds verbal forms.[20] Verbal sexual harassment can include anything from passing but persistent comments on a woman's body or body parts to the experience of an eighteen-year-old file clerk whose boss regularly called her in to his office "to tell me the intimate details of his marriage and to ask what I thought about different sexual positions."[21] Pornography is sometimes used.[22] Physical forms range from repeated collisions that leave the impression of "accident" to outright rape. One woman reported unmistakable sexual molestation which fell between these extremes: "My boss . . . runs his hand up my leg or blouse. He hugs me to him and then tells me that he is 'just naturally affectionate.' "[23]

There is some suggestion in the data that working class women encounter physical as well as verbal forms of sexual harassment more often than middle class and/or professional women, who more often encounter only the verbal forms.[24] However, women's class status in the strict sense is often ambiguous. Is a secretary for a fancy law firm in a different class from a secretary for a struggling, small business? Is a nurse married to a doctor "working class" or "middle class" on her job? Is a lesbian factory worker from an advantaged background with a rich ex-husband who refuses to help support the children because of her sexual preference "upper class"? In any case, most women who responded to the *Redbook* survey, like most employed women, were working at white collar jobs earning between $5,000 and $10,000 a year. Many more were blue collar, professional, or managerial workers earning less than $5,000 or more than $25,000 a year. They report harassment by men independent of the class of those men.

The Working Women United Institute sample, in which approxi-

mately 70 percent reported incidents of sexual harassment, presented
a strikingly typical profile of women's employment history. Almost all
of the women had done office work of some kind in their work life. A
quarter had done sales, a quarter had been teachers, a third file
clerks, 42 percent had been either secretaries or receptionists, and 29
percent had done factory work. Currently, fifty-five were food service
workers with the remainder scattered among a variety of occupations.
The average income was $101–$125 per week. This is very close to, or
a little below, the usual weekly earnings of most working women.[25]

Race is an important variable in sexual harassment in several different senses. Black women's reports of sexual harassment by white
male superiors reflect a sense of impunity that resounds of slavery
and colonization. Maxine Munford,* recently separated and with two
children to support, claimed that on the first day at her new job she
was asked by her employer "if she would make love to a white man,
and if she would slap his face if he made a pass at her." She repeatedly
refused such advances and was soon fired, the employer alleging she
had inadequate knowledge and training for the job and lacked qualifications. His last statement before she left was: "If you would have
intercourse with me seven days a week I might give you your job
back."[26] Apparently, sexual harassment can be both a sexist way to
express racism and a racist way to express sexism. However, black
women also report sexual harassment by black men and white women
complain of sexual harassment by black male superiors and co-
workers. One complaint for slander and outrageous conduct accused
the defendants of making statements including the following:

warning customers about plaintiff's alleged desire to "get in his pants," pointing out that plaintiff had large breasts, stating "Anything over a handful is
wasted," calling plaintiff "Momma Fuller" and "Big Momma," referring to
her breasts, "Doesn't she have nice (or large) breasts?" "Watch out, she's very
horny. She hasn't gotten any lately" "Have you ever seen a black man's
penis?" "Do you know how large a black man's penis is?" "Have you ever slept
with a black man?" "Do you want to stop the car and screw in the middle of
the street?"[27]

One might consider whether white women more readily perceive
themselves as *sexually* degraded, or anticipate a supportive response

---

*Her lawsuit, *Munford v. James T. Barnes & Co.*, 441 F. Supp. 459 (E.D. Mich. 1977), is
discussed in chapter 4, *infra*, at 73 ff.

when they complain, when they are sexually harassed by a black man than by a white man. Alternatively, some white women confide that they have consciously resisted reporting severe sexual harassment by black men to authorities because they feel the response would be supportive for racist reasons. Although racism is deeply involved in sexual harassment, the element common to these incidents is that the perpetrators are male, the victims female. Few women are in a position to harass men sexually, since they do not control men's employment destinies at work,[28] and female sexual initiative is culturally repressed in this society.[29]

As these experiences suggest, the specific injury of sexual harassment arises from the nexus between a sexual demand and the workplace. Anatomized, the situations can be seen to include a sexual incident or advance, some form of compliance or rejection, and some employment consequence. Sometimes these elements are telescoped, sometimes greatly attenuated, sometimes absent. All are variable: the type of incident or advance, the form of response, and the kind and degree of damage attributable to it.

The critical issues in assessing sexual harassment as a legal cause of action—the issues that need to be explored in light of women's experiences—center upon the definition of and the relationship among three events: the advance, the response, and the employment consequence. Critical questions arise in conceptualizing all three. Where is the line between a sexual advance and a friendly gesture? How actively must the issue be forced? If a woman complies, should the legal consequences be different than if she refuses? Given the attendant risks, how explicitly must a woman reject? Might quitting be treated the same as firing under certain circumstances? To get legal relief, must a job benefit be shown to be merited independent of a sexual bargain, or is the situation an injury in itself? When a perpetrator insists that a series of touchings were not meant to be sexual, but the victim experienced them as unambiguously sexual, assuming both are equally credible, whose interpretation controls when the victim's employment status is damaged? These issues will be explored here in the context of women's experiences; suggestions for their legal treatment will be made in chapter 6. In addressing these questions, it is important to divide matters of persuasion from issues of fact, and both of these from issues which go to the core of the legal concept of the discrimination. The first distinguishes the good from the less good case; the second sets a standard of proof; the third draws a line between a legal claim and no claim at all.

Women's experiences of sexual harassment can be divided into two forms which merge at the edges and in the world. The first I term the *quid pro quo,* in which sexual compliance is exchanged, or proposed to be exchanged, for an employment opportunity. The second arises when sexual harassment is a persistent *condition of work.* This distinction highlights different facets of the problem as women live through it and suggests slightly different legal requirements. In both types, the sexual demand is often but an extension of a gender-defined work role. The victim is employed, hence treated, "as a woman." In the quid pro quo, the woman must comply sexually or forfeit an employment opportunity. The quid pro quo arises most powerfully within the context of horizontal segregation, in which women are employed in feminized jobs, such as office work, as a part of jobs vertically stratified by sex, with men holding the power to hire and fire women. In a job which is defined according to gender, noncompliance with all of the job's requirements, which may at the boss's whim come to include sexual tolerance or activity, operatively "disqualifies" a woman for the job. In sexual harassment as a condition of work, the exchange of sex for employment opportunities is less direct. The major question is whether the *advances themselves* constitute an injury in employment.

Quid Pro Quo

This category is defined by the more or less explicit exchange: the woman must comply sexually or forfeit an employment benefit. The exchange can be anything but subtle, although its expression can be euphemistic: "If I wasn't going to sleep with him, I wasn't going to get my promotion";[30] "I think he meant that I had a job if I played along";[31] "You've got to make love to get a day off or to get a good beat";[32] "[Her] foreman told her that if she wanted the job she would have to be 'nice'";[33] "I was fired because I refused to give at the office."[34]

Assuming there has been an unwanted sexual advance, a resulting quid pro quo can take one of three possible shapes. In situation one, the woman declines the advance and forfeits an employment opportunity. If the connections are shown, this raises the clearest pattern: sexual advance, noncompliance, employment retaliation. In situation two, the woman complies and does not receive a job benefit. This is complex: was the job benefit denied independently of the sexual involvement? Is employment-coerced sex an injury in itself or does compliance mean consent? Should the woman in effect forfeit the job opportunity as relief *because* she complied sexually? In situation three, the woman complies and receives a job benefit. Does she have an injury to complain of? Do her competitors? In a fourth logical possibility, which does not require further discussion, the woman refuses to comply, receives completely fair treatment on the job, and is never harassed again (and is, no doubt, immensely relieved). In this one turn of events, there truly is "no harm in asking."[35]

In situation one, the injurious nexus is between the imposition of the sexual requirement and the employment retaliation following upon its rejection. To date, all of the legally successful suits for sexual harassment* have alleged some form of the trilogy of unwanted advances, rejection, retaliation. In Adrienne Tomkins's case** the advances occurred over a lunch that was to include a discussion of her upcoming promotion. She refused to comply, was threatened, demoted, and eventually terminated.[36] In the case of Paulette Barnes,† her supervisor repeatedly insisted that she engage in social and sexual activity with him. When she refused, he took away her duties and eventually abolished her position. A witness in Barnes's case described a classic situation of this type in her own experience with the same man:

Q. Did you ever have any problems working under Mr. Z?
The Witness: Well, the problem started when I took a trip to Puerto Rico with Mr. Z in February of 1971. When we got back he took all of my secretarial duties and gave them to E⎯⎯ M⎯⎯, who was white. Something happened in Puerto Rico, and he used to write me nasty little notes and things like that.
By Miss Barnes:‡
Q. Could you tell us exactly what happened in Puerto Rico or is this confidential information?

---

*These cases are discussed in detail in chapter 4.

**Her lawsuit is reported as *Tomkins v. Public Service Electric & Gas Co.*, 422 F. Supp. 553 (D. N. J. 1977) reversed on appeal, 568 F.2d 1044 (3rd Cir. 1977), discussed in chapter 4, *infra*, at 69–72.

†Her lawsuit is reported as *Barnes v. Costle*, 561 F.2d 983 (D.C. Cir. 1977), discussed in chapter 4, *infra*, at 65–68.

‡Ms. Barnes was not represented by counsel at this point in the proceedings.

A. Well, when we went to Puerto Rico, I was going there as his secretary to take notes on the conferences. . . . When we got there he was supposed to make hotel reservations. He took that out of my hands and when we got there he didn't do it. We waited around until 10:00 or 11:00 that night to get a hotel.

When we got there we went upstairs and put our bags in the room. His bags were in the room, so, he said he had to go and take someone to another hotel, and he would be back to get his things.

When he came back he started undressing, and I told him that he could not stay in the same room with me. He asked me why, and I said—

Mr. H_____: (attorney for Mr. Z) I think we get the picture.

Appeals Examiner: There was a dispute over room accommodations. Is this one of the problems?

The Witness: Right.

Appeals Examiner: You came back and then what happened?

The Witness: He started writing me nasty little notes telling me he no longer wanted me to work for him. He started giving all of his duties to E_____ instead of me, and he even asked me to quit working for him because of what happened.[37]

This structure was also presented in *Alexander v. Yale,* a case complaining of sexual harassment in education. A student who refused a professor's advances allegedly received a low grade in a course.[38] In a related situation, a woman who declined to "join [her employer] in his bed" while on a business trip was reminded at lunch the next day that she was soon to be reviewed for reappointment, that her chances depended largely upon his support and recommendation, and that she would be well served if she "linked both her professional work and her personal life more closely to his own needs." She did not do so. Subsequently she was not renewed, a decision in which his lack of support and negative recommendation were instrumental. He stated publicly that in his decision he regretfully recognized the fact that they had not been able to establish "a closer personal relationship." Women commonly report such a man's insistence that a sexual relationship is essential to their working relationship[39] and that without it the women cannot maintain their jobs.

Some employers use job sanctions to promote the sexual harassment of their female employees by male customers or clients, as well as to assure their own sexual access, and to punish the noncompliant:

June, a waitress in Arkansas, was serving a customer when he reached up her skirt. When she asked her manager for future protection against such incidents, she was harassed by him instead. "They put me on probation," she recalled, "as if I was the guilty one. Then things went from bad to worse. I got lousy tables and bad hours."[40]

In each case, following the woman's refusal, the man retaliated through use of his power over her job or career. Retaliation comes in many forms. The woman may be threatened with demotions and salary cuts; unfavorable material may be solicited and put in her personal file; or she may be placed on disciplinary layoff.[41] In one case, a sexually disappointed foreman first cut back the woman's hours, then put her on a lower-paying machine. When she requested extra work to make up the difference, he put her to sweeping floors and cleaning bathrooms. He degraded and ridiculed her constantly, interfered with her work so it was impossible for her to maintain production, and fired her at two o'clock one morning.[42] In another case, failing to extract sexual favors, the supervisor belittled the woman, stripped her of her job duties, and then abolished her job.[43] In another, a supervisor, following rejection of his elaborate sexual advances, barraged the woman with unwarranted reprimands about her job performance, refused routine supervision or task direction, which made it impossible for her to do her job, and then fired her for poor work performance.[44]

Sudden allegations of job incompetence and poor attitude commonly follow rejection of sexual advances and are used to support employment consequences. When accused of sexual harassment, men often respond that they were only trying to initiate a close personal relationship with a woman they liked very much. In Margaret Miller's situation,* her superior at the bank appeared at her door, bottle in hand, saying, "I've never felt this way about a black chick before."[45] Women who refuse become just as abruptly disliked. In this case, the bank stated that the reason for Ms. Miller's firing was her "insubordination to Mr. Taufer."[46] Under parallel factual circumstances, one judge pointedly concluded: "Ms. Elliott was not terminated because of ... her insubordination except such insubordination as was embodied in her refusal to go along with Lawler's propositions."†[47]

---

*Her lawsuit is reported as *Miller v. Bank of America*, 418 F. Supp. 233 (N.D. Cal. 1976), *appeal pending*, discussed in chapter 4, *infra*, at 61–63.

†Sherry Elliott's lawsuit, *Elliott v. Emery Air Freight*, is unreported; it is discussed in chapter 4, *infra*, at 72–73.

Women whose work had been praised and encouraged suddenly find themselves accused of incompetence or of sabotaging their employer's projects and blamed for any downturn in business fortunes. The investigator in Diane Williams's case* was suspicious:

How did an employee hired in January suddenly become so bad that during the period from July 17 through September 11, a case was built for her separation? . . . I believe a program of faultfinding, criticism and documentation of minor offenses was undertaken.[48]

Some employers do not even bother to create the appearance of actual job incompetence:

The man who was second in command to my boss asked me out and I fielded it. I was charming but I said no. He said that I'd be sorry. . . . Later on, my boss said he had evidence of my inefficiency on which he could fire me, and when I said it wasn't possible, he said he would make evidence. He was supported by the man who had asked me out.[49]

Situation two, the second of the three forms of the quid pro quo, requires inquiry into the impact of compliance. Even less is known about women who comply than about those who refuse. But there is little to suggest that women who meet sexual conditions receive job benefits. More common is the following: "I'm told by the supervisors that the women on the oil slopes and in the camps are fired if they do and also fired if they don't."[50] This suggests that employment sanctions simultaneously prohibit and compel compliance with employment-related sexual advances. Women both must and may not comply—or face the consequences. Constantina Safilios-Rothschild suggests one possible explanation for men's failure to deliver promised job rewards:

Actually it has been quite questionable whether women did in fact obtain economic security through marriage, or desirable occupational advancement in exchange for sexual favors. In the latter case, most often adulterous men, for a variety of motivations (including guilt and fear that their infidelity will be suspected or known) have not returned favors or have done very little. Others have simply not honored the existence of any self-understood or implicit contract of exchange of favors.[51]

---

*Diane Williams's case is reported as *Williams v. Saxbe,* 413 F. Supp. 654 (D.D.C. 1976) and is discussed in chapter 4, *infra,* at 63–65.

This implies that men believe that whenever women are advanced on the job, an exchange of sexual favors must have occurred.

If such a compact were made and broken, a woman attempting to get the benefit of her bargain would encounter little sympathy and probably less legal support. But this misconstrues the issue. Whether or not the woman complies, the crucial issue is whether she was sexually coerced by economic threats or promises. Requiring her to decline would allow the employer to impose such a deal in bad faith, secure sexual favors, and then assert she had no right to complain because she had done what he had no right to demand. Her compliance does not mean it is not still blackmail. Nevertheless, allowing a compliant woman to sue for sexual harassment when an exchange fails leaves open the unattractive possibility of encouraging women to acquiesce in unwanted sex for purposes of career advancement, knowing that they can enforce the man's promise if he does not perform as agreed. For this reason (among others) it would seem preferable to define the injury of sexual harassment as the injury of being *placed in the position* of having to choose between unwanted sex and employment benefits or favorable conditions. From the standpoint of proof, situation two would then make a woman's case weaker (although not impossible) than before she complied. It would simply undercut the plausibility of the argument that her advancement was contingent upon compliance. Such a posture would support women in refusing unwanted sex, and discourage abuse of the cause of action through attempts to get whatever could be gained through sexual compliance and reserving legal resort for times when it did not work out.

"The other side" of sexual harassment is commonly thought to be raised by situation three, in which women who comply with sexual conditions are advantaged in employment over men or over women who refuse. Despite the indications that few benefits redound to the woman who accedes, much folklore exists about the woman who "slept her way to the top" or the academic professional woman who "got her degree on her back." These aphorisms suggest that women who are not qualified for their jobs or promotions acquire them instead by sexual means. Do these stories raise serious difficulties for a conceptualization of sexual harassment as integral to women's employment *dis*advantagement?[52]

Since so few women get to the top at all, it cannot be very common for them to get there by sexual means. Yet undoubtedly some individuals, whether by calculation or in the face of discrimination and lack of recognition of their qualifications, must have followed this course. A mix of these elements is suggested in the following (undocumented) observation: "By using sex, women were able to diminish the social distance between important, rich or powerful men and themselves, and to obtain desirable goods such as economic security and social status through marriage, or a desirable job or promotion through sexual relations with an influential man."[53] Although the author of this statement qualifies it substantially in a footnote, she concludes: "There are, however, even at present a few outstanding examples of professional women, businesswomen, and artists whose occupational success is largely due to a powerful male with whom they have a long-standing and open relationship."[54] This portrays a relationship that appears more like a consensual one than like unwanted sex acquiesced in for career advancement, although it is admittedly difficult to tell the difference.

As discussed earlier, women consistently occupy the lowest-status, lowest-paying jobs, much lower than men of the same education and experience. Given this, it is difficult to argue that women in general receive advantages even remotely comparable with the sexual harassment to which they are subjected. This, after all, is the implication of the supposed "other side": some women are hurt by the practice, it is said, but then look at all the women who benefit from it. Initially, it seems worth asking, as a hypothetical parallel, whether if some blacks are advantaged just because they are black, that is a reason why blacks who are disadvantaged because they are black should continue to be. Next, from the available data on sex discrimination, it cannot be deduced that women in general (and certainly not in individual cases) derive undeserved job opportunities from sexual compliance or by any other means. On the contrary, it would be difficult to show that cooperating women derive advantages commensurate even with the disadvantage of being female. Of course, it is impossible to estimate how much worse women's position might be without the possible contribution of unwanted sex to their side of the bargain. Overall, however, the statistics on discrimination suggest that no fulfillment of any requirement, sexual demands included, results in job status for which women are qualified, much less undeserved advancement.

Presuming for the argument that these stories have some truth, one might look at women who "succeed" this way as having extricated themselves from a situation of sexual harassment. Rather than deriving unfair advantages because of their sex, perhaps they had to meet unfair requirements because of their sex. In this perspective, the woman who "slept her way to the top" may have been the woman who would not have been hired or promoted, regardless of qualifications, without fulfilling sexual conditions, conditions equally qualified men do not have to fulfill. Moreover, for every woman who "got her degree on her back," there were men who offered rewards, supervision, and attention to her development only at a sexual price. To the extent they are true, then, these stories document a point seldom made: men with the power to affect women's careers allow sexual factors to make a difference. So the threats are serious: those who do not comply are disadvantaged in favor of those who do. (It is also seldom considered that a woman might be an attractive sexual object to her superior for the same reasons that *qualify* her for the position.)

Further, there may be compelling explanations for these stories other than their truth. How many men find it unbearable that a woman out-qualifies them in an even competition? Perhaps they assuage their egos by propagating rumors that the woman used her sexuality—something presumptively unavailable to men—to outdistance them. These stories may exemplify a well-documented inability of both sexes to see women in any but sexual terms. Willingness to believe the stories may illustrate the pervasive assumption that, since a career is so intrinsically inappropriate for a woman, her sexuality must define her role in this context, as well as in all others. This dovetails with the prior assumption that if a woman's sexuality is present at all, she must be receiving unfair consideration.

Certainly it is important to establish in individual cases whether a woman is complaining about a failed attempt cynically to use sex to get ahead or a bona fide situation of sex imposed as a career requirement. But to believe that instances raised in situation three symmetrically outweigh the injury that women as a whole suffer from sexual harassment ignores the evidence and provides a convenient excuse not to take the problem seriously. Whatever they mean, people who

do not take sexual harassment seriously are an arm of the people who
do it.

CONDITION OF WORK

In the quid pro quo, the coercion behind the advances is clarified by
the reprisals that follow a refusal to comply. Less clear, and undoubtedly more pervasive, is the situation in which sexual harassment simply makes the work environment unbearable. Unwanted sexual advances, made simply because she has a woman's body, can be a daily
part of a woman's work life. She may be constantly felt or pinched,
visually undressed and stared at, surreptitiously kissed, commented
upon, manipulated into being found alone, and generally taken advantage of at work—but never promised or denied anything explicitly
connected with her job. These events occur both to "token women,"
whose visibility as women is pronounced and who often present a
"challenge" to men,[55] and to women in traditional "women's jobs,"
who are defined as accessible to such incursions by the same standard
that gives them the job at all. Never knowing if it will ever stop or if
escalation is imminent, a woman can put up with it or leave. Most
women hardly choose to be confronted by "the choice of putting up
with being manhandled, or being out of work."[56] Most women are
coerced into tolerance.

This feature of women's lives has sometimes surfaced in other
people's lawsuits, although it has not been previously considered actionable in itself. One case from 1938 presents a zenith in women's
vicarious relationship to the workplace. A long-time employee alleged
(without success) that he was fired because his wife refused his
superior's sexual advances.[57] In another case for reinstatement and
back pay, in which the employer was accused of firing an employee
because of his union activity, one comes upon the following account of
the employee's conduct on the job:

He regularly made lewd remarks and suggestions to the waitresses and customers. . . . He caused at least one waitress to quit her job when he told her
she would have to have sexual relations with him or he would make life
difficult for her. He made similar advances to another waitress. Once Nichols
called a waitress over to where he was seated drinking with a customer and
solicited her to engage in an act of prostitution with the customer.[58]

Sexual harassment is effective largely because women's employment status is depressed. The following account, a composite of several individual accounts, illustrates the interplay of women's feelings of inadequacy with an objective assessment of their options in the labor market. The employer has an eye for energetic, competent, chronically underemployed women in a captive labor market (such as spouses of university men). They are intimidated by the work world. For the first time in their lives, the job gives these women responsibilities, a real salary, a chance to be creative, and quick advancement for good performance. They are grateful; "thrilled." They love the work and feel recognized for their achievements and potential. They work hard and create a niche for themselves. They need the money. Then, beginning on off-times, perhaps when there are unusual work demands, the underlying sexual innuendo is made explicit. Or the man sends the woman on a business trip, shows up at the hotel room where he had booked her, and rapes her.

At this point, otherwise small things come together: all the other women who have precipitously left "such a good job"; the number of women on long, paid leaves that become terminal; the stereotypically attractive appearance of the women, including a ban on long pants at the office. To an individual woman, his demand that she be constantly emotionally available to him; increasingly using her "as a verbal carpet"; his jealousy of her friendships on the job; his casual, even concerned inquiry into her sex life; his lack of desire to meet her husband and his uncomfortableness (or transparent obsequiousness) when he drops in. It becomes clear that his personnel policy is based on his sexual feelings.

Given the woman's insecurity about her work competence, the job may begin to seem like make-work to her, an excuse to keep her available so long as she is sexually compliant, or he thinks she might be. Or the job may continue to be very important to her. Surely she knows there are many women just like her who will take her place if she leaves. Should a woman have to leave a job she needs financially, qualifies for, or finds fulfilling because the employer can make his sexual needs part of it? Or should she have no recourse other than the hope he will stop, or never try again, or that she can stand it just for the chance to work there, or to work at all? Will it ever be different any place else? When workplace access, advancement, and tolerability (not to mention congeniality) depend upon such an employer's good will, women walk very thin lines between preserving their own sanity and self-respect and often severe material hardship and dislocation.

Two recent cases of women seeking unemployment compensation from jobs they left because of employer sexual harassment illustrate the problem, with variations, in somewhat more detail. In a California case,* Nancy Fillhouer[59] left work because she could no longer tolerate the remarks of her employer, which were "slanderous, crude and vulgar," and because he had "tried to exploit her, thus making her job unbearably difficult from an emotional standpoint." In the language of the referee:

She said he was constantly remarking concerning his wishes to have sexual contact with her, and that she reacted in such a way as to certainly inform him that such intentions were not welcome. When she would walk by him, he would occasionally pat her behind. He would make comments to his friends about her figure or legs whenever she wore a dress, implying that she was a loose woman and would do anything with anyone. The claimant asserted that the employer attempted to arrange a liaison with one of his friends for a price. On another occasion, she said one of his friends came to the office and made a comment about the weather being cold, and the employer said that the claimant could keep him warm.[60]

In a similar case in New York State, Carmita Wood[61] reported that she was forced to leave her job because of the physical and emotional repercussions of a superior's sexual advances. He constantly "incorporated palpably sexual gestures into his movements."[62] When speaking to her "he would lean against her, immobilizing her between his own body and the chair and the desk."[63] Sometimes he would "stand with his hands shaking in his pockets and rock against the back of a chair, as if he were stimulating his genitals."[64]

A similar barrage of indignities sustained by one woman in her job as a "photo finishing girl" at a camera store in Oregon† provides a third example. Her complaint alleges that on many occasions her superiors and co-workers, in the presence of other employees and customers, "peer[ed] down plaintiff's blouse from the upper level and stairways above the main sales area of Mr. Pix Camera Store, assisted

---

*This case is discussed in detail in chapter 4, *infra*, at 80–81.

†This case, *Fuller v. Williames*, No. A7703-04001 (Portland, Oregon), is discussed in chapter 6, *infra*, at 168–69.

by binoculars or telephoto lenses." In addition to making frank propositions and references to the large size of her breasts and of their penises, the defendants described the woman as desiring them sexually. Specific statements included:

'Did you just have sex with your husband? What was it like?', 'Is that all you do is have sex with your husband?', 'Do you sleep naked with your husband' pointing out that women were 'better off in bed,' meant 'only for the bedroom or the kitchen,' that plaintiff and other women employees were 'only interested in sleeping with the male employees,' that the former photofinishing 'girl' 'was a good lay. We screwed her down in the basement. We all had sex with her.', 'Do you think your husband would let me take his pants off in front of my camera if I lined him up with a nude female model?', 'Tell your husband I want to do nudes of him. I must photograph him.' that plaintiff was unfit to perform her duties, that women, including plaintiff, were 'not fit for the photography business,' 'incompetent,' unable to work under pressure without bursting into tears,' 'couldn't take it,' 'often stayed home due to headaches,' 'can't be relied upon,' 'possess a lesser ability to photograph,' 'don't know which end of a camera is up,' 'get shows in galleries by sleeping with gallery directors,' 'We've never had a girl selling cameras here. It might be an interesting experiment.' 'We can't hire a woman who has a boyfriend or a husband and have them last any length of time because their partners become very jealous of all us good looking males.'[65]

The connections between sexual desirability and contempt for women, the denigration of women as workers, and exclusion of women from job opportunities have seldom been more vivid. All the careful admissions that women may be oversensitive cannot overwhelm the fact that such comments make women feel violated for good reason. Nor are these remarks aberrations. They make graphic and public the degradation women commonly experience as men's sexual playthings.

At no point in these cases was there an attempt to force the victim into more extensive sexual involvement. But the only reason sexual intercourse was not included was that the perpetrator did not so choose. Nor were the women told that if they did not submit to this molestation, they would be fired, although again this was the employer's choice. The victim's active cooperation with, or submission to, this behavior is relatively irrelevant to its occurrence. Short of physical assault, there is very little one can do to stop someone intent upon visual and verbal molestation, particularly if one has access to few forms of power in the relationship. These are hardly "arm's length"

transactions, with the man as dependent upon an affirmative response as the woman is upon maintaining his good will. They are
transactions which make his sexism a condition of her work.

Sexual harassment as a working condition often does not require a
decisive yes or no to further involvement. The threat of loss of work
explicit in the quid pro quo may be only implicit without being any
less coercive. Since communicated resistance means that the woman
ceases to fill the implicit job qualifications, women learn, with their
socialization to perform wifelike tasks, ways to avoid the open refusals
that anger men and produce repercussions. This requires "playing
along," constant vigilance, skillful obsequiousness, and an ability to
project the implication that there is a sexual dimension to, or sexual
possibilities for, the relationship, while avoiding the explicit "how
about it" that would force a refusal into the open.

A cocktail waitress, whose customer tips measure her success at this
precarious game, reflects upon it.

[A waitress] must learn to be sexually inviting at the same time that she is
unavailable. This of course means that men will take out their lust vicariously
through lewd and insinuating words, subtle propositions, gestures. She must
manage to turn him off gently without insulting him, without appearing
insulted. Indeed she must appear charmed by it, find a way to say no which
also flatters him.[66]

Another waitress makes the economic connection explicitly:

[Men think] they have a right to touch me, or proposition me because I'm a
waitress. Why do women have to put up with this sort of thing anyway? You
aren't in any position to say "get your crummy hands off me" because you
need the tips. That's what a waitress job is all about.[67]

Still another corroborates:

Within my first month as a waitress, it was made very clear to me that if you
are friendly enough, you could have a better station, better hours, better
everything. . . . If you're tricky enough, you just dangle everybody but it
reaches a point where it's too much of a hassle and you quit and take something else. But when you have children, and no support payments, you can't
keep quitting.[68]

While these women's responses do not constitute "compliance" in the
fullest sense, in another sense nonrejection is all the compliance that is
required.

Noncompliance is very problematic when sexual harassment is a working condition. Consider the opportunities for rejection, both immediate and long term, allowed by the situation depicted in the following woman's statement, prepared in an attempt to organize the women in her office:

I, _____, do hereby testify that during the course of my employment with the [company] I have suffered repeated and persistent sexual harassment by Mr. X, [head] of the [company].

Mr. X has directly expressed prurient interest in me on several occasions when he called me into his office as an employee, in his capacity as my superior, during normal working hours. I have been made audience to sexually explicit language and imagery in Mr. X's office during normal working hours. I have been intimidated by his power over my job and future, his connections in [the local government], his reputation for vindictiveness, and the gun he carries, often visibly. In his office, Mr. X has initiated physical sexual contact with me which I did not want.

I believe, and have been made to feel by Mr. X, that my well-being on the job and advancement as an employee of the [company], as well as my recommendations for future jobs, are directly contingent upon my compliance with Mr. X's sexual demands.

It is my opinion that Mr. X's hiring procedures are directly influenced by his sexual interests and that most if not all women who work for the [company] undergo some form of sexual harassment.

Tolerance is the form of consent that sexual harassment as a working condition uniquely requires. The evidence of such cases after they *become* quid pro quo tends to confirm the implicit judgment by the woman who "goes along": it is important, beyond any anticipated delivery, to maintain the *appearance* of compliance with male sexual overtures, a posture of openness. In many cases, the men seem only to want to know they can have a date, to be able "accidentally" to touch a woman intimately at will, or, in a verbal analogue to exhibitionism, say sexy words in her presence, while acting as if something else entirely is happening. The telling aspect is that the decisively nontolerating woman must suddenly be eliminated. Her mere presence becomes offensive; to be reminded of her existence, unbearable. Desperate strategies are devised, including flat lies, distortions, and set-ups, to be rid of her immediately. Something fundamental to male identity feels involved in at least the appearance of female compliance, something that is deeply threatened by confrontation with a woman's real resistance, however subtly communicated. At the point of resistance the quid pro quo that was implicit all along in the working condition—the "tolerate it or leave" in her mind becomes "now that you don't tolerate it, you're leaving" from the boss—is forced into the open, and the two categories converge.

Before this point, the issues are considerably more difficult. The examples suggest that when sexual harassment occurs as a condition of work, it does not require compliance, exactly, on the woman's part. For consummation, nonrejection is not even required; rejection often has no effect. Since little or no active participation or cooperation is required of women in these sexual situations, how explicit should rejection have to be before she can protest the treatment? This is somewhat analogous to asking how ardently a woman must resist rape before she will be considered to have resisted, that is, not to have consented to it. In a case of sexual harassment, it would be paradoxical if, so long as a superior has the power to force sexual attentions by adopting forms of sexual expression that do not require compliance—for example, sitting naked in his office in her presence while giving dictation—a woman would be precluded from legal action or other complaint because she had not properly "refused." How is nontolerance to be conveyed? She can threaten or throw tantrums, but ultimately, what is she supposed to do besides leave work?

Should women be required to counterattack in order to force the man into explicit employment retaliation so she has something to complain about? The problem here is again analogous to a problem with the rape laws: a victim who resists is more likely to be killed, but unless she fights back, it is not rape, because she cannot prove coercion. With sexual harassment, rejection proves that the advance is unwanted but also is likely to call forth retaliation, thus forcing the victim to bring intensified injury upon herself in order to demonstrate that she is injured at all. Aside from the risks this poses to the woman, in a situation not her fault, to require a rejection amounts to saying that no series of sexual advances alone is sufficient to justify legal intervention until it is expressed in the quid pro quo form. In addition, it means that constant sexual molestation would not be injury enough to a woman or to her employment status until the employer retaliates against her *job* for a sexual refusal which she never had the chance to make short of leaving it. And this, in turn, means that so long as the sexual situation is constructed with enough coer-

express any sexuality at all, they just assume you're available to them—you know, just anybody."

As a further result of such attitudes, complaining to the perpetrator usually has little good effect. The refusal is ignored or interpreted as the no that means yes. If the no is taken as no, the woman often becomes the target of disappointed expectations. She is accused of prudery, unnaturalness, victorianism: "What's the matter, aren't you liberated? I thought nothing bothered you." And lesbianism. The presumption seems to be that women are supposed to want sex with men, so that a women who declines sexual contact with this particular man must reject all sex, or at least all men. Noncooperative women (including women who carry resistance to the point of official complaint) are accused of trying to take away one of the few compensations for an otherwise meaningless, drab, and mechanized workplace existence, one of life's little joys.[86] This essentially justifies oppression on the basis of what it does for the oppressor. When the man is black and the woman white, the emotional blackmail, the "you're not the woman I took you for," often becomes particularly unfortunate. The American heritage of racism that portrayed the white woman as "too good" for the black man is now used to manipulate her white guilt, putting her in the position of seeming to participate in that system's castration of the black man if she declines to have sex with him, and in racist repression if she complains officially.

Women's confidence in their job performance is often totally shattered by these events. They are left wondering if the praise they received prior to the sexual incident was conditioned by the man's perception of the sexual potential in the relationship—or is it only that the later accusations of incompetence are conditioned by his perception of the lack of this possibility? Attempting to decline gracefully and preserve a facade of normalcy also has its costs: "We've all been so polite about it for so long to the point we are nauseated with ourselves."

Jokes are another form that the social control over women takes. Women who consider noncompliance dread the degradation of male humor. At Carmita Wood's hearing, when she was describing disabling pains in her neck and arm which vanished upon leaving the job, the referee said, "So you're saying, in effect, that [the professor] was a pain in the neck?" On being told the perpetrator's age, the referee remarked, "Young enough to be interested anyway."[87] As the brief for Ms. Wood put it, "Nowhere is the existence of a persistent sexual harassment . . . questioned, it is merely treated lightly."[88] Trivialization of sexual harassment has been a major means through which its invisibility has been enforced. Humor, which may reflect unconscious hostility, has been a major form of that trivialization. As Eleanor Zuckerman has noted, "Although it has become less acceptable openly to express prejudices against women, nevertheless, these feelings remain under the surface, often taking the form of humor, which makes the issues seem trivial and unimportant."[89]

Faced with the spectre of unemployment, discrimination in the job market, and a good possibility of repeated incidents elsewhere, women usually try to endure. But the costs of endurance can be very high, including physical as well as psychological damage:

The anxiety and strain, the tension and nervous exhaustion that accompany this kind of harassment take a terrific toll on women workers. Nervous tics of all kinds, aches and pains (which can be minor and irritating or can be devastatingly painful) often accompany the onset of sexual harassment. These pains and illnesses are the result of insoluble conflict, the inevitable backlash of the human body in response to intolerable stress which thousands of women must endure in order to survive.[90]

Without further investigation, the extent of the disruption of women's work lives and the pervasive impact upon their employment opportunities can only be imagined. One woman, after describing her own experiences with sexual harassment, concluded:

Many women face daily humiliation simply because they have female bodies. The one other female union member at my plant can avoid contact with everyone but a few men in her department because she stays at her work bench all day and eats in a small rest room at one end of her department.[91]

For many women, work, a necessity for survival, requires self-quarantine to avoid constant assault on sexual integrity. Many women try to transfer away from the individual man, even at financial sacrifice. But once a woman has been sexually harassed, her options are very limited:

If she objects, the chances are she will be harassed or get fired outright. If she submits, the chances are he'll get tired of her anyway. If she ignores it, she gets drawn into a cat-and-mouse game from which there is no exit except leaving the job.[92]

Women do find ways of fighting back short of, and beyond, leaving their jobs.[93] As has been noted, nonrejection coupled with non-compliance is a subtle but expensive form. One shuffles when one sees no alternative. Women have also begun to oppose sexual harassment in more direct, visible, and powerful ways. The striking fact that black women have brought a disproportionate number of the sexual harassment lawsuits to date points to some conditions that make resistance seem not only necessary but possible. Protest to the point of court action before a legal claim is known to be available requires a quality of inner resolve that is reckless and serene, a sense of "this I won't take" that is both desperate and principled. It also reflects an absolute lack of any other choice at a point at which others with equally few choices do nothing.

Black women's least advantaged position in the economy is consistent with their advanced position on the point of resistance. Of all women, they are most vulnerable to sexual harassment, both because of the image of black women as the most sexually accessible and because they are the most economically at risk. These conditions promote black women's resistance to sexual harassment and their identification of it for what it is. On the one hand, because they have the least to fall back on economically, black women have the most to lose by protest, which targets them as dissidents, hence undesirable workers. At the same time, since they are so totally insecure in the marketplace, they have the least stake in the system of sexual harassment as it is because they stand to lose everything by it. Since they cannot afford any economic risks, once they are subjected to even a threat of loss of means, they cannot afford *not* to risk everything to prevent it. In fact, they often must risk everything even to have a chance of getting by. Thus, since black women stand to lose the most from sexual harassment, by comparison they may see themselves as having the least to lose by a struggle against it. Compared with having one's children starving on welfare, for example, any battle for a wage of one's own with a chance of winning greater than zero looks attractive. In this respect, some black women have been able to grasp the essence of the situation, and with it the necessity of opposition, earlier and more firmly than other more advantaged women.

Other factors may contribute to black women's leadership on this issue. To the extent they are sensitive to the operation of racism on an

individual level, they may be less mystified that the sexual attention
they receive is "personal." Their heritage of systematic sexual harassment under slavery may make them less tolerant of this monetized
form of the same thing. The stigmatization of all black women as
prostitutes may sensitize them to the real commonality between sexual
harassment and prostitution. Feeling closer to the brand of the harlot,
black women may more decisively identify and reject the spectre of its
reality, however packaged.

The instances of sexual harassment described present straightforward coercion: unwanted sex under the gun of a job or educational
benefit. Courts can understand abuses in this form. It is important to
remember that affirmatively desired instances of sexual relationships
also exist which begin in the context of an employment or educational
relationship. Although it is not always simple, courts regularly distinguish bona fide relationships from later attempts to read coercion
back into them. Between the two, between the clear coercion and the
clear mutuality, exists a murky area where power and caring converge. Here arise some of the most profound issues of sexual harassment, and those which courts are the least suited to resolve.

In education, the preceptive and initiating function of the teacher
and the respect and openness of the student merge with the masculine role of sexual mastery and the feminine role of eager purity,
especially where the life of the mind means everything. The same
parallel between the relationship that one is supposed to be having
and the conditions of sexual dominance and submission can be seen in
the roles of secretary and boss. Rosabeth Kanter notes that the secretary comes to "feel for" the boss, "to care deeply about what happens to him and to do his feeling for him," giving the relationship a
tone of emotional intensity.[94] Elsewhere, she sees that a large part of
the secretary's job is to empathize with the boss's personal needs; she
also observes that, since the secretary is part of the boss's private
retinue, what happens to him determines what happens to her.
Kanter does not consider that there may be a connection between the
secretary's objective conditions and her feelings—sexual feelings
included—about her boss.

Although the woman may, in fact, be and feel coerced in the sexual
involvement in some instances of sexual harassment, she may not be
entirely without regard for, or free from caring about, the perpetrator. Further investigation of what might be called "coerced caring,"

or, in the most complex cases, an "if this is sex, I must be in love" syndrome, is vital. It is becoming increasingly recognized that feelings of caring are not the only or even a direct cause of sexual desires in either sex.[95] In light of this, it cannot be assumed that if the woman cares about the man, the sex is not coerced. The difficulties of conceptualization and proof, however, are enormous. But since employed women are supposed to develop, and must demonstrate, regard for the man as a part of the job, and since women are taught to identify with men's feelings, men's evaluations of them, and with their sexual attractiveness to men, as a major component of their *own* identities and sense of worth,[96] it is often unclear and shifting whether the coercion or the caring is the weightier factor, or which "causes" which.

This is not the point at which the legal cause of action for sexual harassment unravels, but the point at which the less good legal case can be scrutinized for its social truths. The more general relationship in women between objective lack of choices and real feelings of love for men can be explored in this context. Plainly, the wooden dichotomy between "real love," which is supposed to be a matter of free choice, and coercion, which implies some form of the gun at the head, is revealed as inadequate to explain the social construction of women's sexuality and the conditions of its expression, including the economic ones. The initial attempts to establish sexual harassment as a cause of action should focus upon the clear cases, which exist in profusion. But the implications the less clear cases have for the tension between women's economic precariousness and dependency— which exists in the family as well as on the job—and the possibilities for freely chosen intimacy between unequals remain.

There is a unity in these apparently, and on the legal level actually, different cases. Taken as one, the sexual harassment of working women presents a closed system of social predation in which powerlessness builds powerlessness. Feelings are a material reality of it. Working women are defined, and survive by defining themselves, as sexually accessible and economically exploitable. Because they are economically vulnerable, they are sexually exposed; because they must be sexually accessible, they are always economically at risk. In this perspective, sexual harassment is less "epidemic" than endemic.

4 Sexual Harassment Cases

Sexual harassment, the experience, is becoming "sexual harassment," the legal claim. As the pain and stifled anger have become focused into dissatisfaction, gripes have crystallized into a grievance, and women's inner protest is becoming a cause of action. But this is not a direct process of transliteration. Life becoming law and back again is a process of transformation. Legitimized and sanctioned, the legal concept of sexual harassment reenters the society to participate in shaping the social definitions of what may be resisted or complained about, said aloud, or even felt. Similarly, when a form of suffering is made a legal wrong, especially when its victims lack power, its social dynamics are not directly embodied or reflected in the law. Legal prohibitions may arise because of the anguish people feel or the conditions they find insupportable, but the legal issues may not turn on the social issues that are the reasons they exist. Distanced from social life, yet part of its imperatives, the law becomes a shadow world in which caricatured social conflict is played out, an unreal thing with very real consequences.

Most women who have experienced sexual harassment know that it was done to them, in some sense, as women. Considerations the law requires for determining whether their treatment was based on their sex look like formalistic barriers to recognizing the obvious. Equally apparent to most sexually harassed women is that employers could rectify their situation but instead wink at it, which means that they let it happen. To the victims, employer liability comes down to holding responsible for women's situation the people with the power over it.

Legally, whether sexual harassment is sex discrimination is not nearly so straightforward. Several different interpretations of the meaning of sex discrimination have been applied in this context. In one interpretation, the variable in question must be exclusive to one gender before sex discrimination can occur. An abuse that *can be* visited upon either gender or upon the same gender as that of the perpetrator—as sexual harassment can—cannot be treatment based on sex.[1] In another interpretation, whenever an employment requirement, such as engaging in sexual relations as the price of a job, is fixed upon one gender that *would not,* under the totality of the circumstances, be fixed upon the other, the condition is seen as based on sex.[2] Another approach focuses upon whether the requirement *was in fact* imposed upon one gender and not the other in the case at hand.[3] Still another view might require that sexual harassment be engaged in with intent to deprive women of employment opportunities before it would be considered sex-based.[4]

A similar array of interpretations exists on the issue of whether the employer should be held liable for sexual harassment by employees. In one approach, the closest to the victim's sense of the situation, the fact that the behavior occurred in the course of employment is sufficient to hold the employer responsible. Knowledge is imputed to him because if he did not know about it, he should have.[5] Another interpretation requires that the employer actually know about the abuse, and ignore it or act inadequately to remedy it, suggesting that he ratified or condoned it.[6] A variant suggests that especially stringent standards of employer knowledge should be satisfied because the behavior is sexual.[7] Not yet confronted is the extent to which *pro forma* complaint adjudication can exonerate an employer with notice who does not rectify the situation from the victim's standpoint.[8] Finally, one can imagine an approach requiring knowing acquiescence or active abetting of sexual harassment by the employer with intent to drive women out of their jobs before the employer will be held responsible.[9]

Behind the range of interpretations, basic issues are at stake. Prohibiting sexual harassment as sex discrimination implicitly defines what has been considered private and personal as another dimension of the public order. Of women by men, it suggests a relationship between individual sexual relations and the edifice of unequal gender status as a whole. If women's sexuality is a means by which her access to economic rewards is controlled, relations between the sexes in the process of production affect women's position throughout the society, just as women's position throughout the society makes her sexuality economically controllable. It also suggests that what has been considered among the most "natural" and "normal" of male urges may, in some forms, be sufficiently culturally contingent as well as onerous to give rise to discrimination against women. Boundaries between personal life and work life, the natural and the cultural, are thereby interpenetrated and confounded in the same way that they have become inseparable in women's oppression. Implicit here is whether sexuality is, in itself, a source, form, and sphere of social inequality or whether it is merely a sphere onto which other forms of unequal power—for example, physical force or economic clout—are displaced and imposed, a ground on which other battles (including those of gender) are fought. Behind the doctrinal arguments, conceiving of sexual harassment as unequal treatment based on sex raises fundamental questions of the definitions of, and the relations between, gender, sexuality, and power.

STATEMENT OF CASES

The first women to complain that sexual harassment is sex discrimination—Jane Corne and Geneva DeVane, Paulette Barnes, Margaret Miller, and Adrienne Tomkins—were all unsuccessful in the lower courts. In *Corne and DeVane v. Bausch & Lomb*[10] and *Miller v. Bank of America*,[11] sexual harassment was not considered actionable sex discrimination, in essence because the acts complained of were not seen to be sufficiently tied to the workplace context. In Jane Corne's case, the sexual advances were seen as "a personal proclivity, peculiarity or mannerism";[12] in Margaret Miller's case, the "isolated misconduct" was not considered attributable to employer "policy."[13] In *Corne* the court also found the behavior was not "based on sex" because the sexes of the participants could have been reversed.[14] The district court in Paulette Barnes's case found that sexual harassment is not sex discrimination because it is not treatment "based on sex" within its legal meaning: "The substance of plaintiff's complaint is that she was discriminated against, not because she was a woman, but because she refused to engage in a sexual affair with her supervisor."[15] Alluding to both theories, the district court in *Tomkins v. Public Service Electric & Gas Co.*[16] considered sexual harassment neither employment-related nor sex-based, but a personal injury properly pursued in state court as a tort; however, a firing for complaint about sexual harassment would be discriminatory.

These cases were followed by Judge Richey's holding in *Williams v. Saxbe.*[17] Brought by Diane Williams, a black public information specialist in the Justice Department, this case marked the turning of the tide in favor of women alleging sexual harassment at work. Sexual harassment was first found to be treatment "based on sex" within the meaning of Title VII, leaving the employment-relatedness of the incidents to be determined as a fact at trial. The *Williams* result was followed by reversals on appeal in *Barnes* and *Tomkins,* and was buttressed by the similar holding in *Garber v. Saxon Business Products.*[18] In its reversal in *Barnes,* the Court of Appeals for the District of Columbia held that making sexual compliance a "job retention condition" was a sex-based differentiation under the circumstances because it imposed an employment requirement upon a woman that would not be imposed upon a man, a requirement for which the employer was accountable.[19] In *Tomkins,* the Court of Appeals for the Third Circuit found that the question of sex-basis was an issue of fact to be resolved at trial, and affirmed that an unresponsive employer to whom a victim had complained was complicit, hence liable.[20] In *Garber,* the Court of Appeals for the Fourth Circuit squarely, if inexplicitly as to its reasons, found that a pattern of sexual incidents, "liberally construed," alleged " an employer policy or acquiescence in practice of compelling female employees to submit to the sexual advances of their male supervisors in violation of Title VII."[21] Together these cases gave authority to the claim that sexual harassment violates Title VII. Recent successes in other cases (*Munford*[22] and *Elliott*[23]) at the district court level, and in *Heelan* at trial,[24] appear to confirm that these gains are, at least for now, consolidated.

Corne and DeVane v. Bausch & Lomb

The first reported* adjudication of a sexual harassment claim under Title VII presented the difficult situation of a constructive discharge where sexual harassment was a condition of work. Jane Corne and Geneva DeVane, clerical workers at Bausch & Lomb, alleged that the repeated verbal and physical sexual advances, molestation, and prop-

---

Barnes was decided in 1974 by the federal district court, but it was not first reported until several years later. The original adjudication was thus not widely known until after its reversal on appeal in July 1977.

ositions by their male superior had made their jobs intolerable, forcing them to leave, while women who were sexually compliant received enhanced employment status. Their supervisor's actions, the women alleged, limited them to "the choice of putting up with being manhandled, or being out of work."[25] They argued that the company, by allowing them to be supervised by a man who persistently took unsolicited and unwanted sexual liberties, created sex discriminatory conditions of employment.

Dismissing the claim, Judge Frey held that sexual advances are not sex discrimination, giving in essence four reasons. No employer policy was served by the conduct ("by his alleged sexual advances, Mr. Price was satisfying a personal urge"). Unlike other Title VII cases, the conduct in question did not "benefit the employer." The conduct "had no relationship to the nature of the employment." And "if the conduct complained of was directed equally to males there would be no basis for suit."[26] Since the court read prior Title VII decisions to reach only discrimination that arose out of company policy, the first three considerations were dispositive. As to the fourth, the opinion did not indicate whether the facts of the case specifically provoked this concern. However, if the company's brief on appeal is any indication, ambiguity may have been nurtured to undercut the argument that the harassment of the women was based on their gender: "[nothing plaintiffs] alleged indicated why plaintiffs received the attentions of Price, or that his attentions were based on their gender rather than Price's unknown and perhaps aberrant, taste in such things."[27] The judge also expressed concern about the administrative and social implications of granting relief: "an outgrowth of holding such activity to be actionable under Title VII would be a potential federal lawsuit everytime an employee made amorous or sexually-oriented advances toward another. The only sure way an employer could avoid such charges would be to have employees who were asexual."[28]

Miller v. Bank of America

Miller v. Bank of America turned on and extended, with variations, the issue of "company policy" decisive in *Corne*. Margaret Miller, a black woman, alleged that her white male supervisor "promised her a better job if she would be sexually 'cooperative' and caused her dismissal when she refused."[29] She charged that the Bank of America in policy and in practice permitted men in supervisory positions, in particular her supervisor, to demean women's dignity, and that his sexual advances were a part of this pattern. On the bank's motion to dismiss the action,[30] Judge Spencer Williams framed the issue as: "whether Title VII was intended to hold an employer liable for what is essentially the isolated and unauthorized sex misconduct of one employee to another." It is unclear which issue—sex basis or employer liability—is being addressed. But in *Miller* because they were "isolated," just as in *Corne* because they were "personal," instances of sexual harassment were not considered workplace events for which the employer should be held liable. In order to fall within Title VII, the court in the *Miller* case required an employer policy be alleged "imposing or permitting a consistent, as distinguished from isolated, sex-based discrimination on a definable employee group."[31]

Significantly, and unlike Bausch & Lomb (the defendant company in the *Corne* case), the Bank of America alleged it had a company-wide policy expressly condemning this type of misconduct. In the judge's view, the alleged existence of such a policy undercut employer responsibility for the incident, since the plaintiff had neither complained nor requested an investigation under the existing policy. Exhaustion of company remedies was not held a prerequisite to a suit under Title VII. "Rather, the failure of exhaustion goes more to whether the employer is liable at all."[32] On appeal, it emerged that this "policy" is as follows:

A. POLICY:
  All known and pertinent facts concerning possible acts of dishonest, improper actions or behavior, or other reasons believed to warrant suspension should be reported immediately.
3. ACTS OTHER THAN DISHONEST
  . . . suspensions for acts other than dishonesty, such as moral misconduct or illegal activities, as follows.[33]

As a reason to avoid liability, this policy is shockingly unspecific. Even if it were followed, depending upon the scope of "improper actions or behavior" or "moral misconduct," many incidents of sexual harassment might well escape it. Nor does the mere existence of a written policy resolve allegations that it is not followed, or formalistically followed, in practice.

The court in this case also expressed concern that a federal precedent would stimulate spurious sexual harassment claims every time there was an unfavorable employment decision. Noting further that males and females are mutually attracted, this "natural sex phenomenon . . . [probably] plays at least a subtle part in most personnel decisions."[34] Given this fact, the court concluded that it should refrain from delving into such matters unless an employer policy with the requisite group impact is alleged.

*Williams v. Saxbe (Bell)**

Where *Corne* and *Miller* on the surface turned primarily upon whether sexual incidents at work were considered employment-related, the case brought by Diane Williams against the Justice Department focused more explicitly upon whether retaliation in employment for refusal of sexual advances could be considered discrimination "based on sex." After a tortuous path through the federal bureaucracy,† this case provided the first occasion on which a federal judge held that sexual advances coupled with retaliation for their refusal constituted actionable sex discrimination. Williams, a black woman, alleged that she had a good working relationship with her immediate supervisor, a black man, until she refused a sexual advance. Thereafter, she asserted that he

engaged in a continuing pattern and practice of harassment and humiliation of her, including . . . unwarranted reprimands, refusal to inform her of matters for the performance of her responsibilities, refusal to consider her proposals and recommendations, and refusal to recognize her as a competent professional in her field.[35]

Her supervisor alleged that her poor work performance during this same period was the basis for her discharge. The administrative tribunal to which she first complained thought the evidence did not establish "any causal relationship" between the rejection of her supervisor's sexual advances, his treatment of her, and her termination.[36] The district court to which she appealed sent the case back to the agency, finding that the burden of proof in the administrative hear-

---

*As the heads of federal agencies change, case titles change, since it is the agency that is being sued.

†A detailed account of which can be found in *Williams v. Bell* (Brinson, appellant), No. 76-1833 and *Williams v. Bell,* No. 76-1994, U.S. Ct. App. D.C., Decided September 19, 1978 (slip opinion), at 3-8.

ing had erroneously been upon Ms. Williams to prove sex discrimination rather than upon the government to show its absence. At the second hearing, the examiner inferred, based on evidence of what were termed the supervisor's "personal advances based on sex" and their rejection, together with the lack of prior poor work or bad conduct, that Williams "was discriminated against because of sex in the acts of her immediate supervisor in intimidating, harassing, threatening and eventually terminating her." One piece of evidence was a card with the inscription "Seldom a day goes by . . . without a loving thought of you. Happy Mother's Day" and signed "Harvey." Impaling the supervisor on his own story that Ms. Williams was fired for unsatisfactory work, the examiner drily found it "credible to believe that Mr. Brinson would not have sent such a card to complainant if he had been truly experiencing work performance and/or conduct difficulties with her or was otherwise unsatisfied with her at this time."[37] The examiner further found that the work problems, "in good supervision . . . preventative," occurred because of the situation the supervisor created by his advances and his response to her rejection. The examiner concluded: "The alleged enumerated deficiencies occurring simultaneous with a rejection of personal advances based on sex, lends itself to an inference of sex discrimination."[38] The complaint adjudication officer of the agency rejected this reasoning on the view that the facts did not present a claim within the definitional parameters of Title VII sex discrimination.

In a ground-breaking opinion, Judge Richey held that the retaliatory actions of the male supervisor, taken because the female employee declined his sexual advances, constituted sex discrimination under Title VII. The argument in defense, that "the impetus for the creation of the class must be distinguished from the primary variable which describes the class,"[39] was expressly rejected. The judge held instead that "the conduct of the plaintiff's supervisor created an artificial barrier to employment which was placed before one gender and not the other, despite the fact that both genders were similarly situated."[40] Whether or not discrimination is based on a sex stereotype, Title VII prohibits "all discrimination affecting employment which is based on gender."[41] To the defendant's argument that a criterion which could be applied to both sexes cannot create a class primarily defined by gender, the court noted that it is sufficient for a finding of sex discrimination that a policy is primarily *applied* to one gender. A quality peculiar to one sex is not essential. The contention that sexual harassment is "insignificant" was also rejected.

Centrally, the question of whether the sexual advances constitute a policy or an isolated personal incident was seen as a question of fact, skirting the issue of whether sexual advances to one woman are sex-based as a matter of law. Judge Richey's analysis was that the supervisor's conduct was alleged to be a policy or practice "imposed upon the plaintiff and other women similarly situated."[42] In his view, the defendant's argument that the incident was not a policy but a personal matter

is merely based upon defendants' view of the facts, coupled with a fear that the courts will become embroiled in sorting out the social life of the employees of the numerous federal agencies. . . . [W]hether this case presents a policy or practice of imposing a condition of sexual submission on the female employees of the CRS or whether this was a non-employment related personal encounter requires a factual determination. It is sufficient for purposes of the motion to dismiss that the plaintiff has alleged it was the former in this case.[43]

Unless it is settled, *Williams* will go to trial on the facts.

Barnes v. Train (Costle)

In *Barnes*, the factual and legal configuration was virtually identical to that in *Williams*. Paulette Barnes, a black payroll clerk for the Environmental Protection Agency, argued that the retaliatory actions of a white male supervisor, taken because she refused his sexual advances, were sex discrimination. Her complaint described his "campaign to extract sexual favors," including solicitation for social activities after office hours despite repeated refusals, sexual remarks, and suggestions that her employment status would be improved if she cooperated in a sexual affair.[44] Following her decisive refusal, the supervisor belittled and harassed her, stripped her of job duties, and finally abolished her job. Her supervisor denied the advances, explaining the events as the results of a disagreement with Barnes over the nature of her position and its duties and of his administrative consolidation of the office, which eliminated the need for a job at her level.

After complaining[45] unsuccessfully through the Civil Service Commission apparatus, Barnes sued under Title VII. An opinion by Judge

Smith, echoing the formulation of the administrative tribunal, held that she was penalized because she refused her supervisor's sexual advances, not because of her sex.[46] As the administrative tribunal put it: "complainant's allegation concerning sex discrimination is that her supervisor discriminated against her because of her 'refusal to have an after hours affair' with him, and not because she is female."[47]

On appeal, the *Barnes* case produced the most explicit treatment of the issues to date and a holding that sexual harassment is sex discrimination in employment. Reversing the district court, a three-judge panel held unanimously[48] that Title VII prohibits abolishing a woman's job because she repulses her male superior's sexual advances. This was held to impose a sex-discriminatory "job retention condition."[49] Although the facts before the court presented retaliation for refusal of sexual advances, the language of the court's opinion potentially extends to situations where retaliation has not yet occurred. Sexual compliance may be a condition of job retention long before the point of retaliation for sexual refusal, although it is certainly easier to establish that such a condition exists after that point.

A review of the arguments presented to the court is instructive in interpreting this crucial decision. Ms. Barnes's attorneys had argued that Title VII was intended broadly to prohibit all employment discrimination based on sex and sex stereotypes. Retaliation resulting from a refusal to engage in sexual relations was argued to be a per se violation of Title VII. The primary theory relied upon was that to see women workers as "sexual fair game, and passive, willing recipients of the sexual advances of their male supervisors"[50] is a sex stereotype of the kind Title VII prohibits. The requisite nexus with employment exists because the sexual advances give the woman "the choice of acceding to the sexual demands of her supervisor . . . or of suffering adversely *as an employee*."[51] Sexual harassment was also asserted to have a disparate impact on female employees because the vast majority of supervisors in the federal government are male and the majority of underlings female. Women are far more likely than otherwise comparable men, it was argued, to be required to engage in sexual relations as a condition of government work.

In response, the government argued, as it did in the *Williams* case, that "the impetus for the creation of the class must be distinguished from the primary variable which describes the class."[52] Where the "impetus" may be a sexual stereotype, the "primary variable" must be gender for the Act to apply. The primary variable here, the government argued, is "willingness *vel non** to furnish sexual consideration, rather than gender."[53] Persons outside the class may be women (women on whom the demand is not imposed and women who do not accede) just as persons within the class may be men. As a test for whether the defining characteristic of a class is gender, the government proposed immutability: "If the personal characteristic in question is mutable, such that members of the allegedly aggrieved sex can escape the bounds of class and receive full employment enhancement, then the primary variable is not gender."[54] The characterization of Barnes as one who "decided not to furnish the sexual consideration claimed to have been demanded" emphasized this dimension of mutability, construing her situation as almost voluntary. The government also argued that since the case posed an "inharmonious personal relationship," as distinct from questions of "policy, regulation or statute," the Act did not apply. The spectre was raised of endless judicial time spent reviewing employee claims "that they were not promoted solely because of their sexual attitudes or 'unalluring' physical characteristics."[55]

The theory the Court of Appeals adopted, by contrast, was built upon a strict application of the gender-differentiation prohibition:

So it was, by her version, that retention of her job was conditioned upon submission to sexual relations—an exaction which the supervisor would not have sought from any male. It is much too late in the day to contend that Title VII does not outlaw terms of employment for women which differ appreciably from those set for men and which are not genuinely and reasonably related to performance on the job.[56]

Judge Robinson for the court expressly rejected the government's contention that the plaintiff was denied employment enhancement not because she was a woman but because she refused sexual compliance. The court saw the two as indistinguishable:

But for her womanhood, from aught that appears, her participation in sexual activity would never have been solicited. To say, then, that she was victimized in her employment simply because she declined the invitation is to ignore the asserted fact that she was invited only because she was a woman subordinate to the inviter in the hierarchy of agency personnel. Put another way, she

---

*Vel non means "or not."

became the target of her superior's sexual desires because she was a woman, and was asked to bow to his demands as the price for holding her job.[57]

Nowhere in the legislative history of Title VII were sexual relations between employees and superiors found to be exempted from its coverage. Discrimination against "only one" individual, so long as it is sex-based, was held prohibited, and employers chargeable with discriminatory practices of supervisory personnel, unless the practices were performed without employer knowledge and rectified on discovery.

Taking a position which has been adopted in several subsequent cases, the concurrence in the *Barnes* case strongly urged a narrowing of the majority's standard for vicarious liability. To hold an employer responsible, Judge MacKinnon required a showing of the sexual advance, retaliation by the maker of the advance, and that "other agents of the employer with knowledge of her charges assisted the retaliation or impeded the complaint."[58] This would shift the burden to the employer to disprove callous disregard of Title VII rights. In fact, only one successful sexual harassment case to date (*Elliott,* discussed below) has *not* alleged unproductive attempts to complain about the sexual advances; in both unsuccessful cases, no such complaints were alleged, and in one (*Miller*) that failure was found crucial. Both *Munford* and *Alexander,*[59] the latter a case alleging sexual harassment in education, explicitly affirm the complaint requirement as a prerequisite for employer liability for acts of sexual harassment by subordinates.* Whether *pro forma* complaint processing—as distinct from reaching a result satisfactory to the injured party—would relieve a company or university of liability remains an open question.

Garber v. Saxon Business Products

After *Williams* was decided, and before the appeal in *Barnes* was handed down, the Court of Appeals for the Fourth Circuit, apparently with as little fanfare as possible, decided that sexual advances, if a complaint alleges a company policy compelling or tolerating them, is sex discrimination. The complaint in *Garber v. Saxon Business Products,*

*This is also the case in *Heelan v. Johns-Manville Corporation,* 451 F. Supp. 1382, 1390 (1978), discussed *infra,* at 75 ff.

filed on behalf of an individual woman plantiff and "a class of persons similarly situated," alleged that Darla Jeanne Garber, a secretary, was denied a promised raise and fired "specifically because she refused to engage in illicit sexual relations with her immediate superior."[60] Relief sought, among other things, included one million dollars compensatory damages for mental anguish. The defendant company reportedly argued on appeal that the discharge was not sex-based: " 'She was not allegedly terminated because she was a woman . . .' the company's lawyers told the court. 'Rather her claim is that her employment was affected because she rejected the advances of a superior who found her personally attractive.' " The company also argued that this instance of sexual harassment did not exemplify company policy, but was only "the alleged individual sexual preference of a fellow employee."[61]

The Court of Appeals for the Fourth Circuit remanded the case to the district court for trial, with the following holding:

The district court , without granting leave to amend, dismissed the plaintiff's complaint in which she alleged that she had been discharged for rebuffing the sexual advances of her male supervisor, in violation of Title VII of the Civil Rights Act of 1964, on the ground that the complaint failed to allege a good cause of action. We disagree. We think that the complaint and its exhibits, liberally construed, allege an employer policy or acquiescence in practice of compelling female employees to submit to the sexual advances of their male supervisors in violation of Title VII. The judgment of dismissal must be reversed and the case remanded for further proceedings.[62]

Tomkins v. Public Service Electric & Gas Co.

Tomkins v. Public Service Electric & Gas Co. related a single incident of sexual harassment followed by a series of employment repercussions and complaints to which the company was unresponsive.[63] Adrienne Tomkins, a secretary, was invited to lunch by her boss, ostensibly to discuss his recommendation for her promotion. At a club bar, her boss began drinking heavily. When it became apparent that work was not going to be discussed, Tomkins said she wished to return to work. By threats of retaliation against her as an employee, threats of physical force, and finally exercise of physical restraint, her boss kept her at the bar against her will for several hours. He expressed a desire to have sexual relations with her, saying it was necessary to their satisfactory working relationship. When she tried to leave, he physically prevented her, implying that if she protested, no one at the company would help her. Fearing for her job and physical safety, she remained. Her boss grabbed her and kissed her on the mouth.

At work, Tomkins requested and was promised transfer to a comparable position. When one was not forthcoming, afraid to return to her previous job, she temporarily took an inferior position. Over a period of months, her new superior threatened demotions, charged that she was incapable of holding the position, pressured her to take a salary cut, and solicited and gathered unfavorable material about her and had it placed in her personnel file. She was twice put on disciplinary layoff without just cause and was finally terminated. Her complaints to the company, which was also sued, were not investigated.

Tomkins's attorney argued that the company "knew or should have known" that these actions, part of a pattern and practice of discrimination against women, would occur, yet took no steps to prevent or redress them, and instead retaliated against her. Employer responsibility in employee-supervisor conflicts, she argued, includes not tolerating class-based harassment, "regardless of the fact that the conduct arises from the personal proclivity of the offending employee." The employer was argued to have an obligation to prevent these acts, to halt them on notice, to redress the injury or punish the perpetrator, and to prevent future abuses. A subjective test of harassment, one "depending upon the subjective appraisal of the complaining employee rather than upon the intent of the actor," was urged.[64]

Sexual harassment was argued to be sex-based discrimination on the theory of sex stereotyping. To focus upon the "role of females as sex objects, to the exclusion of individual characteristics" is to judge "female employees on the basis of irrelevant, gender-based stereotypes while evaluating male employees on the basis of their individual qualifications." Finally, employer tolerance of sexual harassment and its pattern of reprisals was asserted to have a disparate impact upon women as a protected class and to be inherently degrading to women.

In his opinion Judge Stern focused on two distinct issues. The first was whether sexual harassment on these facts constitutes sex discrimination as a matter of law. The second was was whether the employer's conduct after the complaint of harassment could amount to sex discrimination. Answering the first in the negative, the court stated that the purpose of Title VII is to remove those artificial barriers to full employment which are based on unjust and long-encrusted prejudice . . . not . . . to provide a federal tort remedy for what amounts to physical attack motivated by sexual desire on the part of a supervisor and which happened to occur in a corporate corridor rather than a back alley.[65]

Further, while here the parties were male and female, "the gender lines might as easily have been reversed, or even not crossed at all," so that "the gender of each is incidental to the claim of abuse."[66] Disagreeing with the approach to employer liability taken in *Corne,* Judge Stern noted that the doctrine of *respondeat superior,* under which employers are liable for some acts of their employees, as well as the explicit proviso of Title VII, would hold an employer responsible for sex discrimination by an employee, were it to be found.

Foreseeing floods of litigants, the judge was apprehensive that "an invitation to dinner could become an invitation to a federal lawsuit if a once harmonious relationship turned sour at some later time."[67] He was not reassured by the Equal Employment Opportunity Commission's suggestion that "only those sexual advances from a superior to a subordinate under the cloak of the superior's authority would be actionable under Title VII, and then only if such a practice contributed to an employment-related decision."[68] Rather,

plaintiff's theory rests on the proposition, with which this Court concurs, that the power inherent in a position of authority is necessarily coercive. . . . every sexual advance made by a supervisor would be made under the apparent cloak of that authority. Any subordinate knows that the boss is the boss whether a file folder or a dinner is at issue.[69]

Having firmly grasped the nettle of hierarchy, Judge Stern rejected the deduction that sexual harassment is properly actionable as sex discrimination. He further held that if a woman were terminated for a *complaint* of sexual harassment, that termination might be sex discriminatory. Regardless of the merits or subject of the complaint, if the company decides to prefer a male employee over the female employee by firing her without investigating the situation, it was held that " the female will be terminated because she is female, that is sex discrimination."[70]

On appeal, alternate theories of liability were proposed on behalf of the plaintiff. The theories correspond to what has been termed here the *quid pro quo,* in which promotion and favorable job evaluation are made conditional upon granting sexual favors, and the condition of work, in which sexual harassment creates an environment of sex-based intimidation, as a barrier to equal employment opportunity. The Court of Appeals for the Third Circuit held that sexual harassment is sex discrimination on the quid pro quo theory, avoiding passing upon the condition of work theory. Sexual demands were found to "[amount] to a condition of employment, an additional duty or burden Tomkins was required by her supervisor to meet as a prerequisite to her continued employment."[71] No light was shed upon the issue of whether sexual harassment of a woman subordinate in the course of employment is sex-based as a matter of law. The court treated it as a matter of fact. Finding that "the essence of her claim is that her status as a female was the motivating factor in the supervisor's conditioning her continued employment on compliance with his sexual demands,"[72] the court treated the question of law—is sexual abuse of women gender-based treatment?—as if it reduced completely to a question of fact in each case: was *this* woman sexually harassed because she is female? It seems more appropriate, not to mention practical, to determine as a matter of law whether the facts of each incident, if proven, amount to sex discrimination. Not having made this distinction, the court nevertheless concluded with a strong statement for the plaintiff:

We conclude that Title VII is violated when a supervisor, with the actual or constructive knowledge of the employer, makes sexual advances or demands toward a subordinate employee and conditions that employee's job status— evaluation, continued employment, promotion, or other aspects of career development—on a favorable response to those advances or demands, and the employer does not take prompt and appropriate remedial action after acquiring such knowledge.[73]

This formulation appears to prohibit under Title VII all knowing invasions of employees' sexuality by employers, either as presumptively sex-based (which was not explicitly held) or whether or not sex-based.

Elliott v. Emery Air Freight

Two more recent cases focus, respectively, upon the issues of reason for termination and the complaint requirement. Since employers can always allege other "reasons" that an employee is undesirable, it is important that courts have seen through them in the sexual harassment context. In *Elliott v. Emery Air Freight,* a Title VII action tried to the court without a jury, Judge McMillan found that Sherry Elliott was terminated because of her refusal to acquiesce in the propositions of a male management employee of the company in violation of Title VII. Parallel with *Williams,* in which the sexual rejection was found to have produced the events to which the firing was then attributed, the judge found:

This [sexual] refusal resulted in Mr. Lawler's placing unusual pressure on Ms. Elliott which produced any strained relationships that may have existed between Ms. Elliott and her co-workers. [The] decision to terminate Ms. Elliott was because of her accusation about Mr. Lawler and was not based in fact on the later-mentioned alleged grounds. Ms. Elliott was not terminated because of her use of profanity, her failure to report her absence to the proper person, her errors, or her insubordination except such insubordination as was embodied in her refusal to go along with Lawler's propositions.[74]

The judge also concluded that "Ms. Elliott would not have been propositioned, pressured, or terminated if she had been a man." No attempt by Ms. Elliott to register a complaint with the company was mentioned in the opinion.

Munford v. James T. Barnes & Co.

In a by now almost tediously familiar story, Maxine Munford, a black woman, was hired as an assistant collections manager by Glen D. Harris, a white man. The next day he asked her to accompany him to another floor to get office supplies, on which errand he "made overt sexual suggestions to Ms. Munford which she rebuffed." Harris indicated that "[her] job might be dependent on whether or not she acceded to his demands."[75] Over the next several days, Harris "made repeated sexual suggestions and innuendos... both verbally and through acts of petty harassment such as leaving cartoons on her desk." When, after repeatedly indicating she was not interested in a sexual liaison with him, she said she would report his behavior to their superior, "Harris replied that she would only succeed in getting herself fired [another version stated "canned"] since Zulcosky [the superior] was his friend."[76] "Harris said [she] had not yet served her ninety days probationary period, that he almost always had his way and when he didn't he held grudges." Shortly thereafter, Harris told Ms. Munford that she would accompany him on a business trip, stay overnight in the same motel room, and have sexual relations with him. She said she would not and was discharged. Upon her protest of her dismissal, the company superior supported the termination.

On the one hand rejecting the reasoning of *Corne* and *Miller* that required the sexual harassment to be pursuant to company policy, and on the other hand steering a middle way between *Williams* and *Barnes,* which were interpreted to hold the employer "automatically and vicariously liable for all discriminatory acts of its agents or supervisors," Judge Freeman held in *Munford* that "an employer has an affirmative duty to investigate complaints of sexual harassment and dea[ ] appropriately with the offending personnel."[77] He quoted with approval the concurrence in *Barnes* limiting liability of a company employer to cases in which a plaintiff can show more extensive employer participation:

The plaintiff's theory is that they are liable under the Act because they ratified without investigation the conduct of defendant Harris. The Court agrees that an employer may be liable for the discriminatory acts of its agents or supervisory personnel if it fails to investigate complaints of such discrimination. The failure to investigate gives tacit support to the discrimination because the absence of sanctions encourages abusive behavior.[78]

The court in this case also held that individual instances of sexual harassment, termed "a personal incident of sexual harassment,"[79] may constitute sex discrimination although "no other women, black or white, are alleged to have been victims of sexual abuse while employed by James T. Barnes & Co."[80]

Morgenheim v. Midnight Sun Broadcasters

With a complaint drafted in the finest frontier lawyer tradition Virginia Morgenheim[81] won a settlement of her claim that she was fired from Midnight Sun Broadcasters, KENI-TV, Anchorage, Alaska, because of her resistance to a superior's sexual advances. Morgenheim, termed "a twenty-seven year old married mother who has an interest in broadcast journalism," and a "conscientious, well trained, efficient and acceptable woman broadcaster," was pushed against a wall and French-kissed by the defendant, Jhan Hiber, alleged to be acting as agent for the company. Surviving her rejection (made "as gently as the circumstances allowed"), "the defendant's next tactic on behalf of Midnight Sun Broadcasters Inc. was to grab her when she least expected it and after he had a sufficient hold, commence to rub her back in what he thought was a passionate manner." In the face of her repeated resistance, Hiber allegedly said that "the only way a woman could succeed in broadcasting was to play the game." Morgenheim replied that she was a qualified broadcaster and could succeed on her merits. She took all reasonable steps to terminate his sexual advances but was discharged for her refusals.

Her complaint asserted a barrage of legal claims, including breach of contract of employment, violation of due process and equal protection under state and federal statutes (including Title VII), and the tort of intentional infliction of emotional distress. Damages were sought for mental anguish, concern for her career, "abject humility" [*sic*], embarrassment, and invasion of her marriage. She also complained of invasion of privacy as guaranteed under the Alaska Constitution, a claim said to cover "the right to work in a legal profession without having to wrestle amorous T.V. managers, reject obscene soliciting, and be man-handled and petted by men superiors." In the event Hiber was not found to have been an agent acting within the scope of his employment, he was alternatively alleged to "be on a folly of his own and is personally liable."

The complaint further alleged negligent breach of the employer's responsibility to inquire into the merits of Morgenheim's recommended termination. The corporation was charged with breach of its "duty to discover truth." In support of this negligence claim, it was alleged that other women had been terminated by the corporation, also on Hiber's recommendation, "because they too would not be sex objects." Avoiding stuffiness on the one hand and grandstanding for sexual freedom on the other, the complaint described Morgenheim as "an emancipated American woman, ... free to have sex with whomever she desires and ... likewise free to refrain from sexual contact by those she does not desire without being penalized by employers for the choice she makes." She reportedly settled these claims.[82]

Heelan v. Johns-Manville Corporation

Mary K. Heelan's case is the first reported sexual harassment case to go to trial. She claimed that her refusal to have sexual relations with her supervisor, Joseph Consigli, resulted in her firing and the company did nothing about it in spite of her complaints. The judge believed her, and held the company responsible, over the supervisor's denial of the advances, and notwithstanding the judge's disbelief of Heelan's denial of a sexual affair with a co-worker during the same period. On the issue of law, the court held that "an employer is liable under Title VII when refusal of a supervisor's unsolicited sexual advances is the basis of the employee's termination."[83] The factual elements needed for making out a *prima facie* case* of sexual harassment as sex discrimination were explicitly enunciated: "(1) submission to sexual advances of a supervisor was a term or condition of employment, (2) this fact substantially affected plaintiff's employment, and (3) employees of the opposite sex were not affected in the same way by these actions."[84]

It must first be proven that the sexual advances occurred, were unwanted, and were refused. The woman's credibility, what the judge termed "worthiness of belief," was considered crucial.[85] That her rejection of these demands (and not some other deficiency) caused her firing was supported by an extensive account of her outstanding employment record. The company had contended that she was terminated for "insubordination, lack of application and general inability to perform at the level required of her position."[86] The judge found that "the only person to question plaintiff's competence is her supervisor, and these criticisms do not appear in any of his formal written evaluations, but only in his oral statements and privately maintained notes"[87] and not until she refused his advances.

The judge's standard for considering that "sexual advances were occasioned as an integral part of her employment"[88] hews closely to the facts of the case, confining it to those instances in which a woman is fired for refusing sexual advances. If she had not been fired, the advances would not have been terms or conditions of employment in this view.

A cause of action does not arise from an isolated incident or a mere flirtation. These may be more properly characterized as an attempt to establish personal relationships than an endeavor to tie employment to sexual submission. . . . Under the facts of this case, the frequent sexual advances by a super-

---

*This means that once the plaintiff has pleaded and proven these facts, the company must rebut them or it loses.

visor do not form the basis of the Title VII violation that we find to exist. Significantly, termination of plaintiff's employment when the advances were rejected is what makes the conduct legally actionable.[89]

By "condition" of employment, the judge clearly had in mind a pre-condition rather than a persistent quality. It is unclear whether the requirement that the advances have a "substantial effect" on plaintiff's employment is to be satisfied independently, or, if so, by a greater or lesser showing of employment-relatedness than the "term or condition" requirement. To the issue of gender as framed here, the company did not prove sexual advances against male employees by any Johns-Manville supervisor,[90] so the advances were considered sex-based.

That Mrs. Heelan complained to the company, although not through any established procedure, was crucial in determining the company's liability. It was found that "she did everything within her power to bring her charges to the attention of top management."[91] She had confided in several employees, including an assistant vice president who was also an administrative assistant to the president. After notice of the termination, she also complained to the executive vice president, who telephoned the perpetrator. "Consigli denied any wrongdoing and the matter was dropped."[92] The court in essence found the company's investigation of the problem inadequate to its notice of it. The depth and scope of the inquiry conducted by the company, which amounted to asking the perpetrator whether he did it or not, were held insufficiently thorough to satisfy its Title VII obligation. The judge concluded that "if the employer fails to respond to a valid complaint, it effectively condones illegal acts."[93] Mary Heelan recovered damages in the form of back pay and lost employment benefits, as well as attorneys' fees.[94]

Unemployment Cases

The first case to hold that sexual harassment as a pervasive condition of work is employment discrimination based on sex is, apparently, Cathy Hamilton's unemployment appeal.[95] The Commission of the Department of Industry, Labor and Human Relations of Wisconsin explicitly found that although there was no evidence of a quid pro quo, sexual harassment as a condition of work was sex discrimination under the Wisconsin Fair Employment Law. *Williams* was cited as authority for this conclusion, although the quid pro quo was crucial to that holding. Hamilton's immediate supervisor and the company's personnel manager were found to have made "repeated sex proposals and advances to Complainant involving requests that she have sexual relations with them and with other individuals for monetary compensation," "the nature and extent of [which] were such as to make them abusive." Hamilton rejected all these advances, complained to her union steward about them, and was eventually discharged. The Commission concluded that she failed to establish that she was discharged because she rejected the sexual advances. "No evidence was introduced to show that Respondent's agents ever linked their sex advances to threats to discharge her if she did not respond favorably." However, the *advances themselves* were held to be discriminatory: "The advances were unsolicited and unwanted. They were directed from higher level supervisory and managerial personnel to a female employee in a subservient position. Given the source of the advances and their intensity and insulting tone, they created a work environment in which Complainant was harassed because of her sex."[96]

Although the results turn on issues of "reasonableness" in leaving work rather than upon constructions of discrimination, two other unemployment compensation cases, on the issue of whether women who leave their jobs due to sexual harassment qualify for unemployment benefits, divide along lines parallel to the Title VII cases. Carmita Wood, referred to previously, claimed she left her job due to the physical repercussions of attempting to ignore sexual harassment, but was denied unemployment compensation.[97] Her leaving was found to be "uncompelling" and "voluntary" under New York law. The claim of sexual harassment, the facts of which were uncontested, was rejected as "an afterthought." Nancy Fillhouer's claim, by contrast, was granted, the California Unemployment Appeals Board finding her sexual harassment a compelling reason for leaving work.[98]

Carmita Wood was an administrative assistant for seven and a half years at a laboratory of a major university. A professor with whom she had almost daily contact in the course of her administrative duties persistently molested her visually, verbally, and physically.[99] She alleged that his movements incorporated sexual gestures, that he stared at her and her secretary in an insinuating way, stimulated his genitals and rocked back and forth in his chair while talking with her, pinned her with his body against her desk, and on several other occasions physically humiliated and accosted her. Affidavits by others confirmed her version of several incidents; one woman reported in an affidavit that the professor had harassed her as well. "Professor [Y] leaned against me and placed his hand on my shoulder and tried to kiss me." Carmita Wood expressed her distress and anxiety to her secretary and other co-workers, complained to another superior, who told her she should try to stay out of these situations, and requested transfer to a comparable position, which she was unable to obtain.

Simultaneously with the incidents, Carmita Wood experienced intensifying physical pain in her hand and arm, pain which made her work extremely difficult and eventually became disabling. During a period when the professor was on leave the pain lessened, becoming again excruciating as his projected return approached. Physical therapy did not improve the condition, nor was an explicit diagnosis made. Hoping that a warmer climate would improve her condition, unable to bear the pain, and dreading exposure to the professor whose return was imminent, Wood left her job. Needing pension fund money to go to a warmer climate, and unable to secure it on a leave of absence, she resigned, citing health, desire to move to another area, and personal reasons. Almost immediately after she left the job, the pain disappeared completely.

The referee in her unemployment hearing found that her reasons for leaving the job were "personal" and "non-compelling," so her leaving was voluntary and without good cause,[100] despite affidavit and testimonial evidence supporting her version of the sexual harassment and expert testimony on psychosomatic response to psychic stress.

In my practice ... I have noted many cases of extreme stress and anxiety related to uninvited sexual molestation. In several cases where such emotional stress and anxiety could not be expressed verbally and thus reestablish self-respect and self-esteem, the patient would express the stress through psychosomatic symptoms.[101]

Never was her sexual harassment disputed; it was merely not seen as a credible reason for leaving work.

On appeal to the Unemployment Appeals Board, counsel for Ms. Wood argued that persistent sexual harassment is an intolerable working condition sufficient for good cause to leave the job; that psychosomatic pain suffered as a result of sexual harassment is fur-

ther good cause for leaving work; and that the referee demonstrated
bias in his findings of fact. The referee's findings were argued to be
unsupported by substantial evidence, indicating that he never took
the issue seriously.[102] The appeals board did not discuss these arguments, stating: "the credible evidence establishes that the claimant left
her employment in order to relocate in Florida in the hope that a
warmer climate would alleviate her neck and shoulder pains."[103] The
board also deemed it significant that Wood could have obtained a
leave of absence "but chose not to do so." Rejected, "as an afterthought," was the contention that she quit because of harassment by a
male supervisor. The expert affidavits on psychosomatic response
were dismissed together with the corroborative affidavits as "largely
opinion in nature." No further appeal was made.

Except for Carmita Wood's physical manifestations of distress,
neither the facts nor the state standards applied substantially distinguish her case from Nancy Fillhouer's successful unemployment
claim, although Fillhouer's employer was more verbally explicit. Ms.
Fillhouer[104] worked as a secretary and receptionist. Although her
mother was very ill and she needed the money, she left work, stating
she could no longer tolerate the sexual harassment of her employer.
The employer stated that she had been discharged for misconduct,
resulting in a denial of unemployment benefits. At the hearing, she
recounted the employer's constant insinuations, advances, pressures,
verbal and physical indignities and liberties sexual in nature, and the
assault on her dignity sustained on an almost daily basis. At one prior
point, she had quit work for these reasons. When the employer asked
her to return, she agreed on condition that she be treated with respect. The employer assented but soon returned to his former practices. Fillhouer had made unsuccessful efforts to find work elsewhere.
In a telephone call (he did not attend the hearing) the employer
admitted using strong language, denied sexual advances, and said he
had employed Fillhouer as a favor to her family.

The referee, denying the claim, purported to apply a test of
whether "the facts disclose a real, substantial and compelling reason
of a nature as would cause a reasonable person genuinely desirous of
retaining employment to take similar action." Actually applying a
kind of "assumption of risk" test instead, the referee stressed several
times that the complainant knew or was aware of the employer's qualities: "The record . . . shows that the claimant was well aware of the

proclivities of the employer when she left her employment the first time. She resumed work with full knowledge of the conditions of employment. She showed a tolerance, therefore, by her resumption of the employment."[105] At the same time the referee noted that "particularly sensitive people may react unreasonably," implying that she was unreasonably *in*tolerant of the conditions of her employment, and ignoring that particularly *in*sensitive people may *act* unreasonably. The referee reportedly inquired at the hearing whether Fillhouer did not think that "today's modern world requires that females in business and industry have a little tougher attitude toward life in general."[106] He also noted that "it is apparent that she could have continued to accept the situation as it was for a longer period" while she looked for other work.

Adopting the referee's statement of fact, the board reversed, citing precedent that good cause to leave work may exist where "the conditions of employment are so onerous as to constitute a threat to the physical or mental well-being of an employee or where the actions of a supervisor are particularly harsh or oppressive."[107] Fillhouer's work context was seen to have "ramifications far exceeding the normal employer-employee relationship," ramifications which were tolerated due only to her need for a job. A previous decision was cited which found in the context of "good cause" for leaving that some things were too personal for the employment relation: "Such supervisorial action and comments upon and prying into the claimant's personal life unrelated in any way to her work can hardly be considered a part of the normal give and take in an employment relationship."[108]

Monge v. Beebe Rubber

Because it presents a striking departure in employment law, a case that arose in New Hampshire on a contract theory deserves review. In *Monge v. Beebe Rubber,*[109] the court held that discharge from employment based upon rejection of sexual advances was breach of contract of employment. Unwritten employment contracts are customarily considered "at will," meaning terminable by either side at any time for any or no reason. Discrimination law qualifies this right. Olga Monge alleged that she was harassed by a foreman she refused to date and that his hostility, condoned if not shared by the personnel manager, ultimately resulted in her firing. The personnel manager's letter stating that Ms. Monge was "deemed a voluntary quit" for failing to report to work for three consecutive days (while hospitalized) was construed as a retaliatory discharge based on her refusal of her foreman's sexual advances. In an action for damages for breach of oral contract of employment, Monge won a jury verdict and damages of $2,500. Beebe Rubber appealed. Justice Lampron for the Supreme Court of New Hampshire held that the jury could draw the "not so subtle inference" from the foreman's overtures, the capricious firing, the manipulation of job assignments, and the "apparent connivance" of the personnel manager that the company, through its agents, acted maliciously in terminating Monge's employment. (The damages for mental suffering were, however, disallowed as improper in a contract action.) The importance of *Monge,* is that, without finding sex discrimination, a public policy exception was made to the usual "at will" rule by applying a stricter contract standard to the employment relation in a case of sexual harassment.

The issue of appropriate relief in sexual harassment cases is far from resolved. It is difficult to calibrate what would make a woman whole for these incidents. Most sexual harassment complaints allege damages for the discrimination, both compensatory and punitive, adopting a tortlike approach; others add a tort claim explicitly. In *Tomkins,* a tentative consent order granted $20,000 in settlement of the tort claims, wide-ranging affirmative policy measures including a management review panel to hear complaints, an appeal procedure, policy affirmations to be communicated directly to employees in writing, and a videotape to be shown at training programs with a portion covering employees' rights to be free of sexual harassment.[110] Diane Williams was granted judgment and $19,147.67 in restitution, which primarily represented back pay.[111] Sherry Elliott was granted back pay up to the time of the termination of the action, and all references to adverse job performance were expunged from her record. Ideally, women who are fired should get their jobs back. But the judge in *Elliott* reflected the difficulty: "I have not decided whether Ms. Elliott should be ordered reinstated in light of the hostility during the course of this controversy. I will entertain alternative remedies that may be suggested by the parties, such as a reasonable amount of front pay."[112]

CRITIQUE OF CASES

The cases that reject sexual harassment complaints—*Corne, Miller, Barnes,* and *Tomkins* at the district level, and *Williams* at the administrative level—consider remarkably superficially (when, indeed, they focus at all) the difficult and central legal issues sexual harassment raises for sex discrimination doctrine. Specifically, they refer only in passing to the key doctrinal issue of whether sexual harassment is conduct "based on sex" in the legal sense.[113] Instead, they present ideological constructs about the nature of women's sexuality and its role in women's social status. These digressions and evasions need to be disposed of in order to clear the ground for confronting the major issues.

Beyond moralizing, the near-universal response of authoritative men—employers and husbands, referees and judges—to womens' complaints of sexual harassment is to consider them "personal" incidents, "natural" expressions, or both. Perhaps the purpose, and certainly the effect, of these labels is to remove the events from the social or political arena, hence from scrutiny, criticism, and regulation by legal intervention. To call something personal is to make it too small, too unique, too infinitely varied, and too private to be considered appropriately addressed by law, which is thought to deal in public social structural generalities. Similarly, but at the other end of the scale, to call something natural or biological (the two are used interchangeably) is to render it too big, too immutable, too invariant, too universal and, thus, too presocial to be within the law's reach. These terms at once monumentalize and trivialize sexual harassment, simultaneously making change seem impossible, unimportant, and undesirable. Both characterizations, while rationalizing legal noninvolvement, make sexual harassment socially and culturally *permissible* by locating its determinants beyond the social and cultural sphere.

Personal

In all the cases in which relief is denied, the terms used to describe women's complaints of sexual harassment are strikingly similar, often identical, even when the cases do not refer to each other. Personal is the most common descriptive term for the incidents. It is usually used

84 **Sexual Harassment Cases**

as if it conclusively renders legal remedies unavailable, as if to the
extent an occurrence can be described as personal the person has no
legal rights. Carmita Wood, who left her job because of the physical
repercussions of attempting to ignore persistent sexual harassment by
a superior, was denied unemployment benefits because her reasons
for leaving work were found to be "personal" and "noncompel-
ling."[114] ("Personal" is also a statutory term here.) At the hearing, a
superior to whom she had reported the incident recalled that he had
found her complaint at the time "greater [than] one of male/
female . . . actually . . . on a different plane" and later termed it "personal."[115] In similarly individuating terms, the referee referred to
Wood's "antipathy" for her superior.[116]

Paulette Barnes charged that her male supervisor "imposed a car-
nal condition upon the enhancement of her employment status"[117]
and then abolished her job when she did not accede. The district
court, holding that no sex discrimination had occurred, observed
"This is a controversy underpinned by the subtleties of an inharmonious personal relationship."[118] In *Corne*, in which two women were
pressured for sexual favors in exchange for employment advancement, the individualization and its effect as a bar to recovery is most
prominent. Judge Frey, finding no sex discrimination, stated: "In the
present case, Mr. Price's conduct appears to be nothing more than a
personal proclivity, peculiarity, or mannerism. By his alleged sexual
advances, Mr. Price was satisfying a personal urge."[119] According to
this logic, because the conduct was personal, it was not company policy, hence not sex discrimination. Building on this opinion, the appeal
brief for defendant Price urged that "such highly personalized and
subjective conduct" is not the proper concern of the courts,[120] and
referred obliquely to the defendant's "personal preference . . . for individual characteristics."[121]

In the case of Nancy Fillhouer, who left work after repeated sexual
advances, the referee who denied her claim individualized the employer's behavior by terming it his "proclivities" and "habits and
traits."[122] Referring to his verbal advances, the referee stated that the
employer's "speech standards were not of the highest." Individualiz-
ing the insults by noting that Fillhouer was "unhappy" with his reference to her "character," he suggested that her response was uniquely
oversensitive, rather than reasonably proportional to the provocation:
"Particularly sensitive people may react unreasonably." Judge Ster-

deplored the actions of Tomkins's boss as "an unhappy and recurrent feature of our social experience" while denying her a cause of action for sex discrimination by terming the behavior "abuse of authority... for personal purposes."[123] In *Alexander,* Yale's attorneys argued that no plaintiff could represent a class of sexually harassed women students to whom the university had allegedly been unresponsive because each incident is "necessarily personal and particularized."[124]

The term personal is used in these cases in four quite distinct ways. In the unemployment cases, outside the sex discrimination context, it is opposed to the "reasonable person" construct. On the one hand, there are personal reasons for leaving work for which unemployment compensation is withheld; on the other hand, there are reasons for leaving work which reasonable persons agree upon, for which unemployment compensation is granted. It is apparent that it is a matter of someone's judgment of the consensus, a judgment that might differ by sex, whether a given reason is sufficiently broadly shared to be considered reasonable by the reasonable person, as opposed to personal to an unreasonable person.[125]

Second, in the sex discrimination cases, personal implicitly stands opposed to *sex-based.* That is, to the extent the sexual advances are conceived as advances toward an individual person, they are seen to lack the requisite group referent to come within the classification "based on sex." Unstressed but clearly present in two successful cases,[126] and a critical omission noted in *Miller,*[127] was the allegation that "other women similarly situated" were sexually harassed. Apparently the group referent considered missing as a matter of law when one woman is sexually harassed is supplied by alleging that other women are similarly treated. This is not an evidentiary requirement, or taken as substantiation that the events occurred, nor is it here a requirement for a class action; it seems to be a legal prerequisite for an *individual* case to be seen as sex-based, in the sense of transcending the personal. It may be telling that in *Miller,* at the point when the advances were first termed "isolated," a footnote stated: "This is not a race discrimination case."[128] This suggests that racial insults to just one black person allege a sufficient group referent, while sexual insults to just one woman are considered too isolated to be seen as sex-based.

Third, the term personal is used to defeat the contention that the incident is employment-related. The underlying sense seems to be that even though the incident occurred on the job, between persons who are working, and in a relationship hierarchically defined by the work situation; and although the job is thereby made unbearable and/or the incident has resulted in loss of job opportunities, somehow the incident has nothing to do with work. This is clearly a matter of point of view. For the perpetrator, it may be a diversion; the victim undoubtedly *wishes* it had nothing to do with work.

The *Heelan* case implicitly distinguishes the personal from the employment-related, finding that the sexual advances made by Heelan's supervisor were *not* personal to the extent that they were terms and conditions of her work. Unlike prior cases, the issue is treated as a matter of fact: were the incidents "isolated" or "mere flirtation," hence "attempts to establish a personal relationship," or were they "an endeavor to tie employment to sexual submission"?[129] What facts are relevant to such a distinction? What is it about some sexual advances that are personal, others that are conditions of work?* At times, the judge focuses upon the "repeated, unwelcome" quality of the supervisor's sexual attention, which, in Mary Heelan's case, "over a two year period developed into a 'term and condition' of employment."[130] He then holds that the signal difference between a personal relationship and a term and condition of work in the sexual context, under the facts of this case, is the noncompliant woman's termination. This readily transforms into a legal requirement: only when the perpetrator acts upon the threat to a woman's job implicit in his sexual demands does a cause of action arise. Can the sexually harassed woman who struggles to endure each day because she has to survive be said to be having a personal relationship with her harasser? One wonders by what magic a termination can transform a personal relationship into a condition of work—and back again, one presumes, if she is rehired.

Fourth, the word personal is used in the sexual harassment cases to undergird the sense of injustice in holding an employer responsible

---

*Mary Heelan's case is particularly well constructed on the facts to underline the distinction, although this point was not so made. She was found to have had a sexual relationship with a co-worker while refusing to have one with her boss. 451 F. Supp., at 1387. This eliminates moralism and prejudice against women's sexual expression from the case and subliminally suggests that relationships that women do choose to have may be legitimately personal.

about it to someone—usually a woman friend, family member, or co-worker. About a quarter of them complain to the perpetrator himself.[75] Those who complain, as well as those who do not, express fears that their complaints will be ignored, will not be believed, that they instead will be blamed, that they will be considered "unprofessional," or "asking for it," or told that this problem is too petty or trivial for a grown woman to worry about, and that they are blowing it all out of proportion. Carmita Wood's immediate supervisor, to whom she had reported incidents with her other superior at length, when asked to recall if she mentioned them, stated: "I don't remember specifically, but it was my impression, it was mentioned among a lot of things that I considered trivia."[76]

Women also feel intimidated by possible repercussions of complaint, such as being considered a "troublemaker,"[77] or other men in their lives finding out about the incidents, men who typically believe they must have been asking for it. One article reports a man "recalling a woman purchasing clerk who had just received a 'really good raise' and then showed up at work 'all black and blue.' Her husband had 'slapped her around' because he thought the raise was a result of 'putting out.'"[78] Women students (and women junior faculty) fear the repercussions of complaint more than the academic and professional consequences of the harassment itself.[79]

Women's worst fears about the impact of complaint are amply justified. "Most male superiors treat it as a joke, at best it's not serious. . . . Even more frightening, the woman who speaks out against her tormentors runs the risk of suddenly being seen as a crazy, a weirdo, or even worse, a loose woman."[80] Company officials often laugh it off or consider the women now available to themselves as well. One factory worker reports: "I went to the personnel manager with a complaint that two men were propositioning me. He promised to take immediate action. When I got up to leave, he grabbed my breast and said, 'Be nice to me and I'll take care of you.'"[81]

Unions' response to women's complaints of sexual harassment by management has been mixed. Some union officials refuse to process grievances based upon claims of sexual harassment. In one such case,[82] the complainant sued the union for breach of its duty of fair representation. Ms. Gates, the company's first and only woman employee, was hired as a janitor on the day shift, then reassigned to the night shift.

While on the graveyard shift she was assigned to clean men's restrooms, to which she did not object except for the treatment which she allegedly received while doing her work. She complained that men were using the urinals while she was cleaning; that on occasions she was propositioned and chased around the restrooms, and that the company refused to place locks on the doors to prevent this from happening.[83]

Her doctor stated that the resulting emotional breakdown made her physically unable to work the night shift. The company then fired her on the grounds that she was unable to perform the work for medical reasons. Through its woman president, the union maintained that the firing was for good cause and urged Ms. Gates to accept the company's offer of reinstatement under the same working conditions. When she refused, the union declined to process her claim, a decision the court held was for the union to make.*

Firm union support was given to four women in another shop who complained to the union of sexual harassment by a male foreman. The National Labor Relations Board reportedly "decided that the foreman would have to apologize to each woman and from then on our relationship would be strictly business."[84] The women found this inadequate. The union continued to pursue the issue, intervening directly in their relations with the perpetrator and working to change the pervasive attitude that "any woman who works in an auto plant is out for a quick make."[85] It should be noted that this assumption is not limited to auto plants. Men in almost every working context attribute sexual desire to women workers based upon their mere presence as workers in that particular environment. This assumption is professed equally about women who are seen as anomalies on the job (any woman who would seek a male-defined work situation must be there because of men) as for those who are in women's jobs (any woman who would choose a feminine job must be looking for a man). Since no working context is excluded, one cannot conclude that women select particular jobs for sexual reasons. As with rape, the situation seems more to be that men wish to believe that women desire to be sexually attacked and to that end construct virtually any situation as an invitation. Constructed according to these images, women who do convey any sexuality whatever are assumed to be unselective: "If you

---

*This case is *Gates v. Brockway Glass Co., Inc.*, 93 L.R.R.M. 2367 (C.D. Cal. 1976). Sex discrimination was apparently not raised.

civeness, subtlety, suddenness, or one-sidedness to negate the effectiveness of the woman's refusal, or so long as her refusals are simply ignored while her job is formally undisturbed, she is not considered to have been sexually harassed.

IMPACT OF SEXUAL HARASSMENT

Women's feelings about their experiences of sexual harassment are a significant part of its social impact. Like women who are raped, sexually harassed women feel humiliated, degraded, ashamed, embarrassed, and cheap, as well as angry. When asked whether the experience had any emotional or physical effect, 78 percent of the Working Women United Institute sample answered affirmatively. Here are some of their comments:

As I remember all the sexual abuse and negative work experiences I am left feeling sick and helpless and upset instead of angry. . . . Reinforced feelings of no control—sense of doom . . . I have difficulty dropping the emotion barrier I work behind when I come home from work. My husband turns into just another man. . . . Kept me in a constant state of emotional agitation and frustration; I drank a lot. . . . Soured the essential delight in the work. . . . Stomachache, migraines, cried every night, no appetite.*[69]

In the Working Women United Institute study, 78 percent of the women reported feeling "angry," 48 percent "upset," 23 percent "frightened," 7 percent "indifferent," and an additional 27 percent mentioned feeling "alienated," "alone," "helpless," or other. They tend to feel the incident is their fault, that they must have done something, individually, to elicit or encourage the behavior, that it is "my problem."[70] Since they believe that no one else is subjected to it, they feel individually complicit as well as demeaned. Almost a quarter of the women in one survey reported feeling "guilty."

Judging from these responses, it does not seem as though women want to be sexually harassed at work. Nor do they, as a rule, find it flattering. As one explanation for women's apparent acquiescence, Sheila Rowbotham hypothesizes that (what amounts to) sexually harassed women are "subtly flattered that their sex is recognized. This makes them feel that they are not quite on the cash nexus, that they

*Ellipses separate different persons' responses.

matter to their employer in the same way that they matter to men in their personal lives."[71] While the parallel to home life lends plausibility to this analysis, only 10 percent of the women in the Working Women United Institute sample and 15 percent of the *Redbook* sample* reported feeling "flattered" by being on the sex nexus. Women do connect the harasser with other men in their lives, but with quite different results: "It made me think that the only reason other men don't do the same thing is that they don't have the power to." The view that women really want unwanted sex is similar to the equally self-serving view that women want to be raped. As Lynn Wehrli analyzes this:

Since women seem to "go along" with sexual harassment, [the assumption is that] they must like it, and it is not really harassment at all. This constitutes little more than a simplistic denial of all we know about the ways in which socialization and economic dependence foster submissiveness and override free choice. . . . Those women who are able to speak out about sexual harassment use terms such as "humiliating," "intimidating," "frightening," "financially damaging," "embarrassing," "nerve-wracking," "awful," and "frustrating" to describe it. These words are hardly those used to describe a situation which one "likes."[72]

That women "go along" is partly a male perception and partly correct, a male-enforced reality. Women report being too intimidated to reject the advances unambivalently, regardless of how repulsed they feel. Women's most common response is to attempt to ignore the whole incident, letting the man's ego off the hook skillfully by *appearing* flattered in the hope he will be satisfied and stop. These responses may be interpreted as encouragement or even as provocation. One study found that 76 percent of ignored advances intensified.[73] Some women feel constrained to decline gently, but become frustrated when their subtle hints of lack of reciprocity are ignored. Even clear resistance is often interpreted as encouragement, which is frightening. As a matter of fact, any response or lack of response may be interpreted as encouragement. Ultimately women realize that they have their job only so long as they are pleasing to their male superior, so they try to be polite.[74]

Despite the feelings of guilt, self-loathing, and fear of others' responses, many women who have been sexually harassed do complain

---

*In both surveys, women could indicate as many feelings as they felt applied to them.

for the unauthorized misconduct of one "individual" employee to another "individual" employee. Here, to be individual means to act on one's own, as well as not to act as a member of a social group. The issue of employer liability needs to be separated clearly from the issue of whether the conduct is sex-based. The former determines how wide the net of responsibility should be cast, not whether sexual harassment is properly sex discrimination.

Having distinguished users of the term personal in these cases, their commonalities should also be observed. One function of all the uses of the term is to individuate, devalue, pathologize, and isolate women's reactions to an experience which is common and shared, practically without variation, by countless women. To label sexual harassment "personal" contributes to the mystification that sexual behavior, because it is sexual, is unique to particular personalities, specific or isolated to particular individuals or types of individuals, necessarily intimate or interpersonally special. As is apparent in the cases, the corresponding legal function served is to distinguish sexual relations from the male/female and employer/employee dimensions, which are legally circumscribed. To have a personal relationship in this sense means to have a relationship that is one's own, that exists irrespective of social determinants—specifically, those social determinants that are legally regulated: gender differences and employment relations.

The often uncontested facts in sexual harassment complaints, the indications in empirical studies, and women's experience contradict this formulation. They document over and over the same basic pattern of advances from a man to a subordinate woman or women, together with impact or reprisals on the job. A workplace superior sexually approaches a subordinate, a man making sexual demands on a woman, to the woman's detriment as a woman in her job. In what meaningful sense can such incidents be said to be extrinsic to male/female, employer/employee relations? Experientially, sexual harassment is hardly "just personal" to the woman who loses her job because of it or has to tolerate it as a working condition. Without the man/woman difference there would be no "sex" in the heterosexual sense that Title VII has interpreted the term; without the employment nexus, Title VII would not prohibit the "harassment." When both elements are so strongly present, the characterization personal merely looks like an attempt to evade the legal categories.

Sexual harassment is also hardly personal in the sense that it little reflects the preferences and desires of the female person involved. If anything, it is personal in the sense that it negates her personhood. As one woman put it:

> I was really crushed that he didn't seem to care, in that all the interaction that I'd had with him over a couple of months meant nothing to him. And if I wasn't going to sleep with him, I wasn't going to get my promotion . . . it made me feel so dehumanized. It made me feel like I wasn't a person—that no one really cared what I was like or was interested in knowing me.[131]

Abuses of the person, such as rape and murder, are not condoned by public policy although they may "satisfy a personal urge" of the perpetrator. Not all urges are given free rein in society, heedless of their impact on others, just because they may be felt to be personal. The underlying point, whereby labeling sexual harassment "personal" avoids legal liability, seems to be that the sexually harassed woman has no personal rights considered worth protecting.

The solution of protecting a woman's interest conceived as a personal one does not, moreover, adequately address the problem. The *Tomkins* and *Barnes* suggestions that sexual harassment be treated as a tort—a private harm—applies, unstated, the view that the interest to be protected is not so much an interest of women as a sex in employment opportunities as it is a personal interest. Torts best redress injuries to one's person, here to individual sexuality as an aspect of the self, rather than to public and shared social existence, here sex in employment. The tort remedy attempts to monetize physical and psychic damage to the person,[132] sometimes including punitive damages representing outrage, rather than to formulate redress in terms of hiring, seniority, or promotion, although these remedies are not precluded. To the extent that tort theory fails to capture the broadly social sexuality/employment nexus that comprises the injury of sexual harassment, by treating the incidents as if they are outrages particular to an individual woman rather than integral to her social status as a woman worker, the personal approach on the legal level fails to analyze the relevant dimensions of the problem.

A parallel with race illustrates the difficulty with the distinction between the personal and the social implicit in these cases. As will be seen in chapter 5, the progress of legal protection against racial abuse (as well as recent regressions) traces (and reverses) a movement from regarding race as a personal matter to grasping its socially determinate character. The assumption that relations between women and men occur in a personal sphere is directly analogous to the assumption once held by whites who lived in intimate daily contact with blacks. These whites were unable to perceive their relationships with blacks as anything other than individual, their feelings and behavior as anything other than personal. Whites had to be convinced that in their personal life they participated in a structure of domination that pervaded society, formed a pattern, was reinforced and reflected in the law, and amounted to the subordination of an entire race. Interracial relationships were felt to be intensely personal. In a sense, they were personal—they simply lacked consciousness of an important social and political determinant of the person. Through a movement in consciousness it became unsustainable to continue to believe that all the characteristics which typify the condition of the two races just happened to be reproduced in two unique individuals in a personal relationship—one rich, one his servant; one formally educated, one a tenant farmer; one assertive and self-confident, the other deferential, and so on. It became clear that the reason such differences could be seen as personal was the same as the reason they were discriminatory: they were seen as appropriate *given each person's place.* In this sense, the examiner in *Williams* most closely captured the dialectical reality when he characterized the supervisor's acts as "personal advances based on sex."[133]

By analogy to race, the fact that a sexual relation between a woman and a man is felt to be personal does not exempt it from helping to perpetuate women's subordinate place in the workplace and in society as a whole. The barriers to recognition of its social structural character are merely very high. Many men go home every night to a person they fully consider themselves to be relating to "as an individual," unconscious of how their feelings, attitudes, and treatment of her might contribute to her subordination and to that of women as a whole. When whites say that they relate to blacks "as people," meaning "without regard to race"—a covert insult in itself to blacks who are affirmatively proud of their racial heritage and do not see it as something to be done "without"—they may mask sheer unconsciousness of the participation of racist social factors in comprising what "a person" means. Race as much as sex comprises part of what a person is "as a person." Physical closeness and daily contact seem to lend the appearance of individuation to relationships, a factor which obscures the group character of social identity and reinforces oppressive institutions at the very moment when it most appears that they are being transcended. It may be that at the very moment treatment appears most individualized one has most *become* the person one is socially determined to be. The social factors that shape that personhood are, at that moment, the most deeply hidden, hence the most determinative.

To view work relations between women and men this way focuses attention upon the operation of socially defined sex roles even in the closest personal relations, relations in which people are accustomed to thinking of themselves as most "themselves," hence most free. For women, as these cases suggest, the reverse often seems to be the case: the measure of the closeness is often the measure of the oppression and the greatest denial of self. The ideological and legal function of considering these matters "personal," as opposed to "sex-based," "reasonable," or "employment-related," is to isolate, individuate, invalidate, and stigmatize women's experience in order to maintain sexual oppression on the job beyond the reach of the law. Once the "personal" is seen to conform to a hierarchical social pattern, it is no more unique to, and without meaning beyond, each individual than are race relations. The "personal" life here protected, and the "natural" law vindicated, is nothing other than men's traditional prerogative of keeping sexual incursions on women beyond scrutiny or change. These most "private" of relations, instead of providing a sphere for particularity and uniqueness, appear in this perspective distressingly stereotypical, as each man and woman, in their own particular way, reproduce in these most personal interactions the structure of dominance and submission that characterizes the entire socioeconomic system.

Natural/Biological

With a tone of "you can't change *that*," the cases rejecting sexual harassment claims repeatedly excuse the incidents as "biological" or "natural." In the *Miller* case, Judge Williams, denying relief, stated with astonishing equanimity and/or candor: "The attraction of males to females and females to males is a natural sex phenomenon and it is probable that this attraction plays at least a subtle part in most personnel decisions."[134] One wonders what this factor has to do with merit and whether subtle racial revulsion is equally permissible. The brief for Bausch & Lomb was similarly explicit in its appeal to nature to exonerate the perpetrator: "Obviously, certain biological differences exist between male and female.... [I]t would appear that in the foreseeable future that the attraction of males to females and females to males will not soon disappear."[135] The *Tomkins* district court also referred to "this natural sex attraction," stating, in a breathtaking but indecisive mid-sentence reversal, "while sexual desire animated the parties, or at least one of them...."[136]

On the level of superficial contradiction, these statements at least concede that the sexual advances derive from a basis *generic* to women and men, as opposed to being purely specific (or "personal") to the individuals involved, as was simultaneously asserted. The only question then is whether this generic basis is accurately termed biological or whether sexual harassment is more open to criticism as a social phenomenon. In the biological view, sexual expression seems presumed to derive from a biological need or genital drive or to be deeply rooted in a natural order that connects biological differences with expressions of mutual attraction. The idea is that biology cannot be questioned or changed, and is legitimate, while society can be, and may be "artificial." Perhaps this presumption underlies the clear doctrinal necessity, if sexual harassment is to be considered sex discrimination under existing conceptions, to establish sexual harassment as less a question of "sexuality" than of gender status: an implicit legal presupposition that sexuality is buried in nature, while gender status is at least in part a social construct. In the above quotations, in an attempt to justify legal nonintervention, sexual harassment is implicitly argued to be an inevitable and integral part of the naturally given, not socially contingent or potentially changeable, sexual relations between women and men.

Upon closer scrutiny, these presumptions about sex have little to do with the occurrence of sexual harassment. Women possess a physical sex drive equal to or greater than that of men,[137] yet do not systematically harass men sexually. Some men, who have nothing wrong with them sexually, seem able to control their behavior. Not all women experience sexual attraction to all men, nor all men to all women. These factors suggest that something beyond pure biology is implicated. Usually, the last thing wanted in these incidents is species reproduction, which removes any connection with a natural drive in that direction. Moreover, not everything deemed natural by defining all sexual behavior as biological is thereby made socially acceptable. If economically coerced intercourse is biological, rape must be also, but it is not legally allowed for that reason.

The image of codetermination in sexual matters by men and women is scrupulously maintained in these cases. But for the unwilling woman, no "attraction" is involved, and little power. Even if the "attractiveness of the sexes for one another" were inevitable, that would not make its expression indiscriminate. Calling sex "natural" means here, in effect, that women are to be allowed no choice of with whom and under what conditions to have sexual relations. In these cases, we are dealing with a male who is allegedly exercising his power as an employer, his power over a woman's material survival, and his sexual prerogatives as a man, to subject a woman sexually. One would have to argue that sexual power is by nature asymmetrical, and hence that it is biological for males to threaten, force, blackmail, coerce, subject, exploit, and oppress women sexually, to conclude that sexual harassment is natural.

More likely, it is only under conditions of women's social inequality (conditions which Congress responded to by the passage of Title VII and other legislation) that sexual harassment is presented as a social inevitability mystified as a natural one.[138] In this view, it is only under conditions in which men systematically hold superior positions to women and are not only willing but able to abuse their position with impunity, and in which women have so few practical alternatives, that so natural an occurrence persists. This is not to deny the existence of social and biological differences, but to question whether the economic subordination of women by sexual means is an inevitable consequence of those differences. Arguably, we are here confronting an inequality in social power rationalized as a biological difference, specifically with a society that rigidly defines role opportunities in terms of sex, and then sanctifies those roles by attributing to them a basis in nature. This is as true for the fact that women are inferiors on the job as it is for the sexual relations that male superiors coercively initiate.

Not a Policy

Arguments that sexual harassment is personal or biological often appear together to defeat the allegation that the treatment complained of is employer "policy" under Title VII. A personal caper is extrinsic to employment; besides, biological facts, like hormone cycles, can hardly be controlled by employer policy. I have addressed each argument separately. Together, they are at the very least contradictory. If an exchange between two persons is "individual" in the sense of being grounded in interpersonal specificity, how is it based on biology? A less particular or unique basis for relations is difficult to imagine. Perhaps romantic poetry better captures the feeling of synthesis of pure individuality with human universlity toward which these court opinions grope. Or perhaps sexual harassment exemplifies the romantic aspect of that "romantic paternalism which, in practical effect, put women not on a pedestal, but in a cage."[139] In any case, women who are sexually harassed do not seem to share any transcendent sense of unity between self and species as a result of this treatment.

Although not discussed in these terms, the question of whether the acts are employer policy serves, however indirectly, to raise the issue of the employment-relatedness of the behavior in question. On one level, as recognized in *Williams,* this may be properly a question of fact:[140] did the employer's sexual advances relate to plaintiff's employment? This poses the question of what acts suffice to bring sexual advances between workplace associates within the legal definition of employment, presuming that sexual harassment in employment is itself considered sex discrimination. The question for legal doctrine here is what suffices to make actions at or arising out of the workplace into actions *of* the workplace in the sense that these acts can be attributed to the employer.

Under usual standards of Title VII, employer policy is nothing more cosmic than employer actions, which expressly includes acts by "agents" of employers within the common law and statutory definitions.[141] Case law supports the inclusion of acts of subordinates as within employer responsibility.[142] "Clearly," the Equal Employment Opportunity Commission (EEOC) has stated, "an employer is responsible for the actions of its supervisors."[143] Liability attaches regardless of employer disclaimer of supervisory conduct as motivated by personal considerations and not by company policy.[144] (The history of the "under color of state law" doctrine illuminates the demise of an analogous attempt to evade official responsibility for officially sanctioned but individually initiated [and/or financially embarrassing] acts.)[145]

The allocation of responsibility between employer and offending

employee might properly vary with the degree of employer involvement or knowing acquiescence. It is possible that punitive damages
would not be imputed to the employer under Title VII,[146] although
they might arguably attach to the individual perpetrator. This var-
iance no more determines *liability* than it would in any other kind of
discrimination. The point is, if sexual harassment is properly discrimination in employment, there should be little legal doubt that the
employer is to some degree accountable. Whether the perpetrator
feels that the incident is personal or biological, the impact is upon the
victim's employment and employment opportunities and the employer is in a position to provide relief. On this issue, sex discrimination by sexual means is no different from sex discrimination by any
other means. The prior questions are whether the conduct is "based
on sex" in the legal sense, and whether the acts are in fact
employment-related.

In this context, the inference drawn in *Corne* that a practice that
"has no relation to the nature of the employment"[147] is not employer
policy, hence cannot ground a discrimination claim, is simply wrong.
On the level on which it is confused, it concedes the point: if they are
sex-based, practices on the job which "have nothing to do with employment" are not job-related, hence discriminatory, when they determine employment opportunities, not "not employer policy." On a
deeper level, the test is insulting. To say that because an allegedly
discriminatory act has nothing to do with the nature of the job it
therefore cannot be discriminatory presumes that usual discriminatory practices have something bona fide to do with the job. The treatment in *Corne* of the test of "employer benefit" confirms this suspicion. In Judge Frey's opinion, one indication that a discriminatory act
is company "policy" is that it benefits the company. Surely Judge Frey
does not think that blacks and women in general do not merit equal
employment, such that policies giving them opportunities equal to
white males are detrimental to companies.

The issue of employer policy as considered in *Miller* was only
slightly more substantial. There, the employer allegedly had a written
policy against "moral misconduct, including sexual advances,"[148] for
which employees who make sexual advances to co-employees, subordinates, or superiors were represented to be reprimanded or dismissed. The court concluded that plaintiff's lack of pursuit of these

internal mechanisms meant that the employer could not be held responsible for any alleged misconduct. Given the statement that this was not an issue of internal exhaustion of remedies, it could be inquired whether a written employer policy against race discrimination would similarly defeat an allegation of race discrimination in practice. Hewing more closely to the allegations, the point might better have been that without attempted pursuit of existing internal remedies, no basis existed for an inference one way or the other as to whether the employer had a policy in practice of allowing these advances. If the policy is challenged as not adequate, a plaintiff who perceived this and did not complain is less an example of its inadequacies than one who did, but is nevertheless arguably injured by its shortcomings. Taking the *Williams* allegations as true, it could be that *in practice* the bank allowed its written policy to be *broken* only in cases of advances from supervisory males to subordinate females. It could even have failed to enforce the policy only in her case out of preference shown this individual man. These are properly issues of fact. Dismissal was thus implicitly grounded upon a negative judgment of the truth of the facts Miller alleged.

Administrative Concerns

According to the foregoing analysis, the entire structure of sexual domination, the tacit relations of deference and command, can be present in a passing glance. To recognize this is to grasp the social reality; it is not fully to delineate a legal cause of action. Few would want every passing glance to be legally actionable sex discrimination. In this sense, what is "sex discrimination" will always be narrower than what is "sexist." But this is no reason for sexual harassment not to be actionable at all, as several courts have suggested.

Judge Frey, in *Corne,* predicted: "An outgrowth of [holding unwelcome verbal and physical advances actionable under Title VII] would be a potential federal lawsuit every time any employer made amorous or sexually-oriented advances toward another."[149] Judge Williams, in *Miller,* expressed a similar concern:

[It] would not be difficult to foresee a federal challenge based on alleged sex motivated considerations of the complainant's superior in every case of a lost promotion, transfer, demotion or dismissal. And who is to say what degree of sexual cooperation would found a Title VII claim? It is conceivable, under plaintiff's theory, that flirtations of the smallest order would give rise to liability.[150]

Judge Frey seems to wish to safeguard the employer's right to make sexual advances free from allegations of job consequences, regardless of any actual connection between them. Reversing the connection between the employment event and the erroneous sexual allegation, Judge Williams seems to wish to protect the employer's right to control an employee's work life free from allegations that sexual advances were a factor, while permitting small-order flirtations on the side. In *Tomkins*, Judge Stern foresees a necessary expansion in the judicial system: "And if an inebriated approach by a supervisor to a subordinate at the office Christmas party could form the basis of a federal lawsuit for sex discrimination if a promotion or a raise is later denied to the subordinate we would need 4,000 federal trial judges instead of some 400."[151]

If sexual harassment is an ubiquitous as these objections recognize, one ought to conclude that women are sexually harassed almost as a matter of routine in the workplaces of America and something should be done about it. Alternatively, the presumption could be that this onslaught, large enough to require an increase in the federal judiciary by a factor of 10, would contain largely unfounded claims. If this is the presumption, the argument should be explicitly made that sexual harassment is more open to false claims than are existing causes of action. One such possible contention, commonly criticized in the rape (as well as the tort) context, is that sexual accusations are easier to make and harder to disprove.

The image of woman as liar and dissembler is probably the source of the myth that women often make false charges of rape against men, even men they do not know. While every person who works in law enforcement knows that false charges are not infrequent, particularly among people who bear grudges against one another, it is only in rape that it is assumed that the usual safeguards in the system cannot protect the accused from a lying witness. The extreme absurdity of this can be seen in a combined burglary-rape-robbery by a total stranger when the defense is mistaken identity. The judge must charge the jury that there is a heavier burden of proof of the rape than of the burglary or robbery even though the same man, whoever he is, committed all three crimes.[152]

As this quotation suggests, the fear of unfounded claims prejudges the facts in individual cases. In general, substantial evidence exists that many more rapes occur than are reported, rather than the reverse.[153]

With sexual harassment "false reporting is unlikely: women have more to lose than to gain from it."[154] Given women's feelings of humiliation and intimidation from the incident, together with the condescension, ridicule, and reprisals that women who report sexual harassment suffer—reactions which legal sanctions might as well be expected to increase as decrease in the short run—it seems unlikely that significant numbers of reports would be fabricated. It is even arguable that most women have more to lose, on an individual basis, from reporting and pursuing *true* incidents than from attempting to ignore them and forget the whole thing. The total cost in terms of reputation, energy, distress, legal fees, and employment opportunities would seem to present sufficient disincentives to pure fabrication as to make the risk worth taking that the legal system would expose prevaricators. Women who genuinely but erroneously see themselves as victims of sexual harassment are probably fewer in number than (or, to give the benefit of the doubt, at least equal to) the number of men who genuinely but erroneously do not see themselves as perpetrators. Thus, the foreseen landslide of sexual harassment complaints must be presumed either potentially bona fide, so that no matter how many there are (or because there are so many) legal redress should be available, or they must be presumed disproportionately likely to be false compared with other legal claims, a sexist and dubious judgment of fact.

Often when courts are confronted with a massive social problem which has been ignored, the first response is "administrative" concern for the legal system. Judicial resistance in similar guise characterized the drive for union rights, recognition coming only after protracted struggle. The same can be said for women's legal rights as a whole and of the rights of racial and national minorities. The objection persists that if such groups are allowed to claim discrimination there will be no end of it. The response is that there will be an end to the claims when there is an end to the discrimination.

The recognition that race discrimination is a legitimate grievance under law—not simply something that inferior persons raise as an excuse for special consideration—was hard won. It was accompanied by the recognition that, as with every other kind of litigation, not every allegation of discrimination is an example of discrimination. To exclude sexual harassment from prohibition as sex discrimination as a matter of law on the ground that not every allegation would prove founded is irrebuttably to presume that *every* charge of sexual harassment is a pretext to attack an employment context or decision that would ultimately be vindicated in court. It is to presume that the risk of abuse (a risk that falls mostly on men) is greater than the benefit of prohibition (a benefit that falls mainly on women). Any law can be abused, and there are two sides to every lawsuit. If sexual harassment is sex discrimination as a matter of law, opponents of its legal prohibition should explain why courts should acquiesce in it and why the application of equal protection doctrine and Title VII should stop short at this point.

These judicial fears may have deeper social roots. Rosabeth Kanter, having analyzed the secretary role as a system of "unequal and non-reciprocal authority" in which the secretary's status is contingent upon the "whim" of the boss and her "personal fealty" to him, describes the major danger to the maintenance of this system: "For the system, the threat of retaliation is what must be guarded against. The danger is that the one-sided authority relations generate resentments that would be turned against former superiors if subordinates ever got authority on their own."[155] Perhaps the underlying fear reflected in these administrative concerns derives from a perception that this cause of action challenges the whole structure of sexual subordination and thus would legitimize something analogous to a slave revolt.

In conclusion, consider the arguments against holding sexual harassment sex discrimination within an altered context.[156] A white male supervisor argues that his former file clerk, a black man, left work, not because of race discrimination as claimed but because of the employer's requirement that he clean the executive bathroom and shine the boss's shoes periodically. The supervisor argued he had a "personal preference" that plaintiff, individually, perform these tasks for him. As a result of the plaintiff's resistance to performing these tasks, the two developed a "subtly inharmonious personal relationship." This was revealed by the supervisor regularly characterizing plaintiff as "that uppity nigger." This reference to his "character" made plaintiff "unhappy," but then he knew that his employer's "speech standards were not of the highest." Unsatisfactory work reports were also filed, since plaintiff began to be absent on days he predicted he would be pressured to clean the bathroom or shine shoes. After a long series of incidents surrounding the bathroom-cleaning and shoe-shining demands, he left work. The unemployment appeals board, denying benefits, found this reason for leaving work "personal" and "uncompelling," and his leaving "voluntary," suggesting that "particularly sensitive people may react unreasonably." His absenteeism was also noted.

To continue the hypothetical case, the file clerk sued for race discrimination. The court found, on the same facts, that "such highly personalized and subjective conduct" evidenced here cannot ground a claim of discrimination. These facts reflect only the racial "practices" of the employer, not conduct based upon racial "characteristics as such."[157] There is no indication that the employer required plaintiff to clean his personal bathroom or shine his shoes *because* he was black. It is uncontested that he was "good at it." Not every black employee was so required; from aught that appears, no other employee of either race was requested to perform these jobs. Without a showing that these task requirements were "a pretext for discriminating" against a "definable employee group," it is better for the courts to avoid involvement in every instance of abuse of authority for personal benefit.

5   *Legal Context*

"One is not born, one rather becomes, a woman," Simone de Beauvoir has said.[1] In this view, biology does not definitively make a woman, the social processes of becoming one do. But the tension that delivers her point lies in the felt experience that what fundamentally defines a woman is not a social construction but the body with which she is born. The relationship between woman's anatomy and her social fate is the pivot on which turn all attempts, and opposition to attempts, to define or change her situation. At every turn, nature appears hand in glove with culture, so that the special definition of woman's place within man's world appears to conform exactly to her differences from him. But the same reality can be seen as the fist of social dominance hidden in the soft glove of reasonableness—the ideology of biological fiat.

The Supreme Court's approach to sex discrimination contains, unresolved, the same tension between physiology and circumstance. Sometimes the Court proceeds upon a conception of sex differences, attributing its roots to nature; sometimes sex inequality is glimpsed, with its foundation in social bedrock. These two approaches are outlined in this chapter,* to be applied in chapter 6 to the legal argument that sexual harassment is sex discrimination. The first approach to sex discrimination implicitly conceives of the social situation of the sexes as an expression of a pattern of sex differences. I term this the *differences* approach. In this view, to prohibit sex discrimination is to prohibit not all differentiations between the sexes but only those that are seen as not well founded, that is, inaccurate or overgeneralized distinctions between the sexes. The test for discrimination is whether

*A more detailed derivation, development, and doctrinal application of these concepts to case materials is contained in Appendix A.

a rule or practice is irrationally grounded upon a sex difference. Discrimination here is what Owen Fiss terms "arbitrariness."[2] The gender difference is lined up against the sex difference in practice, and women are compared with men, to see if the correspondences warrant the application. Expressed doctrinally, the inquiry under the Equal Protection Clause of the Fourteenth Amendment focuses upon a state's purpose in using, and its use of, sex as a criterion, seeing whether sex bears a "rational relationship to a state objective that is sought to be advanced."[3] Under Title VII, courts scrutinize the rationality of the relationship between a sex differentiation and the requirements of employment.*

The second approach implicitly conceives of the social situation of the sexes as unequal, rather than merely—or even basically— different. I term this the *inequality* approach. Inequality is more than discrepancy or disparity. Cases which adopt this view speak in terms of women's imposed inferiority, social disabilities, and the stigma and reality of second-class status. In this view, men's and women's roles are not only different; men's roles are socially dominant, women's roles subordinate to them. The imagery of hierarchy, not just of distinction, animates the opinions. Women as a group are seen to be relegated to work that is not only distinct from men's, but also trivialized, devalued, and undercompensated. While stereotypes of men may cause pain and distortion, social stereotypes of women denigrate and exclude them from the majority of society's pursuits, pursuits which tend to be carried on by men.

Although no legal doctrine exists which fully adopts the inequality approach, several are conducive to it. One is the prohibition on practices which have a "disparate impact" upon one sex while purporting to treat the sexes neutrally or evenhandedly. This is often termed discrimination *in effect*.[4] Another is the now remote possibility that the Supreme Court will consider sex a "suspect classification" under the Equal Protection Clause. This would require that each differentiation

---

*The relevant paragraphs of Title VII are quoted in chapter 1, *supra*, at 6. The Equal Protection Clause of the Fourteenth Amendment provides that no state shall "deny to any person within its jurisdiction the equal protection of the laws." The Fifth Amendment due process clause has been interpreted to provide the same protection against acts by the federal government. *Bolling v. Sharpe*, 347 U.S. 497 (1954). Both provisions will hereinafter be referred to as the "Equal Protection Clause."

between the sexes sustain "strict scrutiny." In the one opinion at the Supreme Court level that took this view, Justice Brennan criticized laws that differentiated between women and men at work, saying they

were not in any sense designed to rectify the effects of past discrimination against women. On the contrary, these statutes seize upon a group—women—who have historically suffered discrimination in employment, and rely upon the effects of this past discrimination as a justification for heaping on additional economic disadvantages.[5]

Implying that even such a substantive view of women's inequality could devolve into an abstract calculus about the sex difference, Ruth Ginsburg poses a question which sharply divides a difference theory from an inequality theory: "In Justice Brennan's view, is sex the suspect criterion or female sex?"[6]

The social position of women has a special place in the inequality analysis, as it does not in an analysis of arbitrary differentiation. In this view, the prohibition on sex discrimination aims to eliminate the social inferiority of one sex to the other, to dismantle the social structure that maintains a series of practices that cumulatively, in Owen Fiss's term, "disadvantage" women. Rational no more than irrational sex differences are legitimate reasons for perpetuating the social inequality of the sexes. The nemesis of the first approach is irrationality; the target of the second, subordination.

Justice Brennan observed the two approaches at work in his dissent in *Gilbert v. General Electric*,[7] in which the Supreme Court reached a pinnacle of differences rationale. The majority held that excluding pregnancy from disability coverage under a private employer's insurance plan was not sex discrimination under Title VII.[8] Justice Brennan thought this case "unusual in that it presents a question the resolution of which at first glance turns largely upon the conceptual framework chosen to identify and describe the operational features of the challenged disability program."[9] The Court's framework, as described by Justice Brennan, perceived General Electric's plan as "a gender-free assignment of risks in accordance with normal actuarial techniques."[10] Sex presented a difference within the risk pool. In this perspective, "the lone exclusion of pregnancy is not a violation of Title VII insofar as all other disabilities are mutually covered for both sexes."[11] Pregnancy provided a sex difference so extreme as to be unique to women. It was considered "extra," over and above the health needs the sexes shared. In addition, because not *all* women can become pregnant, a differentiation based upon pregnancy was not thought a difference in treatment based on gender. Alternatively, in what I call the inequality framework, the Equal Employment Opportunity Commission (EEOC) and the plaintiff saw that pregnancy, a condition creating temporary work disability and a condition affecting only women, had alone been omitted from the plan's coverage. In a clear inequality, "only women [are subjected] to a substantial risk of total loss of income because of a temporary disability."[12]

Far from unusual in underlying a sex discrimination case, these two conceptual frameworks epitomize the way discrimination in general, sex discrimination in particular, has been approached. Pregnancy, because it poses a real sex difference which has also been integral to women's inequality, posed a predictable[13] crisis for the continued coexistence, or mutual obliviousness, of these perspectives.[14] Sexual harassment poses a similarly critical but analytically distinct problem. Sexual differences between women and men are real, although they have probably been socially exaggerated. In the practice of sexual harassment, woman's sexuality is used to perpetuate her inequality. Women's sexuality, like pregnancy, is in one sense unique to women; but unlike pregnancy, women's sexuality—its characteristics and social treatment—can be compared with men's sexuality, so in another sense is not unique. The choice between the inequality and the differences approach is crucial to both issues.

These two approaches have not yet developed into two explicit and recognized legal doctrines. They do mark two conceptually distinct approaches to the purpose of prohibiting sex discrimination, hence to any argument that sexual harassment is within that prohibition. "Presumably," Justice Brennan observed, "it is not self-evident that either conceptual framework is more appropriate than the other. . . ."[15] But it is evident that they present distinct tendencies as social theories, are built upon different perceptions, assumptions, and definitions of the social reality of the sexes, and imply different goals and priorities. Although there are circumstances in which they reach the same result, they tend determinately to diverge on some issues. Preferences for one approach over the other are therefore based on principle.

The difficult cases for sex discrimination law, in light of this analysis, arise when a practice that promotes women's inequality as a sex is predicated upon an actual difference between the sexes. Under the first approach, this is not sex discrimination; under the second approach, it is. *Gilbert* is such a case; so are two others. The *Manhart* case required the Court to choose between compensating women workers in their old age on the basis of their differences from men—leaving them with higher premiums or lower benefits than men because women as a group outlive men—or compensating women equally with men, so that regardless of expected longevity, women would be covered at the same level for the same premiums. In the *Dothard* case, a statute setting minimum height and weight requirements for prison guards was invalidated. Because women's height and weight on the average are less than men's, this standard was found to be discrimination "in effect."[16] Under the differences approach, an accurate but detrimental differentiation (based, for example, on actual sex differences in disabilities, longevity, or build) need not be sex discrimination. Under an inequality approach, detrimental differentiations based on sex are discriminatory whether accurate or not.

The two approaches can be mutually supporting, each reaching the same result for its own reason. Sex stereotypes, for example, are equally forbidden under both theories. Many inequalities are predicated upon untrue generalizations about the sex difference, to women's detriment. Similarly, to be in a subordinate position is to be differentiated from the dominant group, often for reasons that appear arbitrary. But not all subordination lacks a basis in the social actuality of sex, and not all sex-based irrationality produces systematic disadvantage. Sometimes, as has often been the case for men, it produces positive advantages. What the second approach grasps, and the first does not, is that it is not only lies and blindness that have kept women down. It is as much the social creation of differences, and the transformation of differences into social advantages and disadvantages, upon which inequality can *rationally* be predicated. Discrimination is often irrational. But under the inequality approach, that is not all, nor even primarily, what is unjust about it. What is unjust about sex discrimination is that it supports a system of second-class status for half of humanity.

This distinction raises a series of questions about the conceptualization of sex and of discrimination which have never been confronted in a legal context. Is it sex differences that underlie so many of the observed disparities between the sexes, of which some are permissible and ineradicable and some not? Or is the law against sex discrimination facing a systematic social structure that creates women unequal? In other terms, does the policy against sex discrimination seek to eliminate unwarranted accretions upon the sex difference or is its purpose to eliminate the legal supports for male supremacy? Is male supremacy itself nothing more than a collection of encrusted ir-rationalities about the sex difference? Or is it a social system for the maintenance of the advantage of one sex over and against the other? If sex discrimination is a problem of invalid differentiation, true dif-ferences can provide valid grounds for unequal treatment. If sex discrimination is a problem of inequality, as chances for parity be-tween the sexes are opened, women's differences from men must be equally accommodated and equally valued, without penalty or prefer-ence.

Two Theories of Sex Discrimination

Discrimination as a legal concept exists to correct the detrimental application or misapplication of certain kinds of social categories. The law on discrimination is comprised of the variety of circumstances under which group characteristics are judged permissible or imper-missible as bases for distinguishing among individuals. But discrimi-nation theory is not a legal corrective for all social differentiation, however unjust. Discrimination law is an exception to the legal sys-tem's basic unwillingness to intervene in those processes of social selection which systematically produce variances in social outcomes, whether the variations are seen to have an individual or group basis.

There are tensions within discrimination theory at the outset. A detrimental differentiation must contain enough of a group reference to be arguably based on a social category, rather than a unique or individual quality, but it must be presented as an injury to an indi-vidual. Moreover, the group reference must be sufficiently excep-tional to justify singling it out from that vast range of arguably unjust but shared bases for human differentiation which Congress and the courts do not see as their function to police. Examples not prohibited as grounds for employment decisions under Title VII include male effeminacy, government employee status, membership in a racist, anti-Semitic organization, having wages garnisheed, and engaging in unlawful conduct against the employer.[17] Specifically individual "dis-criminations" are not considered discrimination in this sense (al-though they may come into question as bills of attainder or violations of due process). Mass "discrimination," understood as systematic differential treatment, on grounds such as membership in the working class or breathing city air, falls on the other end of the continuum and is also not considered discrimination by the law.

The law has not confronted these questions of boundaries and applications systematically. Instead, a provisional solution to the open-ended list of possible discriminatory factors is achieved by congealing a short list of presumptively suspicious-to-forbidden group characteristics now commonly including race, sex, religion, and national origin—together with a case by case adjudication of the circumstances of their use. But the tensions temporarily resolved for each category and in each individual case reemerge each time a new categorical injustice or a new set of circumstances surfaces.

Sex Differences

The differences approach, currently dominant in sex discrimination law, begins with the usually unarticulated notion that social equality means that equals should be treated equally. This means that people who are the same should be treated the same. The law applies this criterion through the formula that "similarly situated" persons should be treated the same, meaning that persons in relevantly similar circumstances should be treated relevantly similarly. But what is relevant similarity? The same as whom? What is a "fair" relation to those similarities?

Under the Equal Protection Clause, which protects individuals from sex discrimination by the government, similarities and differences are measured in relation to a "legitimate state purpose." For example: "A classification 'must be reasonable, not arbitrary, and must rest upon some ground of difference having a fair and substantial relation to the object of legislation, so that all persons similarly circumstanced shall be treated alike.'"[18] When a classification is scrutinized under the "suspect classification" approach, which sets a stricter standard, the state purpose must be "compelling."[19] Under Title VII, which protects individuals from discrimination in employment, the similarities and differences are measured in relationship to the job. Criteria are not arbitrary if the characteristics on which they rely are relevantly connected to a valid state purpose or to employment decisions.

The first time the Supreme Court found a statute to be sex dis-

criminatory was in 1971, in *Reed v. Reed*. The case challenged a statute
that preferred men over women as administrators of estates.[20] The
Idaho Supreme Court had concluded that administrative efficiency
was served by eliminating women from consideration. It found the
sex distinction was not "so completely without a basis in fact as to be
irrational and arbitrary."[21] The U.S. Supreme Court found sex discrimination under the Equal Protection Clause:

> To give a mandatory preference to members of either sex over members of
> the other, merely to accomplish the elimination of hearings on the merits, is to
> make the very kind of arbitrary legislative choice forbidden by the Equal
> Protection Clause of the Fourteenth Amendment.[22]

Placing women beyond an inquiry into their merits made sex a criterion "wholly unrelated to the objective of that statute."[23]

What made this choice arbitrary was that individual women could
not be chosen on their merits—certainly an evil. An inequality
perspective casts this case in a different light. The inequality principle
would not have reached a different result in the *Reed* case; it would
have reached the same result on a considerably more far-reaching
basis. It would have been considerably more rational, factually based,
not arbitrary, and substantially related to the statutory purpose to
presume that men would be the better administrators if most women
were illiterate and wholly excluded from business affairs. Yet this
reasoning would reveal a society in severe need of prohibitions on sex
discrimination. Further, in a society of female illiteracy, with the *Reed*
opinion as it stands, a legal guarantee of equal consideration would
make little difference to most women, who would merely be rejected
individually as estate administrators on the grounds that they individually could not read.[24] This example suggests that inequality has to
be seen as arbitrary before the differentiations through which it is
effectuated appear irrational.

To illustrate further, a now classic article on Equal Protection doctrine written in 1949 argues that whether a classification is arbitrary
or not depends upon how well it coincides with acceptable social di-
visions. The central inquiry of discrimination is, in the authors' view,
"whether in defining a class, the legislature has carved the universe at
a natural joint."[25] So far as the joint carved corresponds to the conception of the natural, so far the class has "fit," so is not arbitrary, therefore nondiscriminatory. From the inequality perspective, sex may be

such a "natural joint" for all the wrong reasons. A division which produces inequality may seem natural because of inequality so pervasive it has seldom been questioned or been rationally questionable. The social inequality inherent in the lack of physical training for women, for example, may express itself in women's lesser physical strength, a difference which comes to seem natural primarily because it is a physical fact.[26] That the sex division seems natural may measure how deeply sex divides social consciousness better than it measures the givenness of characteristics of the sexes or justifies sex as a foundation for social disparity. That sex seems a natural division may reveal not the appropriateness of the grouping but the degree to which a *social* perception that sex is a matter of differentness has buried itself in nature and reemerged in society clothed as what the society means by a natural difference. The conception of the natural—and its contents—remain social ideas. To pattern a society after what seems natural, in this perspective, is to pattern it after an idea of the natural that is itself social and thereby to sanctify that social idea. Further, while sex may be a "natural joint" at which to carve the universe, it may not be a natural point at which to subordinate one group to the other. The *social* universe is not only carved up, it is also hierarchically ordered.

In these terms, *Brown v. Board of Education*[27] held that racial segregation was arbitrary in public education because race was properly irrelevant to the purposes of education. If discrimination consists in "arbitrariness," to discriminate means to treat differently people who are seen as relevantly the same across the group characteristic in view. *Brown* rejected the reasoning of *Plessy v. Ferguson*,[28] the 1896 case in which "separate but equal" railroad transportation for blacks and whites was held constitutional. But *Plessy* also clearly illustrates the arbitrariness approach. There, the Supreme Court found that it was not arbitrary for Louisiana statutorily to require the separation of the races in public accommodations. Their underlying reasoning was that the racial differences which resulted in racial separation were facts of nature and of social life.

In determining the question of reasonableness it [the legislature] is at liberty to act with reference to the established usages, customs and traditions of the people, and with a view to the promotion of their comfort, and the preservation of the public peace and good order. Gauged by this standard, we cannot say that a law which authorizes or even requires the separation of the two races in public conveyances is unreasonable. If the civil and political rights of both races be equal one cannot be inferior to the other civilly or politically. If one race be inferior to the other socially, the Constitution of the United States cannot put them upon the same plane.[29]

Race was therefore relevant and "reasonably" related to a valid state purpose. Because blacks were socially inferior to whites, it was not at all arbitrary for the law to recognize it. Plainly, the social perspective determined what was "reasonable" in these cases.

What changed between *Plessy* and *Brown* was the implicit standard for what would be seen to be a *reasonable* difference in the social position of the races. In the *Plessy* perspective, the poignant evidence of the damage segregation does to children which supported the *Brown* result[30] could have supported the opposite legal result—that blacks were different, thus deserving of different, that is, separate, educational treatment. In *Brown,* only racial differences which were not based on racial inequality were "reasonable"—hence, there were no reasonable racial differences.[31]

In sex discrimination law, "arbitrariness" consists in utilizing the gender difference in social decision making without justification in what is taken to be gender biology. The unfairness lies in the improper relation between the group characteristic (conceived as biological fact) and its social application. Differential treatment is not permitted when the sexes, although defined in terms of their biological difference, can be considered the same. If the sexes can be considered relevantly the same, "similarly situated," or *comparable* on the dimension in question, differential treatment may be discriminatory; if not, differential treatment merely treats differences differently and is not discriminatory.[32]

Biology, thus, is used to define both the grounds on which different treatment may be recognized as discriminatory and the grounds on which different treatment may be recognized as a consequence of "real" sex differences, hence reasonably based and not discriminatory. One must claim a basis in sex in order to complain of differential treatment; but if there is a real basis in sex for the different treatment, no discrimination occurred. Applied to women, the arbitrariness standard comes down to this: women shall be treated the same as men except in cases where their biology warrants a difference.

This seemingly simple formulation provides no guide to *which* differences are real and hence warrant different treatment. More fatefully, in this approach it is the existence of biological differences that is thought to distinguish the prohibited gender categories in the first place. This reduces the rule to a loaded tautology: biologically different people are to be treated the same except when their biological differences are relevant. The entire determination reduces to a question of which differences, when the groups are defined as groups according to those differences, are to be considered legally relevant under which circumstances, and which sex, as a practical matter, sets the standard against which a "difference" is measured.

Pregnancy exemplifies as real a difference between women and men as can be imagined. *Differential* treatment by sex with respect to pregnancy is impossible because no pregnant men exist to whom pregnant women can be compared. Using exemplary "arbitrariness" logic, Justice Rehnquist for the Court in the *Gilbert* case found pregnancy a *relevant* basis for distinguishing among recipients of temporary disability benefits. What could provide a less arbitrary, hence less discriminatory, reason for differential treatment than a physical condition found only in one sex and never in the other? In this view, the problem was not that coverage was unequal by sex. It was that the risks—due to biology, not policy—to which covered persons are subject are differently distributed by sex. Recognition and assignment of such risks is an accepted technique in the insurance business, a choice to cover some, but not all temporary disabilities. Hence, exclusion of pregnancy is not discrimination, but recognition of a relevant, situated real difference.

As to the area in which the sexes arguably *can* be compared, that is, temporary disability coverage as a whole, an application of the same logic also defeated the discrimination claim. Days covered and dollar benefits received under the plan appeared roughly equal by sex, pregnancy excluded. Thus, Rehnquist found "no proof that the package is in fact worth more to men than to women.... gender-based discrimination does not result simply because an employer's disability benefit plan is less than all-inclusive."[33] This was found to be true despite the fact that only women run the risk of lengthy uninsured absence from work. Must pregnancy be covered because it disables women or may it be excluded because it cannot disable men? In choosing the latter, discrimination law chooses to prevent only differential treatment seen as arbitrarily, sometimes termed "invidiously,"[34] based on sex. It chooses not to equalize social outcomes in the face of biological differences.

The lack of clarity concerning the facts of differences on the one hand and the unequal social consequences of those differences on the other, are revealed even more clearly in *Nashville Gas v. Satty,*[35] a case treating the work consequences of pregnancy after *Gilbert.* There, the employer required a pregnant employee to take a leave of absence, during which she received no sick pay and lost all accumulated job seniority. The Supreme Court held that the policy of denying accumulated seniority to women returning from pregnancy leave, while neutral on its face, discriminates in effect on the basis of sex, because if any employee was forced to take a leave of absence because of disease or disability other than pregnancy, seniority was retained and permitted to accrue. Suddenly pregnancy became comparable with other disabilities. The reasoning was that, in *Gilbert,* there was no evidence that General Electric's policy favored men over women, whereas here, "petitioner has not merely refused to extend to women a benefit that men cannot and do not receive, but has imposed on women a substantial burden that men need not suffer."[36] Noting that *Gilbert* found that Title VII "did not require that greater economic benefits be paid to one sex or the other because of their different roles in the scheme of existence," *Satty* found that "that holding does not allow us to read [the Act] to permit an employer to burden female employees in such a way as to deprive them of employment opportunities because of their different role."[37] However, not awarding sick leave pay to pregnant employees was not found to have a direct effect "upon either employment opportunities or job status," but only to have the effect of "loss of income for the period the employee is not at work."[38] As in *Gilbert,* the scheme was considered facially neutral as to sex, its "only fault is underinclusiveness."[39]

Justice Stevens analyzed this opinion to hold that distinctions based on pregnancy may be facially neutral but have a discriminatory effect if "the employer has a policy which adversely affects a woman *beyond* the term of her pregnancy leave"[40] (emphasis added). Under this test, what is discriminatory about the denial of seniority is that "the formerly pregnant person is permanently disadvantaged as compared to the rest of the work force. And since the persons adversely affected by this policy comprise an exclusively female class, the Company's plan has an obvious discriminatory effect."[41] A loss of money is not seen as a permanent loss, while a loss of seniority, a different form of credit for time worked, is. For this reason, "as the law now stands, although some discrimination against pregnancy—as compared with other physical disabilities—is permissible, discrimination against pregnant or formerly pregnant employees is not."[42]

A pregnant worker may have difficulty cutting herself so fine. Because she is pregnant, she may lose money for time she will never be able to work, but as a worker, she may not lose seniority credit for time she will never be able to work. It is hard to avoid the impression that the real distinction here is that granting seniority credit is a cheap concession which mainly benefits some workers over others, while paying disability benefits is expensive for employers. Doctrinally, to say that the treatment of pregnant persons is not sex-based (and this was implicit in *Gilbert* as well) amounts to saying that pregnant workers are not, for these purposes, to be considered treated as women. To ignore that all pregnant persons are women tends more toward obfuscation—and women's disadvantage—than to sex equality, which is what ignoring gender purports to promote.

The logic of differences theory, its analysis of gender in society, and its interpretation of the purposes of discrimination law, can be further illustrated by an examination of the Court's recent treatment of the issue of discriminatory intent. A policy which is not per se discriminatory under Title VII or the Equal Protection Clause is deemed to become so if it is *intended* as a "mere pretext to effect an invidious discrimination against the members of one sex or the other."[43] Although this is considered doctrinally exceptional, analytically it is of a piece. If pregnancy disability exclusion were purposely used as a "pretext" to deprive all women of employment opportunities, this would be to use a characteristic of some women to the detriment of all women, whether or not pregnant, or potentially so. Such a "subterfuge"[44] would create sex-based discrimination under this theory because it would force the requisite relationship between the policy and gender. The "rational" link between the sex-related criterion and its social application would thereby be broken, making "arbitrary" that which previously was not. The pregnancy disability exclusion was not arbitrary, in this sense, because it applied only to those women who were, in fact, pregnant.[45]

From women's point of view, General Electric's policy would not have done more damage if the company had consciously designed it with intent to damage women rather than to cut costs at pregnant women's expense. Few women have the security of knowing whether or how long they are in the class of "all women" as opposed to the class of "pregnant persons"; no man faces this problem. Women thus buy less employment security for the same insurance contributions. It also seems worth asking whether the law against sex discrimination means more to outlaw malicious attitudes toward women or injuries to women.[46] In other areas of law, variations in the intent with which an act is done may reduce its severity. Negligent torts are considered less heinous than intentional torts; murder without meaning it is manslaughter and is punished less severely. But lack of intent does not transform an injury into a noninjury. The question that defines the injury of sex discrimination is: is the treatment based on sex? Addressing this question to the consciousness of the perpetrator rather than to the objective detriment to the victim focuses upon the state of mind of the institutional policymaker to the neglect of the impact that policies about women's bodies have upon women's work lives. And why should unconsciousness of its sexism exempt a practice, when unconsciousness that it is women who are damaged is integral to the easy disregard that has so long sanctioned women's oppression?

The full reach of the differences approach as well as the problems that may exceed its grasp are illustrated by an examination of the leading interpretation of the Equal Rights Amendment (ERA). The ERA provides that the equal protection of the laws shall not be denied "on account of sex."[47] These words have been interpreted to impose an absolute ban on differential treatment of the sexes by the law.[48] As the Senate Committee on the Judiciary expressed it: "The basic principle on which the amendment rests may be stated shortly: sex should not be a factor in determining the legal rights of men or of women."[49] Differential legal treatment of the sexes would no longer be justified by either a "rational relationship" or a "legitimate" or "compelling state interest." In its basic principle, the ERA rejects sex inequality, regardless of sex differences,[50] so would be a substantial step beyond existing law.

In the leading interpretation, however, an exception to the ban on differential treatment is made for "unique physical characteristics."[51] Unique physical characteristics are defined as those which all or some women but no men have or which all or some men but no women have.[52] This exception is justified by the idea that to treat one sex differently from the other may not be discriminatory if it does not "deny equal rights to the other sex."[53] But what is to define "equal rights" under this theory when a comparison of the sexes cannot be made, owing to differences considered noncomparable? "Where there is no common factor shared by both sexes, equality of treatment must necessarily rest upon considerations not strictly comparable as between the sexes."[54] This reveals the basic logic of differences doctrine: differential treatment is prohibited only so long as the sexes are relevantly the same or enough the same for their treatment to be compared. But whether a common factor even exists for comparison depends upon the conceptual framework chosen. What principle guides the selection of the context within which a factor will appear comparable as opposed to unique? Without question, the proponents of this ERA theory would make a different choice on the *Gilbert* facts than did the *Gilbert* majority, yet the logic of the "unique physical characteristic" exception is the same as that of the *Gilbert* majority: where the sexes are completely different, different treatment can be justified, even if it deprives one sex-defined group.

Within this approach, no argument remains to compel a result one way or the other in a case such as *Gilbert,* or possibly also in cases of sexual harassment.[55] To admit that something is a unique physical characteristic is to concede the only foundation for attacking as discriminatory the unequal treatment based upon it. No assurance exists that women's sexuality will not be seen as a unique physical characteristic. If the basic principle of the ERA—that there shall be no sex inequality—where to be undone by the courts after passage, the undoing might well be achieved through expansion of this exception. So long as the problem of discrimination is understood to be rooted in sex *differentiation,* the exception for unique physical characteristics will be necessary, and results like *Gilbert* will be possible. If the basic principle were defined as a ban upon enforced inferiority by sex rather than upon sex-differentiated treatment, it might be contested which deprivations constituted enforced inferiorities, but no exception for uniqueness would be possible—or necessary.

As a conception of the injustice of discrimination, arbitrariness does not provide a theory of justice that promotes affirmative social diversity, nor does it attempt to. It is not primarily a theory of how real differences are to be justly treated nor of how divergent needs are to be equally accommodated, needs which, due to race or racism, sex or sexism, are not identical or even equivalent. Equality among the differently situated is unintelligible; difference is how *in*equality is jus-

tified. Beyond directing investigation into whether purported differences are real, which is useful, in its most humane application
discrimination as arbitrariness is a theory of the conditions under
which real differences are to be ignored.

Sex Inequality

A view of sex discrimination less frequently adopted by courts, but
which often animates their sympathies, implicitly centers upon the
analysis that discrimination consists in the systematic disadvantagement of social groups. This approach to inequality is marked by the
understanding that sex discrimination is a system that defines women
as inferior from men, that cumulatively disadvantages women for
their differences from men, as well as ignores their similarities. Few
judicial opinions exhibit this awareness, but its spirit moves beneath
most decisions that bestow rights upon women. The *Manhart* decision
is an example.[56] There, the Supreme Court held that requiring
women employees to contribute more than men to their pension fund
violated Title VII. The employer had based the pension plan contributions upon valid mortality tables and its own experience, showing
that women live longer than men. Because women as a group outlive
men, the insurance cost of paying retirement benefits to women could
be expected to be greater than that for men. Justice Stevens, for a
majority of the Court, wrote that the contribution differential discriminates in its "treatment of a person in a manner which but for the
person's sex would be different."[57] Real differences were not allowed
to burden women's social status. Sex equality in *Manhart* meant the
same contributions and the same benefits for women, in the face of
actual differences from men.

This approach has surfaced even more explicitly in a few judicial
decisions prior to *Manhart*. In *Sail'er Inn v. Kirby,* prohibitions on
hiring women as bartenders were characterized as "laws which disable
women from full participation in the political, business and economic
areas" and label women with "the stigma of inferiority and second
class citizenship."[58] In this California decision, sex was held to be a
"suspect classification" because "the whole class [of women] is relegated to an inferior legal status without regard to the capabilities of
characteristics of its individual members."[59] The Supreme Court
plurality in *Frontiero v. Richardson* invalidated a rule that presumed

hat women were dependents of their spouses while the dependency
of male spouses had to be demonstrated.[60] In *Kahn v. Shevin,*[61] decided in 1974, in which a tax preference to widows but not to widowers was not considered sex discrimination, Justice Douglas attributed
women's unequal position to "overt discrimination or . . . the socialization process of a male dominated culture."[62] The differences approach, which allows or disallows classifications based upon similarities or differences, would have investigated whether the practice
were rationally related to the sex difference. The inequality approach taken inquired instead into the substantive consequences that
a male-dominated culture attached to it. *Schlesinger v. Ballard,*[63] decided in 1975, also stands out as having been decided on the latter
theory. The Court there upheld a provision which permitted women
longer tenure in the military before dismissal for nonpromotion, on
the theory that the provision compensated for disabilities suffered by
military women. If one had the choice, a more thorough approach
might have addressed the elimination of such disabilities, so that no
special compensation would have been needed. Doctrinally, *Ballard*
and *Kahn* found sex-based distinctions "justified" under the Equal
Protection Clause because of their remedial purpose or result. They
might also be read as intimations of a substantive approach to sex
discrimination that would overturn the systematic subordination of
women.

A rule or practice is discriminatory, in the inequality approach, if it
participates in the systemic social deprivation of one sex because of
sex. The only question for litigation is whether the policy or practice
in question integrally contributes to the maintenance of an underclass
or a deprived position because of gender status. The disadvantage
which constitutes the injury of discrimination is not the failure to be
created "without regard to" one's sex; that is the injury of arbitrary
differentiation. The unfairness lies in being deprived *because of* being
a woman or a man, a deprivation given meaning in the social context
of the dominance or preference of one sex over the other. The social
problem addressed is not the failure to ignore woman's essential
sameness with man, but the recognition of womanhood to women's
comparative disadvantage. In this approach, few reasons, not even
biological ones, can justify the institutionalized disadvantage of
women. Comparability of sex characteristics is not required because
policies are proscribed which transform women's sex-based dif-

ferences from men into social and economic deprivations. All that is required are comparatively unequal results.

Under the inequality approach, variables as to which women and men are not comparable, such as pregnancy or sexuality, would be among the *first* to trigger suspicion and scrutiny, rather than the last; they would not be exceptions to the rule. From the inequality perspective the question on the *Gilbert* facts would be: is not the structure of the job market, which accommodates the physical needs, life cycle, and family expectations of men but not of women, integral to women's inferior employment status? What can then justify a policy that makes pregnancy, a condition unique and common to women as a gender, into a disadvantage in employment? The affirmative form of the argument is that the health needs of women workers should be accommodated equally with those of men.

The Two Approaches Compared

The distinction between the differences and the inequality theories can be illustrated by contrasting them on the issue of preferential hiring or admissions. Affirmative action plans are problematic under differences doctrine; they are considered "reverse discrimination" in this approach because they use a group characteristic (race, sex) as a criterion for social decision making.[64] The attempt, within the framework, to rationalize the disjuncture between the analysis of the problem and the analysis of the remedy by distinguishing between a differentiation and a differentiation in reverse is analytically uncomfortable to the point of collapse.[65] Contortions are required to support a solution which is based on the criterion, the use of which constituted the injury. If it was the irrelevance or irrationality of the criterion's application that constituted the injustice, one has to bend over backward[66] to make that same criterion suddenly both relevant and the definition of fairness when designing a remedy. A differentiation still looks like a differentiation.[67]

The inequality approach views the entire problem of discrimination in a different way. Affirmative action plans, to continue the example, are steps toward empowering that group whose depowering is the problem. There is no illusion that groups of people are subordinated by abstractions like "race" and "sex," the mechanical reversal of which will result in reverse subordination. These categories are seen to codify and facilitate social inferiority, the agents and beneficiaries of which are not abstractions but other people—in particular, the other half of the abstraction: those whites and men who have been cumulatively advantaged by the subordination and exclusion of blacks and women. In this perspective, white males have long been advantaged precisely on racial and sexual grounds, differentially favored in employment and education *because* they were white and male. To intervene to alter this balance of advantage is not discrimination in reverse, but a chance for equal consideration for the first time.

A fundamental problem with differences logic as a tool for legal redress is its abstraction from the realtity of social inequality. The theory is grounded on the idea that if members of social groups—blacks and whites or men and women—can be viewed *as if* they are the same, then actions predicated upon such a view will produce equal treatment, which will contribute to rational social equality. If members of these groups cannot be viewed as if they are the same, their differences merit inequality. This posture inadequately accommodates two facts: that organized diversity makes human existence social as well as possible and that, socially, women are unequal to men—one of the values the law against discrimination hopes to affirm and the very problem it exists to solve. The abstract legal response does not encourage inquiry into the roots of women's inequality, into the conditions under which one group—the male—has become the standard against which vital differences are judged deviations, hence making differences "relevant," thereby rationalizing the social subordination of women to men.

Antidiscrimination theory, in its antidifferentiation guise, can never confront the issues on which it turns: what social distinctions are based on sex for what reasons, and hence with what permissible consequences? Instead, all a court has to do to circumvent a finding of discrimination is to begin by noticing what, in most instances, is the most obvious of facts: the sexes are neither the same nor, in a sexist society, similarly situated. Simply being a woman may mean seldom being in a position to be sufficiently similarly situated to a man to have unequal treatment attributed to sex bias. Where the sexes are not readily comparable, men and women are compared in terms of a third category in which they must be treated *as if* similarly situated—

120

for example, temporary disability or sexuality*—in order to see if
their different treatment relative to it is based on sex. Any sex loading
in the third, "neutral," category itself is not subject to inquiry. Then
the trap springs: if the sexes are found not equal with respect to this
purportedly neutral standard, the differential treatment can be
termed "discrimination by temporary disability coverage, not sex" or
"discrimination by sexuality, not sex."

Although the two theories are most vivid in counterpose, in a sense
they overlap. One might say that if a given disadvantage were not also
arbitrary—that is, if the inequality were "deserved"—no one would
think that the treatment was discriminatory, no matter how injurious.
Too, no matter how arbitrary a given treatment, if a group is advantaged by it—as whites or men have been—in no sense is it legally
discriminatory *as to them,* no matter how unequal the results. But these
are superficial, almost purely verbal, intersections. In philosophical
underpinnings, political roots and effects, structure and content of
argument, what may look like a distinction in emphasis opens upon
two deeply divergent conceptions of social reality and methods of
approach to their analysis.[68]

Exposed, the two frameworks reveal different philosophical conceptions of the source and function of the gender difference in society
and of women's "nature." The fundamental assumption underlying
the differences view is that a primordial sphere exists in which people
are undifferentially human, the same across the sex difference. Over-
laid is a sphere in which biological differences immutably create gender identity, a sphere in which the sexes are different but equivalent.
Women's different social status is seen to be rationally explained by
these differences. If women's inferiority is noticed at all, it is seen as
"merely" social—meaning an unfortunate, irrational, outmoded, superficial, and quite eradicable mistake.

Confronted with what looks to be a real difference between the
sexes, this approach implicitly attributes it to biology. In this way
substantive judgments are made about which differences between the
sexes are "real" or "relevant" (in terms of permissible differential
consequences) without explicitly investigating which real difference
and consequences may result from sexism itself. The assimilation of
social into natural is always implicit but sometimes apparent, as in the

*Or grooming standards: see Appendix A.

assumption that motherhood includes among its "natural" "joys and blessings" being forcibly laid off without pay.[69] More subtly, pregnancy is considered a work "disability" on the assumption that the job world could not be structured to accommodate this temporary alteration in condition. As a disability, it is then considered an "extra,"[70] an "*additional* risk unique to women."[71] Additional, that is, to *men's* health needs. The inequality of the coverage (no disability unique to men having been excluded) is thereby attributed to women's biology *per se*. What is at issue, however, is the *meaning given* that biology by the model of the job[72] and by the disability plan, which covers women's health needs only up to the cost of covering men's—the result being that men are fully covered and women are not.

Although never judicially expressed, the fundamental assumption of the inequality approach, by contrast, is that the social meaning given to the gender difference has little or no biological foundation, nor is biology itself even particularly relevant. The issue is not that some differences are social while others are biological but which of the social disadvantages of sex courts will prohibit. In this perspective, the point of the *Gilbert* case is that the disadvantage, hence the discrimination, lies not in the biological fact of pregnancy but in the policy which transforms it into a detriment to women who work outside the home. The only relevant meaning in sex difference, in the inequality perspective, is a social creation, springing from social imperatives.

Nor, in this approach, is the social meaning of being biologically female "merely" social in the sense of being superficial, its detriments magically eradicable by being legally ignored. Instead, the society may tend to create women in its image of their inferior status, as a group largely lacking in skills, experience, sense of self, "qualifications." Sexually, women may tend to be passive in accepting male sexual initiation because they have been taught it is feminine and because men give them little choice. Although many women will resist this imposed image, it has reality. Women may be seductive to the same extent and for the same reasons, which may include their survival. These realities are as much a concrete foundation and persistent basis for women's social existence as is pregnancy, and are just as firmly (if not as exclusively) based on sex. To see the natural as social instead—as nature made social—is to see the concrete *content* of the sex difference as the systemic, structural, and determinate subordination of women to men in all social spheres. When this *is* the sex difference, its perpetuation is seen to be not accidental but determinate, in that men as a group are benefitted while women have little choice but to stay in their place.

Examining the legal doctrine of "sex stereotyping" in light of the reality of sex inequality illuminates this point and heightens the contrast between the two theoretical approaches. Under the doctrine of "sex stereotype," disparate treatment of the sexes, to avoid being discriminatory, must derive from a demonstrably "factual basis, as opposed to a commonly held stereotype."[73] The sex stereotype that is prohibited, then, is defined in terms of the absence of a factual basis for sex-differential treatment. What is supposed unjust about a sex stereotype is that it is untrue, either of the individual or of the group, so treatment based upon it is arbitrary. Certainly many untrue stereotypes of women exist; certainly many women do not fit stereotypes that may correctly describe most women. But what about the ones that are true? What about the women whom the stereotypes describe? What if, because a stereotype has set a standard that most women have had little choice but to meet, few women have escaped being measured against and shaped by it? Why should the exceptional individual, who can argue that the stereotype does not apply to her, be the only one who can assert that the stereotype disadvantages her, when most women live a sex-stereotyped reality?

Further, what if the factual basis for the treatment *is* the "commonly-held stereotype?" Is disparate treatment based upon it then nondiscriminatory or justified? Consider, for example, the current stereotype that women are more appropriate as full-time parents of preschool children than men. If men universally bore no responsibility for child care, it would be no sex stereotype for a company to refuse to consider hiring women on that basis,* and it would be small consolation to mothers if women without preschool children—that is, women who met the male standard—were allowed to apply. The answer seems to be that sex-stereotyping based upon illusion is prohibited, while a sex stereotype powerful enough to become a social reality justifies itself.

This doctrinal result in the case of social differences directly parallels the reasoning whereby detrimental treatment based upon female biological differences is not considered arbitrarily "based on sex." To

*See the discussion of the case considering this policy, *Phillips v. Martin-Marietta*, 400 U.S. 542 (1971), in Appendix A, at 225.

return to the pregnancy example as the quintessence of this form of reasoning, if all women became pregnant, the requisite "identity between the excluded disability and gender as such"[74] for the policy to be based on sex would have been established. But if all women became pregnant, could that not (in this case and in many others as well) provide a nonarbitrary "justification" for a sex-based differentiation? It would be neither a "sex stereotype" nor a "sex average." It would be a sex fact, as universal to the gender as women's sexuality. The same proof that would show that a distinction was arbitrarily based on sex would also go to making that distinction "justified."* It seems that the more sex-based the determination is, the less protection the law affords.

Under inequality logic, by contrast, it is neither necessary for all women to get pregnant for that distinction to be sex-based nor possible that such a fact could justify sex-differential treatment. To deprive a woman, for example, of disability pay because she is pregnant discriminates on the basis of sex because pregnancy has a *direct* relation to sex, and produces immediate disadvantages for employment for women only—and that is the end of the argument.

What is and is not taken to be a sex stereotype reveals that the two approaches imply divergent conceptions of the processes that create the observed characteristics of the sexes. For example, in oral argument in *Phillips v. Martin-Marietta*, the case in which disparate hiring policies for mothers and fathers of preschool children were challenged, Chief Justice Burger stated:

Well, I have to assume up to this time, Mr. Senterfitt, that the reason you have 75 or 80 percent women is that again something that I would take judicial notice of, from many years of contact with industry, that women are manually much more adept than men and they do this kind of work better than men do it, and that's why you hire women. . . . For just the same reason that *most men hire women as secretaries, because they are better at it than men*. . . . The Department of Justice, I am sure, doesn't have any male secretaries. This is an indication of it. They hire women secretaries because they are better and you hire women assembly people because they are better.[75] (emphasis added)

Justice Burger has an image of hiring as a rational process based on skills women are (born?) "better at." But female characteristics and

---

*See Appendix A for a fuller discussion of the doctrine of "justification" in this connection.

skills can be viewed as requirements for the occupants of dull, repetitious, dead-end, low-paying, low-status, transient or service-oriented jobs such as those women have been relegated to.[76] One can deduce from Justice Burger's formulation that "most men" do not hire women as executives because women are not good at it; that women do not hire anybody because men are "better at it"; that the Department of Justice could never be guilty of sex bias;[77] that male military secretaries who cannot find a job in the private sector are not encountering entrenched sexism but really are not as good at the job as the women who are hired with half their objective skills. It might be instructive to consider whether women "manually much more adept than men" would do as well at brain surgery as at typing. Four black women in one recent case were discharged because they refused to do heavy cleaning which a white woman was not required to do. This was found discriminatory although the supervisor offered an analogous justification: "[c]olored folks are hired to clean because they clean better."[78]

An inequality perspective thus reverses the causation implicit in the customary "stereotype" view and suggests that a major factor that insures that women will develop personality characteristics, skills, and behavior corresponding to the female stereotype is the availability of jobs which make women's economic survival largely contingent upon such qualities and skills and not others. If women's manual aptitude, sensitivity to the whims of customers and employers, adept cleaning, ability to support egos and anticipate needs, and to make an environment congenial were considered desirable employee qualities in men, men would probably develop them. Occupational motivation studies have not, in general, frontally addressed this question. Judith Long Laws, reviewing studies of female occupational "choice," concludes:

The respondents produce the maps they have learned. . . . These maps reflect, and even exaggerate, the occupationally segregated dual labor market in the United States. Most occupations young women report considering fall within the female job ghetto.[79]

She also notes that occupational outcomes do not reflect women's personal choices or preferences. Rosabeth Kanter gives an interpretation of these data.

Those who are disadvantageously placed limit their aspirations and are less likely to be perceived as promotable, thus completing a vicious cycle. Those who are more advantageously placed are likely to maintain higher aspirations and to be encouraged in keeping them. The sex-typing of jobs in this major corporation, like others, means that a social structural effect might be misleadingly interpreted as a sex difference.[80]

Some might object that this concern with "real differences" involves a few, and easily resolved, instances in which there is an actual difference between the sexes. Such assurance relies upon being able to separate "biological" from "social" sex differences, and upon considering the former unavoidable but few and the latter negligible—so long as legal options exist for individuals to exempt themselves when group characteristics do not apply to them. It tends to presume there are no real differences which are social, that a few biological differences create a narrow sphere of permissible differentiation, and that justice is served by treating most people as "individuals."[81]

What if, as this discussion has suggested, the "merely" social and stereotyped characteristics turn out to be stubbornly deep and pervasively real, as real of most individuals as of groups as a whole? Passing over the question of why biology ought to justify relative deprivation, how many "individuals" have to be afflicted by a social characteristic before the problem is seen as group injustice—the exceptional individuals being those *not* so afflicted? What if most women are actually created more or less in the image of the feminine stereotype? What if they tend to be deprived of male skills, not just of the chance to display them? Would it be so surprising if women came to lack self-confidence as they have been deprived of a sphere for its exercise? In terms of sexual harassment, what if women are deprived of a sense of sexual self worth defending, not only of equal access to money, courts, and a cause of action?

Further, what if, because of unequal treatment from birth, women are deprived not only of qualifications by male standards, not only of equal consideration of their qualifications on these terms, but of the opportunity to set the terms by which their distinctive contributions can be measured? What if the society lacks any sense of the value of those skills and strengths and selves women must and do develop, a form for recognizing women on women's own terms? Surely this is part of the onus of discrimination. These questions may point to the limits of the law for promoting social equality as much as to the shortfall of any of its doctrines. But should the leading interpretation of sex discrimination require that social equality exist before it will be legally guaranteed?

There is a unity to the basic requirement of comparability among the "similarly situated" and the notion that stereotyping refers to a distortion in the eye of the beholder rather than to a distortion of the reality of the beheld. Together, these doctrines reveal that the differences approach, as a requisite to finding discrimination, has in mind people who have not been damaged by racism or sexism, who are in the same position as corresponding whites and men, but have irrationally and arbitrarily been treated differently. The theory proceeds by comparing people who, because of social inequality, are simply noncomparable; clearing that hurdle, it then looks to see if the group on the bottom deserves to be treated equally to the group on the top. To the extent to which such groups really are not equal, their status is found legally justified, each situated "difference" supporting further accumulations of enforced inferiority. The approach protects primarily women who for all purposes are socially men, blacks who for all purposes are socially white, leaving untouched those whose lives will never be the same as the more privileged precisely because of race or sex.

The two theories do not simply supply different "tests" or alternate "doctrines." They contain different conceptions of the problem of sex discrimination and of the way to solve it. Differences doctrine sees itself confronting an exceptional failure of social neutrality which can be corrected by enforced legal neutrality. It searches for a standpoint sufficiently distanced to create a formulation sufficiently abstract that it is blind to sex differences. It seeks a principle sufficiently even, a rule sufficiently ingenious, that when carried sufficiently far it will remedy all inequalities, no matter whose. It searches, in short, for a "neutral principle" of which the cardinal feature, and ground for its claim to principle, is its social abstractness. As Herbert Wechsler, a leading architect of this view, formulates it: "A principled decision, in the sense I have in mind, is one that rests on reasons with respect to all the issues in the case, reasons that in their generality and their neutrality transcend any immediate result that is involved."[82] The problem of social inequality is treated as if it were, in the first instance, a legal problem.

The inequality conception, by contrast, is grounded in an analysis of the balance of power between specific groups with particular social histories. Sex discrimination is treated as a logical and necessary outgrowth of a social whole in which the human sex difference has been transformed into a systematic social inequality—for the benefit of some, to the detriment of others. The "reasons" taken by Wechsler to be intrinsically neutral and general are seen to be socially specific; the abstraction of race and sex becomes the concreteness of blacks and women. Indeed, the best way to preserve a concretely unequal status quo may be by the rigorous application of a neutral standard. Simmel makes this point in its full cultural generality:

> The standards of art and the demands of patriotism, the general mores and the specific social ideas, the equity of practical judgments and the objectivity of theoretical knowledge . . . —all these categories are formally generically human, but are in fact masculine in terms of their actual historical formation. If we call ideas that claim absolute validity objectively binding, then it is a fact that in the historical life of our species there operates the equation: objective = male.[83]

Once insuring that the definition of "qualifications" or "merit" or "reasonableness" will exclude the logical results of the social conditions that shape groups like blacks and women, a rigorous insistence upon sex-blind and race-blind standards—standards "irrespective of race or sex"—will enhance and articulate the inequality.

So conceived, discrimination as a social problem is only secondarily a legal problem. Where differences doctrine searches for the perfectly balanced rule, an inequality theory reaches for a political strategy to guide legal intervention on behalf of the less powerful against those who are not likely to relinquish their place. If the problem of discrimination is arbitrariness, its target is inadvertence, ignorance, caprice, or at most intentional invidiousness. If the problem is inequality, the target is determinate acts, however unconscious, which preserve the control, access to resources, and privilege of one group at the expense of another. The only remedy is redistribution.

THE TWO APPROACHES APPLIED: RACE AND SEX

The primary point of reference for antidiscrimination law has not been the social situation and experience of women, but that of black Americans, or at least black men.[84] In employment as well as in other areas the law against discrimination has emerged in response, however inadequate, to demands by black people for legal equality as a means to social equality.[85] Much of the law on discrimination is best understood as a substantive law on blacks: shaped by their social ex-

perience, tailored to the specific effects of racism and the history of
slavery, and applied only to a limited extent to other groups. The
black experience has shaped what the concept of discrimination
means. This is true even though race discrimination cases are often
couched in broader generalities, and even though they are ultimately
inadequate to the problem of racism.

This focus has been both crucial to the law's growth and limiting.
When no ready analogy exists between a race-based abuse and a sex-
based one, as in pregnancy or sexuality, courts have often seemed at a
loss.[86] In sharp contrast to the best moments of the courts' approach
to racial differences, the socially based, systemic character of the observable differences between the sexes has been neither recognized
nor investigated. Judges have become conscious of many attitudes
and practices as unquestionably racist which are allowed to persist in
their corresponding sexist forms. No Supreme Court justice would
take judicial notice that blacks were "better at" being slaves than
whites, outside an awareness of the social context which made slavery
a virtually exclusive life option. In reaching this perspective on race,
courts did not stop perceiving that racial differences exist. They simply began to view these differences, to the extent blacks were disadvantaged by them, as the results of racism. Differences that derived
from social deprivation were no longer acceptable reasons for inequality, but symptoms of it. This view has not been uniformly embraced by the legal system; it may not survive. But the approach to
race which set the terms of discourse, at least since the school de-
segregation cases in 1954, illustrates and befits an inequality approach. An analogous approach has not been taken—and needs to
be—to the inequality of women.

As a way of extending law to cover "new" facts, it is customary to
proceed by specifying similarities and differences with better known
and better established areas. The social conditions and dynamics
which have created and sustained race-based, contrasted with sex-
based, discrimination are by no means identical. But sufficiently striking similarities in social pathology[87] and legal treatment[88] of blacks
and women as groups have been observed to justify qualified comparison.[89] Further, both race and sex equality have sustained losses on
similar legal and political grounds. Some of the recent regressions in
the Supreme Court's policies on race[90] directly parallel some of those
in the area of sex.

Comparison would seem particularly appropriate under Title VII, since, on its face at least, race and sex are coequal.[91] No court or agency has held that a classification, legislative or practical, that would be discriminatory if based on race is not discriminatory when based on sex. But Justice Powell, writing for the majority of the Supreme Court in the *Bakke* case, saw gender as not on a par with race or ethnicity for purposes of equal protection analysis. Since there are only two genders, the Court stated, sex is more simple than race. "More importantly, the perception of racial classifications as inherently odious stems from a lengthy and tragic history that gender-based classifications do not share."[92] A failure to *perceive* the nature and extent of gender classifications fairly characterizes the consciousness of both the judiciary and the society as a whole. The fact that sex classifications have not been seen as "inherently odious," and racial and ethnic ones now may be, speaks both to the failure of racial and ethnic groups (other than the dominant one) to acquire affirmative cultural dignity as such, and to the success of the whitewash of women's subordination by the myth of inherent differences. The history of sex distinctions in society is at least as long, and no less vicious, wasteful, or unwarranted, than the history of racial distinction. It can be instructive as well as strategic to contrast judicial treatment of an area in which courts have been brought a long way and, at times, have been comparatively sophisticated with an area in which they remain relatively backward and entrenched.

The analogy should not be allowed to obscure the distinctive content and dynamics of sex and race, nor does it imply that sexism and the opposition to it exist only as a derivative of racism and the movement against it. To argue that sex oppression is a pale sister of racial oppression, so that even to compare them mocks the degradation of blacks and minimizes the violence of racism, severely underestimates the degradation and systematic brutality, physical as well as emotional, that women sustain every day at the hands of men.[93] Indeed, it is the invisibility as wrongs of such familiar features of women's social experience as battering, forced motherhood, rape and other assaults of unwanted intimacy that testifies to their acceptability, an acceptability that legitimizes the violence that enforces it. As Elizabeth Cady Stanton stated in 1860:

Prejudice against color, of which we hear so much, is no stronger than that against sex. It is produced by the same cause, and manifested very much in the same way. The Negro's skin and the woman's sex are both *prima facie* evidence that they were intended to be in subjection to the white Saxon man.[94]

The social reality recognized by discrimination law is that blacks, as a group, have been systematically and cumulatively deprived in comparison with whites for many reasons—none of them good. This difference means disadvantage to blacks and advantage, in terms of social hegemony, to whites. Beyond the deprivations blacks suffer due to exclusion from the social privileges whites enjoy, the distinctive qualities of black culture can give rise to further injuries to blacks within a dominant culture that interprets these differences as marks of inferiority. That is, it is seen to be different in social substance to be black than to be white. As Justice Harlan put it in his dissent in *Plessy v. Ferguson:*

Everyone knows that the statute in question had its origin and purpose, not so much to exclude white persons from railroad cars occupied by blacks, as to exclude colored people from coaches occupied by or assigned to white persons. . . . No one would be so wanting in candor as to assert the contrary.[95]

This appropriate recognition of social reality is carried out beneath an often ponderous legal overlay which responds to the norm that the law can and should remain "value neutral," or color-blind,[96] even when choosing to intervene in a reality which is anything but evenly posed or oblivious to color. As a result, whites can and do claim discrimination on the basis of the legal and social abstraction "race."[97] Tenacious clinging to neutrality as all there is to justice, while being confronted with a social inequality that will not go away in the face of such a posture, has created resistance to carrying through on the original insight.* To act against inequality is no longer to be able to maintain neutrality. Of course, to allow it to continue is not neutral either. One reflection of the uneasy coexistence of the two approaches to discrimination is that symmetry remains a logical possibility under the law, while the recognition that provides the force and grounding for the entire attack upon discrimination is the recognition that the social meanings of race and sex are asymmetrical.

To say that there is a substantive law on blacks thus means that the law, while expressing itself in terms of those "neutral principles"[98]

---

*The divided result in *Bakke* is one example.

which would evenhandedly oppose all discrimination on the basis of race or color, instead recognizes the fact of inequality: whites are not systematically and cumulatively deprived in this society by sole reason of being white. A white who suffers harm due to that fact suffers, in this sense, as an individual because he is an exception to his racial group. A black who suffers race discrimination suffers a group injury as a member of the race, because what is done to blacks is not done to each as an individual but, in total derogation of individuality, because they are blacks in a white society, and not as exceptions to that fact. When a white charges race discrimination (for example, due to preferential admissions for blacks) he is protesting the cost in one sphere of his life of a rectification process of an entire system that has tried to destroy all blacks in every sphere of their lives for generations, and could afford to ignore their protests. One delusion of the neutral approach has been that such a change would be costless for whites. So it is not that discrimination against whites based on race is nonexistent or unthinkable or analytically unsound. It is that the implicit and real standard for what has been race discrimination against blacks has not been limited to what would be discriminatory if done to whites. Indeed, more like the reverse is the case.

Although it does not always show on the surface, this recognition of substantive inequality suffuses the law on race. Perhaps the most substantive of any reference to any social group in the Bill of Rights is found in the Thirteenth Amendment, which prohibits "slavery or involuntary servitude."[99] Practices which impose "badge[s] of servitude," including private acts, are prohibited.[100] Women's specific historical forms of subordination—the badges and incidents of sexual servitude—have yet to be the subject of a constitutional prohibition. Similarly, in the most substantive of classifications under the Equal Protection Clause (Fourteenth Amendment), race is a "suspect classification," requiring a rule or practice which is based upon or has the effect of distinguishing between races to sustain "strict scrutiny" of its constitutionality.[101] A majority of the Supreme Court stopped short of extending such strict scrutiny to sex classifications.[102]

Throughout discrimination jurisprudence, racial inequality is treated as a more serious problem than sex inequality. The now classic doctrinal recognition in *Griggs v. Duke Power* that a policy neutral in itself can have a "disproportionate impact" in practice, due to social conditions which neither the law, the defendant, nor the policy in question created, arose in the context of a black challenge to tests and diplomas as hiring requirements.[103] Myriad cases apply *Griggs* to prohibit a wide range of policies and practices which have the effect of disadvantaging blacks, when that effect is seen as due *only* to specific effects of prior, broadly social inequality. Sensitivity to the shape and pervasion of racism has included an acceptance of statistical arguments as evidence of group deprivation. Blacks are seen to be that "discrete and insular minority"[104] stained by the "stigma" of segregation.[105] One culmination of this tradition was reached in the Supreme Court holding that laws prohibiting racial intermarriage as "measures designed to maintain White Supremacy" discriminated against blacks— although miscegenation statutes are obviously equally arbitrary in their treatment of both members of interracial couples.[106]

In what may be the furthest reach of this principle under Title VII, rules or practices have been found racially discriminatory when their disproportionate impact was due only to the specific social concomitants, accompaniments, or effects identifiable (statistically or analytically) as occurring disproportionately among blacks. Some examples of racially associated but by no means racially unique characteristics found discriminatory in effect have included being poor, where wage garnishment resulted in firing, even where poor whites were also fired;[107] having an arrest record;[108] not having a high school diploma;[109] and being dishonorably discharged from the military.[110] When standards are not demonstrated to be job-related, they may not be used to disqualify disproportionate numbers of minority applicants. One case held that an employer cannot raise hiring standards "in a fashion which exempts large groups of whites while restricting most blacks."[111]

The point of these cases is their recognition of the socially created, systemic, historical, and group-defined character of racial status. In such cases, no investigation has been required into whether the specific individual or even blacks in general were in a position that led to more arrests, more undesirable discharges, fewer diplomas, or lower incomes. Such an investigation would have to conclude with either the white supremacist view that blacks as a group are genetically less accomplished, more prone to crime and misconduct, and less deserving of well-paying jobs, or that these results, to the extent observable, are effects of a racist social system, that is, "prior discrimination" in a broadly social sense. Further, it is not the *illusion* that blacks are less likely to have certain job qualifications and are more likely to be poor and to have arrest records or dishonorable discharges that gives rise to the cause of action—it is the *reality*.

Nor did the courts which took this view require a showing that the individual black plaintiffs specifically exemplify the racist conditions presumed to underlie the disparities, although of course they did have to be injured by the practice being litigated. They did not have to show that they were personally innocent of the crimes for which they were previously arrested, individually meritorious yet discriminated against in education or employment, or individually deserving of an honorable discharge. This would establish race as the specific cause of the situation of each individual. Instead, in cases taking the approach premised on racial inequality, individuals are presumed included in the group-defined abuse simply because of their race, not when and because they show themselves specific victims of racism. Statistically speaking, while some individual blacks may have in some sense "deserved" these results independent of race, so long as blacks as a group exhibit these characteristics with greater social frequency than whites, the presumption seems to be that race cannot be considered an independent variable. Until the group results are equal, it is supposed impossible and nonsensical to make an "individual" determination independent of, hence free of, the impact of race. The operative assumption is that racism is a whole system from which no black can be considered exempt; that blacks are disadvantaged cumulatively, systematically, and as a group, not just in occasional, discrete, haphazard, and isolated ways and one at a time.

A related recognition has been that, because of the very pervasiveness of the inequality, there could be no similarly situated white persons. The mere fact that a person is white means that she or he cannot truly be similarly situated. Further, it is these circumstanced differences of the group, which do not meaningfully allow the individual to be conceived in isolation from group characteristics, which constitute the inequality that is the damage of the prior discrimination. To require that whites be similarly circumstanced before blacks could be compared with them, as a prerequisite to being discriminated against, or to suppose that an individual black with specific statistical characteristics is comparable with an individual white with those same characteristics, is to ignore the social factor of race that shaped the circumstances and persons. In short, to treat race cases the same as the sex cases reviewed would quite obviously place the most totally segregated and race-defined situations, persons, and abuses beyond the reach of legal redress.*

It is precisely on these basic grounds that recent Supreme Court reversals of the progress of blacks in the courts have turned. The presumption in *Griggs,* decided in 1971, was that the black plaintiffs were in unequal circumstances because of the social meaning of being black. There was no need to search out an intent to discriminate; patterned differentiation, to their disadvantage, was discrimination enough. Even further, "Good intent or absence of discriminatory intent does not redeem employment procedures or testing mechanisms that operate as 'built-in headwinds' for minority groups and are unrelated to measuring job capability."[112]

A deep change of disposition underlies the case of *Washington v. Davis,*[113] decided in 1976. There, four times as many blacks as whites failed an unvalidated employment test, yet the Supreme Court said there was no showing that plaintiffs failed the test *because* they were black: "Respondents, as Negroes, could no more successfully claim that the test denied them equal protection than could white applicants who also failed. The conclusion would not be different in the face of proof that more Negroes than whites had been disqualified by [the test]."[114] Similar individualism was used to defeat an attack on racist police practices in *Rizzo v. Goode,*[115] in which a group of black plaintiffs requested an injunction against systematic police harassment. The Supreme Court did not think that the misconduct had occurred (nor that it was likely to recur without legal intervention) because of the minority group status of the class the plaintiffs represented. Rather, it saw "a heated dispute between individual citizens and certain policemen."[116]

This approach, together with the requirement of discriminatory intent enunciated in *Washington v. Davis,*[117] is directly analogous to the result in *Gilbert,* in which denial of pregnancy disability benefits was not considered to be "based on sex." The "not all women get pregnant" argument parallels the "not all who fail are black" argument. The commonality in analysis is the lack of identity between the

---

*In some cases, courts have refused to recognize the pattern of social inequality of race, setting significant limits upon the reach of this principle, even in its ascendancy, e.g. *James v. Valtierra,* 402 U.S. 137 (1971); *Hazlewood School District v. U.S.,* 433 U.S. 299 (1977); *San Antonio School District v. Rodriquez,* 411 U.S. 1 (1973).

protected class and the variable (pregnancy or test failure) in question. But just as one can deduce little about the adequacy of individuals when a group failure rate is racially disproportionate, there is nothing biological about which individual women become pregnant that dictates that pregnancy shall be excluded under an insurance plan. Whether the reason for this lack of identity between class and variable is implicitly attributed to individual inadequacies as in *Washington* or to individual biology as in *Gilbert*, the Court's approach in these cases excludes the possibility that the basis for both acts of damaging differentiation is social.

The judicial experience with race cases went far to encourage an awareness of the social and systemic nature of inequality and of the pervasiveness of previous judicial prejudice. Within its limits, this understanding, and with it the growth in sensitivity to the specific concomitants of racism, has neither extended to awareness of systemic sexism nor stimulated a similar investigation by the judiciary into its special effects on women. The functional biological difference between the sexes with respect to human reproduction is still openly adduced to support a wide-ranging set of assumptions about social roles which have nothing demonstrably to do with biology. Many of these assumptions continue to be enshrined in law, much as the biological differences between the races were once considered "reasonably" to support what is now widely recognized as legislative and judicial complicity in the subordination of blacks.

In light of this change in outlook, it is telling to recall the time when racial "differences" were seen to justify racial inequality. As the majority in *Plessy v. Ferguson* reasoned:

A statute which implies merely a legal distinction between the white and colored races—a distinction which is founded in the color of the two races, and which must always exist so long as white men are distinguished from the other race by color—has no tendency to destroy the legal equality of the two races.[118]

This reasoning was based upon the assumption that in matters of race relations, "legislation is powerless to eradicate racial instincts or to abolish *distinctions* based upon *physical differences*."[119] Faced with a social practice which *would* eradicate those differences—racial intermarriage—some judges continued to enforce separation, not any more on the basis of the powerlessness of legislation to abolish these "racial instincts," but on the basis of the powerlessness of the social practice they were engaged in prohibiting to transcend them. In a miscegenation case, where sexual taboos crosscut and intensified racial ones, a Virginia judge stated:

Almighty God created the races white, black, yellow, Malay and red, and He placed them on separate continents. And but for the interference with His arrangement there would be no cause for such marriages. The fact that He separated the races shows that He did not intend for the races to mix.[120]

In a strikingly parallel attribution of authority, deciding that a woman could not legally practice law under a statute which prescribed the qualifications of "persons," an Illinois court stated: "That God designed the sexes to occupy different spheres of action, and that it belonged to men to make, apply, and execute the laws was regarded as an almost axiomatic truth."[121] These separate spheres, seen as based upon sex "differences," have yet to be understood as segregation.

As recently as 1970, upholding against an equal protection attack a statute which prescribes that only males over eighteen shall be prosecuted for sharing the household of a female public assistance recipient when the two are unmarried, the Oregon Court of Appeals gave as the sole ground: "The Creator took care of classifying men and women differently, and if the legislature accepts these differences in a matter like this, we are not prepared to say that the classifications thus made were without good reason."[122] In 1977, in refusing to select a single age of majority for both sexes, the majority of the Supreme Court of Utah stated: "Regardless of what a judge may think about equality, his thinking cannot change the facts of life. . . . to judicially hold that males and females attain their maturity at the same age is to be blind to the biological facts of life."[123] Characterizing the general state of the law on women's equality, Julius Getman recently noted:

It is still widely assumed that certain types of work are for one sex or the other, that men's and women's personalities are unalterably different, and that certain types of behavior which are suitable for men or boys are unsuitable for women or girls. What has been accepted, however, is the principle that the law should not be used to prevent women from full participation in national life.[124]

It is a mystery how women can fully participate in national life when the law continues to reinforce as "suitable" separate (and, as we saw in the employment area, inferior) spheres of work, recognize "unalterable" differences in personality, and enforce dual standards of behavior—unless a "separate but equal" form of participation in national life is presumed to define "full participation" for women. Much like the passive attitude taken toward race cases before *Brown* and, later, in queasiness over affirmative action on race (especially in education), the law on sex reflects the pervasive notion that while the law itself should not openly discriminate, certain social roles are somehow legitimately associated with the sex difference. Or, since the law did not create these differences, there is very little it can do about their social consequences.

Both the difficulty in separating mere differences from discriminatory distinctions, and the contrasting levels of social consciousness in legal recognition of racism and sexism, are revealed in an examination of the Bona Fide Occupational Qualification (BFOQ)* exception to Title VII.[125] Legally, sex can be a BFOQ; race cannot be. As the *Harvard Law Review* put it, "presumably, Congress felt that sex was more likely than race to be a predictor of differences legitimately relevant to employment."[126] The essence of the implicit rationale for this distinction has been, first, that no *biological* difference between the races is legitimately relevant to employment while the sex difference may sometimes be; and, second, as the EEOC guidelines interpret it, sex differences, unlike racial differences, may *culturally* give rise to a legitimate need for "authenticity or genuineness"[127] in certain jobs, such as in acting, which only one sex can provide.

The classic examples on the biological point are the wet nurse and the sperm donor. It is hard to believe that anyone seriously considered these examples. It is not reasonably conceivable that a man would sue for sex discrimination for failing to be hired as a wet nurse, presuming the job description included breast-feeding a child. Being a sperm donor is not even employment. What woman would consider it unlawful if she could not become a sperm donor? It seems obvious that where the rationale for the BFOQ is truly biological, the law is redundant.† Where job qualifications are truly based upon biological differences, and can in fact only be performed by one sex, only a law

---

*When sex can be considered a *valid* requisite for a given job, it is termed a *bona fide occupational qualification.*

†This would be equally true for the "unique physical characteristic" interpretation under the ERA.

which thinks of itself as omnipotent would presume its categories
could matter.

Even when biological differences between the races are considered,
and then with trepidation, a different standard is applied than for
biological differences between the sexes. In reargument in *Gilbert,* the
following dialogue occurred:

Justice Blackmun: Could a plan such as General Electric's exclude sickle cell
anemia?
Kammholz: Sickle cell anemia is a disease that is only contracted by blacks. . . .
Kammholz responded that sickle cell anemia could not be excluded from
coverage under plans such as General Electric's and stated that such exclusion
would amount to a case of race discrimination in light of his understanding that
only blacks could contract the disease. Mr. Justice Stewart then asked whether
the reason for his response was because one condition (sickle cell anemia) is an
illness and the other (pregnancy) is not.
Kammholz: Yes, childbirth is a natural event. It contributes to the well-being
of the mother.[128]

The cultural point is more ambiguous. The EEOC guidelines state:
"Where it is necessary for the purpose of authenticity or genuineness,
the Commission will consider sex to be a bona fide occupational qualification, e.g. an actor or actress."[129] One wonders if it is really less
"authentic" for a male actor to play a woman's part, as was the rule in
Shakespeare's England, or for a male to model women's clothes
(men's bodies often fit the female standard of fashionable flatness
better than women's do) than for a white person to create a black
character or a black actor a white one. Of course, women and men,
like blacks and whites, have their looks as job qualifications and have
had social practice at playing their respective roles. But the complaints
of blacks at being typecast in "black roles" are no different in kind
from actresses' complaints about the restrictiveness of "women's
roles." Authenticity would seem to present both as much and as little a
problem for race as for sex. For other reasons, it seems to have been
decided that it is enlightened for blacks and whites to exchange social
roles, but unseemly for the sexes to do so.

While reinforcing the myth of the immutability of sex roles, the
BFOQ does not support race- or sex-defined groups in affirmatively
maintaining a separate identity, should they choose not to integrate
with the dominant group. Once differences are seen as *nothing but*
excuses for unequal treatment no distinction between separatism and

exclusion can be made. Neither the theater group that specializes in portraying the black experience nor, probably, the women's center (one which hires a staff in numbers above the statutory limit) seems legally to be able to turn its affirmative cultural identification into a BFOQ. If there were a BFOQ for race, presumably the qualities considered part of the black cultural identity could be made into affirmative job qualifications, and anyone who wanted to challenge them would have to argue either that they were not really essential to the job, were equally possessed by whites, or were impermissible racial stereotypes. Depending upon one's view, the point of such a rule might be to make into virtues stereotypical generalizations of blacks in order to maintain racial separation and, thereby, subordination. On the other hand, as for women, there may be many things that, for purely cultural reasons, "all or substantially all"[130] whites could not perform, or perform as well as blacks. But it has not been suggested that this would ever render race a BFOQ, "discriminatory but justifiable" in particular cases, or anything but illegal.[131]

Implicit is not only that hiring on a racial basis is abhorrent to a liberal conscience while hiring on a sex basis is less so. Also present is the doctrinal posture that the BFOQ illustrates, and that broadly underlies the legal approach to race compared with sex, that allows gender but not racial "differences" to be ratified by law. In the case of the BFOQ, they are enshrined into sex-linked job qualifications. This legal posture places the challenger of the BFOQ in the position of having to argue that she is an exception to a statistical reality about women in order to show that a sex generalization is discriminatory as to her. It appears that a statistically true generalization about women created by sexism, if job-related, could only be challenged by a woman who had escaped the reality imposed upon most women. At this point, being judged "as an individual" is a cruel standard, because most women have little choice but to share the fate of most women. For race, by contrast, because no racial generalizations are legally legitimate, group disparities evidence inequality rather than potentially valid differences. Thus, it is precisely because the individual is presumed not to be an exception to the racial pattern that the discrimination as to the individual is demonstrable. It is when the individual black person has *not* escaped the racial generalization that she or he has been a victim of the practices the law seeks to eradicate.

The conception that the trouble with racial differentiation is its arbitrariness has suited the attack on racism up to a point because there is thought to be no functional difference other than the social ones between the indices of race. Skin color per se seems to have no utility. Thus, it is comparatively easy to see that the systematic inferiority of a group of people apparently "based upon" their skin color is arbitrary, because their social station has no relation to its index. Sex, on the other hand, on the average attaches to a functional difference, reproduction. So it has been comparatively easier to say that women should be treated differently because they are different. What has never been said is that men are just as different from women as women are from men, that is, *equally* different. However, while men are equally different from women, men are not equally inferior to women in social terms. Functional difference cannot by itself justify systematic social inferiority. There is nothing in a difference that dictates inferiority; there is only the society that makes the content of those differences into inferiorities. In both cases—race, where the law should be clear by now, and sex, where it has been muddied by reproductive biology—it is the social meaning attributed to the differences that is at stake and determines the social position of the group, not the differences themselves. Thus, when blacks were considered biologically inferior, it was the social meaning attributed to their biology that made it so. Similarly, when women are considered inferior, it is the social meaning of their biology that makes it so.

The limitations of the approach through differences, which identifies arbitrariness as the dynamic and limit of social dominion, are revealed in a passage from Herbert Wechsler's famous article advocating "neutral principles":

In the context of a charge that segregation with equal facilities is a denial of equality, is there not a point in *Plessy* in the statement that if "enforced separation stamps the colored race with a badge of inferiority" it is solely because its members choose "to put that construction upon it." [citation omitted] Does enforced separation of the sexes discriminate against females merely because it may be the females who resent it and it is imposed by judgments predominantly male?[132]

In the context of an attack on *Brown v. Board of Education,* Wechsler's comparison with sex is intended to reduce the point to an absurdity in order to make the point on race unassailable. It succeeds only in exposing the argument from two sides. Blacks are not dominated by whites, nor women by men, because they "choose to put that construction upon it." If social inferiority were a matter of this kind of choice, it would have been thought out of existence long ago. And it is backwards to imply that it is because of enforced separation that social inferiority is resented. Second-class status is resented however it appears. Enforced separation can be one mechanism and expression of it. Enforced integration into the dominant culture and its forms can also be resented. The fact that the sex whose company one keeps *can* be "imposed" on women, by "judgments predominantly male," is the point. How can persons who cannot choose the "judgments . . . imposed" upon them be said to "choose" what "construction to put upon it"—much less the consequences of that judgment in their own lives? If women's judgments could forcibly segregate men, one would see what construction they would put upon it.

6 *Sexual Harassment as Sex Discrimination*

A vision of equality adequate to women's circumstance would balance three elements, in tension. It would guarantee parity based on women's equal personhood with men. It would be sensitive to the systematic damage done to women as a sex through relegation to secondary social status. And it would affirm as strengths the qualities developed through living, and resisting living, women's shared fate. The contradictions between these lines of analysis make sex equality complex. If women have been damaged by inequality, how can they be the equal persons they must be to merit equal treatment? On what basis should women be treated the same as men if they are different? On the other hand, if women are already on a par with men, where is the damage of sexism?

Further, if women have been excluded from that which is socially most valued, making woman's place subordinate, how can the ways women have thereby been formed produce anything beyond a reflection of that exclusion and subordination? How can woman's oppressed image be embraced? Moreover, is not woman's "specialness" the cornerstone of that separate-but-equal logic of complementarity that has assigned her those pursuits and those qualities that are glorified as female but denigrated as human? How can an affirmation of what women share be anything other than an elevation of her deprivation to the most she can expect—to what she has now, to equality *for her*. How can it be said on one breath that women are so much less than what we could be, so much more than what has been taken from us, yet at the very least deserve every chance the same as those who are neither so created nor so destroyed?

Balancing an indictment of the damage with an affirmation of the positivity of womanhood, while claiming women's right to be treated the same as everyone else, is the challenge that women's inequality

poses. The conception of sex equality that lies at the foundation of
what I have termed the *differences* view of discrimination is that of
parity based upon equal personhood. What I have labeled the *inequality* theory of women's situation grows out of a synthesis of the
other two elements and the tension between them. Because the law,
without being particularly conscious of the contradictions between
these positions, has acted upon each of them at various times, it has
been vulnerable from all sides. When the law bestows disproportionate benefits upon women on the basis of women's disproportionate
need, egalitarians see paternalism and insult, stereotyping and rein-
forcement of women's dependency. When it withholds special benefits for women, humanists criticize it as heartless and feminists
criticize it as chauvinistic. Both criticize it for perpetuating women's
depressed social position. A persistent dilemma of discrimination law,
then, derives directly from the tension between the two approaches:
how to lift some of the burdens of inequality without intensifying
them in the same act. One way women have been stigmatized as inferior is through the identification of a sometimes erroneous, usually
exaggerated, always exclusive set of feminine needs. Women's sexuality has been a prime example. It has been hard to avoid branding
woman as inferior long enough to balance a grasp of her dignity with
an analysis of her enforced inferiority, in order to address the specificity of her situation.

That women, too, can be abstract persons is the contribution of the
prohibition on arbitrary treatment based on sex, the contribution of the
single standard. Differences theory elaborates this approach. The
limitation of this view, as it has been applied, reveals the most striking
yet the most concealed flaw of discrimination doctrine: in the guise of
setting a single standard for persons, women are measured by the
standards of men. Such a standard neither grasps the damage done to
women nor values the products of women's social experience. Instead, the standard of men is seen as merely *the* standard. And in a
sense, it is; or at least it has been. But to accept this standard reflects
the very attitudes discrimination law exists to undermine: that the
image of success, of potency, of what it means to do a job is the image
of a man.

Within the differences perspective, the alternative to a male standard appears to be a female standard: measure women by standards
"for women only." But the "different" female standard is implicitly

but inescapably (again, because of the social inequality discrimination law purports to stand against) cast as inferior by comparison with the male standard, which remains the real one. So women come up short either because when compared with men they are less than fully male or because they are measured according to a set of feminine require-ments that are shorted by definition. In Simmel's terms, women are "either to behave like men or they are asked to play female roles that are complementary to the dominant male roles," insuring that they will not live up to "allegedly objectively valid panhuman standards," which turn out to be standards set by and for men.[1]

An examination of some recent case situations exposes this ten-dency at work. The claim to fairness of the prohibition on arbitrari-ness rests upon the application of a neutral standard. In *Gilbert*[2] and *Geduldig*,[3] pregnancy was construed as such a standard, as a sex neu-tral category on the basis of which differentiations were not sex-based. The *Dothard*[4] facts could similarly have been interpreted as imposing a neutral standard of height and weight, such that a "disparate im-pact" upon the sexes would be justified by the real size differences between them, as relevant to the job. Justice Rehnquist. who wrote for the Court in *Gilbert*, implied his agreement with such an interpreta-tion in his *Dothard* dissent.[5] He suggested that had the state argued that it required an "appearance of strength" in prison guards, the size requirement would have been sex neutral.[6] Further taking such a view, different pension contributions for the sexes as in *Manhart*[7] would be seen as based on probable longevity, not sex. That the sexes differ in length of life would be a fact of life and death, not of sex-discrimiratory policy. Women would simply pay more for the proba-bility of receiving more, or pay equally to receive smaller benefits over a longer period. In each case, the standard itself is presented as ra-tional, as merely empirical, as corresponding to reality, so that al-though its application affects the sexes differently—to women's det-riment every time—that is because the sexes happen to be differently situated.

The sex inequality in such results lies not only in each outcome, which places women in a less favorable position than men. The in-equality is buried in the *standard itself*. Although it is nowhere men-tioned in the cases, the practice that is challenged in each one mea-sures women by a standard set according to men's requirements, penalizing women for their deviation. In *Gilbert*, the stacked deck is obvious. To use pregnancy as the standard is not sex neutral since no men become pregnant. But not only does the pregnancy exclusion place no men under a comparable risk of uncompensated disability. Health benefits were found equal by sex because the sexes are found to receive roughly the same dollar amount in benefits. In other words, women's health care needs are to be covered only to the point that their cost coincides with the health care needs of men. In *Dothard,* the human size set for the job, the standard that disqualified a disproportionate percentage of women compared with men is, in fact, the height and weight of the average male. In *Manhart,* if unequal contributions had been found nondiscriminatory (or if women had received smaller pension payments during their retirement years), women would have paid more (or received less) for their "extra" life—extra beyond the average man's life expectancy.* In the differences view, the systematic damage such policies do to women as a sex are not seen to make them discriminatory, nor are contributions specific to women's childbearing capacity, build, or remarkable longevity valued. In an adequate theory of equality, women would be "judged in terms of norms attuned to [their] requirements"[8] as men are.

Current approaches to conceptualizing sexual harassment as sex discrimination should be evaluated for their adequacy in this context. Throughout this chapter, it needs to be asked whether the cases to date, and the arguments advanced, understand sexual harassment to be an expression of sexuality as it has been shaped by conditions of gender inequality. Whether women's sexuality is imagined as potentially within women's own control, rather than as something one group of men protect from another. Whether an exclusive set of rules is being erected for women only, such that the only victims are biologically female, with the result that females tend to be cast, biologically, as victims and little more. Whether women are seen as sexually violated primarily by acts that men can conceive would injure men or primarily by acts understood as injuries to femininity. Whether, if women's sexual treatment is compared with men's, that comparison is equalizing or whether it functions as another way to hold women to

---

*It is a hopeful sign that in both *Dothard* and *Manhart* this approach did not prevail, although it seems not to have been because the issue was seen this way.

men's standards. The issue is ultimately whether the law against sex discrimination will act out sex inequality on the level of analysis.

Most cases to date do not frontally address these issues, but provide examples to illustrate the problems. The district court found that Tomkins's sexual harassment was not treatment based on her gender because:

In this instance the supervisor was male, the employee was female. But no immutable principle of psychology compels this alignment of parties. The gender lines might as easily have been reversed, or even not crossed at all. While sexual desire animated the parties, or at least one of them, the gender of each is incidental to the claim of abuse.[9]

The recognition that the genders could be reversed avoids stigmatizing women as victims. But Judge Stern's formulation suggests that in some cases immutable psychological principle does compel an alignment of parties by gender, making treatment sex-based. Are there any such principles? If they are immutable, can they be discriminatory? The excerpt also suggests that the sexual desire felt by the perpetrator was only incidentally related to the victim's gender. Given the institution of heterosexuality, does one believe this?

By contrast, in *Heelan,* as in several other cases, the court required a showing that "employees of the opposite sex were not affected in the same way by these actions."[10] This seems to mean that Heelan would be shown to have been sexually harassed because of her sex if evidence indicated "no sexual advances against male employees by any JM supervisor,"[11] or if "plaintiff was sexually harassed and males were not sexually harassed by plaintiff's supervisor,"[12] both formulations offered by the court. Would men have been affected in the same way even by the same treatment? Should they have to be for it to be discriminatory? If another JM supervisor of either sex had harassed another employee of the male sex, why would Heelan's treatment not have been based on her sex?

To sharpen the distinctions, recall that both the *Corne* and *Miller* cases (with *Tomkins* quoted above) found that sexual harassment cannot ground a sex discrimination claim by a woman because sexual harassment *can* befall men. *Gilbert,* by contrast, holds that pregnancy cannot ground a sex discrimination because pregnancy *cannot* befall men. (This is similar to *Heelan,* which finds discrimination only if it *does* not befall men.) One view, thus, holds that an act cannot be sex discriminatory when done to one sex if it could be (or is) equally done to both sexes. Another *requires* that an act be able to be done to both sexes before it can be discriminatory when it is done to one.

At this point, the attempt by the majority in *Barnes v. Costle* to distinguish the *Gilbert/Geduldig* rendition of gender-based discrimination, in order to find sexual harassment to be treatment based on sex, is, unfortunately, inadequate. The *Barnes* court read these decisions "not [to] condone . . . sex discrimination against some but not all women."[13] But the point of these cases is that a distinction based on something seen to be *other than* sex (there pregnancy, here sexuality) is not a sex-based distinction. One test for sex-basis is the effect on, or presence in, all women. Thus, the point is not that the *Gilbert* decision does not condone discrimination against some but not all women, but that it construes a factor that affects only some women but only women to be *not* a sex-based factor. The *Barnes* court continues, "When, as in the case before us, a woman is subjected to an employment condition by a superior who leaves all men completely free from that condition, it cannot be said that there is parity of treatment as found in *General Electric* and *Geduldig*."[14] Perhaps courts will view differently a "condition" imposed by nature, such as pregnancy, from one imposed by an employer. But the *employer* in *Gilbert* excluded women from some temporary disability benefits, a condition from which all men were left completely free. And the condition to which women are subjected in sexual harassment, if one chose to see it this way, could be equally predicated upon their "nature"—their sexuality. If the logic of the *Gilbert* and *Geduldig* decisions is read not as aberration but as a consistent culmination of an entire approach to women's equality, an argument that sexual harassment is sex discrimination requires a deeper critique, and a broader alternative, than the *Barnes* majority offers.

Beyond whether sex discrimination law makes plain sense, the doctrinal issues are as follows. If women's sexuality is considered a characteristic of gender, will women's and men's sexuality be viewed as so generically different as not to be reasonably comparable, with the result that sexual harassment will be seen as equal treatment for equal differences? Will the fact that women can sexually harass men exempt the practice from being considered discriminatory when done to women, since it is not based upon a characteristic of the sex? Or will that be the turning point in holding that it *is* sex discrimination, since it is a practice in which treatment of the sexes can be reversed, hence compared? Must sexual harassment mean the same thing to the sexes to be sufficiently comparable to be discriminatory, or will the fact that it does *not* mean the same thing underline the inequality of the practice? If the contrasts between women's and men's sexual expression appear marked, will this be seen as a "sex difference," or will it support a finding that sexuality expresses social inequality?

What Is Sex?

The legal interpretation of the term *sex,* as illustrated by the foregoing, has centered upon the gender difference between women and men, which the law views as a biological given. "Gender *per se*" is considered to refer to an obvious biological fact with a fixed content. Factors "other than gender *per se,*" but correlated with it, may also ground a discrimination claim. These factors are treated in legal discourse as accretions—some biological, some social—upon the biological foundation. These presuppositions about sex and gender have been so widely assumed that it has seldom been considered whether they are appropriate foundations for a social policy directed toward women's equality, or even whether they are, to the best of our current knowledge, true.

One major contradiction within the legal conception of sex as gender was posed by the *Gilbert* analysis. The plaintiff argued that pregnancy was a gender distinction per se because only women become pregnant. The majority of the Supreme Court argued that pregnancy was other than gender per se, in part because it is voluntary, while gender is not; in part because not all women become pregnant, so it is not a characteristic of the sex; and in part because no men become pregnant, so women and men were not being *treated* discriminatorily, they merely *are* different. Defining sex with reference to gender was inadequate to resolve the issue of whether, in order for a classification such as pregnancy to be considered sex-based, all women must be actually or potentially so classified, or whether it is sufficient that all those so classified are women, with no men even potentially included, or whether the fact that no men can be so affected means that the exclusion *cannot* discriminate against women.

To generalize beyond the explicit terms of the Supreme Court's holding, its resolution of this issue could be stated as follows: for differential treatment of the sexes to be considered sex-based, it must occur, or potentially occur, to all members of a group defined by biological gender, but not for reasons unique to that biology. That is, to be sex-based, a treatment (or classification or factor) must be universal to women but not unique to women. It must affect all women and, in some sense, not only women. Pregnancy was considered both not universal to women and unique to women, thus not a gender classification. On this level, the logic of the *Manhart* and *Gilbert* results are reconcilable. *Manhart* presents the mirror image of *Gilbert:* although "extra" longevity is not universal to women, the challenged rule was universally applied to set all women's pension fund contributions; nor is "extra" longevity unique to women, since some men also experience it. So, since the rule affects all women and is based upon a characteristic not of women only, the policy of differential contributions was found to be a gender classification.

Several empirical presumptions are implicit in this approach. It is assumed that a solid physical underpinning exists for the sex difference and that sex is dimorphic. The sexes are understood in terms of their differences and these differences are considered physical and bipolar. It is assumed that a clear, known line can be drawn between those attributes of gender which are biological and those which are other than biological. The relevant referent for the legal meaning of sex is supposed to be primarily in biology rather than society.

The particular place of "sexuality" as one index to maleness or femaleness has never been firmly located in this legal scheme of sex as gender and gender as biology. Other than in the few sexual harassment cases, the question has rarely been posed. One recent EEOC case, justifying the lack of protection for homosexuals under Title VII, distinguished "sexual practice" from "gender as such," the latter defined as "an immutable characteristic with which a person is born."[15] Sexuality, or at least homosexuality, seemed to mean something one does, gender something one is. Similarly, the *Harvard Law Review* implicitly distinguished between sexuality and sex as gender under Title VII as follows: "Although jobs which require sex appeal may exploit their occupants as sex objects, [Title VII] was not designed to change *other* views that society holds about sexuality"[16] (emphasis added). A series of interconnected propositions emerges: "sex in the legal sense is primarily a matter of gender status; gender status is a matter of innate biological differences; homosexuality is a "prac tice," not a matter of gender status, hence not within the ambit of sex discrimination. But what exactly is heterosexuality? What is its relationship to the gender difference? How do gender and heterosexuality interrelate in what discrimination law means by "sex"?

The relationship of sexuality to gender is the critical link in the argument that sexual harassment is sex discrimination. Empirically, gender is not monolithic. Three dimensions can be distinguished: physical characteristics, gender identification, and sex role behavior. Contrary to legal presumptions, current research shows that none of these dimensions is perfectly intercorrelated with, nor strictly predetermines, any other. Gender, then, is not as simple as the biological difference between women and men, nor is that difference itself purely or even substantially a biological one. Sexuality as a complex interaction of (at least) all three is even less simply biologically determinate. It is neither simply a matter of gender status nor a practice without reference to biological differences. Perhaps most significantly, social and cultural factors, including attitudes, beliefs, and traditional practices—quite proper targets for legal change, compared with biological facts—are found to have a substantially broader and more powerful impact upon gender, even upon its biological aspects, than legal thinking on the sex difference has recognized.

Physical characteristics which provide indices of gender include internal and external reproductive organs and genitalia, gonads, hormone balance, and genetic and chromosomal makeup.[17] Strictly speaking, in several of these physical senses gender is not immutable, merely highly tenacious. A transsexual operation, with hormone therapy, can largely transform gender on the physical level, with the major exception of reproductive capacity. But then many born males and females do not possess reproductive capacity for a variety of biological and social reasons. Aside from these characteristics, some evidence of physical differences between the sexes in the aggregate exists in the following areas: body shape, height and weight, muscularity, physical endurance, possibly metabolic rate, possibly some forms of sensory sensitivity, rate of maturation, longevity, susceptibility to certain physical disorders, and some behaviors at birth (irritability, type of movement, and responsiveness to touch).[18] The scientific research stresses the wide, if not complete, mutability of even these differences by social factors such as psychological reinforcements, type of customary physical activity, and career patterns.[19] Moreover, on the biological level, the sex difference is not a polar opposition, but a continuum of characteristics with different averages by sex grouping.

Most characteristics are found in both sexes: the more common difference is in the positive or negative value attached to a characteristic, depending on who has it.... [W]hile it need not and cannot be argued that the individual human being is a biological *tabula rasa* at birth, the slate of *a priori* assumptions concerning the social-biological characteristics should be blank.[20]

Most sexual behaviors which differ by sex or within sex groupings have been found to lack any known biological basis. Choice of sexual object in terms of sex preference for the same or opposite sex is one; intensity of sexual desires and needs is another. Masters and Johnson's research has decisively established that women's sexual requirements are no less potent or urgent than those of men.[21] "There is little factual basis for the belief that males need sex more than do females. It is more likely that men do not exercise so much control over sexual behavior. Male sexual behavior is condoned, even encouraged, whereas females are taught restraint in sexual expression."[22] Social factors rather than biological differences are seen to shape observed differences in sexual needs and patterns of their expression.[23] For example, in spite of physiological differences between women and men, there is no physiological basis for male aggressiveness and female passivity in sexual initiation. Without changing biology, "a woman can be aggressively receptive and a man be motivationally passive in the sexual act."[24] Some scholars locate sexual excitement itself more in society than in nature. "The very experience of sexual excitement that seems to originate from hidden internal sources is in fact a learned process and it is only our insistence on the myths of naturalness that hides these social components from us."[25] Sexual feeling and expression are seen as a form of "scripted" behavior[26] which is as powerfully determined by sexism as by sex.[27] Gagnon and Simon note that "many women's ... participation in sexual activity, has often—historically, possibly more often than not—had little to do with their own sense of the erotic."[28] The social facts of sexual inequality increasingly appear to define this fact of the meaning of sex, rather than the facts of sex differences providing an irrefutable argument against their existence.

Nor is gender *identity* primarily determined by physical attributes, according to current thought and research. Gender identification, defined as the sense one has of being a man or a woman and the presentation of self and acceptance by others as such, is neither a fact nor a sense "with which one is born." Rather, it is assigned and learned. John Money's innovative experiments on hermaphrodites[29] show that gender identity need not correspond to internal organs, external genitalia, hormones, or chromosomes. In cases where, because of external genital ambiguity or deformity, a child's sex is misidentified (in the sense of later proving to be at odds with the body), children after age six persist immovably in the gender identity originally assigned; resistance to change survives even surgical conformity of external genitalia with internal sex organs. Sexual behavior in such cases is socially appropriate to the learned gender rather than to the physical one. Irrespective of sexual biology, the sex socially assigned a child, through deep and early psychological imprinting, becomes the gender identification of the adult. "One is confronted with the conclusion, perhaps surprising to some, that there is no primary genetic or other innate mechanism to preordain the masculinity or femininity of psychosexual differentiation." Money concludes that his research shows "a complete overriding of the sex-chromosomal constitution and of gonadal status in the establishment of gender role and identity."[30]

The importance of Money's research is not that one cannot tell a man from a women, although there are difficulties at times; rather, it is that that element of sex that is made up of a basic gender identification as a man or a woman is not primarily determined by physiological factors. It is secondarily determined by the body, of course, in the social sense. Genital anatomy tends under usual circumstances to determine which gender parents assign a baby, to shape gender-specific social responses, and to elicit reinforcing behavior considered appropriate to each sex. But social factors aside, a female sexual identity does not feel intrinsically out of place in a biologically male body and vice versa. To the extent that one "is" a man or a woman because one takes oneself to be so, sexual biology does not predetermine gender.

The effect of biology on the behavior of the sexes, so often accepted as primary, has been found to be largely secondary. In its place, a vast body of research documents the powerful and pervasive impact of social sex roles on attitudes and behavior, including sexual ones. A "sex role" is a widely held, learned, acted upon, and socially enforced definition of behaviors, attitudes, or pursuits as intrinsically more appropriate or seemly for one sex than for the other. It refers to the cultural practice of allocating social roles according to gender. Socialization is the process by which men and women are socially created to correspond to each society's definition of its "masculine" and "feminine" sex roles. Although scholars differ in their views and evaluations of the origins, social functions, exact transmission processes, contents, and impact upon individual personality of sex roles, the existence of strongly sex-typed social patterns within most cultures is barely disputed.

Choice of occupation, activities, goals, and feelings are strongly associated with masculine or feminine roles in virtually all cultures. The content of these categories varies sufficiently across cultures to suggest that the institutionalization of specific sex role conceptions derives from the specific history and development of each society, rather than from anything intrinsic to the sex difference—even including dimorphism itself.[31] Some societies, for example, have more than two genders.[32] On the whole, sex roles reproduce themselves and tend to describe sex groups in the aggregate, which is not surprising, since people have been molded in their image. As with biology, however, individual characteristics vary as much within sex groups as between them, and sex groups overlap to a considerable extent.[33]

What hermaphrodism does to the concept of biological gender, transsexuality does to the concept of sex roles. The rigid exclusivity of each sex of the other is undercut in the clear presence of some of both. Transsexuals experience a sense of sex identity cruelly trapped in a nonconforming body. Whatever the cause of this sense, it cannot be biological gender, since sex identity stands opposed to the body; nor can it be sex role conditioning alone, since sex identity is also opposed to that. The source of such a thorough rejection of standard sex role conditioning as well as physiology is obscure. But it is testimony to the power of the social correlation of sexual identity with physiology that, in order to pursue the desired behavior patterns fully, transsexuals consider it necessary to alter their *bodies* to accord with their gender identity. A final observation captures both meanings: first, gender identification may be better understood as a social definition of biology than as a biological definition of society, and, second, the power of that definition. Commenting upon the justice of a proposed chromosome test for determining the femaleness of the transsexual tennis player Dr. Renee Richards, one woman observed: "I think nature is not always correct. . . . She looks like a woman, plays like a woman. She *is* a woman. Chromosomes make things scientific, but nature is not always a hundred percent correct."[34]

Socially as well as biologically, gender is not as rigidly dimorphic as it is commonly supposed to be in legal discussions of equality. It is, instead, a range of overlapping distributions with different median points. The majority of women and men are located in the area of overlap. If for most characteristics the majority of women and men fall in the area where the sexes overlap, to premise legal approaches to the sexes on their differences requires the exclusion of those persons whose characteristics overlap with the other sex—that is, most people. The extremes, the tails of both curves, which apply only to exceptional women and men, are implicitly used as guidelines for sex specificity. They become norms, ideals for emulation, and standards for judgment when they are not even statistically representative.

There is a real question whether it makes sense of the evidence to conceptualize the reality of sex in terms of differences at all, except in the socially constructed sense—which social construction is what the law is attempting to address as the *problem*. To require that a given characteristic, in order to be considered a sex characteristic, be universal to the sex grouping is to require something that is not uniformly true even of most of the primary indices of gender. To then require (as the *Gilbert* approach does) that that same characteristic be comparable to, while remaining different from, the corresponding characteristic of the opposite sex, tends to exclude those few characteristics that approach being truly generic to a sex group.

While the biological sex difference has been both exaggerated and used to justify different treatment, sex inequality as a social force has been reflected in the substantive content of sex roles. Sex roles shape the behavior and express the relative position of the sexes. Although social differences between the sexes are far more pronounced than biological differences, to the extent they have been seen as differences they have not been seen as inequalities. It is not at all a distortion of the evidence to characterize the *social* situation of the sexes as largely dimorphic. In fact, the sexes are, and have been, far more dimorphic socially than they are, or have been, biologically. Much of the specific content of sex roles in American culture are those stereotypes that the law prohibits as overt job qualifications: women are weak, good with their fingers, bad at numbers, unable to stand long hours, too emotional for high seriousness. Male sex roles encourage men to be strong, aggressive, tough, dominant, and competitive. These values, which come to be considered "male," do describe conforming and common male behavior in many spheres, including the sexual.[35] Interpreting sexual behavior in sex role terms, Diana Russell argues that rape should be viewed not as deviance but as overconformity to the male sex role.[36] In support, one recent study found that convicted rapists were "sexually and psychologically normal" according to male social norms.[37] Another study quotes a parole officer who worked with rapists in prison facilities: "Those men were the most normal men there. They had a lot of hang-ups, but they were the same hang-ups as men walking out on the street."[38] Although intending to exonerate men as a sex rather than to criticize male sex roles as socially defined, Lionel Tiger makes a corroborative observation that implicitly links rape findings to sexual harassment: "[It] is relatively 'normal' for males to seek sexual access to females who are their subordinates."[39]

As the examples suggest, such behaviors are almost never observed in women. Powerful social conditioning of women to passivity, gentleness, submissiveness, and receptivity to male initiation, particularly in sexual contact, tends effectively to constrain women from expressing aggression (or even assertion) sexually, or sexuality assertively, although there probably is no biological barrier to either. The constraints appear linked to women's relative social position.

[It is] males who are supposed to initiate sexual activity with females. Females who make "advances" are considered improper, forward, aggressive, brassy, or otherwise "unladylike." By initiating intimacy they have stepped out of their place and usurped a status prerogative.[40]

Women are considered synonymous with sex, yet female sexuality is seen as valid only under certain conditions, such as marriage. Even in more permissive ages like our own, there are still limits. One of these is the point where a female can be labeled promiscuous. Another is the point where she attempts to exercise any power: women who initiate and direct sexual activity with male partners find that they have gone too far and are feared and rejected as "castrators."[41]

Implicit in these observations is the view that sexual expression shaped by sex roles prescribes appropriate male and female conduct, defines normalcy, designs sexual rituals, and allocates power in the interest of men and to the detriment of women. In this respect, there definitely is a "difference" between the sexes:

The value of such a prerogative [to initiate intimacy] is that it is a form of power. Between the sexes, as in other human interaction, the one who has the right to initiate greater intimacy has more control over the relationship. Superior status brings with it not only greater prestige and greater privileges, but greater power.[42]

[The] fantasy world that veils [women's] experience is the world of sex as seen through male eyes. It is a world where eroticism is defined in terms of female powerlessness, dependency and submission.[43]

The substance of the meaning of sex roles, in sexuality as in other areas, just as with the social roles allocated to the races, is not symmetrical between women and men. Rather, male and female sex roles complement each other in the sense that one function of the female sex role is to reinforce the impression, and create the social actuality, of male dominance and female subordination. Ellen Morgan describes this asymmetry in sexual relationships as one means through which gender inequality is expressed and maintained in American society:

We have a sexual situation in which the humanity and personhood of the woman, which make her seek autonomy and action and expression and self-respect, are at odds with her socially organized sexuality. We have a situation in which the dominant male sexual culture aggrandizes the male ego whereas the subordinate female style damages the female ego. Sex means different things to women and men by this time.[44]

Behavior by women that aggrandizes the male ego is commonly interpreted by men as attractive or seductive, yet male ego aggrandizement is merely a less charitable way of describing the previously discussed tasks of the secretary or the waitress, the requisite aspects of the demeanor and style. The implications of these roles for interpersonal behavior on the one hand and systemic powerlessness on the other are drawn in the following quotation:

The "trivia" of everyday life—using "sir" or first name, touching others, dropping the eyes, smiling, interrupting and so on ... are commonly understood as facilitators of social intercourse but are not recognized as defenders of the status quo—of the state, the wealthy, of authority, of those whose power may not be challenged. Nevertheless, these minutiae find their place on a continuum of social control which extends from internalized socialization (the colonization of the mind) . . . to sheer physical force (guns, clubs, incarceration).[45]

This examination suggests that the legally relevant content of the term *sex*, understood as gender difference, should focus upon its *social meaning* more than upon any biological givens. The most salient determinants of sexuality, much like those of work, are organized in society, not fixed in "nature." As might be expected, sex role learning, inseparably conjoined with economic necessity when the sexual aggressor is both a man and an employer, tends to inhibit women's effective resistance to "normal" male intrusions and claims upon women's sexuality, whether they come as a look or a rape. In this perspective, sexual harassment expresses one social meaning that sex roles create in the sex difference: gender distributes power as it divides labor, enforcing that division by sexual means.

LEGAL APPROACHES OTHER THAN DISCRIMINATION

Standard legal doctrine in the areas of tort, labor, and crime, which could have moderated the extremes of conventional role expectations when they restrained and damaged women, has, on the whole, institutionalized them. The law has tended to internalize and reflect, and thereby legitimize and enforce, traditional male and female norms. For example, the *act* of rape can be criticized as one expression of the male role of assertive sexual initiation, heedless of women's wishes. To the extent the *crime* of rape is defined to reflect rather than counter this role definition, allowing rape to be *legally* normal as well, rape as women experience it will not be effectively prohibited. Because sexual harassment, too, has appeared so much a part of the normal and expectable behavior between the sexes, the law has fallen short of women's needs and aspirations in similar ways. Prior to the recent cases, the law had failed to grasp the whole configuration of sexual harassment as a distinct theory. Perhaps this is too much to have expected. The greater criticism may be its consistent failure to take the shorter step of recognizing that the constituent acts of sexual harassment were actionable all along if existing doctrines had been applied to them. Contract doctrine, as the *Monge* case illustrates, did not have to be changed to prohibit sexual harassment in employment; it merely had to be applied.[46]

With a little more creativity and a little less sexism, sexual harassment might long have been a recognized tort. But it is even more interesting that without going very far out of mainstream thinking, many of the acts that comprise incidents of sexual harassment, if properly construed (this, after all, is what lawyers do), arguably fit into the traditional torts of assault and battery, with corollary dignitary harm, or, if sufficiently extreme, the tort of intentional infliction of emotional distress. This application has not commonly been made. In the labor area an explicit contractual prohibition of sexual harassment could be bargained over; but incidents could also be arbitrated as grievances—for example, under those clauses in most collective agreements that require "just cause" for termination—but apparently have not been.[47] The Occupational Safety and Health Act could forbid sexual harassment in so many words; sexual harassment could also be—but, again, seems not to have been—interpreted as a workplace "stress" under the existing code, which forbids systematic threats to worker goals, integrity, or well-being.[48]

Examination of the criminal law reveals an arsenal of potential, if partial, approaches that have not been applied to the facts of sexual harassment. Sexual harassment often includes criminal acts such as rape, sexual assault, sexual imposition, deviate sexual intercourse, solicitation, or adultery.[49] Often involved, in addition, are more esoteric or antiquated crimes which still exist in some form in some jurisdictions: lewdness, criminal conversation, fornication, insult, bribery, oppression, exploitation, and blackmail. In the absence of the legitimate employment relation, sexual submission in exchange for material survival is conventionally considered prostitution, which remains illegal in most jurisdictions. A great many instances of sexual harassment in essence amount to solicitation for prostitution. Reported cases and commentaries do not disclose that acts comprising sexual harassment have been prosecuted on any of these criminal grounds, any more than on the foregoing civil grounds. Such a fact of administration confronts the legal system at a point at which its theory and practice converge.

Before a systemic critique is launched, another possible explanation for the lack of legal response to facts amounting to sexual harassment should be considered: sexual incidents in the employment context might not have been reported to those who could initiate legal action. It makes sense that women would not complain to authorities. The

...it and potential for direct reprisals upon exposure, women's previous position in the labor market, and the previously slim chance of access mean that most women, in order to complain officially, would have to take risks that most women are not in an economic position to take. Such an explanation also exposes the social circularity, from women's standpoint, of nonreporting as a justification for legal nonresponse. The law participates in constructing the balance of risks run in reporting. One reason for a lack of complaints may be the lack of legitimation of these injuries *as injuries* which an effective legal prohibition would give. Concretely, when nothing helpful is known to be done, complaint becomes an integral part of the social pathology of the problem, a further aggravation of the injury of the incident itself, instead of a potential solution to it. Together with the psychological impact of sexual harassment upon women's socialized sense of self-worth and the confirmation that a legal nonresponse gives to women's apprehensions about the reactions of others, it seems reasonable that incidents might not be reported. But this indicts more than exonerates the legal system.

Complaints may also have been made but not heard. Wife beating provides a direct analogy. The constituent acts of domestic battery are obvious criminal violations; they are regularly grounds for arrest and, if proven, for conviction in contexts other than husband and wife. Women's attempts to gain legal redress and protection from domestic victimization are infamously ineffectual.[50] This suggests that intimate assaults on women by men are ignored even when they are reported—even when there is an unambiguous doctrinal receptacle for the complaint. The guarantee of impunity seems to be particularly firm when incidents involve either sexuality or violence within a relationship presumed to have a sexual dimension. With the beating of women in the home as well as with the sexual harassment of women on the job (acts which occur when women and men are involved in a relation which is presumptively sexualized, as both home and workplace are) even acts that have been objectively illegal are systematically tolerated.

The legal profession, in addition, has probably seen the nexus between work and sex presented by sexual harassment to introduce "complications" in bringing suits or prosecutions. A clean approach through *either* employment, tort, criminal, or labor law may have appeared impracticable or cumbersome. Neither a quick fix, rich clients, nor a good prospect of large money damages has made such suits attractive. In light of this analysis, the lack of documented legal response to facts amounting to sexual harassment, much less to the totality of the problem, seems less justified by the lack of reports than the lack of reports seems explained by those factors which make sexual harassment a women's problem. The same factors, in turn, begin to explain the effective acquiescence of the legal system.

A more fundamental reason than the absence of reports for the legal system's lack of response to sexual harassment is the conceptual inadequacy of traditional legal theories to the social reality of men's sexual treatment of women. It is no accident that no recognized legal category has been applied with any regularity to the entire fact pattern of sexual harassment. No legal doctrine except sex discrimination, which is relatively new, comfortably accommodates the entire configuration of facts, places them in broad social perspective, or approaches the appropriate relief. Although the facts of sex discrimination have a long history in women's suffering, the prohibition on sex discrimination as such lacks a common law history. Other and older areas of law can contribute the experience, analogues, applicable concepts, and additional avenues for partial or supplementary relief that such a history might have supplied. They illustrate how the law has approached women's sexuality. They provide, moreover, a point of comparison that clarifies the distinctive contribution of sex discrimination as a legal concept and assists in its interpretation. Exploring some illustrative common law attempts to treat intimate violations of women as illegal recaptures and recasts an ongoing history—its contributions and its limitations.

Criminal Law

Many acts of sexual harassment are technically crimes and should be prosecuted. The criminal law has not, however, been generally sympathetic to sexual injuries as women experience them. Unlike most other crimes, and like no other crimes against the person,* corroboration is often required and juries are instructed to be especially careful in evaluating the testimony "in view of the emotional involvement of the witness and the difficulty of determining the truth with respect to

---

*The proof requirements for sexual injuries are most like those for treason.

alleged sexual activities carried out in private."[51] "In private" means more than "while alone." Many crimes are committed in the absence of nonparticipant eyewitnesses. Privacy sanctifies the sphere of the sexual. Because these events so often occur in private, they are safe from public witness. In part because they feel so alone, women are disabled from effective resistance. Such a conception of the "private" becomes a special legal caution that women who accuse men of sexual injury cannot be judged by ordinary standards of credibility. It turns men's "right to be let alone"[52] into a shield behind which isolated women can be sexually abused one at a time.

The Model Penal Code defines sexual assault as subjecting "another not his spouse to any sexual contact" including those circumstances in which "he knows that the contact is offensive to the other person." Sexual contact is defined as "any touching of the sexual or other intimate parts of the person of another for the purpose of arousing or gratifying sexual desire of either party."[53] This suggests that sexual assault, in common with ordinary sexual contact, is motivated by sexual desire. Sexual assault is distinguished from sexual non-assault only by the fact that a wrong person—in this example, a person known to be offended by it—is its object. At what point sexual assault is distinguishable from permissible sexual intimacy is a good question. Here, sexual assault differs from most (if not all) other forms of assault: the proscribed act and the allowed act are the same act. Ultimately, only the meaning to the acted-upon distinguishes them.

Sexual assault as experienced during sexual harassment seems less an ordinary act of sexual desire directed toward the wrong person than an expression of dominance laced with impersonal contempt, the habit of getting what one wants, and the perception (usually accurate) that the situation can be safely exploited in this way—all expressed sexually. It is dominance eroticized. The sense that emerges from incidents of sexual harassment is less that men mean to arouse or gratify the women's sexual desires, or often even their own, and more that they want to know that they can go this far this way any time they wish and get away with it. The fact that they can do this seems itself to be sexually arousing. The practice seems an extension of their desire and belief that the woman is there *for them*, however they may choose to define that. The factors of advantage, the quality of presumption, and the manipulation of occasion may participate in motivating heterosexual contact in ordinary course; they may be constituents or stimuli of ordinary male sexual desire. But to define the crime in the terms of the perpetrator's misplacement of otherwise fine feelings begins the process of distinguishing the sexual from other forms of violation, a process which then extends to an inquiry into what the victim did to arouse this desire and whether she found the assault gratifying.[54] It may be that the normal sexual interactions to which sexual assault is assimilated should be examined in light of the difficulty of distinguishing the two.

An earlier version of the Model Penal Code's sexual assault provision prohibited sexual contact without consent. The requirement was deleted with the following justification: "This seems too strict a standard of criminality, considering the frequency with which tentative sexual advances are made without explicit assurance of consent."[55] The statute prohibits subjection to sexual contact, which presumably should be distinguishable in practice from "tentative sexual advances." At least, advances which subject one to sexual contact, as defined, are not very tentative. More bluntly, this statement reflects the belief that since men so frequently initiate sexual contact without determining whether women want it or not, such acts should not be considered criminal. This approach eviscerates the entire conception of a sexual assault when the unwanted offensiveness of the contact is the only feature that divides it from the noncriminal.

Exactly the conditions that make sexual harassment pernicious may tend to disqualify it as sexual assault. For example, the economic threats that sanction sexual coercion, as well as women's social conditioning to seek men's approval, may prevent women from being sufficiently explicit about the offensiveness of the man's behavior to meet the statutory requirement. Further, it is overwhelmingly clear that male perpetrators do not as a rule experience sexual episodes as the assaults that the victims feel them to be. This must be one reason they can continue to do it. Men who sexually harass women are commonly dumbfounded that the women resent it, even when the women have declined flatly from the beginning and resisted explicitly throughout. Assuming that men's bafflement is sincere, it not only measures monumental insensitivity but also indicates the difficulty of showing that the perpetrator "knew the contact would be offensive." Apparently, men are responsible only if they know they are sexually offensive, and nothing in the law requires (or even strongly encourages) them to know what their conduct means to women.

The rape law is similarly inadequate as a guide to a work-related, gender-specific abuse. It more shows the ambivalence of the law, often its misogyny. Rape ordinarily has referred to a male having "sexual intercourse with a female not his wife" by force or threats to life or physical integrity.[56] "Gross sexual imposition" is the lesser crime for the same act when the woman is under compulsion "to submit by any threat that would prevent resistance by a woman of ordinary resolution."[57] Apparently threat of loss of subsistence has not been found within this prohibition. Consent is a defense. If a woman is threatened with loss of her job if she resists sexual relations, and then does not resist for that reason, she is legally considered to have consented. Menachem Amir summarizes this view: "Threats which may be urgent in terms of the personality and social needs of the victim are known to exist; for example, the threat of loss of a job. . . . Generally, the law refuses to deal with such threats as anything more than reasons for giving consent, which thereby bars conviction of rape."[58] Since the woman's participation has been forced by coercing her consent rather than by coercing the act itself, the intercourse is not considered forced. With the law taking this stance, imagine a complaining witness testifying as follows: "I didn't want to sleep with him but I wanted the job so much and he was holding it over my head, that *I was willing*, right then, to sleep with him, in order to get the job."[59] Because of his power as an employer, the perpetrator gains legal immunity as a man.

Tort Law

Women's bodies, particularly the conditions and consequences of men's sexual access to them, are not a novel subject for the law, as the foregoing examination reveals. The law of torts, or private harms, historically provided civil redress for sexual invasions at a time when social morality was less ambiguous in defining a woman's sexuality as intrinsic to her virtue, and her virtue as partially constitutive of her value, hence as capable of compensable damage. Perhaps with this tradition in mind, several recent sexual harassment cases have suggested—usually as a reason for holding sexual harassment not to be sex discrimination—that sexual harassment should be considered tortious. The federal court in *Tomkins*, implicitly finding that since sexual harassment is a tort it is not discrimination, stated that Title

VII "is not intended to provide a federal tort remedy for what amounts to physical attack motivated by sexual desire on the part of a supervisor and which happened to occur in a corporate corridor rather than a back alley."[60] One appellate judge, concurring in the judgment in *Barnes* that sexual harassment is sex discrimination, observed, "An act of sexual harassment which caused the victim, because of her rejection of such advances, to be damaged in her job, would constitute a tort."[61] Which tort is not specified, although "[t]here is no necessity whatever that a tort must have a name."[62] It is, however, necessary that the definition of the legal wrong fit the conceptual framework of tort law. Brief examination of traditional tort views of sexual wrongs against women illustrates that tort law is not simply wrong, and is partially helpful, but is fundamentally insufficient as a legal approach to sexual harassment.

Sexual touching that women do not want has historically been considered tortious under a variety of doctrines, usually battery, assault, or, if exclusively emotional damage is done, as the intentional infliction of emotional distress. A battery is a harmful or offensive contact which is intentionally caused. While contact must be intentional, hostile intent, or intent to cause all the damages that resulted from the contact, is not necessary. Variously formulated, "taking indecent liberties with a woman without her consent,"[63] "putting hands upon a female with a view to violate her person,"[64] or "intentional touching of a woman by a man without excuse or justification"[65] have been considered battery. Battery is said to include instances in which a compliment is intended, "as where an unappreciative woman is kissed without her consent."[66]

Battery, the actual touching, is often combined with assault, the fear of such a touching. The tort of assault consists in placing a person in *fear* of an immediate harmful or offensive contact. It is "a touching of the mind, if not of the body."[67] The invasion is mental. The defendant must have intended at least to arouse apprehension, and actually have done so. The fear-producing event must be more than words alone, but words can clarify an otherwise equivocal act. Defenses include consent, but only to those acts consented to; consent to a kiss, for example, does not extend to anything further. Nor are provocative words a defense.

Kissing a woman without her consent has been considered actionable under a combination (or confusion) of assault and battery doctrines. In 1899, a husband and wife recovered $700 for assault on the wife for forcible hugging and kissing "against her wish and by force."[68] In 1921, a railroad was found responsible for the embarrassment and humiliation of a woman passenger caused when a drunken man, of whose boisterous conduct and inebriated condition the railroad was aware, fell down on top of her and kissed her on the cheek.[69] In 1895 in Wisconsin, a twenty-year-old schoolteacher recovered $1,000 from the employer of a railroad conductor who grabbed and kissed her several times despite her clear attempts to discourage and repel him.[70]

Other early cases finding sexual incursions actionable reveal that little has changed in men's sexual behavior, although something seems to have changed in the social and legal standards by which it is evaluated. In a case in 1915, a woman recovered damages for assault and battery against a man who squeezed her breast and laid his hand on her face. The defendant denied the whole incident, then characterized the touching as "nothing more than a harmless caress."[71] In a similar case in 1921, a woman recovered for the mental anguish arising from an indecent assault, defined as "the act of a male person taking indecent liberties with the person of a female, or fondling her in a lewd and lascivious manner without her consent and against her will." The judge found it unnecessary for the assault to be made in an angry or insolent manner: "Indecent assaults are not made in that way."[72] Sexual assault—whether or not it was done with bad feeling— is still assault.

Contemporary sexual mores make it difficult to imagine such cases in court. Women are, it seems, supposed to consider acts in this tradition harmless, and litigation in this area is now relatively uncommon.* As recently as 1961, however, an Arizona woman was granted $3,500 actual damages and $1,500 punitive damages in a full-fledged case of sexual harassment in employment brought under the tort theory of assault and battery. The complaint alleged indecent assault by force and violence for an employer's efforts to seduce and offend the dignity of a sixty-five-year-old woman he employed as a caretaker in a trailer park. The situation included the "defendant placing his hand upon the private parts of the plaintiff."[73] The woman resisted the ad-

---

*Such causes of action may also have been pretexts for racial repression. Black men may have been prosecuted and white men not for the same sexual conduct. This hypothesis requires investigation.

vances for two years and was finally discharged. Although this case holds hope for the tort approach, perhaps the desexualization of older women made more than usually credible her assertions that the man's acts were neither desired nor provoked, and that her dignity was violated.

One common rejoinder to charges of sexual harassment is that the individual woman is unduly and overly sensitive to these advances, raising the question of the standards by which an at least partly subjective injury is to be evaluated. Unless the defendant has reason to believe that the individual would permit more or less contact, the tort standard in battery cases prohibits contact that would be "offensive to an ordinary person not unduly sensitive as to his dignity."[74] However, even "innocuous and generally permitted contacts may become tortious if they are inflicted with knowledge that the individual plaintiff objects to them and refuses to permit them."[75] For assault, in which the fear of contact constitutes the injury, the test is what the defendant's conduct "denote[d] at the time to the party assaulted."[76] The standard treatment of the hypersensitive individual is to find liability if the conduct would have been offensive to the person of ordinary sensibilities. If it would have been, the perpetrator is liable for all the damages caused *this* individual, whether she is unduly sensitive or not.

The standard of recovery in the strictly emotional area is particularly instructive. The tort of intentional infliction of emotional distress, codified by the second Restatement of Torts, allows recovery for purely emotional disturbance.[77] The conduct must be extreme and outrageous to a person of ordinary sensibilities. The departure here is that the perpetrator is liable for the emotional distress alone, and for the bodily harm that results from it, without requiring a physical act or invasion. The tort conception of "parasitic damages," in which a tortfeasor is liable for all the consequences of his acts (for example, loss of employment) once he is liable for the tort, raises the possibility of covering the entire range of consequences of sexual harassment in sufficiently aggravated circumstances.

Sexual propositions in themselves have not generally been considered torts where there is no physical incursion upon or trespass against the person, or no physical injury. In Magruder's famous formulation: "Women have occasionally sought damages for mental distress and humiliation on account of being addressed by a proposal of illicit intercourse. This is peculiarly a situation where circumstances alter cases. If there has been no incidental assault or battery, or perhaps trespass to land, recovery is generally denied, the view being apparently, that there is no harm in asking."[78] Expressing attitudes toward women's assertions of sexual injury which have remained largely unchanged to the present day, the court in one case of solicitation of sexual intercourse found the injury of a sexual proposition "generally considered more sentimental than substantial . . . vague and shadowy" and "easily simulated and impossible to disprove." Without physical "impact," the injury of a sexual proposition is considered "remote" and to have a "metaphysical character."[79] It is not an injury *in itself.*[80]

Sexual harassment that consisted solely in propositions as a condition of work apparently would not be tortious unless it became outrageous enough to constitute intentional infliction of emotional distress. One recently filed tort case, *Fuller v. Williames,*[81] makes just such allegations, pleading as intentional infliction of emotional distress a "condition of work" type situation of sexual harassment. The plaintiff complained that the defendants on several occasions, in the presence of others, "unlawfully, wilfully, maliciously, outrageously and contemptuously [did] insult, demean and humiliate plaintiff by making crude remarks of an explicit sexual nature including references to her sexual anatomy and functions and by making remarks deprecating to women in general," knowing that this conduct was likely to cause severe emotional distress. She allegedly

became upset, embarrassed, humiliated, nervous and depressed; suffered frequent tension headaches, had difficulty sleeping, suffered stress in her marriage, and was unable to concentrate on her photographic work and public school and photographic teaching; suffered mental anguish and humiliation and damage to her reputation as a dignified self-respecting woman and impairment of her earning capacity.[82]

Damages included "unpaid wages due." In another case which also pled sexual harassment as sex discrimination, one count complained of intentional infliction of emotional distress through acts of sexual harassment wherein the defendant "disturbed and disquieted the plaintiff by soliciting her to be his sex object if she wished to continue to be employed." The plaintiff "regarded such proposals . . . [as] repugnant, abhorrent, and a shock to her moral sensitivities and ideals of decency and propriety," took steps to end his sexual advances, but they continued under her discharge.[83] The results in these cases may help to clarify the potential of this approach.

Torts prohibiting interference with family relations by sexual means—seduction, enticement, criminal conversation, alienation of affections, loss of consortium, and the like—have blended the enforcement of moral standards with protections for men's possessory interests, whether by design or pattern of administration. Civil recovery usually went to men for loss of consortium, a "relational injury" which included loss of "conjugal affection." Blackstone explains why husbands have recovered for this loss far more often than wives:

We may observe that in these relative injuries notice is only taken of the wrong done to the superior of the parties related . . . while the loss of the inferior by such injuries is totally unregarded. One reason for which may be this; that the inferior hath no kind of property in the company, care or assistance of the superior, as the superior is held to have in those of the inferior, and therefore the inferior can suffer no loss or injury.[84]

This candid admission that women are regarded as inferior parallels the assessment in *Plessy* of skin color as property. Just as the loss of conjugal affection by the inferior in the marital relationship is "totally unregarded," the Supreme Court thought that a property interest in skin color, if it existed, could not be a threatened loss to a black man because he did not have an interest to lose. In questions of race relations, only the dominant race had such an interest.[85] That there can be a property interest in white skin is clearly an atavism of the social system which invested white ownership in black skin. To apply Blackstone's analysis in a racial context, a property interest in an inferior defines the institution of slavery.

Most actions for interference with domestic relations "which carry an accusation of sexual misbehavior" have been abolished by statute. The reasons, as summarized by William Prosser, are instructive on social attitudes toward women's accusations of sexual injury as these attitudes have been reflected in tort law:

It is notorious that [such actions] have afforded a fertile field for blackmail and extortion by means of manufactured suits in which the threat of publicity is used to force a settlement. There is good reason to believe that even genuine actions of this type are brought more frequently than not with purely mercenary or vindictive motives; that it is impossible to compensate for such damage with what has derisively been called "heart balm;" and that no preventive purpose is served, since such torts seldom are committed with deliberate plan. Added to this is perhaps an increasing notion of personal or even sexual freedom on the part of women.[86]

The essence of the first objection is that women lie about sex for money. As to the second, one wonders why bad motives for bringing good suits is not a more common reason for eliminating many other causes of action. Further, money does not adequately compensate for most injuries (for example, wrongful death), yet the cause of action is not eliminated. Then, the sophisticated calculus so basic to tort that distinguishes negligent from intentional harm is abandoned in favor of the proposition that a tort committed without "deliberate plan" is not a tort at all. Money damages are required to serve a deterrent function in these cases, while it suffices for other torts that deterrence is merely a desirable by-product of the point of damages: to help make the victim whole for the injury. These inconsistencies lend themselves to the interpretation that society has increasingly come to view such incidents as not very damaging.

The final reason mentioned by Prosser suggests that the abolished common law actions themselves presupposed that constraints on women's freedom protected the domestic relation, which may be true. Behind this obeisance to women's freedom is a lack of recognition of the double standard that never did see any contradiction between men's freedom and the domestic relation. Nor does the abolition of these actions address the reasons why women continue to be less free in this respect than men, independent of the existence of potential tort recovery. This reference to women's increasing "personal or even sexual freedom" inadequately criticizes the premise common to all these causes of action: that a man's wife's sexuality belonged to him, in the sense that another man was liable to him in damages for sexual acts with her, even with her consent. This attitude may be no less prevalent although it is no longer legally enforceable in this way. The point it not that these common law torts should be revived, but that their statutory abolition for these reasons reveals attitudes toward women's sexuality which can be expected to arise in connection with attempts to impose sanctions upon men's sexual violation of women in employment as well.

The examination of tort shows that the law is quite accustomed to treating cloudy issues of motive and intent, the meaning of ambiguous acts, the effect of words on liability for acts, and the role of excessive sensitivity in determining liability and damages, all in a sexual context. These issues have arisen before. They have not been thought so subtle as to preclude a judicial resolution once a real injury was perceived to exist. This is a recommendation for tort analogies. One major caveat is necessary. Ordinary women probably find offensive sexual contact and proposals that ordinary men find trivial or sexually stimulating coming from women—or that ordinary men consider trivial or stimulating to women. Sex is peculiarly an area where a presumption of gender sameness, or judgments by men of women, are not illuminating as standards for equal treatment, since to remind a man of his sexuality is to build his sense of potency, while for a man to remind a woman of hers is often experienced as intrusive, denigrating, and depotentiating. Making an issue of skin color does not have the same social meaning for blacks as for whites. A corrective "ordinary woman" standard would need to be applied to tort analogies in the discrimination context.[87] Whether sexual propositions in themselves would be actionable in employment should be measured according to this altered standard, and seen as integral to the maintenance of women's depressed economic status.

Most broadly considered, tort is conceptually inadequate to the problem of sexual harassment to the extent that it rips injuries to women's sexuality out of the context of women's social circumstances as a whole. In particular, short of developing a new tort for sexual harassment as such, the tort approach misses the nexus between women's sexuality and women's employment, the system of reciprocal sanctions which, to women as a gender, become cumulative. In tort perspective, the injury of sexual harassment would be seen as an injury to the individual person, to personal sexual integrity, with damages extending to the job. Alternatively, sexual harassment could be seen as an injury to an individual interest in employment, with damages extending to the emotional harm attendant to the sexual invasion as well as to the loss of employment. The approach tends to pose the necessity to decide whether sexual harassment is essentially an injury to the person, to sexual integrity and feelings, with pendent damages to the job, or whether it is essentially an injury to the job, with damages extending to the person. Since it is both, either one omits the social dynamics that systematically place women in these positions, that may coerce consent, that interpenetrate sexuality and employment to women's detriment because they are women.

Unsituated in a recognition of the context that keeps women secondary and powerless, sexual injuries appear as incidental or deviant aberrations which arise in one-to-one relationships gone wrong. The essential purpose of tort law, although it has policy assumptions and implications, is to compensate individuals one at a time for mischief which befalls them as a consequence of the one-time ineptitude or nastiness of other individuals. The occurrence of such events is viewed more or less with resignation, as an inevitability of social proximity, a fall-out of order which can be confronted only probabilistically. Sexual harassment as understood in this book is not merely a parade of interconnected consequences with the potential for discrete repetition by other individuals, so that a precedent will suffice. Rather, it is a group-defined injury which occurs to many different individuals regardless of unique qualities or circumstances, in ways that connect with other deprivations of the same individuals, among all of whom a single characteristic—female sex—is shared. Such an injury is *in essence* a group injury. The context which makes the impact of gender cumulative—in fact, the context that makes it injurious—is lost when sexual harassment is approached as an individual injury, however wide the net of damages is cast. Tort law compensates individuals for injuries while spreading their costs and perhaps setting examples for foresightful perpetrators; the purpose of discrimination law is to change the society so that this kind of injury need not and does not recur. Tort law considers individual and compensable something which is fundamentally social and should be eliminated.

A related defect in the vision underlying the sexual tort cases, from the standpoint of their usefulness as a solution to sexual harassment, is their disabling (and cloying) moralism. The aura of the pedestal, more rightly understood as the foundation of the cage, permeates them. In one case, the judge opined, "Every women has a right to assume that a passenger car is not a brothel and that when she travels in it, she will meet nothing, see nothing, hear nothing, to wound her delicacy or insult her womanhood."[88] Another case reveals an underlying reason for age limits on women's capacity to consent to sex. The ability fully to appreciate the consequences of sex outside of marriage is essential for an act which "when discovered ostracizes her from good society."[89] When it becomes clear that such protections of delicacy and purity have worked women's exclusion from the decisive arenas of social life, while the same society that morally approves economically punishes the sexually independent (that is, noncompliant) woman, more moralism looks like more of the problem. Just as women are tired of being commended rather than paid, they are tired of being considered sexually virtuous rather than hired or promoted—a choice men must seldom confront and a currency of compensation men must seldom settle for. Prohibitions on sexual harassment as acts conceived as moral violations emerge as repressive impositions of state morality. Inventing special rules of morality for the workplace would institutionalize new taboos rather than confront the fact that it is *women* who are systematically disadvantaged by the old ones. Resistance to sexual harassment can be misconstrued as a revival of moral delicacy only until it is grasped that sexual harassment is less an issue of right and wrong than an issue of power. Women are in no *position* to refuse, which is what makes refusal so moral an act and surrender so unfairly the price of survival.

All of this is not to say that sexual harassment is not both wrong and a personal injury, merely that it is a social wrong and a social injury that occurs on a personal level. To treat it as a tort is less simply incorrect than inadequate. The law recognizes that individual acts of racism could be torts in recognizing that the dignitary harm of racist insults can be compensated like any other personal injury.[90] This does not preclude a finding that the same acts of racial invective on the job are race discrimination.[91] Although racial insults impact upon blacks on a personal level, they are systematically connected to the "living insult" of segregation.[92] Although reparations may be due,[93] the stigma is not eradicable by money damages to one black person at a time. As with sexual harassment, the reason these acts can occur and recur, and the source of their sting, is not the breaking of a code of good conduct, but the relegation to inferiority for which they stand.

To see sexual harassment as an injury to morality is to turn it into an extreme case of bad manners, when the point is that it is the kind of bad manners almost exclusively visited upon women by men with the power to get away with it. One can see the social invisibility of blacks as white rudeness, but it makes more sense to see it as racism. The major difference between the tort approach and the discrimination approach, then, is that tort sees sexual harassment as an illicit act, a moral infraction, an outrage to the individual's sensibilities and the society's cherished but unlived values. Discrimination law casts the same acts as economic coercion, in which material survival is held hostage to sexual submission.

It may seem inconsistent to suggest an "ordinary woman" corrective to tort analogies in one breath and to attack as denigrating the special moral rules the law fashioned for women's protection in another. It is not. The double standard is a conception which the rejection of "different treatment" could rightly target. The prohibition on arbitrariness rightly rejects such rules premised upon ascribed status. However, the implicit conception that equality must ascribe sameness avoids the question, "the same as whom?" It thus appears that equality must mean measuring women by the standard of the "ordinary man." The resolution is neither presumptive equivalence nor regression to special moral rules to correspond to special differences. The beginnings lie in women seeking a standard, shaped, in Virginia Woolf's words, "out of their own needs for their own uses."[94]

SEXUAL HARASSMENT AS SEX DISCRIMINATION: AN INEQUALITY ARGUMENT

Practices which express and reinforce the social inequality of women to men are clear cases of sex-based discrimination in the *inequality* approach. Sexual harassment of working women is argued to be employment discrimination based on gender where gender is defined as the social meaning of sexual biology. Women are sexually harassed by men because they are women, that is, because of the social meaning of female sexuality, here, in the employment context. Three kinds of arguments support and illustrate this position: first, the exchange of sex for survival has historically assured women's economic dependence and inferiority as well as sexual availability to men. Second, sexual harassment expresses the male sex-role pattern of coercive sexual initiation toward women, often in vicious and unwanted ways. Third, women's sexuality largely defines women as women in this society, so violations of it are abuses of women as women.

Tradition

Sexual harassment perpetuates the interlocked structure by which women have been kept sexually in thrall to men and at the bottom of the labor market. Two forces of American society converge: men's control over women's sexuality and capital's control over employees' work lives. Women historically have been required to exchange sexual services for material survival, in one form or another. Prostitution and marriage as well as sexual harassment in different ways institutionalize this arrangement.

The impact of these forces, which affect all women, often varies by class. Exclusion of moderately well-off women (that is, women attached to moderately well-off men) from most gainful occupations was often excused by fears that virtuous women would fall victim to sexual predators if they were allowed to work.[95] This exclusion, however, insured their dependence for survival upon bartering attractiveness and sexuality for subsistence, only from different men. Deprived of education and training in marketable skills, excluded from most professions, and disdaining as unsuitable the menial work reserved for their lower-class sisters, such women's adequacy was traditionally measured in large part by sexual allure. As they entered the paid labor force in increasing numbers, the sexual standard they were judged by accompanied them; the class status they held as adjuncts to middle-class men did not. Working-class and poor women did not have the choice between the home and the workplace. And they have always maintained an even more precarious hold on jobs than their male counterparts, with chronically lower wages, and usually without security or the requisites to claim advancement. Because they were women, these factors put them at the mercy of the employer sexually[96] as well as economically. Once in the work force, usually in women's jobs, the class distinctions among women were qualified by their common circumstance, which was sex defined. "Sometimes the employer's son, or the master himself, or the senior stablehand, would have taken them. Men didn't always use brute force, the physical coercion or the threat of it that is the standard definition of rape. Often the threat of dismissal was sufficient."[97]

This point is illustrated in the following excerpt from Olive Pratt Rayner's *The Typewriter Girl* (dated by Margery Davies as late nineteenth century):

Three clerks (male), in seedy black coats, the eldest with hair the color of a fox's, went on chaffing with one another for two minutes after I closed the door, with ostentatious unconsciousness of my insignificant presence.... The youngest, after a while, wheeled around on his high stool and broke out with the chivalry of his class and age, "Well, what's your business?"

My voice trembled a little, but I mustered up courage and spoke. "I have called about your advertisement..."

He eyed me up and down. I am slender, and, I will venture to say, if not pretty, at least interesting looking.

"How many words a minute?" he asked after a long pause.

I stretched the truth as far as its elasticity would permit. "Ninety-seven," I answered. . . .

The eldest clerk, with the foxy head, wheeled around, and took his turn to stare. He had hairy hands and large goggle-eyes. . . . I detected an undercurrent of double meaning. . . . I felt disagreeably like Esther in the presence of Ahasuerus—a fat and oily Ahasuerus of fifty. . . . He perused me up and down with his small pig's eyes, as if he were buying a horse, scrutinizing my face, my figure, my hands, my feet. I felt like a Circassian in an Arab slavemarket.[98]

Millett generalizes this observation: "A female is continually obliged to seek survival or advancement through the approval of males as those who hold power. She may do this through appeasement or through the exchange of her sexuality for support and status."[99]

The generality of "women" and "men" must be qualified by recognizing the distinctive effect of race. Racism does not allow black men to share white men's dominance of economic resources. Black women have not tended to be economically dependent upon black men to the degree white women have been upon white men. To the extent black women are employed by white men, as most have been from slavery until the present, the foregoing analysis applies directly to them, intensified, not undercut, by race. There is little indication that this statement by an anonymous black woman in 1912 is significantly outdated.

I remember very well the first and last work place from which I was dismissed. I lost my place because I refused to let the madam's husband kiss me. . . . he took it as a matter of course, because without any love-making at all, soon after I was installed as cook, he walked up to me, threw his arms around me, and was in the act of kissing me, when I demanded to know what he meant, and shoved him away. . . . I believe nearly all white men take, and expect to take, undue liberties with their colored female servants. . . . where the girl is not willing, she has only herself to depend upon for protection. . . . what we need is present help, present sympathy, better wages, better hours, more protection, and a chance to breathe for once while alive as free women.[100]

Moreover, when black women enter the labor market of the dominant society, they succeed to the secondary place of white females (remaining, in addition, under the disabilities of blacks), while black men succeed at least to some of the power of the male role. Indeed, many of the demands of the black civil rights movement in the 1960s centered upon just such a recovery of "manhood."

Similar to the way in which the status of American blacks of both sexes encompasses personal and economic exploitation, sexual harassment deprives women of personhood by relegating them to subservience through jointly exploiting their sexuality and their work. As women begin to achieve the minimum material conditions under which equality with men can concretely be envisioned, and increasingly consider their skills worth a wage and their dignity worth defending, the necessity to exchange sex for support becomes increasingly intolerable. It is a reminder of that image of a deprived reality in which sexuality and attractiveness to men were all a woman had to offer—and she had very little control over either. The history of the role of sexuality in enforcing women's second-class economic status, sketched only very briefly here, makes sexual requirements of work "uniquely disturbing to women."[101]

It is a reminder, a badge or indicia [*sic*] of the servile status she suffered . . . and which she is now trying to shake off. . . . To make her advancement on the job depend on her sexual performance is to resurrect her former status as man's property or plaything.[102]

But is such status really a thing of the past? The sexual harassment cases and evidence suggest that it is not. Emma Goldman's analysis has no less vitality now than in 1917:

Nowhere is a woman treated according to the merit of her work, but rather as a sex. It is therefore almost inevitable that she should pay for her right to exist, to keep a position in whatever line, with sex favors. Thus it is merely a question of degree whether she sells herself to one man, in or out of marriage, or to many men.[103]

A guarantee against discrimination "because of sex" has little meaning if a major traditional dynamic of enforcement and expression of inferior sex status is allowed to persist untouched. A guarantee of equal access to job training, education, and skills has little substance if a requirement of equality in hiring, promotion, and pay can legally be withheld if a woman refuses to grant sexual favors. A man who is allowed to measure a woman's work by sexual standards cannot be said to employ her on the basis of merit. If a woman must grant sexual consideration to her boss in exchange for employment benefits, her

material status still depends upon her sexual performance, and the
legal promise of equality for women is an illusion.

Sex Roles

In *Stanton v. Stanton,* the Supreme Court spoke of the "role-typing
society has long imposed"[104] on the basis of sex. Congress effectively
recognized the unsuitability of sex-based social role distinctions as
they deprive women of economic opportunities in the original enactment and later extension and strengthening of Title VII, the federal
contract compliance provisions, and in the Congressional passage of
the Equal Pay Act and Equal Rights Amendment. No difference between the sexes was considered to justify the inferior economic status
women were found to occupy throughout the economy, a status which
sexual harassment exploits and promotes.[105] In the vast and growing
scholarly literature investigating social role differentiation by sex in
America,[106] dominance and aggressiveness are found to characterize
the ideal of "masculinity" in general and in sexual relations. Women's
sex roles define the feminine ideal in general and in sex as submissive,
passive, and receptive to male initiative. A major substantive element
in the social meaning of masculinity, what men learn makes them "a
man," is sexual conquest of women; in turn, women's femininity is
defined in terms of acquiescence to male sexual advances. Social expectations, backed by a variety of sanctions ranging from rape to job
reprisals to guilt manipulation, enforce these models by which both
sexes learn to act out, and thereby become, the sex they are assigned.
The inequality in the description is apparent: women are conditioned
to become, and to think of themselves as, the proper subordinates of
men, who learn to define their male identity partly in terms of their
prowess in sexually dominating women. Some men are beginning to
consider that this aspect of male identity not only systematically oppresses women, but, as it aggrandizes men's power, restricts their
humanity.[107]

Sexual harassment is discrimination "based on sex" within the social
meaning of sex, as the concept is socially incarnated in sex roles.
Pervasive and "accepted" as they are, these rigid roles have no place in
the allocation of social and economic resources. If they are allowed to
persist in these spheres, economic equality for women is impossible.
The "sex stereotype"[108] comes the closes to capturing the sex role

argument in legal form. In the sexual harassment cases, some plaintiffs' attorneys have urged it as a theory for prohibiting sexual harassment under Title VII. Difficult as it is to criticize one of the few concepts available, the sex stereotype is ill-suited to the requisite analysis of sexual harassment.

A claim that a practice is discriminatory because it is based upon a sex stereotype is grounded either upon an argument that the stereotype is not, in general, true (hence practices based upon it are arbitrary), or upon an individual woman's claim to be an exception or potential exception to what *is* generally true of women.[109] The concept essentially addresses the use of false images of women in employment. Accordingly, it is useful for attacking sexualized job descriptions and work-related conceptions.[110] It also helps to rebut the misconception that women enjoy sexual harassment, were a kind of "consent" defense to arise. In a sense, a sex stereotype is present in the male attitude, expressed through sexual harassment, that women are sexual beings whose privacy and integrity can be invaded at will, beings who exist for men's sexual stimulation or gratification. The strength of the argument is that it allows men to be considered sincere, if wrong, in their treatment of women according to long accepted, if inappropriate, norms. But as an affirmative argument—that is, that sexual harassment is treatment based on sex because it is treatment based upon a sex stereotype—the argument is unfortunately incomplete.

The sex stereotype concept locates the overgeneralization, the distortion which is the substance of the injury of stereotyping, on the level of *image*, when the injury of sexual harassment is both on the level of image and on the level of reality. In the context of employment, sexual harassment is plainly an arbitrary practice. But it is not only or even fundamentally arbitrariness—in the sense of a divergence between a reality and a behavior purported to be based upon it—that is damaging to women about the practice. To the extent sexual harassment converges with, and mirrors, the accepted social reality of sexual relations, it corresponds to the real social meaning of the sex difference. It does not diverge from or distort this reality. To the extent sexual harassment reflects real social differences between the sexes, it is not arbitrary. If the social meaning of sexuality is accepted, sexual harassment can be seen as a differentiation in treatment due to the social realities of sex.

That is, it is the social reality of sexual relations, as expressed in sexual harassment, that "normally" and every day sexually oppresses women in order to affirm male sexual identity, as socially defined. This reality of treatment, which is the reference point for the argument of stereotyping that the practice is sex-based, is no false picture or illusion. These social relations themselves are shaped by an arguably false but, nevertheless, socially controlling image of relations between women and men. Thus, sexual harassment forms an integral part of the social stereotyping of all women as sexual objects and each individual grievant is but one example of it. So how does the practice lack a "factual basis"? To what true generalization about women is a sexually harassed woman "an exception"? For a heterosexual male so inclined, it is true, not illusory, that only a woman qualifies as the object of sexual harassment, just as for a white racist only a black qualifies as the object of racial harassment. This is true not because of a stereotype from which an exceptional woman might except herself, but because of the pervasively stereotyped social reality women live in.

Diaz v. Pan American World Airways,[111] the leading confrontation between the BFOQ and the sex stereotype, reveals the structure and limitations of the approach. In *Diaz*, a male applicant for a flight attendant position was rejected because the airlines considered only women. They had found women were, on the average, better at performing "the non-mechanical aspects of the job."[112] Passengers preferred being served by women; women were better at reassuring anxious passengers in the flight cabin environment; sex was found the best predictor of these occupational qualities. Sex was therefore, the airlines argued, a BFOQ. The Court of Appeals disagreed. Passenger preference, if as alleged, exemplified "to a large extent, [the] very prejudices the Act was meant to overcome."[113] Only when customer preference is based upon "the company's inability to perform the primary function or service it offers," here safely transporting passengers from one place to another, can it ground a BFOQ. Pan American could not fail to consider all males simply because most males may not adequately reassure passengers. Moreover, "we do not agree that in this case 'all or substantially all men' have been shown to be inadequate."[114] While the ability of individuals to perform the nonmechanical functions of the job could be taken into consideration, sex averaging was not allowed. Presumably, if some abilities were job-related and more women than men applicants exhibited them through a validated predictor, and were therefore hired, a "disparate impact" by sex would be allowed.[115]

One imagines the real situation in *Diaz* as follows. Due to social conditioning, women as a group probably are more supportive toward anxious others; both sexes have learned to accept nurturance and support more readily from women than from men. More basically, stewardesses were preferred because of their sex appeal to male customers who command the financial power to enforce their preferences. That this is economic reality makes it no less sexist, especially since women's corresponding lack of economic power gives them little choice. Stewardesses were originally conceived in part for their qualities as sex objects.[116] Until recently,[117] they had to be unmarried, meet height and weight requirements, and could not wear glasses. These requirements, along with the often provocative dress required, primarily "reassure" men of women's sexual attractiveness to them. The airline did not openly argue that an inseparable part of the stewardess job definition was to look sexy. Would this have presented a sex stereotype in the sense of lacking "factual basis," or would it have been a reality, based upon the fact that women's sexual attractiveness sells tickets in a market within which airlines otherwise lack distinguishing characteristics? What if, in the *Harvard Law Review*'s felicitous legalism, it is argued that "the function of sexual allure cannot be separated from the nonsexual functions of the position without substantial loss of effectiveness."[118] Is sex then a BFOQ?

What would have been the result if a woman with appropriate qualifications who applied for any job with the airlines complained of sex discrimination because she was trained as a stewardess instead of as a pilot? Suppose the airlines claimed sex as a BFOQ for both positions: men are more reassuring to passengers as pilots, women are more reassuring as stewardesses; the more mechanical aspects of the pilot's job utilize male advantages while the nonmechanical aspects give women advantages as stewardesses. There is no sex discrimination. Pan American provides jobs for both sexes—just different jobs, the jobs for which the social experience of each sex best qualifies them. This is merely an extension to the question of justification of the "separate but equal" picture of actuarial selection in *Gilbert*, although the results are just as dramatically unequal. The parallel would be even closer if the airlines argued that the cockpits and instrument panels of planes were arranged according to the size of the

average man, and it would cost too much to change them to accommodate the smaller height and length of extremities of the average
woman. Even the solution of hiring only those women who fit planes
built to male specifications, a solution for a few, only serves to high-
light which sex sets the standard.[119]

Sexuality

Sexual harassment is discrimination "based on sex" in the inequality
approach because women are socially defined as women largely in
sexual terms. The behaviors to which women are subjected in sexual
harassment are behaviors specifically defined and directed toward the
characteristics which define women's sexuality: secondary sex characteristics and sex-role behavior. It is no accident that the English language uses the term *sex* ambiguously to refer both to gender status (as
in "the female sex") and to the activity of intercourse (as in "to have
sex"). The term *sexual* is used in both senses. Further study of the
language reveals that references to sexuality have a pejorative conno-
tation for woman as a gender that is not comparable for men.

Words indicating the station, relationship or occupation of men have remained untainted over the years. Those identifying women have repeatedly
suffered the indignity of degeneration, many of them becoming sexually
abusive. It is clearly not the women themselves who have coined and used
these terms as epithets for each other. One sees today that it is men who
describe women in sexual terms and insult them with sexual slurs, and the
wealth of derogatory terms for women reveals something of their hostility. . . . [T]he largest category of words designating humans in sexual terms are
those for women—especially for loose women. I have located roughly a
thousand words and phrases describing women in sexually derogatory ways.
There is nothing approaching this multitude for describing men.[120]

As a critical convergence of the physiological, psychological, social,
economic, cultural and aesthetic, and political forces, sexuality is
overburdened with determinants. Gender itself is largely defined in
terms of sexuality in that heterosexuality is closely bound up with the
social conceptions of maleness and femaleness.

   Woman's sexuality is a major medium through which gender identity and gender status are socially expressed and experienced. An
attack upon sexuality is an attack upon womanhood. A deprivation in
employment worked through women's sexuality is a deprivation in

employment because one is a woman, through one of the closest referents by which women are socially identified as such, by themselves and by men. Only women, and (as is not the case with pregnancy) all women possess female sexuality,* the focus, occasion, and vehicle for this form of employment deprivation. Few men would maintain that they would have found a given woman just as ready or appropriate a target for sexual advances if she had been sexually male. Indeed, the close association between sexuality and gender identity makes it hard to imagine that a woman would be sexually the same if male. If any practice could be said to happen to a woman because she is a woman, sexual harassment should be one of the more straightforward examples of it.

How the law will conceptualize sexuality on closer consideration is an open question. The question is whether a gender comparison requires that sex characteristics be equivalent or whether it is sufficient that they are analogous. That is, must the sexes possess the same characteristic in order to be considered comparable, or is it enough that each has a corresponding version of its own? Presuming the law's narrow definition of "sex" as "gender," with the implicit heterosexual referent in practice, at least three possible legal approaches come to mind. First, the sexuality of women vis-à-vis men could be considered an aspect of "gender *per se.*" Discrimination "because of sexuality" would be merged with, and subsumed under, discrimination "because of sex." This could be more or less a social or a biological conception, depending upon the understanding of the determinants of sexuality and gender. Second, sexuality could be construed analytically as a variable "other than gender *per se*" as to which the sexes could be compared. Women and men each possess sexuality, so differential treatment with regard to sexuality could be sex discrimination. In a closely related argument, sexuality as in sexual harassment might be considered "other than gender *per se,*" but a "practice," not a status. This approach allows a "pattern or practice" concerning sexuality, as for any other variable, to be alleged to be discriminatory on the basis of the conformity of the practice with gender categories. Such a disparity by gender would produce discrimination "in effect" in that sexual harassment, if allowed, would have a disparate impact upon

---

*Transsexuals and transvestites would probably be considered legally female for this purpose.

women as a gender/sexual group. Third, sexuality could be deemed an aspect of "gender *per se*," but the sexuality of males and females could be considered unique to each sex, as pregnancy was unique to women in the *Gilbert* case. Adverse judgments based upon sexuality would not, in this approach, be sex discrimination because no comparison of unique attributes is possible.

Courts' treatment of women's sexuality in a discrimination context, although rare and backhanded, provides glimpses of some judicial preconceptions and hints at possible resolutions. Women's sexuality has occasionally, if implicitly, been used in attempts to exclude women as a gender group from employment opportunities. In *Eslinger v. Thomas*,[121] the plaintiff successfully challenged an attempt to restrict women's access to jobs by presuming that women might be thought to be sexually used on those jobs. The South Carolina Senate did not hire women as pages. Citing the "public image" of the Senate and its members as the reason, the Senate resolved that the duties of pages—running personal errands, chauffeuring, packing bags, cashing checks, etc.—were "not suitable under existing circumstances for young ladies and may give rise to the appearance of impropriety."[122] The senators' brief argued that the exclusion of women fostered "public confidence" and "avoided placing its employees in a conceivably damaging position, protecting itself from appearing to the public that an innocent relationship is not so innocent."[123]

The Court of Appeals found no fair and substantial relation between the object of the legislation—combatting the appearance of impropriety—and the ground of difference—sex—upon which the classification rested. It adopted an analysis that captured the sexualization of women as a gender:

> On the one hand, the female is viewed as a pure, delicate and vulnerable creature who must be protected from exposure to criminal influences; and on the other, as a brazen temptress, from whose seductive blandishments the innocent male must be protected. Every woman is either Eve or Little Eva—and either way, she loses.[124]

Reaching a contrasting result, the Supreme Court in *Dothard* (1978)[125] held that male sex was a BFOQ for the prisoner contact positions at the male penitentiary. The violent, overcrowded, understaffed "jungle atmosphere" and "rampant violence" in Alabama prisons was given as the reason. The State Commissioner of Corrections had testified that the reason a woman with the same height and weight as a man could not perform all the duties at an all-male correctional institution (a view not adopted) was:

The innate intention between a male and a female. The physical capabilities, the emotions that go into the psychic make-up of a female vs. the psychic make-up of a male. The attitude of the rural type inmate we have vs. that of a woman. The superior feeling that a man has, historically, over that of a female.[126]

The Court's gesture of protection repeated the historical pattern of excluding women from job opportunities, foreclosing women's choices by deciding what risks they will run.

Women's sexuality disqualified *all* women—as a gender—for the job, not just sexy or sexually provocative or attractive women. The majority held that women may be disqualified from employment as prison guards because of the "likelihood that inmates would assault a woman because she was a woman."[127] It is taken for granted that sexual assault is assault "because she was a woman." The rationale for the exclusion of all women from employment on sexual grounds is described as "[t]he employee's very womanhood."[128] In the context of the BFOQ, which makes male sex a bona fide job qualification, it is clear beyond cavil that women are disqualified because of their sexuality, which is equated with their gender. For purposes of women's exclusion, it sufficed to show that the employment treatment was based on gender to suggest that a woman would be treated as a sex object. Incarcerated criminals would *see* a woman guard as a woman, which would provoke misbehavior and upset prison discipline. Justice Marshall's critical response is worth quoting at length:

In short, the fundamental justification for the decision is that women as guards will generate sexual assaults. . . . With all respect, this rationale regrettably perpetuates one of the most insidious of the old myths about women—that women, wittingly or not are seductive sex objects. The effect of the decision, made, I am sure, with the best of intentions, is to punish women because their very presence might provoke sexual assaults. It is women who are made to pay the price in lost job opportunities for the threat of depraved conduct by prison inmates. . . . The proper response to inevitable attacks on both female and male guards is not to limit the employment opportunities of law-abiding women who wish to contribute to their community, but to take swift and punitive action against inmate offenders. Presumably, one of the goals of the Alabama prison system is the eradication of inmates' antisocial behavior patterns so that prisoners will be able to live one day in free society. Sex offenders can begin this process by learning to relate to women guards in a socially acceptable manner. To deprive women of job opportunities because of the threatened behavior of convicted criminals is to turn our social priorities upside down.[129]

Sexual harassment of women prison guards by male prisoners became the reason they should not occupy the job at all. If the extent of sexual assault in all kinds of jobs were known, would women be banished from the workplace entirely? The fact that the Supreme Court conformed women's job opportunities to the behavior patterns of convicted criminals suggests that they may impute sexual harassment to the presence of women's "very womanhood," rather than to men's failure to restrain themselves. To allow sexual violence to be so much a condition of women's work that it keeps women out of workplaces altogether seems to presuppose that male sexual violence is somehow inevitable or unchangeable (perhaps natural?), even in this most controlled of environments. Permitting the normally sexist offender to define the conditions of women's work poses women's sexuality as the threat to prison discipline, when it is the men's attitudes toward women's sexuality that is threatening. When male guards are considered, by contrast, it is not their presence but the prisoners' attitudes and structural relationship to them (as evidenced by assaults, which are common) that are considered threats to discipline. To Justice Marshall, "the only matter of innate recognition is that the incidence of sexually motivated attacks on guards will be minute compared to the 'likelihood that inmates will assault' a *guard* because he or she is a guard."[130] Few would conclude, at least from this, that there should be no guards.

The argument that imposing a sexual condition upon employment is discrimination "by sexual condition," not by sex-as-gender—what might be termed the "sex plus sex" approach—can now be criticized. To separate verbally what is not separated socially by distinguishing a requirement of "sexuality" (or, in a narrow conception of sexuality, genitality) from a gender-based practice cannot eliminate the fact that it is women who are the victims of it. It can only momentarily obscure the doctrinal basis for challenging it.

This argument contrasts with the approach to sex discrimination taken in the *Gilbert* and *Geduldig* cases. An examination of the logic of these cases reveals the deep cleavage over the meaning and purpose of antidiscrimination law that animates the two approaches and their divergent implications for the issue of sexual harassment. In those cases, excluding pregnancy from a disability plan was held not sex discrimination because the differentiation was not sex-based. The reasons were, first, under both California's and General Electric's plans, "There is no risk from which men are protected and women are not. Likewise, there is no risk from which women are protected and men are not."[131] Second, not all women get pregnant, so there is a lack of "identity between the excluded disability and gender as such" requisite for a differentiation to be legally cognizable as sex-based: "The program divides potential recipients into pregnant women and nonpregnant persons. While the first group is exclusively female, the second includes members of both sexes."[132] Third, the intention of the exclusion was not to harm women, but to avoid the cost of covering their pregnancy disabilities. So the policy was not contaminated by a sex-based motive and, in this sense, was not "based on sex."

Gilbert and *Geduldig* exemplify this approach to what is "sex-based," which any argument that sexual harassment is sex discrimination should confront, although all the litigation of the issue has evaded it thus far. The first approach to sex-basis suffers from an ellipsis termed, in formal logic, the fallacy of the undistributed middle. The proper mediate term supplied, what is apparently meant is that there is no risk "*to which both sexes are biologically subject*" for which one is covered while the other is not. The "arbitrariness" to which such a test would be addressed is a refusal, for example, to insure women's broken bones while insuring those of men. Without the middle supplied, statements like the following can be logically deduced: under California's plan, women are protected equally with men from the attendant expenses of prostatitis and circumcision. In fact, the only medical contingency not covered by the plan is pregnancy—neither men's nor women's.

Under *Gilbert,* the requirement for discriminatory insurance coverage seems to be that either one sex is potentially affected by a disability and covered, while the other is potentially affected and not covered, or that only one sex is potentially affected and not covered, with all members of that sex in that position. But the standard set by those disabilities actually covered by both plans is not this standard. There is no disability unique to men which is not covered. The plans do not require all men to be potentially affected by a disability for men's sex-specific ailments to be covered. The class of those with prostatitis includes no women, but the class of those without the disease will include all women and some men. Yet the impossibility of women contracting prostatitis is symmetrical to the impossibility of men getting pregnant. Under the Court's rules, a company is not prevented on sex discrimination grounds from excluding (together with pregnancy-related disabilities) disabilities due to breast cancer or hysterectomy, while covering prostatitis and circumcisions, because these disabilities specific to women do not affect all women. It is plain that the Court allowed these plans to choose to cover all disabilities which affect some men but no women, while excluding a disability which affects many women but no men. Further, although under the Court's rules prostate coverage could be excluded, it is not—and that fact remains, for the *Gilbert* court, itself noncomparable to the pregnancy exclusion. Clearly, if one is in the realm of "sex-specific disabilities," pregnancy and prostate trouble are comparable. But in the realm of "female disabilities" and "male disabilities" presumptive comparisons belie the fact that the categories are divided by a difference: the sex difference. The Court did not compare the standard set by those disabilities included with those excluded to see if sex made the difference.[133]

The hidden requirement of sex-comparability is revealed: before differential treatment will be considered sex-based, both sexes have to be potentially so treated. By this test, pregnancy cannot give rise to a sex-based difference in *treatment* because pregnancy is a risk to which only one sex is subject. Apparently, no exclusion of risk, or anything else that is exclusive to one sex because of sex, could be found discriminatory under this standard. Short of this, it is even open to question whether a factor that *varies* by sex, whether because of sex or sexism, could be challenged when it becomes the basis for variant detrimental treatment of one sex.

The *Dothard* result clearly diverges from this, yet it vindicates—or at least does not pose facts that require a challenge to—the comparability requirement. Height and weight, which vary by sex, were not allowed to be used to exclude women from employment opportunities. Real differences were not allowed to justify unequal outcomes. But women's height and weight can reasonably be compared with men's, so comparison of the underlying variable posed no difficulty. Similarly, in *Manhart*, the fact that women live longer than men was not allowed to justify unequal contributions to the pension plan, to women's disadvantage. The common factor that made comparison seem reasonable was human mortality. These cases restrict the sphere of application of the *Gilbert* approach without really undercutting the approach itself. They do not provide a context for confronting the question of why the sexes should have to be comparable in order for differential treatment of women to be discriminatory. Nor do they clarify the reasons why some factors, such as women's greater longevity and smaller size, are placed in a context which makes them comparable to men's, while other factors, such as pregnancy—both sexes do have temporary disabilities—are conceptualized as unique.

As is to be expected, the *Gilbert/Geduldig* approach to sex discrimination has arisen in the sexual harassment context. In *Williams,* the defendant argued that

> since the primary variable in the claimed class is willingness *vel non* [or not] to furnish sexual consideration, rather than gender, the sex discrimination proscriptions of the act [Title VII] are not invoked. Plaintiff was allegedly denied employment enhancement not because she was a woman, but rather because she decided not to furnish the sexual consideration claimed to have been demanded. Therefore, plaintiff is in no different class from other employees, regardless of their gender or sexual orientation, who are made subject to such carnal demands.[134]

Sexual harassment is argued to be a matter of sexuality, not gender, so it cannot be sex discrimination. The district court in *Barnes* made the same distinction between discrimination "because she was a woman" and discrimination "because she refused to engage in a sexual affair with her supervisor."[135] As the reply brief for defendant in *Corne* stated it: "Plaintiffs do not allege disparate treatment because of sex, but merely the context of advances from a man to a woman."[136]

The "sexuality, not sex" argument ignores the substance of the social meaning of being of the female sex, in which one is largely defined as a female in terms of one's sexuality. Sexual harassment makes of women's sexuality a badge of female servitude. To say that a woman is fired not because she is a woman but because she refuses to have sex with her male superiors is like saying that a black man was fired not because he was black but because he refused to shuffle for his white superiors. (The EEOC, in fact, found it unlawful to discharge a black worker because white co-workers disliked him for being self-confident instead of submissive. The issue of his manner or the dislike it generated was not considered so "personal" as not to be race discrimination but as the form that racism took between the perpetrators and the victim.)[137] To say that sexual harassment is based on sexuality, not sex, is as if an employer defended a charge of racial discrimination against a black by saying the underlying variable was skin color, not race. Perhaps it was to avoid similar pretexts that discrimination on the basis of "color," sometimes a visible index of race, is prohibited, together with race. Will it be necessary legislatively to add "sexuality" to sex discrimination statutes to make the point that female sexuality is part of female sex?*

A combination of "blame the victim" disposition with a presumptive sex symmetry underlies the "sexuality, not sex" formulation. Just as rich and poor alike can sleep under bridges at night and go to jail for stealing bread, men equally with women can be fired for their refusal to engage in a sexual affair with their (male, heterosexual) supervisor. To say that job reprisals occurred because the women declined the invitation, which was her choice, is to conclude from the facts that she was a woman, about which she had no choice, and that she was sexually propositioned, about which she had no choice, that the law should leave her no choice but to submit—or else. An employment standard is proposed which the other sex would rarely be (and is not in most cases alleged to be) required to meet. The plaintiff is then told that it is her failure to meet the standard that caused the job difficulties. Meaning: if only she had engaged in the sexual affair with her supervisor, none of this would have happened. Further meaning: if she does not cooperate as a woman, she will just have to take the consequences as an employee. If only she had not been a woman, she probably would not have been asked.

If, in addition to their status as women, particular women are seen to embody qualities of female sexuality that make them especially subject to sexual harassment in the male mind—that is, they are "attractive" women—this is doctrinally a "sex plus" criterion. She is a woman (sex as gender) *plus* she is "attractive." The addition of the criterion of attractiveness does not, as a doctrinal matter, defeat the

---

*Adding "sexuality" to legislative prohibitions of discrimination based on sex might be a good idea in any case. It might have the added effect, depending upon how the term was interpreted, of expanding gay rights.

argument that the treatment is sex-based. The decision in *Martin-Marietta*[138] prohibited two different hiring policies, one for each sex, each having preschool children. It did not matter that not all women had preschool children. Presumably it would make no difference to a race case if an employer alleged he discriminated only against blacks from Georgia or blacks with curly hair. The attractive woman situation—only attractive women, not all women, are sexually harassed—is no different from a situation in which only unmarried women or women with preschool children were required to fulfill sexual conditions. Really, "sex-plus" in sexual harassment is doubly sex-based, once in its application to women only and again in the application of a sexually stereotyped standard to select the specific victim. According to this approach (which contrasts sharply with the *Gilbert* view), the basis upon which subclasses of women are distinguished from other subclasses of women does not exempt the practice from being discriminatory; it only adds a condition which exempts some women.

As a practical matter for litigation, it might be noted, "attractiveness" will likely arise as an implicit credibility issue that cuts two ways—both against the woman. A conventionally attractive woman will be more likely to be believed when she charges sexual harassment. But it will also be believed that she asked for it, since attractiveness in women so largely consists in the projection of sexual availability, although in veiled and denied ways. Conventionally unattractive women, who would be more credible in asserting that they did not ask for it, by the same token would be less credible in asserting, over a man's derogatory denial, that it happened at all.

The "sexuality, not gender" analysis derived from the *Gilbert* approach was expressed in its most extended form by the government on behalf of the defendants in *Barnes* and *Williams.* "The impetus for the creation of the class must be distinguished from the primary variable which describes the class."[139] In their attempt to distinguish sexual treatment from gender, neither specifies what the "impetus for the creation of the class" is supposed to be. The implication is that it is the sex drive, or something to do with sexuality. In fact, it is the male supervisor's *sexist behavior* which "creates the class." Women are sexually harassed *because they are women,* in the full social meaning of the term. Sexual harassment is a clear social manifestation of male privilege incarnated in the male sex role that supports coercive sexuality reinforced by male power over the job. It is not incumbent upon the victims to explain why a given male chooses to express his sexism in this way, or with them. They need not connect his "impetus" for "creating the class" with its defining variable—their femaleness—to make out a case of sex discrimination. The male supervisor's behavior makes this connection itself by demanding sexual favors of women. In so doing, he "creates the class" and defines its primary variable according to his sexual preferences. In such cases, the distinction between "the creation of the class" and "the primary variable which describes the class" is nothing but the distinction between male and female.

SEXUAL HARASSMENT AS SEX DISCRIMINATION: A DIFFERENCES ARGUMENT

The basic question the differences approach poses is: how can you tell that this happened because one is a woman, rather than to a person who just happens to be a woman? The basic answer, which presupposes sex comparability, is: a man in her position would not be or was not so treated. A presumptive sex equality underlies the placing of one sex in the other's position. This is the sex reversal that forms the basis for the inference of differentiation. The central conceptual difficulty (which often occurs as a difficulty of proof) arises because of the necessity to infer from a context, a frequency distribution, a single event, or proximate circumstances that a given discrimination is sex-specific, without deeply investigating the concrete social meaning of gender status. To take the differences approach requires temporary suspension of the fact that the sexes are substantively unequal, not just different, a fact which calls into question the appropriateness of presuming equality in order to measure disparity.

An argument under the differences approach can, nonetheless, be made against sexual harassment. The Supreme Court distinguishes between disparate treatment, in which "the employer simply treats some people less favorably than others because of their race, color, religion, sex, or national origin,"[140] and disparate impact, which "involves employment practices that are facially neutral in their treatment of different groups but that in fact fall more harshly on one group than another and cannot be justified by business necessity."[141] In the disparate treatment case, "proof of discriminatory motive is critical, although it can in some situations be inferred from the mere fact of differences in treatment."[142] "Proof of discriminatory motive . . . is not required under a disparate impact theory."[143] The discussion here is accordingly divided into arguments that support each of these theories.

Disparate Treatment

As a practice, sexual harassment singles out a gender-defined group, women, for special treatment in a way which adversely affects and burdens their status as employees. Sexual harassment limits women in a way men are not limited. It deprives them of opportunities that are available to male employees without sexual conditions. In so doing, it creates two employment standards: one for women that includes sexual requirements, one for men that does not. From preliminary indications, large numbers of working women, regardless of characteristics which distinguish them from each other, report being sexually harassed. Most sexually harassed people are women. These facts indicate that the incidents are something more than "personal" and "unique" and have some connection to the female condition as a whole.

To argue that sexual harassment is an "arbitrary" practice based on sex, it is necessary either to explain why the differences approach to gender classification need not apply to the sexual harassment situation or to meet its requirements. As we have repeatedly seen, disability benefits for pregnancy provided a critical test for the conflict between two conceptions of sex discrimination. Pregnancy disability posed a "real" difference between the sexes as the basis for an employment practice by means of which only women were disadvantaged. Sexual harassment also poses a "real" difference between the sexes, together with an employment practice based upon it, most victims of which are women. But the differences between the *Gilbert* and *Geduldig* facts and situations of sexual harassment, in relation to the applicable doctrine, are several and striking. The most basic is that, unlike pregnancy, the treatment of women and men in employment can be compared on the underlying variable: sexuality. Sexuality is not unique to women. Women have female sexuality, men have male sexuality. Both sexes can be victims of the practice. When one gender is the victim of a practice as to which the treatment of the sexes can be compared, the practice can be considered sex-based.

Sexual harassment can be further distinguished from the *Gilbert* pregnancy disability conceptualization. First, sexual harassment is a precondition of employment or a condition of work, not a discretionary benefit. There is no employer choice not to have working conditions or employment criteria at all, an option that was thought important in the case of temporary disability insurance.[144] Since the sphere for the discrimination cannot be cast as employer largesse in the first place, the argument that no arbitrary differentiation should exist within it is strengthened. Second, the impact of sexual harassment upon women's work provides a measure of the detrimental effect of the challenged practice, rather than a reason the distinction may be felt to be proper in employment, consistent with the profit motive. Pregnant women leave work and seek compensation; sexually harassed women cannot work well or at all and seek relief.

Third, in *Gilbert,* the dimension along which women and men arguably could be compared—temporary disability coverage—militated against a finding of discrimination, since aggregate benefits were found to be distributed roughly equally by sex, pregnancy excluded. Even if all employees were paid more instead of provided benefits, the ultimate cost of coverage for pregnancy would have been higher. By no measure does sexual harassment, in general, fall equally upon women and men. If it does, that is a defense.[145] Sexual harassment makes the employment experience as a whole more injurious, more stressful, more insecure, and less economically beneficial for women than for men, for reasons having nothing legitimately to do with the job or with women's work performance. Fourth, unlike pregnancy, there is nothing about unwanted sexual solicitation and pressure that, even within social values as they are, arguably "contributes to the well-being" of the woman,[146] once the incidents are distinguished from good clean fun. Especially when women decline or reject the advances, their participation cannot be said to be voluntary. Even when they comply with or ignore the advances, voluntariness, under the circumstances, is a question of fact.

Specific contextual factors have supported findings of sex-based discrimination in situations analogous to, and highly suggestive for, sexual harassment. In a Commission Precedent Decision, the EEOC found "sex-based intimidation" under circumstances in which an employer demoted a recently promoted female employee from her supervisory position because her male inferiors harassed her and refused to assist her in performing job tasks which required team-work.[147] The only evidence in the opinion that the practices occurred because of sex was that the supervisor was a woman and the harassing workers were men. Perhaps the EEOC understood that a woman supervising men was in a socially unusual and exposed position. A man who failed to elicit cooperation from female inferiors might, by this logic, simply be considered an ineffective supervisor. It was not argued, apparently, that if a man were not assisted by male or female co-workers it would not have been sex discrimination, so, therefore, should not be here. The treatment might arguably have been "intimidation" to either sex, but a man in her position would not have been and was not so treated.

Focusing upon the "sexual" rather than the "harassment" aspect, another EEOC decision involved a female employee who was discharged for having a sexual affair with a male employee, while the male employee was only "talked to" about it. The EEOC held that at least part of the reason the female employee was disciplined more severely than the male was that she was female. "Where similarly placed persons of different sexes receive dissimilar treatment, it is reasonable to infer that sex was a factor in the dissimilar treatment."[148] Without agonizing about the place of "sexuality" in gender, the EEOC simply found that women's sexuality and men's sexuality were differently treated while the sexes were similarly situated.

Ignoring the factor of the woman's apparent consent, this case parallels a common situation of sexual harassment in which the offending superior is "talked to" while the woman loses her job. Perhaps due to a common assumption that men are generically "human" while women are defined by sexuality, men are not usually thought to be sexually defined in these situations in a way that bears comparison with women. For whatever reason, no sexual harassment case has relied upon the theory of differential employer treatment of the perpetrator and the victim on the basis of sex, due to such handling of a sexual incident.[149]

Sexual harassment, in most cases, is an employment practice that would not have occurred if the victim's sex had been different. Some difficulties in proving that the practice is not individual affinity but sex-based arise when women who sexually comply are benefited on the job. This does not mean that sexual harassment as a practice is not sex-based. The woman who complies is in a different legal position from the woman who resists, but she is still a victim of the practice. Should women have no recourse from sexual exactions because, due to their lack of recourse, they have been forced to submit? Having allowed employers to require women sexually to submit as the price of a job, can the law use the fact of women's sexual submission as a reason they are not injured by such a requirement? When women perform sexually because they must, should their compliance exonerate the employer who requires it? Men have required that women act sexy in order to get jobs and perform sexual services in order to keep or advance in them. Having been reduced to submissive sex objects on the job, had their economic desperation exploited, having been forced into sexual subservience through threats of material retaliation, women are then criticized for acting sexy, being submissively dependent, and complying sexually. Having been forced into a position in which their employment goals can sometimes be achieved (if at all, and then precariously) only by sexual means, women are branded as unworthy of a legal prohibition on these exactions because they have complied. The so-called benefits of sexual compliance, the scraps thrown the "good nigger" as the reward for apparently voluntary submission, are considered the reason such requirements should be allowed. In this logic, women are first excluded from employment opportunities free of sexual extortion and then stigmatized by having the behavior that the context produced in them (that is, their survival skill), singled out as the reason they are unfit for the guarantees of equality. Their degradation is further mocked when the situation is considered a net benefit. This resembles the white supremacist logic of depriving blacks of the tools of an education, calling them nonintellectual and ignorant when they challenge the system of unequal educational opportunities, and concluding that they must be happy that way when they are defeated.[150]

If sexual compliance is required *in addition* to all the job-related standards the women involved must meet, as is most often the case, the practice can be attacked by any victim, whether she complied or not, although the victim who rejected the advances has the better legal case. Having to meet a sexual standard is an injury in itself, whether or not another employment interest was consequentially damaged. If sexual compliance is required of women *in lieu of* meeting job-related standards, which seems to be much less usual, it is open to clearest attack by men, who are not given an equal opportunity to meet the real requirements of the job, which depend upon female sexuality. It is also open to attack by arguably qualified women who were never sexually approached, as well as by noncompliant women who refused. The fact the latter were approached with a promise of employment benefits in exchange for sex suggests that these women met the employer's *other* requirements for the job, whatever they were. These situations represent the furthest reach of the concept, probably beyond the currently imaginable reach of most courts. Otherwise nonqualified benefited women, by contrast, may be casualties of the sex war, but they are not in a good position to charge sex discrimination. The factual difficulty arises in distinguishing among benefited women between the qualified and the nonqualified when sexual harassment intervenes as a substitute selection procedure. So long as this is kept properly a question of fact, women will at least have a chance to argue their qualifications. At last, the ugly suspicion will be exposed that whatever women achieve is due to the extraordinary power of their sexuality, and whenever women fail it is due to the ordinary deficiencies of their gender.

Women need not be compliant to reap the benefits of misogyny, nor does a benefit given to another woman automatically mean that a practice is not sex-based. One federal district judge has held that if one woman benefits from a practice whereby another woman is disadvantaged, that fact in itself does not defeat a conclusion that Title VII sex discrimination has occurred. In *Skelton v. Balzano,*[151] a supervisor reneged on a promise to advance one woman and instead advanced another, with the intent (which the judge found credible) that the two women would develop conflicts and "devour" each other. Rejecting the defense that as a matter of law there can be no sex discrimination when one woman is advanced over another, the court held: "It is enough to show by a preponderance of the evidence *that if plaintiff had been a man she would not have been treated in the same manner,* and at the very least would have been afforded genuine opportunity to advance."[152]

In light of these standards for the inference that a practice is "based on sex," the *Tomkins* result at the district court level is bizarre in a way that bears analysis. The court held that firing for refusal of sexual advances is not sex discrimination, but firing for *complaining* about sexual advances without an investigation might be. Such a result would be either redundant or contradictory. Title VII prohibits only adverse consequences that result from acts illegal under Title VII. If summary firing for complaining about sexual harassment might be sex discrimination, it is only because the complaint is protected under the Act. This would be the case only if a firing for sexual harassment would be sex discrimination if proven.

At the same time, sexual advances were not considered "gender-based" in *Tomkins* because either gender could have been involved, while the court inferred from the sex of the parties alone that the summary firing could have been sex discrimination.

In brief, it [the firing] may reflect a conscious choice to favor the male employee over the female complainant on the ground that a male's services are more valuable than a female's. Such a preferential practice may violate the act even though the grievance procedures do not by their terms implicate characteristics peculiar to either gender.[153]

From the bare fact that one party is male and the other female, the judge infers that the company's failure to investigate might be a determination "based on sex," but sexual advances from a man to a woman are thought to lack the requisite connection with gender. Surely a company could fire a male without investigation on the ground that his female superior was more valuable than he. Perhaps firing renders employment-related an incident which otherwise would not be, but that was not argued. On what grounds ought a stricter standard of gender-connectedness apply to sexual harassment than applies to a firing for complaining about it?

Further, what if, upon investigation, the plaintiff's version of the story were found true? Unless she is protected under Title VII from being fired for refusal of sexual advances, she could still legally be fired. If she *is* then protected by Title VII, there was no distinction between the two issues in the first place. It should be evident that, if the plaintiff *is* protected under the Act if her story is true, the supervisor's conduct is illegal in itself, and the employer merely further collaborated by firing her; if she is not protected under the Act, she has no more cause of action for being fired for complaining about the conduct than for the conduct itself.

Intent and Motive   Partially supported by evidence that the supervisor did not like "pushy women," the *Skelton* court also stated that if the supervisor "was motivated by antipathy for women in his mistreatment of plaintiff, this will also suffice to fall within the strictures of the act."[154] Women's experiences suggest, and some evidence supports the view, that male sexual advances may often derive as much from fear and hatred of women and a desire to keep them in an inferior place as from a genuine positive attraction or affection, although the perpetrator may be unaware of his feelings. At least in the heterosexual context, misogyny and an active sex life are not necessary contradictions.[155] The well-established legal rule on the relationship of motivation to discrimination is that evidence of negative attitudes toward women as a class can help support an inference that an employment deprivation was "based on sex"; positive attitudes will support "good faith."[156] But a benevolent motivation will not save behavior which, in fact, discriminates,[157] so long as the action is not accidental.[158] It would not matter, then, whether a supervisor alleged that his sexual advances sprang only from good, affectionate feelings if his actions met standards of employment discrimination based on sex.

Should sexual harassment not be found to be sex-based treatment under other tests, the intent requirement would be difficult to meet, for all the wrong reasons. Most men do not sexually harass women with an intent to injure the female sex. To act with an intent to subordinate women is to acknowledge the atrocity of the act, when it is precisely that it is considered totally normal that is its most atrocious feature. It is exactly because men can feel that their acts spring from sexual attraction to an individual woman that they can feel justified in abusing their power as employers in the service of their sexual gratification as men. Acts that oppress women are typically well-meant. If men could see their acts as women often see them (that is, as degrading and hostile to their survival), the transformation in consciousness to which a prohibition against sexual harassment might contribute would already be substantially achieved. Only clinically sick men would sexually harass women and it would be relatively rare. That sexual oppression can be so much of a habit, so much a part of the definition of normalcy, and so unconsciously done is part of the pathology that requires legal intervention to show employers that ignorance and unconsciousness are no excuse.

Motivation must also be distinguished from "intent" as formulated in *Gilbert*. There, the existence of a "pretext to discriminate"[159] would render sex-based a distinction which, in itself, was neither "gender *per se*" nor "discrimination in effect." The intent approach leaves

untouched the rule that good motives are irrelevant to defend otherwise discriminatory conduct. The latter policy makes particular
sense for sexual harassment. The male point of view, from which
standpoint advances may be benign, is not the female point of view,
from which standpoint they may be a nightmare.

Women's feelings and experience on this subject have not up to
now been reflected in law. Accustomed to the view that "there is no
harm in asking,"[160] courts now leap to the opposite extreme to suppose that precipitate and automatic liability will suddenly attach to
any and all acts of sexual interest previously thought harmless. Exposing extreme or repeated incidents, which distinguish clearly between
"asking" as a common feature of male sex roles (whatever one might
think of the convention) and demands sanctioned, particularly (but
not necessarily) with proximate job retribution, should help dispel this
reservation. Actually, there is little danger to the truly well-meaning,
particularly assuming incrementally greater sensitivity which potential liability would encourage. If the motive is benevolent, and no
coercion is involved, one firm contraindication should suffice. Moreover, an employer who acts resolutely and promptly upon learning of
unauthorized employee misconduct would probably not be held liable.[161]

Gay and Bisexual Harassment   Gay sexual harassment is a closet issue in
the sexual harassment cases. It is always present in a differences approach to sexuality because the method abstracts from social content
and reverses social categories in pursuit of fairness in treating sex
differences. Homosexuality is usually unnamed and often obliquely
or hypothetically raised. It has a far larger place in the conceptual life
of sex discrimination law than it does in its practice. At the same time,
these intimations are often the sum total of the conceptual consideration of the question of whether sexual harassment is "based on sex" in
the legal sense. Specifically, in much the same way that the spectre of
homosexual marriage is used to undermine the Equal Rights
Amendment, bisexual or gay sexual harassment is used as an implicit
reductio ad absurdum to defeat legal prohibition of sexual harassment
of women by men. In *Tomkins,* for example, the district judge found
that heterosexual harassment could not be sex-based because "gender
lines might as easily have been reversed, or even not crossed at all."[162]
The judge in *Corne* made the same point: "It would be ludicrous to

hold that the sort of activity involved here was contemplated by the Act because to do so would mean that if the conduct complained of was directed equally to males there would be no basis for suit."[163] Apparently the court means that if a male employer sexually harassed men as well as women, no cause of action would lie in sex discrimination. As factual speculation, this is irrelevant. Without an allegation of bisexual harassment, to conclude that this *possibility* disposes of the issue as a matter of law is simple error. Further, this argument takes seriously the sexual harassment of nobody, but rather attempts to turn the possibility of gay (or bisexual) harassment into a reason that no likely victim, neither gays nor women, should be protected: because any prohibition would cover gays, women should not be covered from harassment by men. This attempt fails as a *reductio* the moment protecting both is recognized as not absurd.

As a matter of law, no area of discrimination doctrine has ever required that because allegedly discriminatory treatment *could* be leveled equally against another group, when it is leveled against one, the reversed possibility destroys the group referent. Instead, the whole reason that discrimination can be "arbitrary" is that other groups could be, but are not, so treated. The fact that the law does not need to protect all groups equally often—here, because most employers are men and practice heterosexuality—is a social fact which does nothing to undercut the presumptive equipoise of the differences doctrine.

Specifically, reversed possibilities in logic and life do not present barriers to a prima facie case (or to recovery) in sex discrimination situations alleged on grounds other than sexual abuse. In the *Martin-Marietta* situation, for example, a company could have discriminated against fathers of preschool children because they thought these fathers would be less attentive, less single-mindedly devoted to work, or less mobile than non-fathers. When, in fact, mothers of preschool children were excluded, the *possibility* of discrimination against similarly situated fathers did not bar finding a sex-based classification. If parents of both sexes had been discriminated against, just as with bisexual harassment under current theories, the sex discrimination argument would probably fail. In *Diaz*,[164] the airlines could have hired only male stewards, alleging that the strong masculine presence reassured anxious customers. But since the airlines in fact hired only women, the possibility of hiring only men was not a barrier to a finding of sex discrimination. It was instead a possibility which identified the discrimination and pointed the direction in which hiring could be sex-equalized. Some courts, *Gilbert* notwithstanding, might consider sex discriminatory a disability scheme which which covered all risks including pregnancy and childbirth, *except* prostate conditions, circumcisions, and hemophilia. Yet this *possibility* was never held to be a reason to preclude a finding that exclusion of pregnancy from such plans constitutes sex discrimination, even by those courts which found, as *Gilbert* did, pregnancy exclusions non-sex-discriminatory. In no case of alleged racial discrimination has the possibility that whites *could* be discriminated against in the same way prevented a finding of race discrimination when in fact only blacks were so treated. In fact, this possibility is what makes the treatment "arbitrary": it could be done to whites or men, but is done only to blacks or women.

When a woman imposes sexual conditions on male employees, the result should be identical to that with the sexes reversed—and, given existing sex roles, will probably be only slightly more common than occurrences of a man raped by a woman or incest initiated by women against male children. Women should not be exempt on the basis of mere biology for behavior that would be actionable if done by men. For example, if a woman professor or corporate executive sexually harasses male students or workplace subordinates, she should not escape liability because she is a woman. She has succeeded to the forms of power which traditionally have been the province of men, and has attained the protection and legitimacy of such a male-defined position. She derives the power to insist from those structures that traditionally have sanctioned men's demands. She has also succeeded to that aspect of sex role that has been peculiarly male cultural behavior: the imposition of unwanted sex upon the less powerful. If she is in a position to make sexual demands with relative impunity, as men have been, and uses that position to play the sex role men have played, she should succeed to the legal liability men in positions of power incur for abusive sexual practices. If nothing else, such an argument should demonstrate that the determinants of sexual behavior are not so much biological as deeply social. The rarity of such instances demonstrates how deep the social determinants go. But the woman who functions socially as if she were a man should be viewed by the law according to the social power she wields, regardless of body.

By the logic of the differences argument, if a sexual condition of employment were imposed equally upon both women and men by the same employer, the practice would no longer constitute sex discrimination because it would not be properly based on the gender difference. Title VII, as interpreted, does not concern itself with abuses of human sexuality, only with impermissible differential consequences of the gender distinction in employment. Arguably, a sexual requirement placed on both a man and a woman would not have the same impact upon each. And some potential exists that an argument of disproportionate impact might bring even these facts under the ambit of the sex discrimination prohibition. One race case suggests such an approach. In *Stamps v. Detroit Edison Co.*[165] the fact that some whites as well as blacks had been assigned to some of the employer's low opportunity jobs—jobs to which blacks had *customarily* been assigned—did not overcome the inference under Title VII that blacks had been assigned to those jobs because of their race. The "severe disproportion test"[166] suggested the argument that even if not all persons sexually harassed are women, if most are, those who are are so treated because of their sex, because it is customary gender-specific treatment sexually to harass women.

But with differences doctrine in its current posture, a sexual condition that disadvantages both sexes, not one, is probably not sex discrimination—it is merely exploitative, oppressive, and an abuse of power. To draw this conclusion does not, as some of the sexual harassment cases have concluded,[167] undercut the major argument. It properly creates an affirmative defense. This "bisexual defense," where applicable, should be pleaded and factually proven, not stated coyly, left for guesswork, or raised as a matter of law.[168] The alternative is to begin with the presumption that the sexes are *not* sexually equal. The legal conclusion would then be that only a bisexual can *discriminate,* because only to a person with an equal sexual preference for each sex would the sexes be sufficiently comparable to engage in a detrimental differentiation. One hopes that such a result reveals the untenability of its premise.

Exclusively homosexual advances are doctrinally more ambiguous. Although they may be open to change, the EEOC and the courts

(unless under a specific state or local statute) do not generally interpret sex discrimination under Title VII to prohibit loss of employment opportunities because a person is gay.[169] The wisdom or logic of
this position might be questioned in many contexts, but few more
persuasively than sexual harassment. Sexual preference, usually including sexual expression, is what distinguishes gay men and lesbians
from their heterosexual counterparts. (Looked at this way, the social
definition of heterosexuals is their opposite-sex preference, by virtue
of which fact alone they are not customarily deprived of employment
opportunities.) Given a gender-defined sexual preference, gay and
non-gay sexual harassment, if exclusive, equally fit the definition of a
prohibited practice under the differences approach as employment
based on gender. (From an inequality perspective, too, the vulnerability of gays is analogous to that of women. The use of the criterion of
heterosexual preference to deprive lesbians and gay men of employment opportunities is clearly arbitrary and an imposition of the power
of a dominant group over a subordinated one.) Whether there should
be a difference in the legal approach to homosexual harassment in
employment—that is, same-sex sexual harassment on the job—and
the treatment of homosexuals in employment—that is, exclusions of
gays from jobs because they are gay, not because they refuse to comply sexually—is a question of the scope of sex discrimination doctrine
in the same-sex context, and the relationship between gender difference and sexuality in legal terms.

Doctrinally, the problem with gay harassment is that it does not
involve a difference between the sexes in the sense that the EEOC and
the courts take gender differentiation as the touchstone for the term
sex under Title VII. Sex-sameness defines homosexual practice and is
thought to be symmetrical as between women and men.[170] A recent
EEOC decision so conclusively rejected a discrimination complaint
based on homosexuality as to find itself without subject matter jurisdiction over the issue. Homosexuality was held to be "a condition
which relates to a person's sexual practices or proclivities, not to his or
her gender." In the most inauspicious possible language for prohibiting sexual harassment in a gay context, the EEOC further stated: "in
enacting Title VII Congress [did not intend] to include a person's
sexual practices within the meaning of the term sex."[171] Hostility to
male homosexuality is exemplified by a recent federal district court
holding that Title VII does not forbid employment discrimination

based on an applicant's "affectional or sexual preference," so was not violated by an employer who declined to hire a man applicant on the ground that he was "effeminate."[172] One wonders if an effeminate woman would have been similarly treated. The predictable analysis of gay sexual harassment is that abuse of gay *sexuality* merits no more protection than any other employment deprivation of gay people as such or than any other deprivation due to sexuality as such—that is, none. Until discrimination on the basis of homosexuality is considered sex discrimination for other purposes one can predict (but not recommend) that gay sexual harassment will probably not be considered sex discrimination. This is one of the clearer inadequacies to flow directly from the differences approach.

Paradoxically, however, sexual harassment is one context in which the EEOC and the courts might consider same-sex discrimination sex discriminatory. To do so, they would have to find not in favor of the gay party, but in favor of the person who refused the homosexual contact. Faced, for example, with a man or a woman who suffered employment reprisals for affirming society's definition of manhood or womanhood (heterosexuality), the EEOC might find unwanted sexual advances to be an unreasonable, offensive, and arbitrary term and condition of employment based upon gender. As a matter of fact, it might perceive this *more* easily in a case of homosexual advances than with advances from a man to a woman. Many men, for example, find it credible that homosexual advances are unwanted, unsolicited, and coercive, and blame the perpetrator instead of the victim, while women are widely supposed to "want" heterosexual relationships which they reject. According to sex roles and accompanying social attitudes, coercive male initiation to women is "natural," while to other men it is not. Sexual coercion from a gay male superior presents one of the few situations in which an uninterested male employee has a chance of facing a situation similar to that which many women employees commonly confront every day—except that he stands a better chance of ruining his employer's career if he exposes it.

Women probably wish to choose whether and with whom to have sexual relationships, on a noncoerced basis. They do not find a man attractive or wish to have a sexual relationship with him just because they practice heterosexuality and the initiator is male, in very much the same way that a male might wish to reject homosexual advances. Forced homosexual relations cannot be presumed to be any more repugnant or demeaning to a man, or less wanted or consented to, than forced heterosexual relations are for a woman. Nor, ultimately, can coercive sexual advances from a gay superior to a same-sex inferior, whatever the sexual preferences of the inferior, be said to be noncoercive if they are not wanted. A woman who is fired because of her refusal to submit to a lesbian supervisor is just as fired—and her firing is just as related to her gender—as if the perpetrator were a man. It would be strange, if efficient, if a landmark sexual harassment case were decided in a homosexual context, simultaneously recognizing that sexual harassment and employment deprivation in a same-sex context—in a sense due to sexual preference—can be sex discrimination. But stranger things have happened than a simultaneous legal precedent for gays and for women sexually harassed by men—for reasons deriving from that moment in sexism where male supremacy and homophobia converge.

Disparate Impact

Sexual harassment could under some circumstances be seen as a pattern or practice which, in effect, has a "disparate adverse impact" upon women employees.[173] To qualify under this test, a purportedly evenhanded practice has disproportionately to injure one sex. Unwanted sex could be imposed neutrally upon both sexes. Compared with men, however, women are far more likely to be sexually harassed. Within the differences approach, a case with this structure would require an allegation that a company required, or acquiesced in a practice, that employees tolerate or fulfill sexual conditions at work. Then, when most superiors are male and heterosexual and most subordinates female, such a policy would have, or be likely to have, a disparate impact upon women employees. The argument would have more practical effect if companies were held to have a duty to respond to complaints about sexual harassment, or to institute adequate procedures to process such grievances. Then if they did not perform, it could be argued that the lack of a procedure for fair adjudication of complaints adversely affected women because they were more likely to (and disproportionately did) need one. An inequality approach to the disparate impact theory would argue that sexual harassment is both more likely to happen to women and is more damaging to women because men are sexually dominant in the society, and control women's work destinies, making women's potential for linked sexual and economic coercion greater than men's. An employer's toleration of sexual harassment would damage women more, and more often.

A question which recurs throughout sex discrimination cases, one which an adverse impact theory raises in particular, is the relationship between one individual, or one "isolated" event, and the group referent needed for an injury to be sex-based.* Concretely, this problem arises when employers defend charges of sexual harassment as sex discrimination by invoking an otherwise unblemished record in women's employment or by arguing that neither one individual man's harassment of one individual woman nor one woman being sexually approached only once makes the pattern necessary to show a basis in sex. Cases in contexts other than sexual harassment have repeatedly held that one victim of one practice is enough, provided the practice itself is based on sex as a matter of law.

It is not necessary to demonstrate that all women, even all women in a given work environment, are victims of a practice to show that the practice occurred to a given individual because she is a woman. All those of one sex need not be affected in individual cases of a group-based discrimination. In the *Bakke* case, not all whites were excluded from the medical school at the University of California at Davis; the form of the *Bakke* analysis (whatever one thinks of its substance) is that *one* white was given an unequal competitive chance for admission because of his race.[174] Similarly, in one case in which different hair length rules for men and women was held to be sex discrimination, the judge stated: "it would not matter that such a dress rule would affect only those males whose hair length contravened the employer's standards, and not all males."[175] Further, if in many factual contexts there are *no* men with whom an impact on women can be compared, this fact only underlines the context of sex segregation and sex classification of occupations which the employer's hiring practices promote, practices which themselves may be prohibited. The lack of men who are "similarly situated"—meaning here in the same working context but not sexually harassed—does not protect the practice, but

---

*An additional but distinct set of relations arises between an individual's situation, the requisite group referent, and the class action form.

underlines conditions which aggravate it. Permitting sexual harassment may support a segregated work context as much as a segregated work context conduces to the practice.

SEXUAL HARASSMENT IS EMPLOYMENT DISCRIMINATION[176]

Sexual harassment threatens women in their jobs. It "hinders [women] in getting, enjoying and keeping a job."[177] It is not intrinsically non-work-related because it is sexual. When it has an impact upon fundamental employment decisions and upon the workplace atmosphere,[178] sexual harassment is discrimination in employment. Title VII explicitly prohibits sex discrimination in "terms, conditions, and privileges of employment." In many circumstances, sexual requirements are used to deny women access to "privileges" of employment. In situations in which sexual threats and coercion shape a woman's job definition and working environment, or cases in which job-related pressures are used to coerce sexual acquiescence or involvement, sexual harassment is a "term" and "condition" of work. It can be a prerequisite for employment and a persistent quality of it. As a practice, sexual harassment distinguishes women for undesired compulsory sexual attention to their detriment as working people, whether they are compelled to comply or are able to resist. The employment discrimination consists not only in retaliation for refusal of advances, but also in the imposition of the sexual condition itself, which places the woman in the position of having to choose between tolerating or complying with sexual demands on the one hand and suffering employment deprivation on the other.

Practices that differentially damage a statutorily designated group *in and at work* constitute discrimination in employment. When compliance with sexual demands is a quid pro quo for an employment benefit, sexual harassment imposes a "condition precedent"[179] upon employment which limits and burdens the acquisition and enhancement of job status. Combined with circumstances such as knowledge of a promotion request, a pending job review, or a job interview, a single physical advance or verbal proposition may be sufficient to support an inference of an exchange of sex for a job benefit. As an extension of the expectations of the job, sexual harassment expresses and reinforces a sex-stereotyped perspective that women hired for

"women's jobs" are to be at the service of men in every way, are fair
game for male sexual advances, desire to be sexually used, and owe
men sexual liberties—all of which works to their disadvantage as
women workers. One incident or several, depending upon the sever-
ty and the circumstances, should suffice. With "extreme or coercive"
sexual attention, "even one incident may be too many,"[180] particularly
f coupled with constructive or actual discharge upon resistance.

In most jobs performed mostly by women, there is little nonsexist
connection between the content of the jobs and female sexuality. If a
job is allowed to be so pervasively sexualized as to include sexual
harassment within its very definition without being considered discriminatory, there is no limit to what an employer can buy with a
wage. "There is a serious problem in our society when men think that
access to the female body is, if not a divine right, at least a monetary
right."[181] Any woman employee, from topless dancer to law professor, should be able to refuse sexual intercourse and quid pro quo
pressures without job consequences. In a very few extreme cases the
degree of permissible sexual harassment might vary with the erotici-
zation of the job. Because of the nature of the work, a topless dancer
might be expected, without considering herself discriminated against,
to tolerate more catcalls, insults, and even some sexual advances from
customers than women in most other occupations. In these situations,
more than is impermissibly the case for most women's jobs, without
the sexual harassment, there *is* no job. Until all women *need* no longer
sell their physical attractiveness, there is no point in the law prohibiting all such behaviors in these contexts. Of course, in these situations
female sex would also be a BFOQ. But the reason that an employee
might be expected to tolerate some sexual harassment is independent
of the reasons sex is a BFOQ, illustrating the separability of biology
from job-related sexuality. Sexual harassment is no more acceptable
for a wet nurse than for a babysitter. If the sexual dimension of the
behavior, particularly verbal comments, is *properly* job-related, it
would be difficult to argue that the employee did not consent to it,
although extreme abuse, especially if accompanied by explicit dis-
avowal of consent, might be actionable.

Sexual harassment is a condition of work within the meaning of
Title VII. It makes women's jobs immensely more difficult, adding
onerous demands and distractions. It inhibits job performance by

placing women under pressure to tolerate or fulfill sexual conditions or leave work. Men do not labor under such burdens. The necessity to escape sexual harassment discourages women from remaining at one job long enough to acquire seniority and experience, to their detriment in employment. Employers are under an obligation to eradicate such discriminatory conditions from the working environment. No woman should have to leave work in order to enforce her right to work free from sex discriminatory conditions.

Working conditions that differ by sex are sex discriminatory. Sexism should be no more acceptable a working condition than racism, verbal forms no less than physical forms. The problems of proof are no greater in the sexual context than in the racial one. The EEOC found reason to believe that race discrimination in the form of harassment existed when an employee was called racist names like "nigger"[182] or "little black Sambo."[183] Analogous derogatory and insulting sexist labeling and epithets should be considered sex discrimination. Racial harassment has extended to include the practice of using titles (Mr., Mrs., Miss) for white employees while calling blacks by first names.[184] An analogous practice, similarly presuming upon intimacy and inferiority, is to call women by their first names, men by the honorific. In one combined far-reaching race and sex discrimination case, the EEOC found race discrimination when black adult women were addressed as "girl," and *sex* discrimination when adult women employees, both white and black, were persistently addressed as "girl."[185] Disparate working conditions, in historical context, were seen to imply inferiority: "We cannot ignore the historical pattern of referring to male employees as men, while referring to female employees as 'girls.' Inherent in the historically disparate treatment is an implication of female inferiority."[186] At least for white women, being called "girl" pales by comparison with the verbal assaults on womanhood that typify incidents of sexual harassment.

The EEOC has not reported a decision on sex bias in the verbal sexual harassment of a female employee. The case which comes closest contains no specifically sexual references, and the employer was found to have abused his male employees equally.[187] However, in *Rogers v. EEOC*,[188] Judge Goldberg offered a sensitive and insightful interpretation of "terms and conditions of employment" that could cover verbal as well as physical sexual harassment.

The phrase "terms, conditions, or privileges of employment" in Section 703 is an expansive concept which sweeps within its protective ambit the practice of creating a working environment heavily charged with ethnic or racial discrimination. I do not wish to be interpreted as holding that an employer's mere utterance of an ethnic or racial epithet which engenders offensive [*sic*] feelings in an employee falls within the proscription of Section 703. But by the same token I am not willing to hold that a discriminatory atmosphere could under no set of circumstances ever constitute an unlawful employment practice. One can readily envision working environments so heavily polluted with discrimination as to destroy completely the emotional and psychological stability of minority group workers, and I think Section 703 of Title VII was aimed at the eradication of such noxious practices.[189]

Consistent with other areas of discrimination law, the EEOC has consistently held employers affirmatively responsible for the elimination of discriminatory working conditions, regardless of whether the practice was a deliberate policy. The sense of these cases is that, since few employers have deliberately discriminatory policies, the only way a policy (for example, on sexual harassment) would be expressed would be through actions that would probably be disavowed the moment they were authoritatively questioned, although up to that time they had been ignored. In cases where racial insults and ethnic jokes and other derogatory remarks about minority employees were uttered (in one case written on bathroom walls, hardly the usual index of employer policy)[190] the EEOC has found an abrogation of employer responsibility to "maintain an atmosphere free of racial and ethnic intimidation and insult"[191] and "racial invective."[192] Although the employees were not always individually identified, the presence of these practices established employer responsibility by showing that the employer knew of, but did nothing to discourage or punish, these actions. A single verbal incident would probably not suffice to show "atmosphere," but a sufficiently derogatory, coercive, or threatening remark, or circumstances supporting company knowledge and support, may. Many certainly should.

Unauthorized nonsupervisory sexual harassment may also be covered. Recently the EEOC found the use of the term "nigger" in an ethnic joke at the end of a paid training program by a district manager "in the normal course of agency" sufficient reason to believe race discrimination had occurred.[193] Verbal sexual remarks could similarly violate protected rights. In a case (discussed previously) in which the employer demoted a recently promoted female worker from her supervisory position when male subordinates harassed and refused to cooperate with her, the EEOC held the employer responsible for the unauthorized individual nonsupervisory employees' behavior. Perhaps the EEOC would think that an employer has greater authority over job performance than over what is done at moments when employees are not directly engaged in the production process. But sexual harassment is as integral to women's work life as are the tasks themselves, and it is the ambience of the workplace that the prohibition on discrimination in "conditions of work" has been interpreted to encompass. Noting that an employer's demotion in such circumstances cooperates with, rather than opposes, the discrimination, the Commission stated flatly: "Title VII requires an employer to maintain a working environment free of sex-based intimidation. That requirement includes positive action where positive action is necessary to redress or eliminate employee intimidation."[194]

The explicit involvement of sexuality as a factor does not alter this responsibility. Raising sexual conduct *sub rosa,* another EEOC case presumed the employer was responsible for the sexual conduct of employees when the employer's response affected women's job opportunities. The EEOC found reason to believe that an employer was guilty of sex discrimination who restricted male/female share-driving by means of limiting female truck drivers to single runs. The protest by the male drivers' wives, who did not want their husbands sharing driving assignments with women, was found not to be a valid business justification. In striking parallel, a major study of sex roles at work reported that the wives of working men often express fear of the sexual potential of their husbands' working situation: "A few men played on these concerns and then used their wives' jealousies as reasons why women should not be hired for certain jobs, like those that involved travel with men."[195] Instead of allowing women to be excluded from jobs on this basis, the EEOC suggested, "Respondent may prescribe reasonable standards of on-the-road conduct equally applicable to both males and females, and take proper action to insure adherence to these standards."[196] The presumption that employers *could* prescribe such standards undercut the employer's justification for the share-driving practice: that discriminating against women drivers was the only way to avoid the problem. In this case, sexual activity was only feared, not alleged, and by third parties. When direct victims of actual sexual harassment complain, such a standard seems no less applicable for assessing what an employer who undertook to prevent sexual abuse of workers on the job could have done.

7 Conclusion

Sexual harassment, I have argued, is sex discrimination within two approaches: one seeing its role in women's inequality, the other seeing it as arbitrary differentiation. Having sharply contrasted the two conceptual approaches, I should explain how the two arguments can be true at the same time. One approach proceeds from an examination of the social substance of sexual inequality. In this analysis, the sexuality of women and men cannot be treated as the same. This comes perilously close to an admission, fatal for the other approach, that with regard to sexuality women and men cannot be "similarly situated" so cannot be compared, so no discrimination because of sex can result.

To the extent that women and men are not similarly situated sexually, the reason is pervasive social inequality. It is not biological difference or personal choice. Moreover, it is questionable that people should be required to be similarly situated before they can be found to be unequally treated, since due to systematic inequality, people often are not in similar situations. Further, that women's and men's sexuality are not substantively the same does not mean that their treatment is not comparable. It has never been thought that simply because people are black, their situation is so noncomparable with that of whites that it is impossible to tell whether blacks are compatively disadvantaged. Yet it is widely recognized that the content of the social meaning of being black is very different from that of being white, such that black and white skin color cannot be treated as if they are the same. As with skin privilege, so also sex privilege. Both genders possess sexuality. Women and men can, then, be compared with regard to the underlying variable: sexuality in the context of employment. Both sexes can be sexually harassed. When women's sexuality is treated differently from men's sexuality, similarly situated women and men will have been differentially treated, to women's comparative disadvantage, and that is sex discrimination.

The argument that sexual harassment is arbitrarily based on sex is that men are not placed in comparable positions to women when they are comparably circumstanced. The inequality argument is that under current social conditions, no man would be in the same position as a woman, even if he were in identical circumstances. The question which divides the approaches is: if both sexes were equally sexually harassed, would the treatment of the two be different, so equal, or would it be different, so unequal? Is it reasonable to compare the sexual harassment of women with the sexual harassment of men? Logically, biologically, and presuming equality between the sexes, it is, which is all the comparability required. In this society, it is not, because of that social inequality which discrimination law exists to eliminate.

The analysis of sexual harassment presented here has social implications for an understanding of women's work as integral to her social status. Sexual harassment at work critically undercuts women's potential for work equality as a means to social equality. Beyond survival, employment outside the home may offer women some promise of developing a range of capacities for which the nurturing, cleaning, and servant role of housework and child care provide little outlet. A job, no matter how menial, offers the potential for independence from the nuclear family, which makes women dependent upon men for life necessities. The marketplace promises limits with its impersonality. A woman may even be hired to be a man's individual servant, but he is supposed to own only her services, not herself. Even if the substance of the work is identical to that performed in the home, she is paid in a medium she can control in exchange.

Sexual harassment breaks the marketplace nexus. When a woman is seen as a provocative anomaly in the workplace, her sexuality is a condition of her subsistence, its delivery part of the definition of her productive activity. The woman's financial dependence on a man—this time her employer in place of her husband—is again sealed on a sexual basis. Gender and sexuality become inseparable as the dynamics of the home and marketplace converge. Sexual harassment on the job undercuts a woman's autonomy outside the home by sexualizing her role in exactly the same way as within the family:

sexual imposition combined with a definition of her work in terms of tasks which serve the man, sanctioned by her practical inability to create the material conditions of life on her own.

This relationship between women's sexuality and her material survival is stunningly evoked in the statement by Roberta Victor, a prostitute:

[My first trick] wasn't traumatic because my training had been how to be a hustler anyway. I learned it from the society around me, just as a woman. We're taught how to hustle, how to attract, hold a man, and give sexual favors in return. . . . It's a market place transaction. . . . the most important thing in life is the way men feel about you. . . . It's not too far removed from what most American women do—which is to put on a big smile and act. . . . What I did was no different from what ninety-nine per cent of American women are taught to do. I took the money from under the lamp instead of in Arpege. What would I do with 150 bottles of Arpege a week?[1]

Sexual harassment at work expresses the truth of these connections. If anatomy is not destiny as a biological matter, it can certainly appear all-inclusive as a social matter. Women learn early to be afraid that men will not be attracted to them, for they will then have no future; they also learn early to be afraid that men will be attracted to them, for they may then also have no future.

Americans are accustomed to thinking of themselves as freely choosing rather than as determined by social imperatives. Personality or character is defined largely in terms of this opposition. Becoming a person is thought to involve overcoming social determinants, forces which are impediments to individual choice, hence individual self. Women have little choice but to become "women" in the sense of having to become those persons who will then freely choose women's roles. Equally important, and pulling toward change, they struggle against this condition. Once having determined to equalize economic opportunities by sex, the law's role is not to try to overthrow these constructs but to support women who wish to resist the sexualization of their economic insecurity.

Sexual harassment has been analyzed throughout, with shifting emphasis, as the reciprocal enforcement of two inequalities: the sexual and the economic. The way the sexual subordination of women interacts with other forms of social power men have can now be more precisely delineated. Economic power is to sexual harassment as physical force is to rape. Recent examinations of rape, focusing upon attempts to understand what is wrong with it, provide an instructive parallel to the role of economic coercion in sexual harassment.

Rape has recently been conceptualized as a crime of violence, not sex. Sexual harrassment, so conceptualized, would be an abuse of hierarchical economic (or institutional) authority, not sexuality. According to this analysis, rape is an act of violence, an assault like any other, not an expression of socially organized sexuality. The first to state this interpretation, Susan Griffin defined rape as "an act of aggression in which the victim is denied her self-determination. It is an act of violence."[2] Susan Brownmiller applied and developed this analysis. *Against Our Will* examines rape under conditions of coercion, with coercion defined in other than sexual terms. Rape is systematically examined in the context of riots, wars, pogroms, and revolutions; rape by police, of children by parents, rape in prison, and rape as an expression of racism are analyzed.[3] Lorenne Clark and Debra Lewis, similarly, see the injury of rape to lie in the denial of the victim's physical autonomy. In their interpretation of the rape victim's perspective, "the fact that this assault was directed against her sexual organs is—at least at the time—irrelevant."[4] Carolyn Shafer and Marilyn Frye argue that what is wrong with rape is that it is "the ultimate disrespect . . . the exercise of the power of consent over another person."[5] Susan Peterson submits that "rape is first and foremost a crime of violence against the body, and only secondarily (though importantly) a sex crime."[6]

Driving a wedge between sexuality and power is the point of these interpretations. Rape is an abuse of physical force, not an expression of male sexuality. The power that makes rape effective, as well as injurious, derives from some other source—guns, strength, race, age, the state. Power is considered inappropriately displaced onto the sexual rather than being, in any sense, a part of sexuality. Rape is an expression of physical force that just happens to be acted out in sex, not an expression of male sexuality acted out a little more forcefully than usual. Power is ultimately reducible to physical force,[7] however mediated through social institutions, and sex is something, anything, else. Dominance can take sexual forms, but it does not have sexual sources. Particularly for Brownmiller, although rape is seen as widespread, it is rarified. It is not analyzed in normal circumstances, in everyday life, in ordinary relationships. The radical distinction between rape and intercourse—rape is violence, intercourse is sexuality—is both the most basic and the least examined premise of the approach.[8]

The motive for this bifurcation is not difficult to understand. A major obstacle to prohibiting rape effectively is that it has been seen as a natural expression of male sexual desires for women's bodies. Accused rapists are often found not guilty, or women's complaints considered unfounded, because the incident is seen in this light, as not extraordinary enough. A great many incidents women consider rape are, in effect, considered "normal" by the legal system.[9] As one accused rapist put it, he hadn't used "any more force than is usual for males during the preliminaries."[10] Taking rape from the realm of "the sexual," placing it in the realm of "the violent," allows one to be against it without raising any questions about the extent to which the institution of heterosexuality has defined force as a normal part of "the preliminaries."

This literature shares a starting point with the system it criticizes: both attempt (equally implicitly) to distinguish sexual abuses from sexuality which must be healthy, eternal, and natural, from that which must be normal and allowed in order to justify punishing some acts as abuses of it. But is ordinary sexuality, under conditions of gender inequality, to be presumed healthy? What if inequality is built into the social conceptions of male and female sexuality, of masculinity and femininity, of sexiness and heterosexual attractiveness? Incidents of sexual harassment suggest that male sexual desire itself may be aroused by female vulnerability. Much of what seems to make subordinate women so sexually irresistible is that they are so defenseless. Men feel they can take advantage, so they want to, so they do. Examination of sexual harassment, precisely because the episodes appear commonplace, forces one to confront the fact that sexual intercourse normally occurs between economic (as well as physical) unequals. In this context, the apparent legal requirement that violations of women's sexuality appear out of the ordinary before they will be punished helps prevent women from defining the ordinary conditions of their own consent.

If power is shaped outside the sexual sphere, rape, conceptualized as an abuse of such power, need have nothing specifically to do with the condition of women, with gender, or with sexism. So understood, neither does sexual harassment, although both can be considered wrong because of the inappropriate (arbitrary) conflation of power from one sphere with advantage in another. But if socially defined sexuality, its pattern of initiative and acquiescence, is understood to express sex inequality, the cases that consider rape "normal," are, in a backward way, correct. The problem is that the appearance of rape as similar to normal heterosexual encounters is not seen as an indictment of normal heterosexual encounters, but as a reason the behavior should be allowed. But if rape *is* very like normal intercourse, it is, further, no mystery that convictions are so difficult. If most men do similar things all the time, on what grounds should this individual man be sent to jail? Similarly with sexual harassment: if unwanted sex imposed by a man upon a woman who is in no position to refuse only expresses the usual situation in unusually vivid terms, on what grounds should it be illegal?

At this point, the law of discrimination has a distinctive contribution to make. Sex discrimination law can keep sexual violation of women in full view of the social setting within which it occurs. This social context has defined as normal a structural situation in which women can be and are systematically subordinated to men sexually and in other ways. Sexual harassment at work connects the jobs most women do—in which a major part of their work is to be there for men—with the structure of sexual relations—in which their role is also to be there for men—with the denigrated economic status women as a gender occupy throughout the society. Women's place at work and in sexual relations can be seen as socially constructed, not naturally given; public and structural, not private and individual; separate and subordinate and not equal. Discrimination law exists to remedy such disparities. If sexual harassment expresses the pervasive reality of normal relations between the sexes, and if these relations express unequal social power, then the feelings and practices that emerge are not reasons that the practices should be allowed. They support and evidence the discrimination. Violations that would not be seen as criminal because they are anything but unusual may, in this context, be seen as discriminatory for precisely the same reason.

Analysis of sexuality must not be severed and abstracted from analysis of gender. What the current interpretations of rape fail to grasp (indeed, seem to avoid most strenuously as they approach) is the argument most conducive to conceiving sexual harassment as sex discrimination: a crime of sex *is* a crime of power. Sexual harassment (and rape) have everything to do with sexuality.[11] Gender *is* a power division and sexuality is one sphere of its expression. One thing wrong with sexual harassment (and with rape) is that it eroticizes women's subordination.[12] It acts out and deepens the powerlessness of women as a gender, *as women*.[13] If sexuality is set apart from gender, it will be a law unto itself.

Setting sexuality within an analysis of gender is a task sex discrimination law is peculiarly well suited to perform. The two approaches to sex discrimination, taken together, can encompass the social meaning of women's sexuality without institutionalizing it as an emblem of women's inferiority. Together, they guarantee an equality that begins to comprehend womanhood as distinct *and* fully human. The distinctive contribution of differences doctrine to this synthesis is that, because the sexes can be reversed in theory, sexual victimization is not exclusively identified (even in its prohibition) with women as a biological group. Inequality theory, by making a substantive critique, insures that sex discrimination doctrine is not debased by becoming enmeshed in the abstractions of neutral principles. Differences doctrine alone could allow female sexuality to be considered unique to women, male sexuality unique to men. This would be to accept as inevitable, or as the correct legal point of reference, the current social meaning of gender. Men have long been dominant to women, while being just as different from women as women are from men. Differences doctrine presumes a symmetry of power between the sexes, when women have been subordinate as well as distinct. Women want to be equal and different, too.

Appendix A: *Application of the Two Theories to Sex Discrimination Doctrine*

The two conceptual frameworks, the *inequality* approach and the *differences* approach, have been sketched in the text. This appendix applies them to the broader range of sex discrimination doctrine. Taken as a whole, assuming the requisites for a cause of action are otherwise met (for example, state action under the Equal Protection Clause, employment relation under Title VII), the judicial approach to sex discrimination can be summarized in four questions: (1) was there a differentiation? (2) did it deprive the complainant(s)? (3) was it based on sex? and (4) was it justified? Differentiation and deprivation (questions 1 and 2) are usually, although not always, either self-evident and uncontested or questions of fact. Questions 3 and 4, together with whether the proper resolution is at the level of 3 *or* 4, are the focus of dispute in most sex discrimination litigation. As to these key issues, sex basis and justification, the inequality approach and the differences approach require different arguments and set different standards for their resolution. Although the two approaches are often confused, and sometimes support each other, in critical instances they appear on opposite sides of the basic issues and tend toward disparate results.

SEX BASIS

Sex is both a group classification and an attribute of individuals. The reality of such a simple observation, and the consequences of what it means for an action or policy to be "based on sex," is extremely complex. Is there such a thing as an individual woman, as such, apart from the group context which socially defines what a woman is? Is there such a thing as a group called *women,* above the accumulated

characteristics of its individual constituents? From one's conception of
the relationship between sex as an individual attribute and sex as a
group classification flows one's conception of the project of prohibiting discrimination based upon sex. Should a law against sex discrimination primarily prohibit injustice to groups or irrationality to individuals?

Before swiftly affirming that it should do both, consider whether
there are rational treatments of individual women that might work a
group injustice; conversely, whether there are injustices to women as
a group that would be socially rational as treatment of individuals. At
issue here is whether an individual irrationality due to sex is meaningful only as a group injustice in microscopic form, or whether a group
injustice is intelligible only as an aggregation of irrationalities to individuals. Further, if there is no such thing as a sex-based irrationality to
one woman out of the context of women as a group, is such a
generalization of one woman into all women part of the problem of
sexism—a stereotyping on the level of analysis—or is it a reflection of
that unity of all women's experience which grounds a thoroughgoing
critique of the gender division? Stated in terms of the law against
discrimination, the question becomes: does, or should, the law against
discrimination aim at the dismantling or overturning of the social
meaning of sex, as a pervasive injustice, or should it mitigate only
those irrationalities which lurk as exceptions on the fringes of a fundamentally rational and just (or at least unchangeable) allocation of
roles based on sex differences?

On the surface of the law, the starting point of the analysis of
sex-basis is typically the EEOC's rule, in which the term *sex* refers to "a
person's gender, an immutable characteristic with which a person is
born."[1] The Commission thus considers sex-based those differences
in treatment it attributes to gender. Courts have variously reworded
this and the language of Title VII, "because of such individual's sex,"[2]
the restatements emphasizing the strictly biological factor to varying
degrees. The most narrow tests prohibit differences in treatment
"solely because of the fact of female gender,"[3] when "based on immutable characteristics,"[4] or when "based on a physical condition peculiar to her sex."[5] Other decisions more broadly prohibit differential
treatment where sex "was a factor" in the dissimilar treatment,[6] when
the treatment was "related to immutable characteristics"[7] or to factors
due to "a condition attendant to their sex,"[8] or bearing "a significant

correlation to . . . sex"[9]—the latter even when not all those persons affected by the practice were women. These tests, placed together, suggest some latitude in the required correspondence between gender as a physical reference for sex and the practice questioned. An understanding of the substantive meaning attributed to "sex" itself in its group and individual manifestations, however, requires investigation of the logic of its application in context.

In the differences approach, a differentiation is based on sex when it can be shown that a person of the opposite sex in the same position is not treated the same. This requires that a person of the opposite sex can reasonably be in a comparable position. A clear example is *Phillips v. Martin-Marietta,* in which mothers but not fathers of preschool children were excluded from applying for jobs. Lacking evidence of "bias against women as such," the Supreme Court prohibited "one hiring policy for women and another for men—each having preschool age children."[10] In an analytically identical result, the Supreme Court found sex discrimination in a social security survivorship policy which allowed male wage earners to purchase more security for their families than female wage earners, each for the same amount of work.[11]

The logic of the inequality approach, by contrast, requires no comparability of situation, only that a rule or practice disproportionately burden one sex because of sex. Under the facts of *Phillips v. Martin-Marietta,* suppose the lower court had found that family obligations presented a greater job conflict for mothers than for fathers of preschool children. In this approach, the differential hiring rule would still be discriminatory because it would reinforce the traditionally disproportionate burden of parenthood on women. As it was, the court suggested that such a finding on remand might support a Bona Fide Occupational Qualification (BFOQ)*[12] for men for the job, over Justice Marshall's concurring protest. But this was a correct result under the court's differences approach. Mothers of preschool children *are* less "qualified" for jobs than fathers, if the "qualifications" related to the job include freedom from child care obligations, and fathers who apply are not so burdened. In effect, this is no less true if each

---

*When it is legal to have sex itself be a job qualification, sex is termed a *bona fide occupational qualification.* See the discussion *supra,* at 137-39, for a critique of this conception, and *infra,* at 300, n. 12, for relevant legal citations.

mother's qualifications are *individually* considered than if her application is flatly barred by a BFOQ, although the former gives individual women a chance to be exceptional, so is, of course, preferable. In the differences perspective, dissimilar circumstances can legitimately ground sex-unequal results, even if the situated differences are themselves the product of a sexist distribution of social responsibilities.

If its logic is dissected, the differences approach implicitly grounds a conception of sex upon a conception of biology. The inequality framework emphasizes the grounding of sex in the *social* meaning of biology. Translated into doctrinal terms, under the differences approach, the closer a variable comes to sexual biology, or to those social differences which are seen to be biologically necessary, the less a differentiation will tend to qualify as "gender as such." This is the opposite of the result one would expect for a doctrine that ostensibly *prohibits* different treatment of two groups that are defined by the biology of sex. But different treatment based upon factors close to that difference are not considered sex-based differences because the doctrine effectively requires that a sex-neutral category in terms of which the sexes can be compared exist. The closer one gets to gender biology, the less comparable the sexes appear, so different treatment does not appear unequal, to the point that it does not seem sex-based, but instead based upon the gender factor itself. (Implicit in this approach is a conception that sex is an individual attribute, with sex groups being collections of individuals possessing this attribute, rather than an attribute formed out of social interaction of the groups themselves.)

For example, since pregnancy is unique to women, no differentiation from men with regard to pregnancy exists to be compared. This is because women as a sex are so "different." Thus, in *Manhart,* the proponents of the *Gilbert* approach argued that *because* there *is* a difference between the sexes in longevity, differentiation is based on a "factor *other than* sex," so is nondiscriminatory. That is, real situated differences justify different treatment, *especially* if those differences arise from sex itself. Taking this logic one step further, the doctrine on justification shows that, to the extent a factor is seen as "real," even (in fact, especially) a distinction seen as "based on sex" can be "justified."[13] The BFOQ is the final expression of this approach. At this point, the danger that sexual harassment will be seen as treatment based upon real differences, that is, upon sexuality, not sex, is not fanciful.

According to an inequality approach, the differences conception of the injustice of discrimination fails to grasp the nature of the problem it is trying to solve. Due to the fact that the society defines and treats women as a group, as a distinct and subordinate category of being on the apparent basis of biological femaleness, this treatment will shape the actual characteristics, personalities, circumstances, qualifications, even many of the physical qualities and attributes of individuals of both sexes. To the extent the law allows sex-based differences to be a reason for considering that differential outcomes are not sex-based, it will allow the very factors the law against discrimination exists to prohibit to be the reason not to prohibit them.

Illustrations of the divergence between the two approaches, and of the deep incoherence of the differences approach, exist throughout sex discrimination adjudications of the issue of sex-basis. Some courts have found that holding men to one grooming standard regulating their beards and hair length, when women are not held to this or any standard, is discrimination in employment based on sex.[14] Other courts, applying differences logic, find it nondiscriminatory to have two different policies for women and men, so long as the policies are based on something other than gender *per se,* that is, grooming standards.[15] This is termed "discrimination by grooming code, not by sex."[16] *Rafford v. Randle Eastern Ambulance* presents a striking example of this reasoning, holding that the discharge of pregnant women and bearded men does not violate Title VII because "only women become pregnant, and only men grow beards."[17] This observation is intended to indicate that the differentiation is *not* sex-based because "in neither instance are similarly situated persons of the opposite sex favored."[18] Only too true: there *are* no similarly situated persons of the opposite sex, precisely because of the sex difference.

In a conceptually identical maneuver, many lower courts prior to *Gilbert*[19] had found sex discrimination when companies had one temporary disability policy for men which covered every contingency, and another for women, which covered all but one common major disability unique to women: pregnancy and pregnancy-related disabilities.[20] Beginning to approach this question in the perspective of sex inequality, Chief Judge Brown, dissenting in *Phillips v. Martin*

Marietta, argued: "Is this sex-related? Nobody—and this includes Judges, Solomonic or life-tenured—has yet seen a male mother. A mother, to oversimplify the simplest biology, must then be a woman."[21] To require that a pregnant mother take leave deprives only women and no men; it is thus a differentiation based on sex. As another court stated the argument in a discharge case:

[Mrs.] Cerra and other pregnant women are singled out and placed in a class to their disadvantage. They are discharged from their employment on the basis of a physical condition peculiar to their sex. This is sex discrimination pure and simple.[22]

Other courts, pursuing the logic of differences ultimately adopted in *Gilbert,* held that it was not discriminatory to exclude some temporary disabilities, as long as the exclusion was based on something other than gender per se, that is, on pregnancy.[23] Denying a woman sick pay for a maternity leave is not sex discrimination because:

If a class is based on some reasonable quality other than sex, the classification is not sexually discriminatory even though that quality may be possessed only by persons of the female sex.[24]

A pregnant woman is disadvantaged in employment in this approach not because she is a woman, but because she is pregnant. Judge Haynesworth explains why:

The fact that only women experience pregnancy and motherhood removes all possibility of competition between the sexes in this area. No man-made law or regulation excludes males from those experiences, and no such laws or regulations can relieve females from all the burdens which naturally accompany the joys and blessings of motherhood.[25]

Minus the romanticism, the *Gilbert* and *Geduldig* cases applied the same analysis to support the result that excluding pregnancy from a disability plan was not sex discrimination because the differentiation was not sex-based. To further illustrate the distinction, consider the concurrences in *Gilbert.* Justices Stewart and Blackmun stated that plaintiffs failed to prove that the rule excluding pregnancy disability benefits constituted "discrimination in effect."[26] Under the inequality approach, this could only refer to a failure to prove that (a) denial of disability benefits to pregnant women disadvantaged them in employment, or (b) not all pregnant women were denied disability benefits under the plan, or (c) that not all (or most) of those denied pregnancy disability benefits were women. Under the differences approach, the discrimination must be grounded upon a comparison between the sexes: the failure to demonstrate that benefits were unequally distributed by sex due to the pregnancy exclusion. The factual basis for such a demonstration would exist only if, in fact, the distribution of women's needs for disability coverage *including* pregnancy-related disabilities were the same as men's. That is, sex discrimination due to *different* coverage would only be discriminatory if, as a proportion of their health needs, men's and women's sex-specific ailments, or ailments as a whole, gave rise to equal amounts of temporary disability. Why one should require the sexes to *need* the same amount of health care in order to insure those needs equally fully is unexplained. Yet only women risk a long uncompensated period of absence from work for a sex-specific disability. The explanation that *was* given for pregnancy exclusion was cost; thus, in *Gilbert,* cost was *not* a *justification* for allowing a distinction that is "based on sex,"[27] but a reason why the distinction was not sex-based. This example suggests that the goal of antidiscrimination law, in this view, is to prohibit inequality "in effect" only to the extent that the sexes are the same. When they diverge, male requirements set the standard against which women's requirements are judged "different"; the inequality of women is thus legitimized.

JUSTIFICATION

The justifiability of sex-based differentiation is often confused with the question just discussed, whether a detrimental differentiation is "based on sex." This confusion persists because of an implicit notion about "differentness": if there is a "good reason" for treating the sexes differently, such treatment, not being arbitrary, is not properly "discrimination." As often phrased, with emphasis but without explication, it is not "invidious"[28] discrimination. In this way, what is termed a "discriminatory but justified" distinction, referring to a detrimental differentiation based on sex that is nevertheless legally permitted, is commonly collapsed, together with failures to prove a differentiation to be sex-based, into a "nondiscrimination" category. A separate analysis keeps these elements distinct. Even if kept distinct, there is always a danger that an argument of sex-basis will succeed, only to find that too much was proven: the behavior is so much based upon sex that it is justified.

Within the differences framework, a detrimental sex-based differentiation can be doctrinally "justified" in two ways: (1) by reference to sex itself, as in the BFOQ[29] and the "unique physical characteristic"[30] exceptions, or (2) by reference to some other important value, showing the distinction has a "rational relation to a compelling state interest" under the Equal Protection Clause,[31] or (possibly) by showing it is "job-related" under Title VII[32] or by showing it has a remedial purpose. Available doctrinal limitations on these justifications, standards for what are *not* "good reasons" for sex-based differentiation, include the "sex stereotype"[33] for the BFOQ and "sex averaging"[34] for the "unique physical characteristic." That is, just as a valid unique physical characteristic may not be based upon a sex average, a valid BFOQ may not be based upon a sex stereotype.

The BFOQ presents courts with the need to consider, in light of alleged sex differences, the duties, hence the qualifications, for a job. The sex stereotype constraint upon the BFOQ requires courts to consider whether a job legitimately requires one sex. Thus, disparate treatment by sex must derive from a "factual basis, as opposed to a commonly held stereotype"[35] and the qualification must be "*necessary* to the business . . . not merely tangential,"[36] or convenient.[37] The sex stereotype cases can be read as investigations of the supporting myths of women's separate status.[38] Some courts have gone even further with the sex stereotype argument, allowing it, in the absence of a BFOQ defense, to ground an affirmative attack on a range of sex-biased job practices.[39]

Both the sex stereotype and sex averaging prohibitions hold up individual, not group, characteristics as the proper criteria for social determinations. The sex stereotype argument focuses upon showing that the attributed characteristics are not true of all women, in particular of a given individual; the sex averaging objection focuses upon characteristics which may be true of the group as a whole, or of group members on the average, but are not true of each, or (necessarily) of any one, individual in the group. The requirement challenged in *Manhart*—that all women contribute more to the pension fund because women on the average outlive men—would probably be an example of sex-averaging under the ERA. Beyond the criticism that the longevity criterion may be untrue of many women, the "arbitrariness" which makes such a sex-based differentiation unjust lies in the group, as opposed to individual, referent: the criterion treats each individual woman as if a true generalization about women applies to her, without allowing her to prove that she might be an exception.

In the inequality approach, by contrast, there are no justifications for group detriment. Most issues are resolved at the level of the third question ("is it sex-based?"), assimilating the judgment of "justifiability" to the judgment of whether the deprivation is based upon the social meaning of the sex difference, that is, whether it inures to the systematic disadvantage of one sex. The entire notion that a detrimental differentiation based on sex can be "justified," in the inequality framework, amounts to recognizing the potential validity of the inferiority of one sex to the other. The mistake of this type of analysis has been to confound differences with detriments. Treatment that recognizes or benefits differences, injuring no one, has never been the issue. Detriments supposedly corresponding to sex differences—usually women's differences from the male standard—have been. To justify sex-based detriments enshrines as an exception to the law requiring equal treatment the very incidents of social inferiority the law proposes to change. Not a case of the exception swallowing the rule, this is a matter of translating the legal mandate of equality into a doctrine that allows social inequality to be a limiting condition upon its own delivery.

Appendix B: *A Brief*

As women alleging sexual harassment increasingly seek relief on the theory that it constitutes sex discrimination and favorable precedents accumulate, a short accessible statement of the legal argument is needed in a form readily adaptable to varying facts and issues. This appendix is meant to assist plaintiffs' attorneys in briefing responses to defendants' motions to dismiss for legal insufficiency, the usual procedural posture in which the challenge to sexual harassment as sex discrimination is posed. The legal analysis spread throughout the book, and developed in depth, is brought together in outline here. While employment remains the primary context, the application to education is sketched as well. The two approaches to sex discrimination structure the presentation with the analytic labels removed. Courts would doubtless find them distracting.

Sexual harassment states a claim of sex discrimination. The plaintiff has alleged that defendant's practcies and policies with respect to the sexual harassment of women employees (or students) by male superiors or co-workers (or faculty and administrators) discriminates on the basis of sex. On the factual allegations and under applicable law, if it is not "without doubt that the plaintiff can prove no set of facts in support of [her] claim which would entitle [her] to relief," the plaintiff should be allowed to maintain the action. *Conley v. Gibson,* 305 U.S. 41, 45-46 (1957); *Hospital Building Co. v. Trustees of Rex Hospital,* 425 U.S. 738, 742 (1976). The plaintiff advances a claim that has been received favorably by the three federal appellate courts that have considered it, *Barnes v. Costle,* 561 F.2d 983 (D.C. Cir. 1977); *Tomkins v. Public Service Electric & Gas Co.,* 568 F.2d 1044 (3rd Cir.

The assistance of Anne E. Simon in preparing this appendix was particularly valuable.

1977); *Garber v. Saxon Business Products, Inc.*, No. 76-1610 (4th Cir. 1977), and a claim that has grounded relief in federal district courts, in additional cases, e.g., *Williams v. Saxbe,* 413 F. Supp. 654 (D.D.C. 1976); *Munford v. James T. Barnes & Co.,* 441 F. Supp. 459 (E.D. Mich. 1977); *Heelan v. Johns-Manville Corp.,* 451 F. Supp. 1382 (D. Colo. 1978); *Elliott v. Emery Air Freight* (D.N.C. June 21, 1977). *But cf. Corne v. Bausch & Lomb,* 390 F. Supp. 161 (D. Ariz., 1975), *vacated and remanded,* 562 F.2d 55 (9th Cir. 1977); *Miller v. Bank of America,* 418 F. Supp. 233 (N.D. Cal. 1976), *appeal docketed* No. 76-3344 (9th Cir. 1978). It is a claim that is soundly based in principle.

Because the cause of action is relatively new, it is useful to consider the claim of sex discrimination in two analytically separable but related parts: is there a discrimination based on sex, and does it have the requisite relationship to employment (or educational program) to come within the statutory proscriptions.

The contours of a legal understanding of the problem of sexual harassment of women are only beginning to emerge. As more cases are brought and courts become more familiar with the essence of the claim, law on sexual harassment as sex discrimination is developing. The principal forum for that development has been the law against sex discrimination in employment under Title VII, 42 U.S.C. §2000-e, although a comparable claim in education under Title IX, 20 U.S.C. §1681, with its associated regulations, 45 C.F.R. Part 86, has been acted upon favorably. *Alexander, et al. v. Yale University,* 459 F. Supp. 1 (D. Conn. 1977). The handful of employment cases to date, while increasingly tending to be resolved in the plaintiff's favor, have been divided in their results, sometimes unclear in their rationale, and often strained in their interpretation of the allegations.

A failure to recognize the social context and implications of incidents of sexual harassment has been a major element in those court decisions which have declined to find discrimination. The court in *Corne v. Bausch & Lomb,* 390 F. Supp. 161, 163 (D. Ariz. 1975) found the supervisor's conduct "nothing more than a personal proclivity, peculiarity, or mannerism," and thus not within the reach of Title VII. Similarly, in *Miller v. Bank of America,* 418 F. Supp. 233, 234 (N.D. Cal. 1976), the court held that the plaintiff had alleged "essentially the isolated and unauthorized sex misconduct of one employee to another," not an injury cognizable under Title VII. In the District Court's opinion in *Tomkins v. Public Service Electric & Gas Co.,* 422 F.

Supp. 553, 556 (D.N.J. 1976), *rev'd.*, 568 F.2d 1044 (3rd Cir. 1977), the sexual harassment was described as "physical attack motivated by sexual desire on the part of a supervisor." To the court, this individual action did not amount to the kind of "artificial barrier to full employment" proscribed by Title VII. Faced with allegations of repeated sexual pressure from the plaintiff's supervisor, which she refused, followed by abolition of her job, the District Court for the District of Columbia observed that "this is a controversy underpinned by the subtleties of an inharmonious personal relationship." *Barnes v. Train*, 13 F.E.P. Cases 123, 124 (D.D.C. 1974), *rev'd. sub nom. Barnes v. Costle*, 561 F.2d 983 (D.C. Cir. 1977).

In all of these cases, the courts seemed to think that the incidents alleged, being merely "personal," did not rise to the level of a public problem within the purview of the statute. This view neglects both the negative impact on the woman's employment opportunities (Barnes and Tomkins lost their jobs as a result; Corne and coplaintiff DeVane quit under the pressure of the harassment) and the fact that each incident reproduces, with very little personal variation, the inequitable social structure of male supremacy and female subordination which Titles VII and IX seek to eliminate in proscribing sex discrimination as a factor in employment and in education.

Far from being simply individual and personal, sexual harassment is integral and crucial to a social context in which women, as a group, are allocated a disproportionately small share of wealth, power, and advantages compared with men as a group. When women work outside the home, they typically occupy jobs that are low on the ladder of financial reward and personal satisfaction independent of their aspirations, preparation, or potential. Often they are shunted to dead-end "women's jobs." In this context, the problem of sexual harassment is revealed as both a manifestation and perpetuation of the socially disadvantaged status of women. A man in a position of authority, whether a supervisor or a teacher, uses his hierarchically superordinate role to place conditions of sexual compliance on his female subordinate's access to the benefits of her job or her educational program. The necessity of dealing with sexual pressures that are, by virtue of the man's position and actions, bound up with the woman's desired goal (getting a job, doing a job, getting an education) burdens and restricts her access to the means of survival, security, and achievement. In a society in which women as a group are at a comparative disadvantage to men, the negative impact that sexual harassment has on the maintenance or improvement of women's position contributes to the continuation of their socially inferior condition. Viewed in such a light, sexual harassment can be seen as the kind of sex discrimination which Title VII and Title IX were intended to redress.

This analysis is grounded in the cases to date. As developed in *Barnes v. Costle*, the critical issue is whether the injury suffered by the plaintiff is the result of differential treatment based on gender, 561 F.2d 983 at 989. In none of the decided cases is there any evidence (as opposed to speculation, for example, *Corne v. Bausch & Lomb*, 390 F. Supp. 161 at 163–164, *Tomkins v. P.S.E.&G. Co.*, 422 F. Supp. at 556) that a male subordinate in the plaintiff's position was treated in the same way as the plaintiff. A man *could* have been sexually harassed, but was not. Indeed, in a dominantly heterosexual society, in which it is men who overwhelmingly decide both men's and women's employment and educational destinies, male subordinates are generally treated very differently. Men tend to go about their business, doing jobs or taking courses, without having sexual demands routinely being made on them and without needing to invest care and energy continually to attempt to avoid or manage such demands. It is the injury of having to meet sexual criteria in addition to the other criteria in the situation, while similarly situated men could but do not have to meet such additionally imposed criteria, that creates the sex discrimination. See *Barnes v. Costle*, 561 F.2d 983 at 992; *Williams v. Saxbe*, 413 F. Supp. 654, 657–58 (D.D.C. 1976); *Garber v. Saxon Business Products, Inc.*, 552 F.2d 1032 (4th Cir. 1977).

In order to dispose of the kind of speculation that has plagued earlier cases, it is important to consider directly the impact of sex reversal and of same-sex harassment on the analysis just presented. The behavior would be just as sex-based and discriminatory if the genders were reversed, as noted in *Barnes v. Costle*, 561 F.2d 983, 990 n. 55. Depending upon the theory, it might be proscribed if the sexes were the same. As a matter of social fact, those instances are probably rare and appear to have produced no litigation. Moreover, it is both procedurally sensible and substantively illuminating to follow the suggestion in *Barnes* in cases of a bisexual superior who harasses subordinates in a way that shows no gender bias. Such a circumstance is properly raised as a matter of fact, to be pleaded and proven, and if shown, goes to negate the claim of sex discrimination.

The conduct that constitutes sexual harassment takes many specific forms. The cases reveal situations of persistent verbal suggestion, unwanted physical contact, straightforward proposition, and coerced intercourse. By analogy, the law with respect to racial discrimination is well developed and instructive. Personal insults or intimidation having a racial basis or referent have repeatedly been found to be discriminatory by the EEOC. An atmosphere that creates psychological strain and emotional distress because of race-based treatment is likewise a violation of Title VII. *Rogers v. EEOC*, 454 F.2d 234, 237–38 (5th Cir. 1971), *cert. denied*, 406 U.S. 957 (1972); *Gray v. Greyhound Lines, East* 13 F.E.P. Cases 1401 (D.C. Cir. 1976). Insult, pressure, or intimidation having gender as its basis or referent should be equally proscribed.

It is no answer to try to split the harassment into two parts—the incidents, which are not discriminatory, and retaliation, which is. This leads to the conceptually incoherent result that a woman is protected from sexual harassment if she is fired or otherwise penalized for complaining, but is unprotected if her complaint is merely ignored. Title VII contains specific prohibitions against retaliation for complaint, which suggests that Congress did not contemplate that retaliation is a necessary element for all conduct to be considered discriminatory. The treatment of the issue of retaliation in *Williams* shows that the impact of the relationship between the job and the sexual demands goes to the core of the woman's dilemma and damage, rather than to a later official response. Not only is the plaintiff in the situation of being harassed on the job "only because she was a woman subordinate," *Barnes v. Costle*, 561 F.2d 983, 990, but the retaliation against her job status by the rejected supervisor is necessarily implicit in the original incidents. It is precisely the ever-present availability of the supervisor's or teacher's hierarchical authority that *conditions* the woman's accession to benefits upon her compliance with, or nonrejection of, his sexual demands.

The fixation with the "personal" sometimes argued to preclude an incident from being sex-based also emerges in those cases in which courts question the employer's responsibility for supervisor actions when the perpetrator is not himself the employer. *Miller*, 418 F. Supp. at 236; *Corne*, 390 F. Supp. at 163. The better view, and general rule in employment discrimination cases, is that discriminatory acts of supervisors are chargeable to employers. *Barnes v. Costle,* 561 F.2d, 993, n. 71 (*collecting cases*); *Tomkins,* 422 F. Supp. at 566, n.; 51 *New York U. L. Rev.,* 149, n. 17 (1976); Ginsburg and Koreski, "Sexual Advances by an Employee's Supervisor: A Discrimination Violation of Title VII?" 3 *Employee Relations L.J.* 83 (1977). *Cf.* the concurrence in *Barnes v. Costle,* 561 F.2d 995–99. The disagreement about the extent and nature of properly attributable employer responsibility has led to unsound results in some cases. It is less likely to arise in cases in which there are allegations of actual notice to responsible officials. At that point, failure to act would support liability even on the most narrow and misguided understanding of vicarious liability standards.

The nexus with educational deprivation is similar. A woman who is attempting to pursue a course of study is in a position, with respect to her professors, analogous to a female employee's position with respect to her male supervisor. In each case, the male superior can allocate benefits, rewards, and punishments that materially affect the woman's future in the institution or company, and often beyond it. A professor's imposition of sexual conditions on the student's educational progress creates a barrier to her access to equal educational opportunity.

The effect of sexual harassment in both an employment and a university setting on a motivated woman who thinks of herself as, and is, a serious worker or student is potentially devastating. Beyond the exclusionary and restrictive results, the intrusion of the feeling that she is not valued for her productivity, accomplishments, or promise, but for her woman's body can cast a pall of resentment and self-doubt over her working or academic career, when it does not drive her out of the pursuit altogether.

This situation would be discriminatory even if only one person were affected, as long as the requisite showing of sex basis were made. *Barnes v. Costle,* 561 F.2d 983 at 993. The group referent requisite for the claim that the injury is "based on sex" is legally distinct from the allegation that the injury has affected a class of persons whom the plaintiff purports to represent. The group referent is a question of whether the practice is sex-based, which has been addressed. When a plaintiff additionally alleges a class of victims, questions about its size and composition are reserved to the time of certification, and are not relevant to the legal sufficiency of the claim on a motion to dismiss.

Notes

1. Sexism is by no means unique to American culture. This discussion, for purposes of application to American law, focuses upon its forms in this culture.

2. Houseworkers (paid and unpaid) are excluded from this discussion of working women not because I think they do not work, nor because they do not suffer from sexual harassment. Most are not covered by Title VII's limitation to workplaces with fifteen or more employees. For one review of quantitative studies which discuss the contribution of unpaid housework to the Gross National Product, see Juanita Kreps, *Sex in the Marketplace: American Women at Work* (Baltimore: Johns Hopkins University Press, 1971), chap. 2.

3. "Sexual Harassment on the Job: Questions and Answers" (Ithaca, N. Y.: Working Women United Institute, 1975 [mimeograph]).

'4. Lin Farley, testimony given before the Commission on Human Rights of the City of New York, Hearings on Women in Blue-Collar, Service and Clerical Occupations, "Special Disadvantages of Women in Male-Dominated Work Settings," April 21, 1975 (mimeograph). The data are based upon the study reported at chap. 3, *infra*, note 5.

5. *Barnes v. Costle*, 13 F.E.P. Cases 123 (D.D.C. 1974), *rev'd*, 561 F.2d 983 (D.C. Cir. 1977); *Williams v. Saxbe*, 413 F. Supp. 654 (D.D.C. 1976), *sub nom. Williams v. Bell*, Nos. 76-1833, 76-1994 (D.C. Cir. September 19, 1978) (slip opinion); *Corne v. Bausch & Lomb*, 390 F. Supp. 161 (D. Ariz. 1975), *vacated and remanded*, 562 F.2d 55 (9th Cir. 1977); *Miller v. Bank of America*, 418 F. Supp. 233 (N.D. Cal. 1976), *appeal docketed*, No. 76-3344 (9th Cir. 1976); *Tomkins v. Public Service Electric & Gas Co.*, 422 F. Supp. 553 (D.N.J. 1976), *rev'd*, 568 F.2d 1044 (3rd Cir. 1977); *Garber v. Saxon Business Products, Inc.*, 552 F.2d 1032 (4th Cir. 1977); *Munford v. James T. Barnes & Co.*, 441 F. Supp. 459 (E.D. Mich. 1977); *Elliott v. Emery Air Freight*, No. C-C-75-76 (W.D.N.C. June 21, 1977); *Heelan v. Johns-Manville Corp.*, 451 F. Supp. 1382 (D. Colo. 1978). A case of sexual harassment brought as a contract action is *Monge v. Beebe Rubber*, 316 A.2d 549 (N.H. 1974). Three unreported actions for unem-

ployment compensation are based upon allegations of sexual harassment. *In re Nancy J. Fillhouer,* App. No. 75-5225, California Unemployment Insurance Appeals Board (July 25, 1975); *In re Carmita Wood,* App. No. 207, 958, New York State Department of Labor, Unemployment Insurance Appeals Board (October 6, 1975); *Cathy Hamilton v. Appleton Electric Co.,* E.R.D. Case 7301025, State of Wisconsin Department of Industry, Labor and Human Relations (October 1, 1976). In education, see *Alexander v. Yale,* 459 F. Supp. 1 (D. Conn. 1977), *supplemented,* June 30, 1978.

6. Ann Hill, "Protective Labor Legislation for Women: Its Origin and Effect" (unpublished paper, Yale Law School, 1970); Ann Hill, "Protection of Women Workers and the Courts: A Legal Case History" (unpublished paper prepared for the Conference on Protective Legislation and Women's Employment, Smith College, Northampton, Massachusetts, November 3–5, 1977); Ronnie Steinberg Ratner, "The Paradox of Protection: Changes in Hours Legislation in the United States" (unpublished paper, prepared for the same conference.)

7. The Supreme Court has held that disability insurance plans that do not cover pregnancy or pregnancy-related disabilities in employment are not illegal sex discrimination. *Geduldig v. Aiello,* 417 U.S. 484 (1974) (state plans, under the Fourteenth Amendment); *Gilbert v. General Electric,* 429 U.S. 125 (1976) (private plans, under Title VII). In October 1978, the House of Representatives agreed to the conference report on S. 995, a bill to amend Title VII to prohibit discrimination on the basis of pregnancy as sex discrimination. *Congressional Record Daily Digest,* vol. 124, no. 168, part V, October 14, 1978, D 1574 (*Congressional Record* at H13494–H13496). Congress (with the approval of the President) can thus modify the result of *Gilbert,* but it cannot so directly alter the reasoning on the meaning of sex discrimination which produced it. (The Congressional action also leaves the *Geduldig* result standing.)

8. Georg Simmel, *Philosophische Kultur* (Leipzig: Werner Klinkhardt, 1911), quoted in Lewis A. Coser, "Georg Simmel's Neglected Contributions to the Sociology of Women," *Signs: Journal of Women in Culture and Society,* vol. 2, no. 4 (Summer 1977), at 872, 873.

9. Professor Fiss, in a recent article, develops a similar distinction in his examination of equal protection cases on race. Owen Fiss, "Groups and the Equal Protection Clause," 5 *Philosophy and Public Affairs* 108 (1976). His article provided labels for the two theories and advanced and clarified them. The two theories, as I develop them, differ from his in several respects. Most obvious is that he does not directly consider whether women could be a "disadvantaged" group. The essential purpose of his theory is to justify affirmative action for blacks in higher education. The outside requirements for a group to be "disadvantaged" are not clear, especially where the criteria of biology and mutability are involved. At one point, apparently stating reasons that qualify the case for some groups to be considered disadvantaged groups,

he states that "some . . . socially disadvantaged groups can be defined in terms of characteristics that do not have biological roots and that are not immutable; the Clause might protect certain language groups and aliens." This clouds whether it is biology and immutability that qualify blacks as disadvantaged (and would also qualify women), or whether, as he more generally seems to think, blacks are disadvantaged because of their social characteristics. He continues, "the court may even develop variable standards of protection. . . . it may tolerate disadvantaging practices that would not be tolerated if the group was a 'pure' specially disadvantaged group. Jews or women may be entitled to less protection than American Indians, though nonetheless entitled to some protection" (155) (citations omitted). Treatment of the poor, a group that is, after all, totally socially created, is grudging to the point of exclusion. However strategic this may have been—in order to promote affirmative action for blacks, it is necessary to convince courts that they are not opening the door to redress of all inequalities—it does not bode well for women. His interpretation of equal protection disadvantagement would allow a legislative judgment that "the plight of tbe poor may be bad but, so the legislator or administrator should be allowed to say, not as bad as that of the blacks" (162). Given that the majority of blacks are poor, this recognizes as disadvantagement only that poverty which is attributable to racial, as distinct from economic, causes, a difficult distinction to make. Since poverty is not seen to be completely all-pervasive, cultural, disabling, maintained by false consciousness, and as difficult to change as the meaning of being black, it seems unlikely that women would fare well under this interpretation.

10. 429 U.S. 125 (1976).

11. *City of Los Angeles, Department of Water and Power, et al. v. Manhart, et al.*, 98 S.Ct. 1370 (1978).

12. Title VII of the Civil Rights Act of 1964, as amended by the Equal Employment Opportunity Act of 1972, Section 703 (a) (1) and (2), codified at 42 U.S.C. Section 2000 e (2) (a) (1) and (2). (Hereinafter, "Title VII" refers to this quoted section, unless specifically noted otherwise.) Section (b) applies the quoted section to employment agencies, (c) to labor organizations, and (d) to training programs. Section (e) provides for an exception under which sex may be shown a bona fide occupational qualification; Section (h) excepts bona fide seniority and merit systems; Section (j) prohibits "preferential treatment" based upon existing numerical or percentage imbalance.

13. *United States Constitution,* Amendment XIV.

CHAPTER 2

1. Women's labor force participation has been increasing dramatically and continuously since 1940 both in rate and in numbers. In 1975, 35 million women participated in the labor force, representing 39.3 percent of all work-

ers, 45 percent of all women. In March 1940, 25.4 percent of workers were women, 28.9 percent of all women; in 1960, 33.3 percent and 37.4 percent, respectively. Women's Bureau, *1975 Handbook on Women Workers* (hereinafter, *1975 Handbook*), Bulletin 297, U.S. Department of Labor, Employment Standards Division (1975), table 2, at 11. See also Valerie Kincade Oppenheimer, "The Female Labor Force in the United States: Demographic and Economic Factors Governing its Growth and Changing Composition" (Berkeley, California: Institute of International Studies, University of California, 1970), and Lise Vogel, "Women Workers: Some Basic Statistics" (Boston: New England Free Press, 1971).

2. Lapidus uses these analytic dimensions. Gail Warshofsky Lapidus, "Occupational Segregation and Public Policy: A Comparative Analysis of American and Soviet Patterns," *Signs: Journal of Women in Culture and Society,* vol. 1, no. 3, part 2 (Spring 1976), at 120.

3. In a good review of recent studies of women's labor force participation, Elizabeth M. Almquist concludes: "The major recommendations, then, are that research should become less generalized and more specific, less concerned with outcomes and more concerned with the process of status attainment, less attentive to the decisions women make and more attentive to the decisions employers make, less abstract in orientation and more focused on the day-to-day transactions between workers and boss." "Women in the Labor Force," *Signs: Journal of Women in Culture and Society,* vol. 2, no. 4 (Summer 1977), at 854. Research on sexual harassment meets all these requirements.

4. U.S. Census, 1960 Occupational Characteristics, quoted and discussed at table 5.1 by Harriet Zellner, "Determinants of Occupational Segregation," in Cynthia Lloyd, ed., *Sex, Discrimination and the Division of Labor* (New York: Columbia University Press, 1975), at 126.

5. Barbara B. Bergmann and Irma Adelman, "The 1973 Report of the President's Council of Economic Advisors: The Economic Role of Women," *American Economic Review,* vol. 68 (September 1973), at 510: See also *Statistical Abstract of the United States,* 1971, "Employed Persons, by Major Occupation and Sex: 1950–1971," at 222.

6. These calculations are based upon data in *1975 Handbook,* at 84 and 86. For a sensitive analysis of these dimensions of working women's lives, see Nancy Seifer, "Absent from the Majority: Working Class Women in America" (New York: Institute of Human Relations, National Project on Ethnic America of the American Jewish Committee, 1973). See also Nancy Seifer, *Nobody Speaks for Me! Self-Portraits of American Working Class Women* (New York: Simon and Schuster, 1976), for oral histories on the subjects discussed statistically in this chapter.

7. *1975 Handbook,* at 86–87.

8. *1975 Handbook,* table 36 (Manpower Report of the President, April 1974), at 84. As shown in this table, 15.6 percent of working women are in a

"professional, technical" category. Depending upon its precise parameters, given the miniscule representation of women in the professions and the lack of congruence in status between professionals and particularly lower level technicals, this category seems inapt. The vast majority of these women are probably lower level technical workers, with more in common with clericals, service workers, and factory workers than with women professionals.

9. *1975 Handbook,* at 89–91, table 38, "Employed Persons in Selected Occupations by Sex, 1973 Annual Averages."

10. Janice N. Hedges, "Women Workers and Manpower Demands in the 1970's," *Monthly Labor Review* 93 (June 1970), at 19.

11. *1975 Handbook,* at 91–92.

12. Seifer (1973), *supra,* note 6, at 29.

13. Georgina Smith, "Help Wanted—Female: A Study of Demand and Supply in a Local Job Market" (1964), quoted in Babcock, Freedman, Norton, and Ross, *Sex Discrimination and the Law: Cases and Remedies* (Boston: Little, Brown, 1975), at 209. See Babcock *et al.* for supportive materials on "sex stereotypes that make sex discrimination acceptable," at 208 ff.

14. Harry Braverman, *Labor and Monopoly Capital: The Degradation of Work in the Twentieth Century* (New York and London: Monthly Review Press, 1974), especially at 293–358; Margery Davies, "Woman's Place is at the Typewriter: The Feminization of the Clerical Labor Force," *Radical America,* vol. 8, no. 4 (July–August 1974).

15. Seifer (1973), *supra,* note 6, at 31–32; see also *1975 Handbook,* at 64 ff.

16. See C. Wright Mills, *White Collar* (New York: Oxford University Press, 1956), at 192–193.

17. Andrea Dworkin, "Phallic Imperialism: Why Economic Recovery Will Not Work For Us," *Ms.,* vol. V, no. 6 (December 1976), at 104. For data, see Ester Boserup, *Woman's Role in Economic Development* (New York: St. Martin's Press, 1970).

18. Data from *1975 Handbook,* at 97. Rosabeth M. Kanter, *Men and Women of the Corporation* (New York: Basic Books, 1977), at 17, draws a similar conclusion.

19. *1975 Handbook,* at 94–96.

20. *1975 Handbook,* at 115. For further empirical documentation of the existence, depth, and dimensions of sex segregation, see Bergmann and Adelman, *supra,* note 5, at 509–514; Francine D. Blau, "Pay Differentials and Differences in the Distribution of Employment of Male and Female Office Workers," (Ph.D. diss., Harvard University, 1975); Francine Blau Weiskoff, " 'Women's Place' in the Labor Market," *American Economic Review* 62 (May 1972), at 161–166; John E. Buckley, "Pay Differences Between Men and Women in the Same Job," *Monthly Labor Review* 94 (November 1971), at 36–39; Edward Gross, "Plus ça change...? The Sexual Structure of Occupations Over Time," *Social Problems* 16 (Fall 1968), at 198–208; Oppenheimer,

supra, note 1; Elizabeth Waldman and Beverly J. McEaddy, "Where Women Work—An Analysis by Industry and Occupation," *Monthly Labor Review* 97 (May 1974), at 3-14; and Francine Blau and Carol L. Jusenius, "Economists Approaches to Sex Segregation in the Labor Market: An Appraisal," *Signs: Journal of Women in Culture and Society,* vol. 1, no. 3, part 2 (Spring 1976), at 181-199. See generally the entire volume of *Signs: Journal of Women in Culture and Society* devoted to "The Implications of Occupational Segregation," based on a conference on occupational segregation held at Northampton, Massachusetts, May 21-23, 1973, vol. 1, no. 3, part 2 (Spring 1976 Supplement).

21. Women's Bureau, U.S. Department of Labor, Employment Standards Administration, "Women with Low Incomes" (November 1977) (hereinafter Women's Bureau, 1977), at 1.

22. U.S. Department of Commerce, Bureau of the Census, *Current Population Reports,* P-60, No. 101 (1974), issued January 1976.

23. U.S. Department of Commerce, Bureau of the Census, "Money Income of Families and Persons in the U.S.," *Current Population Reports, 1957-1975.* U.S. Department of Labor, Bureau of Labor Statistics, *Handbook of Labor Statistics,* 1975. One man's experience attempting to apply for such a "woman's job" illustrates the reality behind these data: "Galvan Pool and Sauna needs a 'Gal Friday,' and you can type, file, and transcribe from a dictaphone. The woman on the phone apologizes, 'We're only offering $95 a week, so we only want a woman.'" Rik Myslewski, "But can he type?" *Sister, Connecticut's Feminist Publication,* vol. V, no. 10 (New Haven, November 1976) at 10.

24. Women's Bureau, U.S. Department of Labor, Employment Standards Administration, "The Earnings Gap Between Women and Men" (1976), at 2-3.

25. Women's Bureau, 1977, at 5.

26. Six recent econometric studies reviewed by Bergmann and Adelman *supra,* note 5. Larry Suter and Herman Miller, in "Income Differences Between Men and Career Women," demonstrate that women receive smaller increments of income for equal increases in educational level and occupational status. In Joan Huber, ed., *Changing Women in a Changing Society* (Chicago: University of Chicago Press, 1973), at 21-22. The Carnegie Commission on Higher Education reveals a similar pattern, concluding that women faculty members earn an average of $1,500-$2,000 per year less than men in comparable positions with comparable qualifications. *Opportunities for Women in Higher Education* (New York: Carnegie Commission, 1973). See also Myra Strober, "Lower Pay for Women: A Case of Economic Discrimination," *Industrial Relations* II (May 1972), at 279-84.

27. *1975 Handbook,* at 2. Congress noted the "profound economic dis-

crimination against women workers" at H. Rep. No. 238, 92d Cong., 1st Sess., *reprinted in* [1972] *U.S. Code Cong. & Ad. News* 2137, *et seq.*

28. "The median earnings of white men employed year-round full-time is $7,369, of Negro men $4,777, of white women $4,279, of Negro women $3,194. Women with some college education both white and Negro earn less than Negro men with 8 years of education. Women head 1,732,000 impoverished families, Negro males head 820,000. One-quarter of all families headed by white women are in poverty. More than half of all headed by Negro women are in poverty. Less than a quarter of those headed by Negro males are in poverty. Seven percent of those headed by white males are in poverty." This was in 1970. "A Matter of Simple Justice, The Report of the President's Task Force on Women's Rights and Responsibilities," U.S. Government Printing Office (April 1970), at 18. See also Robert Stein, "The Economic Status of Families Headed by Women," *Monthly Labor Review* 93 (December 1970), at 7. The figures had changed little by 1972. See Women's Bureau, U.S. Department of Labor, Employment Standards Administration, "Facts About Women Heads of Households and Heads of Families" (April 1973), at 8, and *1975 Handbook,* at 141–142. Data for 1976 can be found in Women's Bureau, "Women with Low Incomes" (November 1977).

29. Women's Bureau, 1977, at 1.

30. *Id.,* at 5.

31. *1975 Handbook,* at 124.

32. *1975 Handbook,* at 19–21.

33. Women's Bureau, 1977, at 6.

34. *Id.,* at 8.

35. *1975 Handbook,* at 21.

36. Women's Bureau, 1977, at 6.

37. All data from Edna E. Raphael, "Working Women and their Membership in Unions," *Monthly Labor Review* (May 1974); see especially table 3, "Union Membership of Private Wage and Salary Workers, by occupation of longest job, industry and sex, 1970." (The author attributes her data to the Bureau of Labor Statistics.)

38. See Janice Madden, *The Economics of Sex Discrimination* (Lexington, Mass.: Heath, 1973), chap. 2.

39. Barbara Bergmann, "Economics of Women's Liberation," *Challenge,* vol. 16 (May/June 1973), at 14.

40. Mary Stevenson, "Women's Wages and Job Segregation," *Politics and Society,* vol. 4, no. 1 (Fall 1973), at 93.

41. Barbara Deckard and Howard Sherman, "Monopoly Power and Sex Discrimination," *Politics and Society,* vol. 4, no. 4 (1974), at 477.

42. A review of the growing empirical literature in this field is provided by

Andrew I. Kohen, *Women and the Economy: A Bibliography and a Review of the Literature in Sex Differentiation in the Labor Market* (Columbus, Ohio: Center for Human Resource Research, Ohio State University, 1975).

43. For a specific review of theoretical approaches to sex segregation, see Francine D. Blau and Carol L. Jusenius, *supra*, note 20, at 181–199.

44. Paul Brest, *Processes of Constitutional Decisionmaking: Cases and Materials* (Boston: Little, Brown, 1975), at 489.

45. Owen Fiss, "Groups and the Equal Protection Clause," 5 *Philosophy and Public Affairs* 108, 117 (1976). Neither Professor Fiss nor Brest considers whether it would violate equal protection of whites, if the black students wanted, for reasons of racial solidarity, to hold their own graduation, or to sit together at a regular graduation, or even to sit on the opposite side of the stage from whites.

46. The data on sex segregation in the labor force presented earlier documents this; the following commentators analyze it. Margery Davies, *supra*, note 14, at 22–23; Braverman, *supra*, note 14, at 326–348; Jean Tepperman, "60 Words a Minute and What Do You Get? Clerical Workers Today" (Somerville, Mass.: New England Free Press, n.d. [approx. 1976]); Jean Tepperman, *Not Servants, Not Machines: Office Workers Speak Out* (Boston: Beacon Press, 1976).

47. 83 percent of all "waiters, waitresses, and helpers" are female. All data for 1973 from *1975 Handbook*, at 89–91.

48. Talcott Parsons and Robert F. Bales, *Family, Socialization and Interactive Processes* (Glencoe, Ill.: Free Press, 1956), at 313.

49. Paddy Quick, "Women's Work," *The Review of Radical Political Economics* (issue on the political economy of women), vol. 14, no. 3 (July 1972), at 17.

50. Thorstein Veblen, *The Theory of the Leisure Class* (New York: Viking Press, 1964), at 51.

51. Lynn O'Conner Gardner, "Strategic View of the Labor Force: Who Can Take Power," *The Second Page* (San Francisco, April 1972), at 27.

52. Bernard M. Bass, Judith Krusell, and Ralph A. Alexander, "Male Managers' Attitudes Toward Working Women," *American Behavioral Scientist*, vol. 15, no. 2 (November–December 1971), at 221–236, 228, 232.

53. Kanter, *supra*, note 18, at 73.

54. *Id.*, at 86 and at 78, respectively.

55. Kanter, *supra*, note 18, at 234, 235.

56. Sylvia Federici, "Wages Against Housework" (Bristol, England: Falling Wall Press, 1976), at 28.

57. Paddy Quick, *supra*, note 49, at 17.

58. Lynn O'Conner Gardner, *supra*, note 51, at 27.

59. Sheila Rowbotham, *Woman's Consciousness, Man's World* (London: Penguin, 1973), at 90.

60. Kanter, *supra*, note 18, at 107. Kanter does not customarily question whether the first person reports of her subjects are right or wrong, particularly without further evidence adduced.

61. Mary Kathleen Benet, *The Secretarial Ghetto* (New York: McGraw-Hill, 1972), at 2–3.

62. W.I.T.C.H. (Women Incensed at Telephone Company Harassment), "AT&T Switchbored" (New York mimeograph, n.d.).

63. David Gurupert, "Women's Liberation Has All But Bypassed the Katy Gibbs Chain," *Wall Street Journal,* March 15, 1974, quoted in Kanter, *supra,* note 18, at 76.

64. Herbert Marcuse, *One-Dimensional Man: Studies in the Ideology of Advanced Industrial Society* (Boston: Beacon Press, 1967), at 74–75.

65. David Riesman, *The Lonely Crowd: A Study of the Changing American Character* (New Haven: Yale University Press, 1950), at 154.

66. "On the Job Oppression of Working Women: A Collection of Articles" (Boston: New England Free Press, n.d.).

67. Susan Rautenberg, "Serving Food: $elling $miles," *City Star* (New York), repr. in *Women: A Journal of Liberation,* vol. 4, no. 2 (Spring 1975), at 4.

68. Susan Madar, quoted by Enid Nemy, "Women Begin to Speak Out against Sexual Harassment at Work," in John H. Gagnon, ed., *Human Sexuality in Today's World* (Boston: Little, Brown, 1977), at 243. The relationship between employment opportunities and the need to "look a certain way" is further commented upon, with its implications for sexual harassment, at 1 *Sister Courage* 9 (October 1975), and "An Ugly Story: Homely People Need Not Apply," *Chomp: Boston's Food and Dining Magazine* (September 1976), at 13.

69. Working Women United Institute, "Speak-Out on Sexual Harassment" (Ithaca, N.Y., May 4, 1975 [typescript]), at 35.

70. In 1952 Helen Hacker observed similarities between black people as a group and women as a group. (Presumably, black women are doubly burdened.) In particular, the deferential manner in blacks corresponds to this flattering manner in women, together with careful study of points at which the dominant group is susceptible to influence, as a survival strategy. Helen Mayer Hacker, "Women as a Minority Group," *Social Forces* 30 (October 1951), at 61, reprinted in many places, including in part by Leo Kanowitz, *Sex Roles in Law and Society: Cases and Materials* (Albuquerque: University of New Mexico Press, 1973), at 1–9.

71. Ntozake Shange, *for colored girls who have considered suicide when the rainbow is enuf* (New York: Macmillan, Inc., 1977), at 39.

CHAPTER 3

1. Claire Safran, *Redbook Magazine* (November 1976), at 149 (hereinafter, *Redbook*). That respondents were self-selected is this study's most serious

drawback. Its questions are perceptively designed to elicit impressionistic data. (The questionnaire was published in the January 1976 issue.) When the results are interpreted with these characteristics in mind, the study is highly valuable. Scholars who look down upon such popular journalistic forays into policy research (especially by "women's magazines") should ask themselves why *Redbook* noticed sexual harassment before they did.

2. Much of the information in this chapter is based upon discussions with ten women who shared their experiences of sexual harassment with me from five to twenty or more hours apiece. In addition, I have studied lengthy first person written accounts by five other women. Several women reported the situations and feelings of other women who were being sexually harassed by the same man they were discussing with me. Where permission has been sought and obtained, some of this material will be quoted or referenced throughout. Where quotations in this chapter are unattributed, or statements of fact (such as the racial characteristics of victims and perpetrators) or feelings (such as caring about the man involved) are not otherwise footnoted, they are derived from one or several women from my own research.

Finally, although the context was education rather than employment, much of my grasp of sexual harassment as an experience is owed to the extensive investigation conducted at Yale from 1976 to 1978 by the plaintiffs and the Yale Undergraduate Women's Caucus Grievance Committee in connection with *Alexander v. Yale*, 459 F. Supp. 1 (D. Conn. 1977). In this research, incidents involving at least half a dozen faculty members or administrators and a total of about fifty women were systematically uncovered and pursued, to the extent the victims were willing.

3. Sex on the job has not gone entirely unnoticed; it is only sexual harassment conceived as such that has been ignored. Two examples illustrate. One study entitled "Rape at Work" reports rapes of women on their jobs by hospital or prison inmates, students or clients; employers, superiors, or co-workers are not mentioned. Carroll M. Brodsky, "Rape at Work," in Marcia J. Walker and Stanley L. Brodsky, eds., *Sexual Assault, the Victim and the Rapist* (Lexington, Mass.: D. C. Heath & Company, 1976), at 35–52. This study is useful, however, for observing dynamics of on-the-job rape that are also true for sexual harassment, whether it includes rape or not. Rape at work was experienced as worse than at other places because it had been seen as a safe place, where the woman did not have to be constantly on guard (at 43–44). And the site of the assault is difficult to avoid (at 44). In another study of "occupations and sex," the examination is divided between jobs "where the occupation involves sex"—cab driving, vice squad duty, and gynecology—and jobs "where the occupation is sex"—stripteasing and prostitution. James M. Henslin, *Studies in the Sociology of Sex* (New York: Appleton-Century-Crofts, 1971). This defines as the universe for study the rarified extremes of the

convergence of sexuality with work to the neglect of the common experience of thousands of women. See, however, Carroll M. Brodsky, *The Harassed Worker* (Lexington, Mass.: Heath, 1976), at 27–28 for a useful if brief discussion.

4. Recent attempts to understand women's experience from women's point of view have produced upheavals in standard conceptions in many academic disciplines. One clear example is in the field of history. See Gerda Lerner, *The Female Experience: An American Documentary* (Indianapolis: Bobbs-Merrill, 1977), especially the introduction; Joan Kelly-Gadol, "The Social Relation of the Sexes: Methodological Implications of Women's History," *Signs: Journal of Women in Culture and Society*, vol. 1, no. 4 (1976), at 809–824; Hilda Smith, "Feminism and the Methodology of Women's History," in Berenice A. Carroll, ed., *Liberating Women's History* (Chicago: University of Illinois Press, 1976), at 369–384.

5. References to this survey come from three sources. One is my own interpretation of a simple collation of the marginals from the survey, generously provided by Working Women United Institute (hereinafter, WWUI). The total is 145 women, because 5 women both attended the speak-out and worked in Binghamton. Whenever possible, I will refer to the published article which reports some of the data and provides some analysis. Dierdre Silverman, "Sexual Harassment: Working Women's Dilemma," *Quest: A Feminist Quarterly*, vol. III, no. 3 (1976–1977), at 15–24 (hereinafter, Silverman). Finally, Lin Farley's testimony before the Commission on Human Rights of the City of New York, Hearings on Women in Blue-Collar, Service and Clerical Occupations, "Special Disadvantages of Women in Male-Dominated Work Settings" (April 21, 1975) (mimeograph) refers to the same study.

6. United Nations Ad Hoc Group on Equal Rights for Women, Report on the Questionnaire xxxvi, Report on file at the New York University Law Review, reported in Note, 51 *New York U. L. Rev.* 148, 149, n. 6.

7. Letter of December 8, 1976, from Marie Shear, public information officer of the division, to Lynn Wehrli, copy in author's file.

8. *Redbook*, at 217, 219.

9. Nancy Seifer, "Absent from the Majority: Working Class Women in America" (New York: Institute of Human Relations, National Project on Ethnic America of the American Jewish Committee, 1973), at 11.

10. *1975 Handbook*, at 28.

11. *Redbook*, at 217. The only study I have found that sheds further light upon the statistical prevalence of sexual harassment of women is Diana E. H. Russell's 1978 pretest interviews of ninety-two women randomly selected from San Francisco households. The general purpose of the study was to investigate sexual assault and rape. Her question #46a was: "Some people

have experienced unwanted sexual advances by someone who had authority over them such as a doctor, teacher, employer, minister, or therapist. Did you ever have any kind of unwanted sexual experience with someone who had authority over you?" Responses to this question were 16.9 percent yes, 83.1 percent no. From an examination of the rest of the marginals, it seems possible that these results are low. The more specific and detailed the questions became, the higher the affirmative responses tended to be. A woman who was sexually harassed by more than one authority figure would be counted only once. The percentage of affirmative responses to this question is about the same as to the question about sexual experiences with close relatives, but lower than to those about rape. Several questions were asked about rape. Perhaps more questions on authority figures would have increased the prevalence figures. Since the sampling was done by households, the incidence of sexual harassment might not be as high as it would be in subsamples, for instance, of employed women only. Nevertheless, nearly one-fifth of *all women* is a lot of women. The most startling result of the pretest is that thirty-four respondents reported a total of sixty-five incidents of rape and attempted rape in the course of their lives, with a pair or group assault counted as one attack. This means that approximately one-third of all women have been raped, or experienced an attempted rape. The preliminary analysis of the full sample of 935 interviews will be available April 1, 1979. Information from Diana E. H. Russell, "The Prevalence of Rape and Sexual Assault," *Summary Progress Report,* March 31, 1978; Appendix IV: Edited Interview Schedule with Marginals. This research was sponsored by the National Institute of Mental Health and funded through the Center for the Prevention and Control of Rape.

12. *Redbook,* at 217; Silverman, at 18.

13. Working Women United Institute (now at 593 Park Ave., New York, N.Y. 10021) seems to have been the first to use these words as anything approaching a term of art, at first in connection with the case of Carmita Wood in October, 1975 (*infra,* note 61). The concept was also used and developed by the Alliance Against Sexual Coercion (P.O. Box 1, Cambridge, Mass. 02139), for example in their "Position Paper #1" (September 1976) and appears in Carroll Brodsky, *The Harassed Worker* (Lexington, Mass.: Heath, 1976), at 27–28.

14. Sheila Rowbotham, *Woman's Consciousness, Man's World* (London: Penguin, 1973), at 29–30.

15. Adrienne Rich, *The Dream of a Common Language, Poems 1974–1977* (New York: W. W. Norton & Co., 1978), "Cartographies of Silence," at 17.

16. This statement is supported by every study to date and by my own research. These dimensions of sexual harassment were further documented at a speak-out by Women Office Workers, 600 Lexington Avenue, New York,

N. Y., in October 1975. Accounts of the event, and WOW's complaint to the Human Rights Commission, can be found in *Majority Report,* November 1–15, 1975; Paula Bernstein, "Sexual Harassment on the Job," *Harper's Bazaar* (August 1976); *New York Daily News,* April 22, 1976; *New York Post,* April 22, 1976.

17. WWUI.

18. Silverman, at 18.

19. The information from the *Redbook* study in this paragraph is at 217, 149.

20. WWUI.

21. *Redbook,* at 217.

22. The use of pornographic videotapes is reported in "2 Phone Executives Called Promiscuous—Witnesses Tell of Sex in Offices as Trial on Wrongful Death Nears End in Texas," *New York Times,* September 3, 1977. The legal action is for the wrongful death of the man who committed suicide on being accused of a fact pattern seeming to amount to sexual harassment of many women employees.

23. *Redbook,* at 149.

24. Silverman, at 18; *Redbook,* at 217, 219.

25. WWUI; in May 1974, the median weekly earning for women working full time was $124.00. *1975 Handbook,* at 126.

26. The quotations are Ms. Munford's allegations from the Joint Pre-Trial Statement in her case, at 7 and 8, respectively. The decision in the case is *Munford v. James T. Barnes & Co.,* 441 F. Supp. 459 (E.D. Mich. 1977). In addition to Munford, the plaintiffs in *Alexander* (Price), *Barnes,* and *Miller* (see chap. 1, *supra,* note 5) are black women charging sexual harassment by white men. (Diane Williams is a black woman charging sexual harassment by a black man.)

27. First Amended Complaint for Outrageous Conduct and Slander; Law Action for Unpaid Wages; Demand for Jury Trial, Count IX, *Fuller v. Williames,* No. A7703-04001 (Ore. Cir. Ct. 1977).

28. See the discussion of vertical stratification in chap. 2.

29. See the discussion of sex roles and sexuality, in chap. 5.

30. Working Women United Institute, "Speak-Out on Sexual Harassment," Ithaca, N. Y., May 4, 1975 (typescript), at 15.

31. *Id.,* at 30.

32. Peggy A. Jackson, quoted in Jane Seaberry, "They Don't Swing to Sex on the Beat," *Washington Post,* October 13, 1975.

33. *Monge v. Beebe Rubber,* 316 A.2d 549, 560 (N.H. 1974).

34. *Redbook,* at 149.

35. See discussion in chap. 6, beginning p. 167. The reference is to the classic formulation by Herbert Magruder of the position that a man should

not be liable in tort for emotional harm resulting from his sexual advances. Magruder, "Mental and Emotional Disturbance in the Law of Torts," 49 *Harv. L. Rev.* 1033, 1055 (1936).

36. *Tomkins v. Public Service Electric & Gas Co.*, 442 F. Supp. 553 (D.N.J. 1976), *rev'd*, 568 F.2d 1044 (3d Cir. 1977).

37. Transcript of administrative hearing 171, 174, *quoted in* Brief for Appellant at 18–20.

38. *Alexander v. Yale*, 459 F. Supp. 1 (D. Conn. 1977).

39. My own research and, for example: "her new supervisor asked her to lunch to discuss a promotion. Over the meal, in a nearby hotel, he said that he wanted to go to bed with her that afternoon and that it was the only way they could have a working relationship." Ann Crittenden, "Women Tell of Sexual Harassment," *New York Times,* October 25, 1977.

40. Leslie Phillips, "For women, sexual harassment is an occupational hazard," *Boston Globe,* September 9, 1977.

41. *Tomkins, supra,* note 36 illustrates these consequences.

42. *Monge v. Beebe Rubber,* 316 A.2d 549 (N.H. 1974).

43. *Barnes v. Train,* 13 FEP Cases 123 (D.D.C. 1974), *rev'd sub nom. Barnes v. Costle,* 561 F.2d 983 (D.C. Cir. 1977). On this motion the allegations of fact are provisionally considered as if they were true.

44. *Williams v. Saxbe,* 413 F. Supp. 654, 655–6 (D.D.C. 1976). Order denying motion to dismiss and motion for summary judgment by Judge Richey.

45. Clerk's Record, *quoted in* Brief for Appellant, at 39.

46. *Id.,* at 80.

47. *Elliott v. Emery Air Freight,* No. C-C-75-76, slip opinion, at 2 (W.D.N.C. June 21, 1977).

48. Investigative Report, No. 8, 1972, *quoted in* Brief of Appellee, at 4.

49. Quoted in Enid Nemy, New York Times News Service, *Newark Star-News,* August 24, 1975. This is identical to the fact pattern in *Munford v. James T. Barnes & Co.,* 441 F. Supp. 459 (E. D. Mich. 1977).

50. *Redbook,* at 217. A recent complaint filed in the Alaska federal district court alleged that the woman was rejected for the position of equal employment officer with a pipeline contractor because she refused sexual relations with the employer's senior management official. *Rinkel v. Associated Pipeline Contractors, Inc.,* 16 E.P.D. IP#8331 (D. Alaska 1977). See also Kerri Weisel, "Title VII: Legal Protection Against Sexual Harassment," 53 *Washington Law Review* 123 (1977), at 124.

51. Constantina Safilios-Rothschild, *Women and Social Policy* (Englewood Cliffs: Prentice-Hall, 1974), at 66.

52. The legal import of this and other possible complications for sexual harassment as a cause of action is discussed in chap. 6.

53. Rothschild, *supra,* note 51, at 66.

54. *Loc. cit.*

55. See Rosabeth M. Kanter, *Men and Women of the Corporation* (New York: Basic Books, 1977), at 233–236. Gloria Steinem has suggested that "sexual harassment might be called the taming of the shrew syndrome." "Women Tell of Sexual Harassment," *New York Times,* October 25, 1977. This may be true for women who are perceived as powerful, but my investigations suggest that as many, if not more, women are sexually harassed whom the perpetrators perceive as powerless.

56. Brief for Appellants, at 17, *Corne v. Bausch & Lomb,* 562 F.2d 55 (9th Cir. 1977).

57. *Comerford v. International Harvester Co.,* 235 Ala. 376, 178 So. 894 (1938). Discharge in revenge for what was termed "the superior's failure to alienate the affections of the employee's wife" was held to impose no employer liability under a contract of employment. Here, the contract expressly provided that the employee would not be terminated as long as his services were satisfactory. The supervisor had reported that the plaintiff's services were unsatisfactory in revenge for the employee's wife's refusal of the supervisor's sexual advances. The discharge, although found malicious and improper and based on a false report of unsatisfactory performance, was held within the employer's right under the contract. This is not atypical of judicial interpretation of employment contracts.

58. *NLRB v. Apico Inns of California,* 512 F.2d 1171, 1173 (9th Cir. 1975).

59. *In re Nancy J. Fillhouer,* No. SJ-5963, California Unemployment Insurance Appeals Board (May 12, 1975) (Referee), *rev'd,* Appeals Board Decision No. 7505225 (July 2, 1975).

60. This and prior statement are contained in the statement by the referee of allegations of claimant, Decision of the Referee, at 1.

61. *In re Carmita Wood,* App. No. 207, 958, New York State Department of Labor, Unemployment Insurance Division Appeal Board (October 6, 1975).

62. Brief for Claimant-Appellant, at 1.

63. *Id.,* at 2; Affidavit of Carmita Wood, at 3.

64. Affidavit of Carmita Wood, at 3.

65. *Fuller v. Williames,* No. A7703-04001 (Ore. Cir. Ct. 1977).

66. Shulamith Firestone, "On the Job Oppression of Working Women: A Collection of Articles" (Boston: New England Free Press, n.d.).

67. An unnamed woman quoted in Nemy, *supra,* note 49.

68. *Id.* (This is a different woman from that quoted in the foregoing quotation.)

69. Silverman, at 18, 19.

70. *Redbook,* at 149; WWUI; *all* my own cases.

71. Rowbotham, *supra,* note 14, at 90.

72. Lynn Wehrli, "Sexual Harassment at the Workplace: A Feminist Analysis and Strategy for Social Change" (M.A. thesis, Massachusetts Institute of Technology, December 1976).

73. Silverman, at 19.

74. All my cases and all the studies comment upon a need to be polite during the incident, or to exit politely.

75. WWUI; Silverman, at 19.

76. Statement by [Mr. X], Lab. of Nuclear Studies, Transcript at 37, *In re Carmita Wood,* Case No. 75-92437, New York State Department of Labor, Unemployment Insurance Division (Referee).

77. *Redbook,* at 219; all my own cases mentioned this fear as substantial, even paralyzing.

78. Bill Korbel, quoted in Lin Farley, "Sexual harassment," *New York Sunday News,* August 15, 1976, at 12.

79. One Yale graduate student observed: "A student making a major complaint would expose herself in a way that's more harmful than harassment. The complaint could have a much more profound effect on your future and the focus of your education than the instance of harassment." Quoted by Alice Dembner, "A Case of Sex Discrimination," *Yale Graduate-Professional,* vol. 7, no. 14 (March 6, 1978), at 7. See also "Sexual Harassment: A Hidden Issue" (Project on the Status and Education of Women, Association of American Colleges, 1818 R. Street, N.W., Washington, D.C. 20009, June 1978), at 3; and Donna Benson, "The Sexualization of Student-Teacher Relationships" (unpublished paper: Berkeley, California, 1977).

80. Lin Farley, quoted by Enid Nemy, *supra,* note 49; see also Farley's testimony, *supra,* note 5.

81. *Redbook,* at 219.

82. *Gates v. Brockway Glass Co., Inc.,* 93 L.R.R.M. 2367 (C.D. Cal. 1976).

83. *Id.,* at 2367. See also the account by Morris Stone, "Backlash in the Workplace," *New York Times,* June 11, 1978, Business Section, p. 3.

84. Michele Noah, "Sexual Harassment on the Job," *Sister Courage* (Boston, May 1978), at 9.

85. *Loc. cit.*

86. Transcript, Permanent Commission on the Status of Women, Public Hearing, New Haven, Connecticut, January 22, 1975. A study of the role of sex in the life of the cab driver suggests a similar attitude. James M. Henslin, *Studies in the Sociology of Sex* (New York: Appleton-Century-Crofts, 1971).

87. Transcript of hearing, *In re Carmita Wood,* Case No. 75-92437, New York State Department of Labor, Unemployment Insurance Division, at 19, 37.

88. Brief for Claimant-Appellant, *In re Carmita Wood,* App. No. 207, 958, New York State Department of Labor, Unemployment Insurance Division Appeal Board (October 6, 1975), at 19.

89. Eleanor L. Zuckerman, "Masculinity and the Changing Woman," in Zuckerman, ed., *Women and Men: Roles, Attitudes and Power Relationships* (New York: Radcliffe Club of New York, ca. 1975), at 65.

90. Lin Farley, testimony, *supra,* note 5, at 6.

91. Transcript, Permanent Commission on the Status of Women, *supra,* note 86, at 5.

92. Lin Farley, testimony, *supra,* note 5, at 3.

93. One example is provided in a recent news article which reported a strike by eight waitresses against sexual harassment by the management at a restaurant in Madison, Wisconsin: "Ellen Eberle, a waitress at Dos Banditos said that sexual harassment by the management was a constant problem. ' Pete says he never touches 'his girls' but it's not true. He's touched me a number of times and I didn't like it and I've told him so. It's perverted and it makes me sick. He's very blatant about it and he makes gross jokes.' " The strike was called after the owners and management refused to listen to the grievances; the waitresses went back to work after a settlement that they described as a "complete victory." *Off Our Backs,* vol. VIII, no. 5 (May 1978), at 10.

94. Kanter, *supra,* note 55, at 88.

95. See discussion at 156–58, *infra.*

96. For commentary on this point written by men, see Jack Litewka, "The Socialized Penis," and other articles in *For Men Against Sexism,* Jon Snodgrass, ed. (Albion, Cal.: Times Change Press, 1977), at 16–35.

CHAPTER 4

1. *Corne v. Bausch & Lomb,* 390 F. Supp. 161, 163 (D. Ariz. 1975), *Tomkins v. Public Service Electric & Gas Co.,* 422 F. Supp. 553, 556 (D.N.J. 1976).

2. *Barnes v. Costle,* 561 F.2d 983, 989 (D.C. Cir. 1977).

3. *Williams v. Saxbe,* 413 F. Supp. 654, 660 (D.D.C. 1976).

4. This is one position that might be argued from *Gilbert v. General Electric,* 429 U.S. 125 (1976) and *Geduldig v. Aiello,* 417 U.S. 484 (1974). For an application of this logic to race, see *Regents of the University of California vs. Bakke,* 98 S. Ct. at 2748, n. 27 (1978).

5. This would be to apply the doctrine of *respondeat superior* or a strict rule of agency in the Title VII context.

6. *Barnes v. Costle,* 561 F.2d 983, 999–1000 (D.C. Cir. 1977); *Heelan v. Johns-Manville Corp.,* 451 F. Supp. 1382, 1389–1390 (D. Colo. 1978).

7. *Miller v. Bank of America*, 418 F. Supp. 233, 236 (N.D. Cal. 1977). *Corne v. Bausch & Lomb*, 390 F. Supp. 161, 163 (D. Ariz. 1975) also seems to suggest this. See also *Barnes v. Costle*, 561 F.2d 983, 999 (D.C. Cir. 1977).

8. *Barnes v. Costle*, 561 F.2d 983, 995 (D.C. Cir. 1977) (MacKinnon, J., concurring). *Alexander v. Yale*, 459 F. Supp. 1 (D. Conn. 1977). The most recent case to address this issue, *Heelan v. Johns-Manville Corp.*, 451 F. Supp. 1382 (D. Colo. 1978), does not fully resolve it because the company's procedures were found inadequate to its notice of the problem's existence. *Heelan* holds that the company's investigation was insufficiently broad, deep, or thorough to satisfy its obligation under Title VII, given that the plaintiff "did everything within her power to bring her charges to the attention of top management." *Id.*, at 1389. The court therefore does not need to reach the more difficult issue of inadequacy of result in the face of adequacy of procedure.

9. See *supra*, note 4.

10. 390 F. Supp. 161 (D. Ariz. 1975), *vacated and remanded*, 562 F.2d 55 (9th Cir. 1977). Although the reporter indicates nothing about the remand, it apparently concerns the issue of deferral to the state agency, not the issue of sexual harassment as such.

11. 418 F. Supp. 233 (N.D. Cal. 1976), *appeal docketed*, No. 76-3344 (9th Cir. 1976).

12. 390 F. Supp., at 163.

13. 418 F. Supp., at 236.

14. 390 F. Supp., at 163.

15. *Barnes v. Train*, 13 FEP Cases 123, 124 (D.D.C. 1974).

16. 422 F. Supp. 553 (D.N.J. 1976).

17. 413 F. Supp. 654 (D.D.C. 1976). Both *Williams* and *Barnes* arose under provisions of Title VII covering federal employees, which language is slightly more activist in tone than corresponding provisions covering private employees (see chap. 1, *supra*, note 12), although nothing has been made of this difference in the cases. 42 U.S.C. Section 2000e-16(a) as amended, 1972, states: "All personnel actions affecting employees . . . in executive agencies [of the United States] . . . shall be *made free from* any discrimination based on . . . sex" (emphasis added).

18. *Garber* was reversed and remanded, 552 F.2d 1032 (4th Cir. 1977).

19. *Barnes v. Costle*, 561 F.2d 983 (D.C. Cir. 1977).

20. *Tomkins v. Public Service Electric & Gas Co.*, 568 F.2d 1044 (3d Cir. 1977).

21. *Garber v. Saxon Business Products Inc.*, 552 F.2d 1032 (4th Cir. 1977).

22. *Munford v. James T. Barnes & Co.*, 441 F. Supp. 459 (E.D. Mich. 1977).

23. *Elliott v. Emery Air Freight*, No. C-C-75–76 (W.D.N.C. June 21, 1977).

24. *Heelan v. Johns-Manville Corp.*, 451 F. Supp. 1382 (1978). *Corne, Miller,*

Tomkins, and *Garber* all arose on defendants' motions to dismiss for failure to state a claim. In order to resolve the issue of whether these facts present a good *legal* claim, the alleged facts are provisionally treated as true, for purposes of the resolution of the legal issue only. *Barnes* and *Williams* included, in addition to motions to dismiss, plaintiffs' motions for judgment. *Williams* arose on review of an administrative record. In a review of the administrative record, with motion for judgment, the truth of the facts pleaded is not disputed, although the adequacy of the factual record is. In *Williams,* the major issue finally appealed was whether the plaintiff should have a trial *de novo* (a whole new trial) or whether a court review of her claim on the basis of the administrative record was sufficient. The issue of sexual harassment as sex discrimination was briefed on appeal but settled out of court. For the chronology, see *Williams v. Bell,* No. 76-1833 (D.C. Cir. September 19, 1978) (slip opinion, at 8, n. 33).

25. Brief for Appellants, at 17.

26. 390 F. Supp., at 163.

27. Brief for Appellees, at 30.

28. 390 F. Supp., at 163–164.

29. 418 F. Supp., at 234.

30. The individual supervisor was, apparently, not joined.

31. 418 F. Supp., at 236.

32. 418 F. Supp., at 236, n. 2.

33. Quoted in Plaintiff's Response to Defendant's Motion to Dismiss and for Summary Judgment, February 23, 1976, at 5.

34. 418 F. Supp., at 236.

35. 413 F. Supp., at 655–656. On appeal, the Organization of Black Activist Women filed a brief *amicus curiae,* which is of special interest since both the perpetrator and victim were black.

36. Complaint Adjudication Officer, December 21, 1973, *quoted in* the district court's opinion, 413 F. Supp., at 656.

37. Report of Hearing Examiner, *quoted in* Brief of Appellee to the United States District Court for the District of Columbia, *Bell. v. Williams,* 413 F. Supp. 654 (D.D.C. 1976).

38. Decision of Hearing Examiner, at 4 (February 21, 1975), as quoted in the district court's opinion, 413 F. Supp., at 656.

39. 413 F. Supp., at 657.

40. 413 F. Supp., at 657–658.

41. 413 F. Supp., at 660.

42. 413 F. Supp., at 660, n. 8.

43. 413 F. Supp., at 660.

44. Complaint of plaintiff, *quoted in* Brief for Appellant, at 5.

45. Barnes originally complained of race discrimination.

46. *Barnes v. Train,* 13 FEP Cases 123, 124 (D.D.C. 1974).

47. The Civil Service Board of Administrative Review, *quoted in* Brief for Appellee at 12.

48. *Barnes v. Costle,* 561 F.2d 983 (D.C. Cir. 1977). The concurrence agreed with this result on the question of law.

49. *Id.,* at 994.

50. Brief for Appellant, at 14.

51. *Id.,* at 13 (emphasis in original).

52. Brief for Appellee, at 19.

53. *Id.,* at 20.

54. *Id.,* at 21, n. 12. See also at 23.

55. *Id.,* at 27.

56. 561 F.2d, at 989–990.

57. 561 F.2d, at 992, n. 68.

58. 561 F.2d, at 1000 (MacKinnon, J., concurring).

59. Before the opinion was filed, the Government moved for a remand on the ground that the Civil Service Commission had concluded, with the benefit of a change in administration, that the behavior complained of was a good cause of action under Title VII. "[C]onditioning employment benefits upon an employee's compliance with his or her supervisor's demands for sexual favors—if true, constitutes sex discrimination within the meaning of Title VII." Motion to Remand, *Barnes v. Train,* 13 FEP Cases 123 (D.C. Cir. 1977). This shift in position toward the view that sexual harassment is sex discrimination appears to insure that neither *Barnes* nor *Williams* will go to the Supreme Court on this issue.

60. Complaint, *Garber v. Saxon Business Products, Inc.,* C.A. No. 75-778-4, Filed E.D. Va., October 28, 1975, at 3.

61. Bill McAllister, "Woman Refusing Sex to Boss Can Sue, Court Holds," *Washington Post,* February 15, 1977.

62. 552 F.2d 1032 (4th Cir. 1977).

63. Account from brief for plaintiff, Memorandum in Opposition to Defendant Company's Motion to Dismiss Plaintiff's Title VII Claim at 1–3.

64. Memorandum in Opposition to Defendant Company's Motion to Dismiss Plaintiff's Title VII Claim, *Tomkins v. Public Service Electric & Gas Co.,* 422 F. Supp. 553 (D.N.J. 1976), at 11.

65. 422 F. Supp., at 556.

66. *Id.*

67. *Id.,* at n.

68. 422 F. Supp., at 557.

69. 422 F. Supp., at 557. On appeal, the EEOC as *amicus curiae* argued against this view, stating that not every sexual advance affected employment opportunities. "We simply do not share that particularly jaundiced view of human nature that every sexual advance contains an implied threat that non-

compliance will bring forth employment retaliation." Brief of the Equal Employment Opportunity Commission as *amicus curiae,* at 15.

70. 422 F. Supp., at 557.

71. 568 F.2d 1044, 1047 (3d Cir. 1977).

72. *Id.,* at 1047.

73. 568 F.2d at 1048–1049.

74. No. C-C-75-76 (W.D.N.C. 1977), at 1–2.

75. From Memorandum Opinion, *Munford v. James T. Barnes & Co.,* Civil No. 6-72240 (E.D. Mich, Southern Division 1977). Defendants stipulated to the facts for purpose of the motion for summary judgment. As reported, see *Munford v. James T. Barnes & Co.,* 441 F. Supp. 459 (E.D. Mich. 1977).

76. Joint Pre-Trial Statement, *Munford v. James T. Barnes & Co.,* disputed fact, at 8.

77. 441 F. Supp. 459, 466 (E.D. Mich. 1977).

78. 441 F. Supp., at 466.

79. *Id.,* at 466.

80. *Id.,* at 466–467.

81. Complaint, *Virginia A. Morgenheim v. Jhan Hiber and Midnight Sun Broadcasters Inc,* Superior Court, State of Alaska, Third Judicial District at Anchorage, December 29,1975. All following quotations are from the complaint.

82. *Media Report to Women,* November 1, 1976.

83. 451 F. Supp. 1382, 1390 (D. Colo. 1978).

84. 451 F. Supp., at 1389.

85. *Id.,* at 1385. The judge noted that he had, in determining credibility, taken into account motive, state of mind, strength of memory, demeanor, manner while on the witness stand, factors which affect recollection, opportunity to observe and accurately relate the matters discussed, whether the testimony was contradicted or supported by other evidence, the bias, prejudice, and interest of the witnesses, their relations, and the manner in which each might be affected by a decision in the case. *Id.,* at 1385.

86. *Id.,* at 1385.

87. *Id.,* at 1385.

88. *Id.,* at 1387.

89. *Id.,* at 1388, 1390.

90. *Id.,* at 1389, n. 5.

91. *Id.,* at 1389.

92. *Id.,* at 1388.

93. *Id.,* at 1390. It is also noteworthy that the court had "considered and reject[ed] JM's argument that plaintiff failed to take advantage of JM's internal grievance procedures. First, the evidence fails to establish the existence of any such procedure and second, during her tenure plaintiff advised top management of her allegations." *Id.,* at 1389.

94. *Id.*, at 1391. "Appropriate considerations include the difference between the salary plaintiff would have made had she remained in the JM organization and that which she actually made since her departure by way of unemployment compensation, wages, and the like." *Id.*, at 1391.

95. *Hamilton v. Appleton Electric Co.*, Findings of Fact, Conclusions of Law, Order and Memorandum Decision, E.R.D. Case #7301025, State of Wisconsin Department of Industry, Labor and Human Relations, October 1, 1976.

96. *Id.*

97. *In re Carmita Wood*, Case No. 75-92437, New York State Department of Labor Unemployment Insurance Appeals Board, Decision and Notice of Decision, March 7, 1975 (unreported).

98. *In re Nancy J. Fillhouer*, Case No. 75-5225, California Unemployment Insurance Appeals Board, Referee's Decision No. 55-5963, *reversed on appeal*, July 24, 1975 (unreported).

99. The account of the facts is from Brief on Behalf of Claimant-Appellant at 1–7. Affidavit of C——— K——— contained the quotation following.

100. Referee #75-92437, referred to in Decision of the Board, New York State Department of Labor, *supra*, note 97.

101. Examination of Ms. Wood revealed this pattern. (Affidavit of Sara Pines, psychotherapist.)

102. Brief on Behalf of Claimant-Appellant, *supra*, note 99.

103. Decision of the Board, New York State Department of Labor, *supra*, note 97.

104. Facts from Decision of the Referee, *In re Nancy J. Fillhouer*, Case No. SJ-5963, William J. Costello, Referee (San Jose Referee Office, April 28, 1975).

105. *Id.*

106. Quoted in Rina Rosenberg, "A Woman Must Persevere in Battle Against Sexism," *Santa Clara Sun*, August 26, 1975, at 6.

107. Appeals Board Decision No. P-B-139 (California), citing Appeals Board Decision No. P-B-126 (California), as cited in *Fillhouer, supra*, note 104.

108. Appeals Board Decision No. P-B-139 (California), as cited in *Fillhouer, supra*, note 104. Legislatures are beginning to propose unemployment insurance benefits for women who quit or are fired due to sexual harassment. A proposed Amendment to the New York State Unemployment Insurance Law, which died in committee in 1978, would have included sexual harassment as "good cause" for "voluntary separation" from work, thus entitling the worker to benefits. The language was:

A voluntary separation shall be deemed to be for good cause if it occurred as a consequence of physical or verbal harassment based upon the claimant's age, race, creed, color, national origin, sex or disability. Such a claimant shall not be denied unemployment benefits solely because the employer had no knowledge of such harassment if the claimant's supervisor knew of such harassment or should have known had he or she used due diligence in the exercise of his or her supervisory functions." A-7614, S-5215, Proposed Amendment to Section 593 (1) (a) of Article 18, New York State Labor Law.

The legislative history would have had to clarify that sexual harassment is harassment "based on sex," since the term of the provision itself does not guarantee such an interpretation, nor does the judicial history of the issue.

The Wisconsin bill #450 is more carefully drafted in this latter regard. Proposed by State Representative James Rutkowski, the bill provides that a person who quits a job because of sexual harassment may not be deprived of unemployment benefits (under Section 108.04 (7) *Wisconsin Statutes*). The language of the bill, which was signed on May 2, 1978, reads:

Paragraph (a) [prohibiting unemployment benefits if an employee quits] shall not apply if the department determines that the employe [*sic*] terminated because the employer made employment, compensation, promotion or job assignments contingent upon the employe's consent to sexual contact or sexual intercourse as defined in Section 940.225 (5).

The reference is to Wisconsin's new sexual assault statute, which defines "sexual contact" as

any intentional touching of the intimate parts, clothed or unclothed, of a person to the intimate parts, clothed or unclothed, of another, or the intentional touching by hand, mouth or object of the intimate parts, clothed or unclothed, of another, if that intentional touching can reasonably be construed as being for the purpose of sexual arousal or gratification.

"Intimate parts" is defined as a human breast, buttock, anus, penis, vagina, or pubic mound. "Sexual intercourse" is defined as "cunnilingus, fellatio, anal intercourse or any other intrusion, however slight, of any part of a person's body or of any object into the genital or anal opening of another." Section 940.225 (5) *Wisconsin Statutes*. The new sexual harassment law also amends the Wisconsin Fair Employment Act to include sexual harassment. It amends Section 111.32 (5)(g) which reads "it is discrimination because of sex" to add: "For any employer, labor organization, licensing agency or person to make hiring, employment, admission, licensure, compensation, promotion or job assignments contingent upon a person's consent to sexual contact or sexual intercourse as defined in Section 940.225 (5)" (the sexual assault statute recounted *supra*). Although this law is a tremendous improvement, it does take a rather narrow view of what contact is sexual. In addition, the application of the criminal definition does not appear to prohibit verbal sexual harassment *per se*, but only allows it to be part of a showing that consent to physical acts was required as a job condition. Short of physical touching as defined by the assault statute, it would seem necessary to show that it was consent to these particular criminal acts that a harasser had in mind in his verbal sexual advances, rather than allowing the verbal advances to be injuries in themselves.

109. 316 A.2d 549 (N.H. 1974).

110. Consent Order, 422 F. Supp. 553 (D.N.J. 1976).

111. Order, C.A. No. 74-186 (D.D.C. June 30, 1976). Paulette Barnes settled for $18,000. Gloria Berger, "GS-5 is awarded $18,000 in Sexual Harassment Suit," *Washington Star,* March 1, 1978.

112. *Elliott v. Emery Air Freight,* No. C-C-75-76 (W.D.N.C. June 21, 1977). A case alleging "firing for resisting the amorous advances of her immediate supervisor" was tried to a jury, according to the *San Juan* (Puerto Rico) *Star* of September 19, 1975, winning a verdict of $70,000 ($20,000 compensatory, $50,000 punitive) on September 26, 1975, according to the Commission on the Status of Women, Santa Clara County, San Jose, California. *Madeline Leon Salas de Vila v. Cruz Ayala.* Confirmation of these facts has been obtained from Attorney Judith Berkan (December 1977, personal communication). The government's motion to set aside the verdict is undecided as of May 1978.

113. A critical analysis of this issue, given its minor place in the cases to date, but its major role in the affirmative argument here advanced, is deferred for full development in chap. 6.

114. *In re Wood,* quoting the referee.

115. *In re Wood,* transcript of hearing, at 36.

116. *In re Wood,* referee quoted in Brief on Behalf of Claimant-Appellant, at 19.

117. *Barnes v. Train,* Brief for Appellee, at 2. (This is the government's formulation of plaintiff's complaint.)

118. Memorandum and Order, John Lewis Smith, J., August 9, 1974, *quoted in* Brief for Appellant, at 7, and in the Joint Appendix, at 165. Reported at *Barnes v. Train,* 13 FEP Cases 123 (D.D.C. 1974).

119. 390 F. Supp., at 163.

120. Brief for Appellee, at 33.

121. *Id.,* at 28.

122. *In re Fillhouer, supra,* note 98.

123. 422 F. Supp., at 553, 556.

124. Memorandum in Support of Motion for Stay of Discovery (May, 1978), *Alexander v. Yale,* 459 F. Supp. 1 (D. Conn. 1977).

125. *State of Washington v. Wanrow,* 559 P.2d 548 (Wash. 1977).

126. *Williams,* 413 F. Supp. at 60, n. 8; complaint in *Garber,* pars. 4–7.

127. 418 F. Supp. 233, 236 (N.D. Cal. 1976) ("consistent" is distinguished from "isolated" and impact is sought on "a definable employee *group*" [emphasis added]).

128. *Id.,* at 234, n. 1. The conclusion itself was also disputed by the plaintiff on appeal. Note also that the protection from discrimination, at least in the racial context, is often stressed as a "*personal* right." *Shelley v. Kraemer,* 334

U.S. 1, 22 (1948). See also *Regents v. Bakke,* 98 S.Ct. at 2753 1978 and *Furnco Construction Corp. v. Waters,* 57 L. Ed. 2d 957, 969 (June 29, 1978).

129. 451 F. Supp. 1382, 1388 (D. Colo. 1978).

130. *Id.,* at 1389.

131. Speak-Out transcript, chap. 2, *supra,* note 67.

132. But some courts grant recovery in tort for dignitary harm on a racial theory, see chap. 6, *infra,* note 90.

133. Quoted at 413 F. Supp. 654, 656. (emphasis added).

134. 418 F. Supp. 233, 236 (N.D. Cal. 1976).

135. Answering Brief for Defendants-Appellees, at 32–33.

136. 422 F. Supp. 553, 556 (D.N.J. 1976).

137. "It can hardly be claimed any longer that men have greater 'sex drives' and therefore, a lesser expression of sex must be attributed to an inhibition on the part of women to display sexual interest in this manner." Nancy Henley, "Power, Sex and Nonverbal Communication," in Thorne and Henley, eds., *Language and Sex: Difference and Dominance* (Rowley, Mass.: Newbury House, Publishers, 1975), at 193. G. Schmidt and V. Sigusch in a study entitled "Women's Sexual Arousal" reported little gender difference in physiological or self-ratings of sexual arousal in response to erotic stimuli, in J. Zubin and J. Money, *Contemporary Sexual Behavior: Critical Issues in the 1970s* (Baltimore: Johns Hopkins University Press, 1973), at 117–143. Such differences are widely attributed to cultural factors. See, for example, W. J. Gadpaille, "Innate masculine-feminine differences," 7 *Med. Asp. Hum. Sexuality* 141–157 (1973) and references in chap. 6, *infra,* notes 17–45.

138. Vivien Stewart in "Social Influences on Sex Differences in Behavior" notes, "the contemporary feminist movement has made us so aware of the malleability of what were once considered 'eternal verities' that the impact of social forces on sex differences in behavior hardly seems to require documentation," in M. Tietelbaum, ed., *Sex Differences: Social and Biological Perspectives* (Garden City, New York: Anchor Press, Doubleday, 1976), at 138. The article summarizes research on social mechanisms and processes by which "babies born with male and female physical characteristics *are transformed into* 'masculine' and 'feminine' adults." *Id.,* at 138 (emphasis added). Reviewing the mass of evidence in his chapter entitled "Biological Influences on Sex Differences in Behavior," Ashton Barfield comes to a similar conclusion about sexual behavior in particular. "Adult androgen [male hormone] levels may contribute to libido, but so can experience and attitude. . . . Cultural factors influence the types of stimuli which cause arousal and the choice of sex object." Tietelbaum, at 108. See also references in chap. 6, *infra,* note 106.

139. Justice Brennan for the plurality in *Frontiero v. Richardson,* 411 U.S. 677, 684 (1973).

140. 413 F. Supp. 654 (D.D.C. 1976). "Whether this case presents a policy or practice of imposing a condition of sexual submission on the female employees of the CRS or whether this was a non-employment related personal encounter requires a factual determination." *Id.*, at 660. See also *Price v. Lawhon Furniture Co.*, 16 E.P.D. IP #8342 (D. Ala. 1978).

141. 42 U.S.C. 2000(e)(b).

142. This was recognized in *Tomkins*, 422 F. Supp. 553, 556 (D.N.J. 1976). See also *Anderson v. Methodist Evangelical Hospital*, 464 F.2d 723 (6th Cir. 1972); *Tidwell v. American Oil Co.*, 332 F. Supp. 424 (D. Utah 1971); *Slack v. Havens*, 7 F.E.P. Cases 885 (S.D. Cal. 1973).

143. [1973] EEOC Decisions (CCH) ¶6347 (1972).

144. EEOC Decision No. 71-1442.

145. See *Monroe v. Pape*, 365 U.S. 167, 187 (1961).

146. See *Clairborne v. Illinois Central R.R. Co.*, 401 F. Supp. 1022 (E.D. La. 1975), *but cf. Richerson v. Jones*, 551 F.2d 918 (3d Cir. 1977).

147. 390 F. Supp. 163.

148. 418 F. Supp. 233, 234. Apparently, its *written* policy did not include the term *sexual advances*.

149. 390 F. Supp., at 163, meaning, presumably, another "person (employee)."

150. 418 F. Supp. 233, 234.

151. 422 F. Supp. 553, 557.

152. *Report of the District of Columbia Task Force on Rape*, July 9, 1973, at 4–5; Lynn Wehrli, "Sexual Harassment at the Workplace: A Feminist Analysis and Strategy for Social Change," (M.A. thesis, Massachusetts Institute of Technology, December 1976), pursues the parallel between conceptions of rape and sexual harassment throughout, particularly in chap. 6. See also *People v. Rincon-Pineda*, 123 Cal. Rptr. 119, 126, 538 P.2d 247 (1975).

153. Menachem Amir, *Patterns in Forcible Rape* (Chicago: University of Chicago Press, 1971), at 26–29, 279–291. Of course, this does not allow predictions to be made in individual cases.

154. Wehrli, *supra*, note 152, at 39.

155. Kanter, *Men and Women of the Corporation* (New York: Basic Books, 1977), at 83.

156. The example is adapted from an actual case, *Slack v. Havens*, 7 FEP Cases 885 (S.D. Cal. 1973), *aff'd*, 522 F.2d 1091 (9th Cir. 1975). See also EEOC Decision No. 71-2227 (1971). (Two black female employees selected for personal service at employer's home found discrimination based on race and sex in terms and conditions of employment.)

157. The EEOC case making this distinction as to sex is discussed in chap. 6, *infra*.

CHAPTER 5

1. Simone de Beauvoir, *The Second Sex* (New York: Alfred A. Knopf, 1952, Bantam ed., 1970), at 249.

2. Owen Fiss, "Groups and the Equal Protection Clause," 5 *Philosophy and Public Affairs* 108 (1976).

3. *Reed v. Reed*, 404 U.S. 71, 76 (1971). The stiffest "arbitrariness" standard is illustrated by *Flemming v. Nestor*, 363 U.S. 603 (1960), which held that a statute which withheld noncontractual Social Security benefits from the class of aliens deported for Communist Party membership would have been illegal only "if the statute manifest[s] a patently arbitrary classification, utterly lacking in rational justification." *Id.*, at 611. This stringent approach has been applied in many recent cases, not in sex discrimination context. *Mathews v. DeCastro*, 429 U.S. 181 (1976) (distinguishing between divorced and married women in Social Security benefits); *Mathews v. Lucas*, 427 U.S. 495 (1976) (denying benefits to a class of illegitimates under Social Security); *Weinberger v. Salfi*, 422 U.S. 749 (1975) (requiring widows to be married nine months to be a recipient of Social Security benefits permitted). A similar approach was taken in *Jefferson v. Hackney*, 406 U.S. 535 (1972); *Richardson v. Belcher*, 404 U.S. 78 (1971); *Dandridge v. Williams*, 397 U.S. 471 (1970). But compare, in illegitimacy context, *Jimenez v. Weinberger*, 417 U.S. 628 (1974); *Weber v. Aetna Casualty and Survivorship Co.*, 406 U.S. 164 (1972); *Levy v. Louisiana*, 391 U.S. 68 (1968). This analysis is supported by citations in Emily Leader, "Equal Protection and Sex Discrimination: Evolution of a Constitutional Safeguard in *Califano v. Goldfarb*," 4 *Women's Rights Law Reporter*, 115, 117, nn. 38 and 40.

4. The test is from a race case, *Griggs v. Duke Power*, 401 U.S. 424 (1971). Recent considerations of applications to sex can be found at *Gilbert v. General Electric*, 429 U.S. 125, 137 (1976), *City of Los Angeles, Department of Water and Power v. Manhart*, 98 S. Ct. 1370, 1386 (1978) (Marshall, J., concurring).

5. *Frontiero v. Richardson*, 411 U.S. 677, 689 n. 22 (1973).

6. Ruth B. Ginsburg, *Constitutional Aspects of Sex-Based Discrimination* (St. Paul, Minn.: West Publishing Co., 1974), at 89.

7. 429 U.S. 125 (1976).

8. Section 703 (a)(1) and (2) of Title VII, 42 U.S.C. Section 2000e-2 (a)(1) and (2). Since *Gilbert* was decided, the state courts of four states have declined to follow its reasoning and reached opposite results under state discrimination laws. *Brooklyn Union Gas Co. v. New York State Human Rights Appeal Bd.*, 41 N.Y. 2d 84 (1976); *Anderson v. Upper Bucks County Area Vocational Technical School*, 36 Pa. Comnwl. Ct. 103 (1977); *Time Ins. Co. v. Departments of Industry and Human Relations*, No. 154-423 (Wis. Cir. Ct., Dane County, January 3, 1978); *Massachusetts Electric Company v. Massachusetts Commission Against Dis-*

crimination, 375 N.E.2d 1192 (Mass. 1978). *But cf. Narragansett Electric Co. v. Rhode Island Commission for Human Rights,* 374 A.2d 1022 (R.I. 1977).

9. 429 U.S. 125, at 147 (Brennan, J. dissenting).

10. *Id.,* at 147.

11. *Id.*

12. Brief by the Equal Employment Opportunities Commission, as *amicus curiae,* at 12, quoted at *id.*

13. Diane Zimmerman in an excellent article essentially predicted the *Gilbert* result through implicitly examing but not fully generalizing a theory of the two approaches. "*Geduldig v. Aiello:* Pregnancy Classifications and the Definition of Sex Discrimination," 75 *Columbia Law Review* 441 (1975).

14. For a review of the issues for sex discrimination raised by pregnancy, see Peratis and Rindskopf, "Pregnancy Discrimination as a Sex Discrimination Issue," 2 *Women's Rights Law Reporter* 26 (1975).

15. 429 U.S. 125, 148.

16. *Dothard v. Rawlinson,* 433 U.S. 321 (1977).

17. In order, the cases are: *Smith v. Liberty Mutual Insurance Co.,* 395 F. Supp. 1098 (N.D. Ga. 1975); *Tomlin v. U.S. Air Force Medical Center,* 369 F. Supp. 353 (S.D. Ohio 1974); *Bellamy v. Mason's Stores Center,* 368 F. Supp. 1025 (E.D. Va. 1973); *Johnson v. Pike Corporation,* 332 F. Supp. 490 (C.D. Cal. 1971); *McDonnell Douglas Corporation v. Green,* 411 U.S. 792 (1973).

18. *Royster Guano v. Virginia,* 253 U.S. 412, 415 (1920), *quoted in .Reed v. Reed,* 404 U.S. 71, 76 (1971).

19. For a discussion of this approach, see *Frontiero v. Richardson,* 411 U.S. 677 (1973) and citations therein.

20. 404 U.S. 71 (1977). To be resolved was "whether a difference in the sex of competing applicants for letters of administration bears a rational relationship that is sought to be advanced by the statute." *Id.,* at 76.

21. *Reed v. Reed,* 93 Idaho 511, 514 (1970).

22. 404 U.S. 71, 76 (1971).

23. *Id.,* at 76.

24. In fact, the appellee had argued that the mandatory preference for male applicants was reasonable since "men [are] as a rule more conversant with business affairs than [women]" and "it is a matter of common knowledge that women still are not engaged in politics, the professions, business or industry to the extent that men are" as quoted in *Frontiero v. Richardson,* 411 U.S. 677, 678, n. 11 (1973). Which is true, sex discrimination being what it is.

25. Tussman and tenBroek, "The Equal Protection of the Laws," 37 *California Law Review* 341, 346 (1949). The authors did not use the term *fit,* but their diagrams illustrating overinclusiveness, *id.,* at 351 (or overbreadth) and underinclusiveness, *id.,* at 348, in classifications suggested the term, which is now commonly used. See Ely, "The Constitutionality of Reverse Discrimina-

tion," 41 *Chicago Law Review* 723, 727, n. 26 (1974) and Fiss, *supra*, note 2, at 111 and 112, nn. 2 and 3 (1976).

26. Even apparently biological facts may be socially caused. "A significant part of the longevity differential may be explained by the social fact that men are heavier smokers than women. . . . perhaps even the lingering effects of past employment discrimination" might affect the differential. 98 S.Ct. 1370, 1376, 1376 n. 17. When justices Burger and Rehnquist, in their dissent in *Manhart*, observed that "for whatever reasons or combination of reasons," 98 S.Ct. 1370, 1384 (1978), women and men differ in longevity, they missed an important point. The reasons matter.

27. 347 U.S. 483 (1954).

28. 163 U.S. 537 (1896). In holding that "separate educational facilities are inherently unequal" *Brown v. Board of Education*, 347 U.S. 483, 495, was taken by many to overrule *Plessy*, and the reasoning of *Plessy* was expressly "rejected," 347 U.S., at 494–495. But because *Brown* was not a transportation case, others set *Plessy*'s explicit demise at the affirmance, without opinion, of the lower court ruling in *Gayle v. Browder*, 352 U.S. 903 (1956), two years later. It appears, in point of fact, that although *Plessy* presumably has no remaining vitality, it has never been overruled by the Supreme Court in so many words.

29. 163 U.S., at 551–552.

30. 347 U.S. 483, 494, n. 11 (1954).

31. It is perhaps well to recall that there was a time when racial differences were considered matters of biological fact, supported by scientific evidence, and believed determinative of the inferior social status occupied by "inferior" races. Abraham Lincoln illustrates: "and I will say . . . that there is a physical difference between the white and black races which I believe will forever forbid the two races living together on terms of social and political equality. And inasmuch as they cannot so live, while they do remain together there must be the position of superior and inferior, and I as much as any am in favor of having the superior position assigned to the white race." Quoted in Thomas S. Gossett, *Race: The History of an Idea in America* (New York: Schocken Books, 1965), at 254. See also W. R. Stanton, *The Leopard's Spots: Scientific Attitudes Toward Race in America, 1915–1959* (Chicago: University of Chicago Press, 1960); W. D. Jordan, *White Over Black: American Attitudes Toward the Negro, 1550–1812* (Williamsburg, Va.: University of North Carolina Press, 1968).

32. The other possibility, that the treatment is "discriminatory but justified," is considered at Appendix A.

33. 429 U.S. 125, 138–139 (1976).

34. See, *e.g., Geduldig v. Aiello,* 417 U.S. 484 (1974).

35. 98 S.Ct. 347 (1977).

36. *Id.,* at 351.

37. *Id.*, at 351. Brief consideration of sexual harassment in this context reveals the inadequacy of this distinction. If a woman is forced to comply with sexual demands as the price for promotion, is her refusal, with the result of nonpromotion, a "withholding of benefits" or an "imposing of burdens"? Clearly a benefit is being withheld, but it is being withheld over her refusal to have a burden imposed upon her. She could act to secure the benefit by meeting the burden imposed. Much like the distinction between rights and privileges, benefits withheld are not readily differentiable from burdens imposed.

38. 98 S.Ct., at 352-353.

39. *Id.*, at 351. Smelling inequality in these practices, Justice Powell would have allowed the plaintiff on remand, to attempt to prove that the sick leave policy was worth more to men than to women. The combined operation of the mandatory maternity leave policy with the denial of accumulated sick-pay benefits might yield "significantly less net compensation" for female employees than for male employees, since only the women endured forced absence from work without compensation of any kind. Male workers were not subjected to any mandatory leave policy and are "eligible to receive compensation in some form for any period of absence from work due to sickness or disability." *Id.*, at 356. This contrasts with the *Gilbert* approach since it treats pregnancy as a work disability like any other.

40. *Id.*, at 358.

41. *Id.*, at 358-359.

42. *Id.*, at 359.

43. In *Geduldig*, 417 U.S., at 496-497, n. 20. Applied in *Gilbert*, 429 U.S., at 135.

44. 429 U.S., at 136.

45. Knowing with any exactness which working age women will become pregnant is virtually impossible although the risks vary. If all women would forseeably become pregnant, most jobs would probably have male sex as a BFOQ, and no talk of "pretexts" would be necessary. As it is, pregnant women distinguish themselves from all women, both to themselves and to their employers, only after it is too late to tell (or to matter) whether pregnancy was excluded from disability coverage in order to discriminate against all women or only to exclude from benefits those women who become pregnant.

46. See, for further discussion, *Sims v. Sheet Metal Workers Local 65*, 353 F. Supp. 22, 25 (N.D. Ohio 1972); Tussman and tenBroek, *supra*, note 25, at 358-360.

47. The Equal Rights Amendment states: Section 1. Equality of rights under the law shall not be denied or abridged by the United States or by any State on account of sex. Section 2. The Congress shall have the power to enforce, by appropriate legislation, the provisions of this article. Section 3. This amendment shall take effect two years after the date of ratification. 86 Stat. 1523 (1972).

48. Brown, Emerson, Falk, and Freedman, "The Equal Rights Amendment: A Constitutional Basis for Equal Rights for Women," 80 *Yale Law Journal* 871 (1971).

49. S. Rep. No. 92-689, 92d Cong., 2d Sess. 2 (1972). See also H.R. Rep. No. 359, 92d Cong., 1st Sess. 5–8 (1971).

50. Brown *et al., supra,* note 48, at 889–893.

51. *Id.,* at 893.

52. *Id.*

53. *Id.*

54. *Id.,* at 894. Under the ERA, "strict scrutiny" would probably then follow.

55. Applied as intended by its proponents, ERA theory would probably conceptualize pregnancy as a facially neutral factor which, in the disability context, is applied to disadvantage one sex. Brown *et al., supra,* note 48, at 896–900. But I do not think that pregnancy, in fact, is a neutral factor. Pregnancy is also a physical characteristic unique to women. The choice of whether to measure equality in terms of dollar amount of benefits conferred—in *Gilbert,* the choice of result—cannot be made within the theory alone.

56. *City of Los Angeles, Department of Water and Power v. Manhart,* 98 S.Ct. 1370 (1978).

57. *Id.,* at 1377.

58. 5 Cal. 3d 1, 485 P.2d 529, 95 Cal. Rptr. 329 (1971).

59. *Id.* See also Appellants' brief in *Reed v. Reed* characterizing the legislative distinction between the sexes challenged there as "mandating *subordination* of women to men without regard to individual capacity . . . arbitrarily ranking the woman as *inferior* to the man." As quoted in Ginsberg, *supra,* note 6, at 63 (emphasis added). In most of these examples, the criticism of the collapsing of individuals into the group, while accurate, misses the fact that most members of the group are, individually, in the same position as the group as a whole. The logic of the differences approach, which stresses differences between individuals as well as between the sexes, is imported to support a position, as here, premised upon an awareness of inequality across differences. Similarly, the majority decision in *Manhart* mixes the individualism of the differences approach with a consciousness of group inequality. Although the generalization based upon sex in *Manhart* was accurate, the Court found it important that fairness to individuals precluded treating them simply as members of the group. How to compute actuarial probabilities on an individual basis was left unclear, since, individually, there is no telling when one will die. This incoherence (from the point of view of inequality theory) aside, the definition of equality for women as a group remains.

60. 411 U.S. 677 (1973).

61. 416 U.S. 351 (1974).

62. *Id.*, at 353.

63. 419 U.S. 498 (1975).

64. Examples of cases protesting this are *Defunis v. Odegaard*, 82 Wash. 2d. 11, 507 P.2d 1169 (1973) (the Supreme Court avoided the question by holding the case moot, 416 U.S. 312 (1974); *Bakke v. Regents of University of California*, 132 Cal. Rptr. 680, 553 P.2d 1152, *aff'd*, 98 S.Ct. 2733 (1978).

65. For example: "The lesson of the great decisions of the Supreme Court and the lesson of contemporary history have been the same for at least a generation: discrimination on the basis of race is illegal, immoral, unconstitutional, inherently wrong, and destructive of democratic society. Now this is to be unlearned and we are told that this is not a matter of fundamental principle but only a matter of whose ox is gored. Those for whom racial equality was demanded are to be more equal than others. Having found support in the Constitution for equality, they now claim support for inequality under the same Constitution." Alexander M. Bickel, *The Morality of Consent* (New Haven: Yale Univeristy Press, 1975), at 133.

66. An example is Chief Justice Burger's opinion for the Court in *Swann v. Charlotte-Mecklenberg Board of Education*, 402 U.S. 1 (1971).

67. In *Gilbert*, Justice Rehnquist sees this problem, but sees no way around it:

The difficulty with their [Gilbert's] contention that General Electric engaged in impermissible sex discrimination is vividly portrayed in their closing suggestion that "[if] paying for pregnancy discriminates within the sphere of classification by sex, so does the failure to pay." [citation omitted] As that statement, and its converse, indicates, perceiving the issue in terms of "sex discrimination" quickly places resolution of this issue in a no-win situation. 429 U.S., at 140, n. 18.

In his dissent in *Craig v. Boren*, Justice Rehnquist took an approach that saw beyond this impasse. The majority invalidated a statute that set a different age for male and female purchasing of 3.2% beer on grounds of sex discrimination. Dissenting, Justice Rehnquist found objectionable the majority conclusion "that *men* challenging a gender-based statute which treats them less favorably than women may invoke a more stringent standard of judicial review than pertains to most other types of classifications." 429 U.S. 190, 217 (1976). Men, he noted, do not present "a history or pattern of past discrimination," *id.*, at 219, to justify special scrutiny: "[t]here is no suggestion in the Court's opinion that males in this age group are in any way peculiarly disadvantaged, subject to systematic discriminatory treatment, or otherwise in need of special solicitude from the courts," *id.* He criticized using "gender classification as a talisman ... without regard to the rights involved or the persons affected," *id.*, at 220. The affirmative version of such an argument would distinguish between gender classifications that disadvantage women from gender classifications that disadvantage men, elevating disadvantageous distinctions to women to a higher level of scrutiny. (It is also worth noting that the passage of the Equal Rights Amendment may make a difference in Justice Rehnquist's assessment of sex as a classification to be distinguished from other types of classifications.)

In *Califano v. Goldfarb*, however, in which a widower challenged a preference for widows as sex discrimination, Rehnquist also saw a way around the dilemma, recognizing women's inequality: "The very most that can be squeezed out of the facts of this case in the way of cognizable 'discrimination' is a classification which favors aged widows," a classification he found "rationally justifiable, given available empirical data, on the basis of 'administrative convenience'... and is in fact explainable as a measure to ameliorate the characteristically depressed condition of aged widows." 430 U.S. 199, 242 (1977). At the least, this suggests that if a legislative choice had been made to cover pregnancy under disability plans (such as in *Geduldig*, the same case as *Gilbert* under the Equal Protection Clause), and if it were challenged by men who said such plans provided more total benefit payments to women than to men, the author of the opinion that found the distinction based on pregnancy not sex-based might have found it sex-based but "rationally justifiable."

This suggests that the "no-win situation" arises only as a problem within the abstractions of differences doctrine.

68. This distinction is clearly illustrated by the concurrences in *Gilbert*. See Appendix A at 228–29 for a fuller discussion of the implications.

69. *Cohen v. Chesterfield County School Board*, 474 F.2d 395, 397 (4th Cir. 1973) *rev'd* 326 F. Supp. 1159 (E.D. Va. 1971). See Appendix A, note 21, for a fuller discussion and critique of this view.

70. 429 U.S., at 139, n. 17.

71. *Id.*, at 139.

72. In a society with different values and organization, women's reproductivity could as well provide a reason for a pay bonus as for a layoff. Pursuing the *Gilbert* logic in the *Manhart* context, women's greater longevity could be used as a reason to require women to work until a more advanced age, while making the same contributions to the pension fund, thus receiving benefits for no longer than men.

73. *Weeks v. Southern Bell Telephone*, 408 F.2d 228, 235 (5th Cir., 1969). *Weeks* held that an employer must show a "factual basis for believing, that all or substantially all women would be unable to perform safely and efficiently the duties of the job involved," *id.*, at 235, here, to lift more than thirty pounds. This is also the position of the EEOC guidelines at 29 C.F.R. Section 1604.2 (a)(1)(ii). But at least one court has held that the BFOQ can be a matter of "efficient mode of operation," *Gudbrandson v. Genuine Parts*, 297 F. Supp. 134 (D. Minn. 1968) (allowing policy against hiring women because job requires lifting weights over 140 lbs. even though some women may have been able to perform the work). And a chaplain at a Youth Authority facility must, according to one California case, be a man. *Long v. California State*

Personnel Board, 116 Cal. Rptr. 562 (Ct. App. 1974). This case is also important for establishing the principle that the same evidence which substantiates a BFOQ under Title VII establishes a "compelling state interest" for Equal Protection purposes.

74. *Geduldig v. Aiello,* 417 U.S., at 496–497, n. 20 (1974), also cited in *Gilbert v. General Electric,* 429 U.S. 125, 135 (1976).

75. Quoted in I *Women's Rights Law Reporter* II, (1971), at 19–20.

76. It might be considered whether these jobs are ideologically "sold" to women workers, much like the housewife role, as fulfilling to their femininity, as a form of compensation in lieu of wages.

77. The Justice Department was Diane Williams's workplace. See chap. 4, at 63–65, for a discussion of her sexual harassment claim.

78. *Slack v. Havens,* 7 FEP Cases 885, 889 (S.D. Cal. 1973), *aff'd.,* 522 F.2d 1091, 1093 (9th Cir. 1975).

79. Judith Long Laws, "Work Aspirations of Women: False Leads and New Starts," *Signs: Journal of Women in Culture and Society,* vol. 1, no. 3, part 2 (Spring 1976), at 38–39.

80. Rosabeth M. Kanter, "The Impact of Hierarchical Structures on the Work Behavior of Women and Men," *Social Problems,* vol. 23, no. 4 (April 1976). Kanter proceeds throughout as if the sex difference is primarily biological. She then objects to treating as if they are sex differences social products which can be observed in men as well as women who are relegated to subordinate roles. She does not consider whether these social products themselves might essentially constitute the sex difference, so that to speak about "sex differences" is to speak about these "social structural effects."

81. In this view, the suspicion that any stereotype is untrue is allied with a belief that determinations should be made on an individual basis. There is a view that each person must be treated as an individual, meaning not on the basis of characteristics *generally, often falsely,* attributed to a gender group. In the formulation of *Manhart* in the district court, the intent of the sex discrimination prohibition was framed thus: "to strike at the entire spectrum of disparate treatment of individual men and women resulting from sex stereotypes" 387 F. Supp. 980, 984 (1974). In this context, when the stereotype is true, is there not a point in Chief Justice Burger's dissenting *Manhart* opinion that actuarial tables "treat [women] as individually as it is possible to do in the face of the unknowable length of each individual life"? 98 S.Ct. 1370, 1385.

82. Wechsler, "Toward Neutral Principles of Constitutional Law," 73 *Harv. L. Rev.* 1, 19 (1959).

83. Georg Simmel, *Philosophische Kultur* (Leipzig: Werner Klinkhardt, 1911), quoted in Louis A. Coser, "Georg Simmel's Neglected Contributions to the Sociology of Women," *Signs: Journal of Women in Culture and Society,* vol. 2, no. 4 (Summer 1977), at 872.

84. See Diane K. Lewis, "A Response to Inequality: Black Women, Racism, and Sexism," *Signs: Journal of Women in Culture and Society,* vol. 3, no. 2 (1977), at 349. Pauli Murray states that in spite of black women's participation, "the aspirations of the black community have been articulated almost exclusively by black males. There has been very little public discussion of the problems, objectives or concerns of black women." "The Liberation of Black Women," in Jo Freeman, ed., *Women: A Feminist Perspective* (Palo Alto, Calif.: Mayfield Publishing Co., 1975), at 354. Further, "It is clear that when translated into actual opportunities for employment and promotional and educational benefits the civil rights movement really meant rights for black men." Christina M. Carroll, "Three's a Crowd: The Dilemma of the Black Woman in Higher Education," in Alice Rossi and Ann Calderwood, eds., *Academic Women on the Move* (New York: Russell Sage Foundation, 1973), at 177.

85. *Griggs v. Duke Power Co.,* 401 U.S. 424 (1971); *Albemarle Paper Co. v. Moody,* 422 U.S. 405 (1975); *Franks v. Bowman Transportation Co.,* 424 U.S. 747 (1975); *Bridgeport Guardians, Inc. v. Civil Service Commission,* 482 F.2d 1333 (2d Cir. 1973); *McDonnell Douglas Corp. v. Green,* 411 U.S. 792 (1973); *Teamsters v. United States,* 431 U.S. 324 (1977) are examples.

86. This has been noted by several commentators, among them Katharine T. Bartlett, "Pregnancy and the Constitution: The Uniqueness Trap," 62 *California Law Review* 1532, 1548–1549 (1974).

87. See Gunnar Myrdal, Appendix 5, "A Parallel to the Negro Problem," *An American Dilemma* (New York: Harper and Brothers, 1944); Shirley Chisolm, "Racism and Anti-Feminism," 1 *Black Scholar* 44–45 (January–February 1970); Catharine Stimpson, "'Thy Neighbor's Wife, thy Neighbor's Servants': Women's Liberation and Black Civil Rights," in Vivian Gornick and Barbara K. Moran, eds., *Woman in Sexist Society* (New York: Basic Books, 1971), at 622–657; Helen Hacker, "Women as a Minority Group," 30 *Social Forces* 60 (1951); Beverly Jones and Judith Brown, "Toward a Female Liberation Movement" (Boston: New England Free Press, n.d.), mention the parallel eleven times, as noted by Stimpson, *supra,* at 649: "1. Women, like black slaves, belong to a master. They are property and whatever credit they gain redounds to him. 2. Women, like black slaves, have a personal relationship to the men who are their masters. 3. Women, like blacks, get their identity and status from white men. 4. Women, like blacks, play an idiot role in the theatre of the white man's fantasies. Though inferior and dumb, they are happy, especially when they can join a mixed group where they can mingle with The Man. 5. Women, like blacks, buttress the white man's ego. Needing such support, the white man fears its loss, fearing such loss, he fears women and blacks. 6. Women, like blacks, sustain the white man: 'They wipe his ass and breast feed him when he is little, they school him in his youthful years, do his clerical work and raise him and his replacements later, and all through his life in the factories, on the migrant farms, in the restaurants, hospitals, offices, and

homes, they sew for him, stoop for him, cook for him, clean for him, sweep, run errands, haul away his garbage, and nurse him when his frail body alters.' 7. Women, like blacks, are badly educated. In school they internalize a sense of being inferior, shoddy, and intellectually crippled. In general, the cultural apparatus, the profession of history, for exemple, ignores them. 8. Women, like blacks, see a Tom image of themselves in the mass media. 9. Striving women, like bourgeois blacks, become imitative, ingratiating, and materialistic when they try to make it in a white man's world. 10. Women, like blacks, suffer from the absence of any serious study on the possibility of real 'temperamental and cognitive differences' between the races and the sexes. 11. The ambivalence of women toward marriage is like the ambivalence of blacks toward integration."

88. For some examples of courts that have noted parallels between race and sex discrimination, see *Frontiero v. Richardson*, 411 U.S. 677, 685–686 (1973) (Brennan, J., for a plurality); *Sail'er Inn, Inc. v. Kirby*, 5 Cal. 3d 1, 485 P.2d 529, 540–541, 95 Cal. Rptr. 329, 340 (1971) (exclusion of women as bartenders); *Seidenberg v. McSorleys' Old Ale House, Inc.*, 317 F. Supp. 593, 597 (S.D.N.Y. 1970) (exclusion of women from ale house service); educational opportunities: *Brenden v. Independent School District 742*, 477 F.2d 1292, 1296–1297 (8th Cir. 1973) (exclusion of women from high school sports program); *Kirstein v. Rector and Visitors of the University of Virginia*, 309 F. Supp. 184 (E.D. Va. 1970) (exclusion of women from state university); criminal sentencing: *State v. Chambers*, 63 N.J. 287, 307 A.2d 79 (1973); *Commonwealth v. Daniel*, 430 Pa. 642, 243 A.2d 400 (1968). A report of the Senate Committee on Labor and Public Welfare noted that "recent studies have shown that there is a close correlation between discrimination based on sex and racial discrimination, and that both possess similar characteristics." S. Rep. No. 92-415, 92d Cong., 1st Sess. 7 (1971).

89. One notable recent attempt to analyze the race and sex comparison with legal applications in mind is Richard Wasserstrom's "Racism, Sexism, and Preferential Treatment: An Approach to the Topics," 24 *U.C.L.A. L. Rev.* 581 (1977). Although his perspective on women is sympathetic and informed, he persists in discussing sex in terms of "distinctions" and "differences," while seldom losing sight of race as a matter of oppression and domination. He never speaks of men "dominating over" women as he does of whites over nonwhites, and most of his passion emerges on racial issues. He courageously attacks the pretense that society is a meritocracy except for affirmative action (*id.*, at 619–620) and sees that whatever problems might characterize affirmative action, they are not the problems of racism.

It is difficult to disagree with his major argument that racism and sexism can be distinguished in some ways, while criticizing both. It is just that the distinctions he offers do not withstand scrutiny. He observes, for example, that "the race of an individual is much more than a fact of superficial physiology. It is, instead, one of the dominant characteristics that affects both the way the individual looks at the world and the way the world looks at the individual" (*id.*, at 581) without seeing that the same is most emphatically true for sex. He does, however, recognize that it is the social differences between the sexes that tend to matter (*id.*, at 609).

In the reverse of the Supreme Court majority's position in *Bakke*, Wasserstrom sees sex as more complex than race, since the ideology of sexism both idealizes and denigrates women: "at best [women] are viewed and treated as having properties and attributes that are valuable and admirable for humans of this type" (*id.*, at 590). Wasserstrom neglects that this is a prominent feature both of the white racist, who greatly admires the human qualities of the black maid, and of the white liberal, whose exaggerated guilt allows no criticism of anything connected with a black person. It seems apparent that both race and sex are similarly complex but different. Wasserstrom's contrast between the meanings of race- and sex-segregated bathrooms might also be questioned in light of the deep social image of women as dirty and impure and contaminating. And his use of eye color as the paradigmatic socially irrelevant category fails to recognize that both sex objectification (in which eye color often becomes a fetish) and racism (placing a value upon light eyes comparable to that upon light skin, see e.g., Toni Morrison, *The Bluest Eye* (New York: Holt, Rinehart & Winston, 1970) attribute socially significant, however irrational, meanings to it. The truly irrelevant social category may prove as elusive as the truly neutral standard—for the same reasons.

90. On race, see *Washington, Mayor of Washington v. Davis*, 426 U.S. 229 (1976), discussed here at 134; *Keyes v. School District No. 1, Denver, Colorado*, 413 U.S. 189 (1973).

91. How similarly the prohibition on discrimination is to be applied to the categories in Title VII is not firmly established. In *Espinoza v. Farah Manufacturing Co., Inc.*, 414 U.S. 86 (1973), for example, in which the Supreme Court held that the "national origin" prohibition did not cover a refusal to employ an alien with Mexican citizenship, Justice Douglas, dissenting, noted: "*Griggs*, as I understood it until today, extends its protective principles to all, not to blacks alone. Our cases on sex discrimination under the Act yield the same result as *Griggs*." 414 U.S. at 97 (citations omitted).

92. *Regents of the University of California v. Bakke*, 98 S.Ct. (1978) at 2755 opinion by Justice Powell; for a contrasting view, see the separate opinion by four other justices at *id.*, 2784.

93. See, for example, *The Victimization of Women*, Jane Roberts Chapman and Margaret Gates, eds. (New York: Russell Sage Yearbooks in Women's Policy Studies, 1978) and the *Proceedings of the International Tribunal on Crimes Against Women*, Diana E. H. Russell and Nicole Van de Ven, eds. (Millbrae, Cal.: Les Femmes, 1976). The many recent books on domestic battery of women document this point further. Erin Pizzey, *Scream Quietly or the*

Neighbors Will Hear (England: Ridley Enslow, 1977); Del Martin, *Battered Wives* (San Francisco: Glide Publications, 1976); Roger Langley and Richard Clevy, *Wife Beating: The Silent Crisis* (New York: Simon & Schuster, 1977); Susan Steinmetz and M. A. Straus, *Violence in the Family* (New York: Dodd, Mead & Co., 1974); R. Emerson Dobash and Russell P. Dobash, "Wives: the 'Appropriate' Victims of Marital Violence," *Victimology: An International Journal*, vol. 2, no. 3–4 (1977), at 426–442.

94. Quoted in William H. Chafe, *Women and Equality: Changing Patterns in American Culture* (New York: Oxford University Press, 1977), at 44.

95. 163 U.S. 537, 557 (1896) (Harlan, J., dissenting).

96. "Our Constitution is color-blind, and neither knows nor tolerates classes among citizens." 163 U.S. 537, 559 (Harlan, J., dissenting). Note that the metaphor implies a nonseeing of something that is, in fact, there.

97. *DeFunis v. Odegaard*, 82 Wash. 2d 11, 507 P. 3d 1169 (1973), *vacated and remanded*, 416 U.S. 312 (1974); *Regents of the University of California v. Bakke*, 98 S.Ct. 2733 (1978).

98. Wechsler, *supra*, note 82.

99. U.S. Constitution, Thirteenth Amendment, §1, states, "Neither slavery nor involuntary servitude, except as a punishment for crime whereof the party shall have been duly convicted, shall exist within the United States, or any place subject to their jurisdiction."

100. The quotation is from Justice Harlan's dissent in *Plessy v. Ferguson*, 163 U.S. 537, 562 (1896). The amendment itself has been invoked only a few times, and then to invalidate state legislation. Section 1 has not been used against private parties. See *Jones v. Alfred H. Mayer Co.*, 392 U.S. 409 (1968) and *Palmer v. Thompson*, 403 U.S. 217 (1971).

101. *Korematsu v. U.S.*, 323 U.S. 214, 216 (1944), in which the "rigid scrutiny" of the Supreme Court allowed Japanese-Americans to remain in concentration camps.

102. *Frontiero v. Richardson*, 411 U.S. 677 (1973). For an analysis of the split in the Supreme Court on this issue, see Ruth Bader Ginsberg, "Comment: *Frontiero v. Richardson*," 1 *Women's Rights Law Reporter* 5 (Summer 1973), at 2–4. See also *Eisenstadt v. Baird*, 405 U.S. 438, 447, n.7 (1972).

103. *Griggs v. Duke Power*, 401 U.S. 424 (1971). The first case to hold that a rule neutral on its face could not legally be *applied* to effect discrimination was also a race case, although the plaintiff was Asian. *Yick Wo v. Hopkins*, 118 U.S. 356 (1886).

104. Justice Stone, *U.S. v. Carolene Products*, 304 U.S. 144, 153, n. 4 (1938).

105. *Brunson v. Board of Trustees*, 429 F.2d 820, 826 (5th Cir. 1970) (Sobeloff, J., concurring).

106. *Loving v. Virginia*, 388 U.S. 1 (1967). The question of who is injured by social differentiations by sex arose in *Califano v. Goldfarb*, 430 U.S. 199 (1977), in which a widower challenged a rule under the Social Security Act

that presumed the dependency of widows but required that widowers demonstrate dependency upon a deceased woman wage earner. This rule was challenged as discriminatory against women, who could not buy the same amount of insurance benefits for their families for the same amount of work as did wage-earner men, and against men, who were required to prove eligibility which was presumed for women. Justice Brennan, for a plurality, found the provision discriminated against the woman wage earner. Justice Stevens, concurring, found the law discriminated against widowers but not against their wage-earner wives. 430 U.S. 217–224. Even a benign purpose to help women would not, to him, justify "a statute which was actually based on 'archaic and overbroad' generalizations." *Id.*, at 224, citing *Weinberger v. Wiesenfeld*, 420 U.S. 636, 643 (1975). "Women are given the benefit of a broad vague definition of 'dependent' while men are held to a harsh arithmetic standard." *Id.*, at 222, n. 8. Yet he observed that the disparate treatment was "merely the accidental by-product of a traditional way of thinking about females." *Id.*, at 223.

107. *Johnson v. Pike Corporation of America*, 332 F. Supp. 490 (C.D. Cal. 1971); *Wallace v. Debron Corporation*, 7 FEP Cases 595 (8th Cir. 1974).

108. *Gregory v. Litton Systems, Inc.*, 316 F. Supp. 401 (C.D. Cal. 1970), *aff'd*, 472 F.2d 631 (9th Cir. 1970); EEOC Dec. 74-08, 6 FEP Cases 467 (1973). See also Sarratt, "Arrest records as racially discriminatory employment criterion," 6 *Harv. C.R.C.L. Rev.* 165 (1970).

109. *Griggs v. Duke Power Co.*, 401 U.S. 424 (1971); also, with regard to testing and examinations, see *Douglas v. Hampton*, 512 F.2d 976 (D.C. Cir. 1975); *Padilla v. Stringer*, 395 F. Supp. 495 (D. N.M. 1974); see also *Stevenson v. International Paper*, 516 F.2d 103 (5th Cir. 1975).

110. *Dozier v. Chupka*, 395 F. Supp. 836 (S.D. Ohio 1975). In *Douglas, Padilla and Dozier* the requirements were found not job-related.

111. *Hicks v. Crown Zellerbach Corporation*, 319 F. Supp. 314 (E.D. La. 1970), *terminated in part on other grounds and reaffirmed in part*, 321 F. Supp. 1241 (E.D. La. 1970). See also *Chance v. Board of Examiners*, 330 F. Supp. 203 (S.D.N.Y. 1971), *aff'd*, 458 F.2d 1167 (2d Cir. 1972); *Castro v. Beecher*, 459 F.2d 725 (1st Cir. 1972).

112. 401 U.S. 424, 432 (Burger, C.J., for a unanimous court).

113. 426 U.S. 229, 246 (1976) (Justice White for the majority) (arising under the due process clause of the Fifth Amendment and the Fourteenth Amendment).

114. *Id.*, at 246. This case held that governmental action which discriminates "in effect" is not unconstitutional unless intent to discriminate is shown. The scope of Title VI of the Civil Rights Act of 1964 appears to be constricting to this size, *Regents of the University of California v. Bakke*, 98 S.Ct. 2733 (*compare* 2747 with 2768) just as *Gilbert* constricted Title VII to *Geduldig* limits.

115. 423 U.S. 362 (1976).

116. *Id.,* at 371.

117. 426 U.S. 229 (1976). See also *Hazelwood School District v. U.S.,* 433 U.S. 299 (1977), which held that intent to discriminate on the basis of race must be shown before state practices which have a racially disparate impact will be considered a violation of the Equal Protection Clause of the Fourteenth Amendment.

118. 161 U.S. 537, 543 (1896).

119. *Id.,* at 551 (emphasis added).

120. The lower court judge was quoted by the Supreme Court in *Loving v. Virginia,* 388 U.S. 1, 3 (1967).

121. Opinion for the majority of the Illinois Supreme Court, quoted in *Bradwell v. Illinois,* 16 Wall 132, 133 (1873).

122. *State v. Bearcub,* 1 Or. App. 579, 465 P.2d 252, 253 (1970).

123. *Stanton v. Stanton,* 429 U.S. 501, 503 (1977), the Supreme Court of Utah, at 522 P.2d 112, 114 (1976).

124. Getman, "The Emerging Constitutional Principle of Sexual Equality," 1972 *The Supreme Court Review* 157, at 164–165.

125. See Appendix A, at 225–30.

126. 84 *Harv. L. Rev.* 1109, at 1176 (1971).

127. 29 C.F.R. 1604.2(a)(2).

128. 45 U.S.L.W. 3297 (1976), summary and quotation by *United States Law Week.* Mr. Kammholz is an attorney for General Electric. One court did not agree that sickle cell anemia was race-based, at least not enough to require a showing of business necessity before an employee whose back ailment was possibly caused by the disease could be discharged. Even if such a rule would discriminate against blacks, the need for a manual laborer to have a good back was found to be an obvious occupational requirement, not an "arbitrary, unnecessary" barrier to employment. *Smith v. Olin Chemical Corp.,* 555 F.2d 1283, 1286 (5th Cir. 1977).

129. 29 C.F.R. 1604.2(a)(2).

130. This test is adapted from *Weeks v. Southern Bell Telephone,* 408 F.2d 228 (5th Cir. 1969).

131. So long as there is no BFOQ for race, all racial distinctions or disparities in employment are either unlawful discriminations or must be justified on an individual basis as business necessities. The operative difference between the "business necessity" test in a racial challenge to disproportionate impact and the "business necessity" requisite for a sex BFOQ is not large; both have been restrictively interpreted. The doctrinal difference, however, is that once a BFOQ is established a business can then hire on the basis of sex. Once a practice that has the effect of discriminating racially is found justified by business necessity, a racially "disparate impact" is allowed, but no business may then proceed intentionally to hire on the basis of race—even though race

has, in effect, been found to be a reasonably good predictor of success in an area necessary to the business.

132. Wechsler, *supra,* note 82, at 33.

CHAPTER 6

1. Georg Simmel, *Philosophische Kultur* (Leipzig: Werner Klinkhardt, 1911), quoted in Lewis A. Coser, "Georg Simmel's Neglected Contributions to the Sociology of Women," *Signs: Journal of Women in Culture and Society,* vol. 2, no. 4 (Summer 1977), at 873.

2. *Gilbert v. General Electric,* 429 U.S. 125 (1976).

3. *Geduldig v. Aiello,* 417 U.S. 484 (1974).

4. *Dothard v. Rawlinson,* 433 U.S. 321 (1977). For the requirements challenged, see *id.,* at 324, n. 2.

5. *Id.,* at 337–340. (Rehnquist, J., dissenting.)

6. *Id.,* at 340.

7. *City of Los Angeles, Department of Water and Power et al. v. Manhart et al.,* 98 S.Ct. 1370 (1978).

8. Simmel, as quoted by Coser, *supra,* note 1, at *loc. cit.*

9. *Tomkins v. Public Service Electric & Gas Co.,* 422 F. Supp. 553, 556 (D.N.J. 1976).

10. 451 F. Supp. 1382, 1389 (D. Colo. 1978).

11. *Id.,* at 1389.

12. *Id.,* at 1390.

13. *Barnes v. Costle,* 561 F.2d 983, 992, n. 68 (D.C. Cir. 1977).

14. *Id.*

15. 2 Empl. Prac. Guide (CCH) ¶ 6493 (1976).

16. 84 *Harv. L. Rev.* 1109, 1184 (1971) (emphasis added). The context is a discussion of the BFOQ.

17. John Money, "Developmental Differentiation of Femininity and Masculinity Compared," in Farber and Wilson, eds., *The Potential of Woman* (New York: McGraw-Hill, 1963), at 56; John Money and Patricia Tucker, *Sexual Signatures: On Being A Man or A Woman* (Boston: Little, Brown, 1975); R. Stoller, *Sex and Gender: On the Development of Masculinity and Femininity* (London: Hogarth, 1968); R. Green and J. Money, *Transsexualism and Sex Reassignment* (Baltimore: Johns Hopkins University Press, 1969); Edward S. David, "The Law and Transsexualism: A Faltering Response to a Conceptual Dilemma," 7 *Conn. L. Rev.* 288 (1975); J. Money and A. Erhardt, *Man and Woman, Boy and Girl* (Baltimore: Johns Hopkins University Press, 1972); J. Money, *Sex Errors of the Body* (Baltimore: Johns Hopkins University Press, 1968); Note, *Transsexuals in Limbo,* 31 *Md. L. Rev.* 236 (1971).

18. Ashton Barfield, "Biological Influences on Sex Differences in Be-

280

Notes to Pages 151–153

havior," in M. Tietelbaum, ed., *Sex Differences: Social and Biological Perspectives* (Garden City, New York: Anchor Press, Doubleday, 1976), at 107. Bibliography of research supporting this summary at *id.*, 110–121.

19. Eleanor F. Maccoby, ed., *The Development of Sex Differences* (Stanford: Stanford University Press, 1966). See also *infra*, note 106.

20. Barfield, *supra*, note 18, at 109, 110.

21. Robert Masters and Virginia Johnson, *Human Sexual Response* (Boston: Little, Brown, 1966).

22. R. Staples, "Male-female sexual variations: functions of biology or culture," 9 *Journal of Sexual Response* (1973), at 11–20.

23. A. C. Kinsey *et al.*, *Sexual Behavior in the Human Male* (Philadelphia: W. B. Saunders Co., 1948). Kinsey's famous studies of sexual arousal in women and men in the 1930s and 1940s seemed to confirm that the sexes differed substantially in this respect. Culturally, his results were used to endow men with animal lust, women with demure passionlessness. (Demonstrating that obscure ability of racism to survive evidence, the stereotype of the black woman as sex-crazed was never apparently confronted by these findings purporting to represent the sexuality of all biological females.) A recent replication of Kinsey's studies suggests that cultural repression of women's sexuality largely accounts for his findings. Sigusch and Schmidt conclude that sexual arousability "is as strongly and quite similarly structured for both women and men." They explain the difference between their results and Kinsey's as follows:

His findings cannot serve as evidence for a lesser capacity of women to become sexually aroused by pictoral and narrative stimuli. They reflect one aspect of the cultural de-sexualization of women in western societies which 20 to 30 years ago, when Kinsey collected his data, was more extensive than today.

V. Sigusch and G. Schmidt, "Women's Sexual Arousal," in Zubin and Money, *Contemporary Sexual Behavior: Critical Issues in the 1970s* (Baltimore: Johns Hopkins University Press, 1973), at 118–119.

24. J. Marmor, "Women in Medicine: The Importance of the Formative Years," *Journal of American Medical Women's Association* (July 1968), at 621.

25. John H. Gagnon and William Simon, *Sexual Conduct: The Social Sources of Human Sexuality* (Chicago: Aldine Publishing Company, 1973), at 9.

26. *Id.*, at 19–26.

27. See Judith Long Laws and Pepper Schwartz, *Sexual Scripts: The Social Construction of Female Sexuality* (Hinsdale, Ill.: The Dryden Press, 1977), who apply Gagnon and Simon's concept to women's sexuality specifically.

28. John H. Gagnon and William Simon, eds., *The Sexual Scene* (Chicago: Aldine Publishing Company, 1970), at 4.

29. See *supra*, note 17.

30. Money, in Farber and Wilson, *supra*, note 17, at 56.

31. Margaret Mead, *Sex and Temperament in Three Primitive Societies* (New York: Dell, 1935); Margaret Mead, *Male and Female: A Study of the Sexes in A Changing World* (New York: William Morrow & Co., 1975), at 7–8; Michele Rosaldo and Louise Lamphere, eds., *Woman, Culture and Society* (Palo Alto, Cal.: Stanford University Press, 1974); Rayna R. Reiter, ed., *Toward an Anthropology of Women* (New York: Monthly Review Press, 1975).

32. See Anna S. Meigs, "Male Pregnancy and the Reduction of Sexual Opposition in A New Guinea Highlands Society," *Ethnology: An International Journal of Cultural and Social Anthropology,* vol. xv, no. 4 (October 1976), at 393–407; C. S. Ford and F. Beach, *Patterns of Sexual Behavior* (New York: Harper, 1951) provides background and several illustrative examples.

33. See citations *infra,* note 106.

34. *New York Times,* August 22, 1976, (Sports Section) at 3. See also the discussion by Germaine Greer of transsexual April Ashley, *The Female Eunuch* (New York: McGraw-Hill, 1970), at 54–55, *but cf.* the legal decision in the same case, *Corbett v. Corbett,* [1971] P. 83 (P. P. Div'l Ct.) (England).

35. A very different approach to analyzing sexuality for legal purposes can be found in the psychoanalytic interpretations collected in Ralph Slovenko, *Sexual Behavior and the Law* (Springfield, Ill.: Charles C. Thomas, 1965).

36. Diana E. H. Russell, *The Politics of Rape* (New York: Stein & Day, 1975), at 260.

37. Andrea Medea and Kathleen Thompson, *Against Rape* (New York: Farrar, Straus & Giroux, 1974), at 29–30.

38. Susan Griffin, "Rape: The All-American Crime," *Ramparts,* vol. 10 (September 1971), at 26–35, repr. in Jo Freeman, ed., *Women: A Feminist Perspective* (Palo Alto, Cal.: Mayfield Publishing Co., 1975), at 26.

39. Lionel Tiger, *Men in Groups* (New York: Random House, 1969), at 271. Lynn Wehrli, "Sexual Harassment at the Workplace: A Feminist Analysis and Strategy for Social Change," (M.A. Thesis, Massachusetts Institute of Technology, December 1976) makes the same connection, at 86.

40. Nancy Henley and Jo Freeman, "The Sexual Politics of Interpersonal Behavior," in Freeman, ed., *Women: A Feminist Perspective* (Palo Alto, Cal.: Mayfield Publishing Co., 1975), at 393–394.

41. Linda Phelps, "Female Sexual Alienation," in Freeman, *id.,* at 20.

42. Henley and Freeman, in *id.,* at 393–394.

43. Phelps, in *id.,* at 19.

44. Ellen Morgan, "The Erotization of Male Dominance/Female Subordination," University of Michigan Papers in Women's Studies 2 (1975), at 112–145, reprinted by Know, Inc., at 20. See also Nancy M. Henley, *Body Politics: Power, Sex and Nonverbal Communication* (Englewood Cliffs: Prentice-Hall, 1977), at 94–123.

45. Henley, "Power, Sex and Nonverbal Communication," in Barrie

Thorne and Nancy Henley, eds., *Language and Sex: Difference and Dominance* (Rowley, Mass.: Newbury House, Publishers, 1975), at 184.

46. See the discussion of *Monge v. Beebe Rubber*, 316 A.2d 549, 551-2 (N.H. 1974).

47. Of course, this requires that women be unionized; few are. See chap. 2, *supra*, note 37. See also, *Gates v. Brockway Glass*, 93 L.R.R.M. 2367 (C.D. Cal. 1976).

48. The Occupational Safety and Health Act of 1970 mandates that the National Institute of Occupational Safety and Health conduct research into the psychological factors involved in worker safety and health. 29 U.S.C. §§669, 671.

It does not appear that sexual harassment has been studied in this connection, although suggestive work has been done in the field of occupational stress generally. See, for example, Alan McLean, ed., *Occupational Stress* (Springfield, Ill.: Charles C. Thomas, 1974). One article therein notes in passing that "racial prejudice, felt or real, can be a source of stress for the worker, independent of the requirements or nature of the job." Bruce K. Margolis and William H. Kroes, "Occupational Stress and Strain," *id.*, at 17. See also *id.*, at 94, and Alan McLean, *Mental Health and Work Organizations* (Chicago: Rand McNally, 1970).

49. See, for example, *Model Penal Code* (1962), §251.1 (lewdness); §213.1 (1) (rape); §213.2 (deviate sexual intercourse by force or imposition); §213.3 (seduction); §213.4 (sexual assault); §5.02 (solicitation); §213.1(2) (gross sexual imposition), and the discussion of views of the criminal law on women's sexuality at 161-64, *infra*.

50. *Carmen Bruno et al. v. Michael Codd, Commissioner of New York City Police Department et al.:* "For too long, Anglo-American law treated a man's physical abuse of his wife as different from any other assault, and, indeed as an acceptable practice." 90 Misc. 2d 1047, 1048, 396 N.Y. S.2d 974, 975 (Sup. Ct. 1977). The favorable result to the complaining women in this case was recently reversed. *Bruno v. Codd*, 407 N.Y.S. 2d 165 (App. Div. July 20, 1978).

51. *Model Penal Code*, §213.6(6).

52. The phrase "the right of a person to be let alone" is the classic definition of the right to privacy, usually attributed to T. Cooley, *A Treatise on the Law of Torts*, §135 (2d ed., 1888), and cited to *Roberson v. Rochester Folding Box Co.*, 171 N.Y. 538, 64 N.E. 442 (1902). See also Warren and Brandeis, *The Right to Privacy*, 4 *Harv. L. Rev.* 193 (1890).

53. *Model Penal Code*, §213.4(1) and §213.4.

54. For a similar, but not identical, analysis of rape, see Susan Brownmiller, *Against Our Will: Men, Women and Rape* (New York: Bantam Books, 1976). For discussion, see chap. 7, *infra*, at 218-20, and works referenced.

55. *Model Penal Code*, at 149.

56. *Model Penal Code*, §213.1(1).

57. *Model Penal Code*, §213.1(2)(a).

58. Menachem Amir, *Patterns in Forcible Rape* (Chicago: University of Chicago Press, 1971), at 21.

59. Working Women United Institute, "Speak-Out on Sexual Harassment," Ithaca, N. Y., May 4, 1975 (typescript).

60. *Tomkins v. Public Service Electric & Gas Co.*, 422 F. Supp. 553, 556 (D.N.J. 1976) *rev'd*, 568 F.2d 1044 (3d Cir. 1977).

61. *Barnes v. Costle*, 561 F.2d 983, 995 (D.C. Cir. 1977) (MacKinnon, J., concurring).

62. W. Prosser, *The Law of Torts*, 3.

63. *Id.*, at 36.

64. *Hough v. Iderhoff*, 69 Or. 568, 139 P.931, 932 (1914).

65. *Gates v. State*, 110 Ga. App. 303, 138 So.2d 473, 474 (1964). This was a criminal battery, the quotation taken from another criminal battery case, *Goodrum v. State*, 60 Ga. 509 (1878). "If to put the arm, though tenderly, about the neck of another man's wife, against her will, is not an assault and battery, what is it? . . . There was nothing to excite rapture or provoke enthusiasm. Why should he embrace her? Why persist in caressing her? . . . He took the risk of not meeting with a responsive feeling in her, and must abide all the consequences of disappointment" *id.*, at 510, 511. On the question of what is and is not a sexual touching, see *People v. Thomas*, 91 Misc. 2d 724 (1977).

66. Prosser, *supra*, note 62, at 36, n. 85.

67. *Kline v. Kline*, 158 Ind. 602, 64 N.E. 9, 10 (1902), cited in Prosser, *supra*, note 62, at 38.

68. *Ragsdale v. Ezell*, 20 Ky. 1567, 49 S.W. 775, 776 (1899).

69. *Liljegren v. United Rys. Co. of St. Louis*, 227 S.W. 925 (Mo. Ct. App. 1921). She was awarded $500, which corrected for inflation is $1,684 in 1977. Similarly corrected for inflation to 1977, the damage awards for sexual harassment tort cases, *infra*, are as follows. The actual awards are in parentheses. *Skousen* (1961), $7,350 ($3,500) actual, $3,015 ($1,500) punitive, for $10,065 ($5,000) total damages; *Hatchett* (1915), $2,969 ($500); *Martin* (1920), $1,354 ($450); *Kurpgeweit* (1910), $9,670 ($1,500); *Ragsdale* (1899), $5,051 ($700); *Craker* (1895), $7,220 ($1,000); *Davis* (1905), $26,740 ($4,000) (note that the *Davis* jury award was overruled).

70. In a situation familiar to sexually harassed women, the perpetrator simply did not believe her when she told him she wanted him to leave her alone. Their dialogue reportedly ended as follows: "'Look me in the eye, and tell me if you are mad.' I said, 'I am mad.'" *Craker v. The Chicago and Northwestern Railway Company*, 36 Wis. 657, 659, 17 Am. Rep. 504 (1895). She apparently was. Her report precipitated his immediate firing; she proceeded criminally (for criminal assault and battery) and won, and then sued the

employer for civil damages. The *Craker* decision is notable in several respects. The treatment of the size of the damage awarded—which amounts to an inquiry into how much this woman's bodily integrity and sexual feelings are worth—is incisive and sympathetic: "who can be found to say that such an amount would be in excess of compensation to his own or his neighbor's wife or sister or daughter?" 36 Wis., at 679. The judge's refusal to separate the woman's sense of wrong at the injustice done her from her mental suffering and pain, holding both proper objects of *compensatory* damages, would be considered pathbreaking had it been more widely followed:

And it is difficult to see how these are to be distinguished from the sense of wrong and insult arising from injustice and intention to vex and degrade. The appearance of malicious intent may indeed add to the sense of wrong; and equally, whether such intent be really there or not. But that goes to mental suffering, and mental suffering to compensation.... What human creature can penetrate the mysteries of his own sensations, and parcel out separately his mental suffering and his sense of wrong—so much for compensatory, so much for vindictive damages? 36 Wis., at 678.

The decision further held the employer responsible for this intentional tort by the employee, an unusual departure. The standard view is that employers are only responsible for employee negligence.

One employing another ... would be as little likely to authorize negligence as malice.... [T]he true distinction ought to rest ... on the condition whether or not the act of the servant be in the course of his employment.... If we owe bread to another and appoint an agent to furnish it, and the agent of malice furnish a stone instead, the principal is responsible for the stone and its consequences. In such cases, negligence is malice. 36 Wis., at 668–69.

71. *Hatchett v. Blacketer,* 162 Ky. 266, 172 S.W. 533 (1915).

72. *Martin v. Jensen,* 113 Wash. 290, 193 P. 674 (1920). By analogy with the law of trespass to property, recovery for mental anguish alone was allowed where suffering "is the result of a wanton or intentional trespass on the person of a woman." 193 P., at 676.

73. *Skousen v. Nidy,* 90 Ariz. 215, 367 P.2d 248 (1961).

74. Prosser, *supra,* note 62, at 37.

75. *Id.,* at 37.

76. *Id.,* at 41.

77. Restatement (Second) of Torts §46 (1965).

78. Magruder, "Mental and Emotional Disturbance in the Law of Torts," 49 *Harv. L. Rev.* 1033, 1055 (1936). It is interesting that the cases commonly cited in support of Magruder's proposition do not squarely support it. Some hold that the facts were improperly pleaded. *Prince v. Ridge* states that an attempt by words of persuasion to induce a female to have sexual intercourse does not constitute an assault, but finds that the instant case presents sufficient acts for a battery, an assault, or both. 32 Misc. 666, 66 N.Y.S. 454, 455 (Sup. Ct. 1900). It would seem usual that more than simply asking would be involved.

Other cases referenced to support the formulation require that a physical *injury*, not merely an *act*, must be alleged to make out an assault. As is often the case where sex is involved, this requirement confuses the basic doctrine. The doctrine of assault requires only an act, not an injury. An example of a correct application of assault doctrine requiring physical acts, not physical injuries, is one 1880 Vermont case, in which a blind traveling music teacher, sleeping overnight in the defendant's house, was propositioned. "During the night he stealthily entered her room, sat on her bed, leaned over her person, and made repeated solicitation to her for sexual intimacy, which she repelled." *Newell v. Witcher*, 53 Vt. 589 (1880), quoted in *Reed v. Maley*, 115 Ky. 816, 74 S.W. 1079, 1081 (1903). The defendant was found liable for trespass and assault on the person for sitting on the bed and leaning over her. (Although it was the defendant's property, the sleeping room was considered exclusively the plaintiff's for the night.) The assault finding meant that the plaintiff was found in fear of sexual touching from the proposition; the cited physical acts were sufficient to ground actionable assault, while the proposition alone would not.

Davis v. Richardson, 76 Ark. 348, 89 S.W. 318 (1905), by contrast, required physical *injury*. In this case, a fifteen-year-old girl was seized and embraced "in a rude and indecent manner" by a man who kissed her with "violent and indecent familiarity" and "acted like he was going to do something else." The damage award of $4,000 ($26,740 in 1977) was overturned because an instruction allowed the jury to conclude that the mere proposal was actionable, although acts sufficient for both assault and battery were evidenced. *Bennett v. McIntire*, 121 Ind. 231, 23 N.E. 78 (1889) similarly took the approach of requiring some physical invasion of itself actionable before any recovery could be allowed for sexual propositions. In a case for seduction and debauching of his wife, the plaintiff pleaded a cause of action in trespass. Defendant was argued to have gained permission to come upon plaintiff's property by fraud, then seducing his wife. It was held that since he was on the property by permission, albeit fraudulent, no damages were recoverable. Trespass was the only cause of action apparently considered, with seduction as aggravation of damages.

Similarly, in *Reed v. Maley*, 115 Ky. 818, 74 S.W. 1079 (1903), in which a man solicited a woman to have sexual intercourse, no cause of action was held to exist.

79. 74 S.W., at 1080 (referring to several other cases).

80. The judge posed a reverse familiar to readers of the early sexual harassment cases:

Suppose a bawd should solicit a man upon a public street to have sexual intimacy with her; he certainly could not maintain a civil action against her. If an action could be maintained by a woman against a man for such solicitation, the same right to maintain one would exist in his favor. Whilst he might not suffer the same anguish and humilia-

286

tion on account of such solicitation as the woman, yet the right of recovery would be the same. The amount of it would only be determined by reason of the difference in effect such a solicitation would have upon one or the other. 74 S.W., at 1081.

Although a proposition would have a different impact upon the sexes, it is nevertheless argued that because a man "certainly could not maintain a civil action" for a proposition by a woman (why not is not considered), a woman should be similarly precluded.

The dissenting judge in this case urged that a sexual proposition should be actionable as solicitation to commit adultery. It should be prohibited not because it preys upon women, but because "if unsuccessful, it is liable to lead to violence and bloodshed at the hands of the [one supposes male] relatives of the woman; and if successful it defeats the end for which marriage is intended, and destroys the woman." 74 S.W. 1079, 1083. He thought punitive damages appropriate for reasons that combined solicitude for the woman's shattered virtue with an eye toward her undone housework: "The purity of woman and the sanctity of the marriage relation lie at the basis of our whole social fabric. . . . The natural effect of an indecent proposal of this character to a virtuous woman would be to upset her nerves and unfit her for discharging for the time her domestic duties." 74 S.W. 1074, 1083–1084.

81. No. A7703-04001 (Or. Cir. Ct. 1977).

82. First Amended Complaint, *Fuller v. Williames et al.*

83. Complaint, *Morgenheim v. Hiber and Midnight Sun Broadcasters* (Alaska Superior Court, filed December 29, 1975).

84. 3 *W. Blackstone Commentaries* 142–143, quoted and discussed by Leo Kanowitz, *Women and the Law: The Unfinished Revolution* (Albuquerque: University of New Mexico Press, 1969), at 82.

85. "It is claimed by the plaintiff in error that, in any mixed community, the reputation of belonging to the dominant race, in this instance the white race, is property, in the same sense that a right of action, or of inheritance is property. Conceding this to be so, for the purposes of this case, we are unable to see how this statute deprives him of, or in any way affects his right to, such property. If he be a white man and assigned to a colored coach, he may have his action for damages against the company for being deprived of his so called property. Upon the other hand, if he be a colored man and be so assigned, he has been deprived of no property, since he is not lawfully entitled to the reputation of being a white man." *Plessy v. Ferguson*, 163 U.S. 537, 549 (1896).

86. Prosser, *supra*, note 62, at 887. The final reason, with which it is difworth maintaining."

87. For an analogous approach to the one suggested, see *State of Washington v. Wanrow*, 559 P.2d 548 (Wash. 1977), which held, *inter alia*, in a prosecution for murder where self-defense was claimed, that an instruction

using an objective standard of self-defense was erroneous under Washington law and also violated the woman's right to equal protection.

In our society women suffer from a conspicuous lack of access to training in and the means of developing those skills necessary to effectively repel a male assailant without resorting to the use of deadly weapons. . . . The [instruction] not only establishes an objective standard, but through the persistent use of the masculine gender leaves the jury with the impression the objective standard to be applied is that applicable to an altercation between two men. . . . The respondent was entitled to have the jury consider her actions in light of her own perceptions of the situation, including those perceptions which were the product of our nation's "long and unfortunate history of sex discrimination" (citation omitted).

The instruction was found to misstate the law of "reasonableness" by focusing exclusively upon immediate circumstances, and then "compounds the error by utilizing language suggesting that respondent's conduct must be measured against that of a reasonable male individual finding himself in the same circumstances." *Id.*, at 558–559. By this logic, a reasonable woman might react quite differently to (hetero)sexual advances than would a reasonable man, or then a man would think reasonable in a woman.

88. *Craker v. The Chicago and Northwestern Railway Co.*, 36 Wis. 657, 674, 17 Am. Rep. 504 (1895).

89. *Hough v. Iderhoff*, 69 Or. 568, 139 P.931 (1914).

90. See, for example, *Alcorn v. Ambro Engineering, Inc.*, 468 P.2d 216, 36 Cal. Rptr. 216 (Sup. Ct. 1970); *Wiggs v. Coursin*, 355 F. Supp. 206 (S.D. Fla. 1973); *Gray v. Serruto Builders*, 110 N.J. Sup. 297, 265 A.2d 404 (1970).

91. See EEOC cases discussed at 210, *infra*.

92. *Brunson v. Board of Trustees*, 429 F.2d 820, 826 (1970).

93. See Boris Bittker, *The Case for Black Reparations* (New York: Random House, 1973).

94. Virginia Woolf, *Three Guineas* (New York: Harcourt, Brace & World, Inc., 1938).

95. See Mary Bularzik, "Sexual Harassment at the Workplace: Historical Notes," *Radical America*, vol. 12, no. 4 (July–August 1978), at 25–43, especially the discussion at 29–31; Robert Smuts, *Women and Work in America* (New York: Schocken Books, 1971), at 88; Louise A. Tilly, Joan W. Scott, Miriam Cohen, "Women's Work and European Fertility Patterns," *Journal of Interdisciplinary History*, vol. 6, no. 3 (1976), at 463–470.

96. See William Sanger, *A History of Prostitution* (New York: Medical Publishing Co., 1858), repr. in Rosalyn Baxandall, Linda Gordon, and Susan Reverby, *America's Working Women* (New York: Random House, 1976), at 96; Richard B. Morris, *Government and Labor in Early America* (New York: Columbia University Press, 1946), repr. at *id.*, at 26–29.

97. Edward Shorter, "On Writing the History of Rape," *Signs: Journal of Women in Culture and Society*, vol. 3, no. 2 (Winter, 1977), at 475.

98. Bliven, *Wonderful Writing Machine,* at 75–76 (no date given), repr. in Margery Davies, *Woman's Place Is At the Typewriter: The Feminization of the Clerical Labor Force* (pamphlet), at 13, repr. from *Radical America,* vol. 8, no. 4 (July-August 1974).

99. Kate Millett, *Sexual Politics* (New York: Avon, 1969), at 54.

100. Gerda Lerner, *Black Women in White America* (New York: Vintage Books, 1973), at 149–150.

101. Memorandum in Opposition to Defendant Company's Motion to Dismiss Plaintiff's Title VII Claim at 10, *Tomkins v. Public Service Electric & Gas Co.,* 422 F. Supp. 553 (D.N.J. 1976).

102. *Id.,* at 14–15.

103. Emma Goldman, *The Traffic in Women* (New York: Times Change Press, 1970), at 20.

104. 421 U.S. 7, 15 (1975) (*Stanton I*). (Justice Blackmun for the majority).

105. In any argument to extend the coverage of Title VII, the issue of legislative intent requires disposition. No specific evidence of Congressional contemplation of sexual harassment was found. The view is widely held that the term *sex* was included in Title VII as a joke, by a fluke, or in an attempt to overload the legislation. There is evidence that certain members of Congress were less than sincere in their commitment to eliminating sex discrimination when they included the term in the original act. However, first, since the original enactment, courts have taken Congress at its word. The issue is, thus, whether sexual harassment comes within the term *sex,* as interpreted. Second, the appropriateness of understanding the legislative history of Title VII together with that of its amendments in 1972 and the Equal Pay Act is apparent. See *Barnes v. Costle,* 561 F.2d 983, 987 (D.C. Cir. 1977), and the following comments by Bessie Margolin, for 25 years Assistant or Associate General Counsel for the Department of Labor:

The most illuminating measure of the significance of both the Equal Pay Act and the "sex" amendment requires particular emphasis because the mistaken idea has been circulating that, in contrast to race, color and creed discrimination, there is little or no legislative history or documentation bearing on the legislative intent or objectives of the "sex" amendment to Title VII. Anyone who asserts that the case against sex discrimination has not been documented prior to the inclusion of sex discrimination in Title VII, or that "the legislative history was virtually blank" and "the intent and reach of the amendment were shrouded in doubt" has manifestly overlooked the overwhelmingly impressive documentation presented at the hearings on the Equal Pay bills. This documentation is certainly no less thorough and convincing than the documentation of discrimination against the Negro. The chronology of the enactment of the Equal Pay Act and the Civil Rights Act, and the extensively documented facts and statistics emphasized at the hearings and in the debates on the Equal Pay bills can leave no doubt, I submit, of the direct relevance of this legislative history of the "sex" amendment of Title VII of the Civil Rights Act. . . . It seems fair to say, therefore, that only ignorance or thoughtless oversight of the pertinent legislative background, if not simply "entrenched prejudice" rooted in a psychological downgrading of women generally, can explain the view that the inclusion of sex discrimination in Title VII was no more than a "fluke" not to be taken seriously. . . . Commissioner Graham in his speech to the Personnel Conference of the American Management Association of February 9, 1966, specifically denounced the "fluke" charge and warned against the negative approach implicit in that characterization. He also made clear that the Commission is quite aware of the impressive legislative background underlying the Equal Pay Act and its manifest pertinence to the "sex" amendment of Title VII."

(Bessie Margolin, "Equal Pay and Equal Opportunities for Women," N.Y.U., 19th Conference on Labor, 1967, at 297, 301, 306.) Third, Congress has had numerous opportunities to eliminate the term *sex* if it was not serious about its inclusion, but has chosen rather to strengthen and extend the provisions. On the occasion of the 1972 amendments, additional legislative history supports a commitment to ending sex discrimination. For example, Senator Percy said: "Even among the resolution's opponents, there seems to be little question but that tradition and law have worked together to relegate women to an inferior status in our society. In many cases, this has been intentional, based on an archaic precept that women, for physiological or functional reasons, are inferior." 118 Cong. Rec. 9595 (1972). In response to such perceptions, Congress extended coverage to previously exempted federal employees (leaving administration for federal employees to the Civil Service Commission, 42 U.S.C. §2000e-16; see also *Parks v. Dunlop*, 517 F.2d 785, 787 (5th Cir. 1975), lowered the statutory minimum of number of employees over which coverage extends from 25 to 15 and conferred significant enforcement power on the EEOC. These strengthening, enforcement, and extension provisions would not have been made by a Congress that thought sex discrimination was a joke.

106. There are numerous excellent reviews and collections of sex role research. A classic in the field is Eleanor E. Maccoby, ed., *The Development of Sex Differences* (Stanford, Cal.: Stanford University Press, 1966). A bibliography of research conducted from 1973 to 1974 can be found in *Women's Work and Women's Studies, 1973—74, A Bibliography* (The Barnard College Women's Center, 1975), at 285-302, and a list of bibliographies on the subject at *id.*, 321-322. Recent books on varying levels include Carol Tavris and Carole Offir, *The Longest War: Sex Differences in Perspective* (New York: Harcourt, Brace Jovanovich, 1977); Nancy Reeves, *Womankind: Beyond the Stereotypes* (Chicago: Aldine Publishing Company, 1977); Shirley Weitz, *Sex Roles: Biological, Psychological and Social Foundations* (Oxford University Press, 1977). For a political perspective on sex roles in terms of power, see, *e.g.*, Nancy Hartsock, "Political Change: Two Perspectives on Power," *Quest: A Feminist Quarterly* (Summer 1974), at 10-25. An application to the law is Barbara Kirk Cavanagh, "A Little Dearer than His Horse: Legal Stereotypes and the Feminine Personality," 6 *Harv. C.R.C.L. Rev.* (1970), at 260-287.

107. Jon Snodgrass, ed., *For Men Against Sexism* (Albion, Cal.: Times Change Press, 1977) contains the best essays from this perspective to date. Warren Farrell, *The Liberated Man* (New York: Bantam, 1974) also treats this subject, substantially less well.

108. Initially a qualification on the Bona Fide Occupational Qualification (BFOQ), but sometimes used affirmatively. See Appendix A, *infra*, note 12, and accompanying text.

109. See Appendix A, *infra*, notes 33 and 39, and accompanying text.

110. See Appendix A, *infra*, notes 35–39 and accompanying text.

111. 442 F.2d 385 (5th Cir. 1971), *cert. denied*, 404 U.S. 950 (1971) (for the lower court opinion, see 311 F. Supp. 559 (S.D. Fla. 1970).

112. 442 F.2d 385, at 387.

113. *Id.*, at 389.

114. *Id.*, at 388.

115. EEOC Guidelines state that a BFOQ ought not be based on "the refusal to hire an individual because of the preferences of co-workers, the employer, clients or customers." 29 C.F.R. Section 1604.1(ii).

116. This fact was documented in the lower court hearing in *Diaz*, at 311 F. Supp. 562.

117. *Laffey v. Northwest Airlines*, 374 F. Supp. 1382 (D.D.C. 1974), *supplemented* 392 F. Supp. 1076 (D.D.C. 1974).

118. "Developments in the Law—Title VII" 84 *Harv. L. Rev.* 1109, 1184 (1971).

119. In *Boyd v. Ozark Air Lines*, a similar result was reached. 419 F. Supp. 1061 (E.D. Mo. 1976). The airline met its burden of showing that a height requirement is a business necessity. "The evidence shows that pilots must have free and unfettered use of all instruments within the cockpit and still have the ability to meet the design eye reference point. In view of the cockpit design, over which defendant has little control, a height requirement must be established." *Id.*, at 1064.

120. D. Schulz, "The Semantic Derogation of Women," in Barrie Thorne and Nancy Henley, eds., *Language and Sex: Difference and Dominance* (Rowley, Mass.: Newbury House, Publishers, 1975), at 67, 71.

121. 476 F.2d 225 (4th Cir. 1973).

122. Resolution S. 525 quoted at 476 F.2d at 227 (4th Cir. 1973). On the impact of good faith upon liability and damages, see *id.*, at 229–230.

123. *Dothard v. Rawlinson*, 433 U.S. 321 (1977).

124. Johnston and Knapp, "Sex Discrimination by Law: A Study in Judicial Perspective," 46 *New York U. L. Rev.* 675, 686 (1971), quoted at 476 F.2d 225, 231 (4th Cir. 1973).

125. *Dothard v. Rawlinson*, 433 U.S. 321 (1977).

126. 433 U.S., at 344, n. 2.

127. *Id.*, at 335.

128. *Id.*, at 336.

129. *Id.*, at 345–346.

130. *Id.*, at 346.

131. *General Electric Co. v. Gilbert*, 429 U.S. 125, 135 (1977) quoting from *Geduldig v. Aiello*, 417 U.S. 484, 496–497 (1974).

132. 417 U.S., at 496–497, n. 20.

133. Discussions with Barbara D. Underwood of the Yale Law School, helpful throughout, were crucial in clarifying this aspect of the analysis. The contribution of her advice here is gratefully acknowledged; at the same time she must be absolved of responsibility for the consequences of my selectivity in following it.

134. Brief for the government, *Williams v. Saxbe*, 413 F. Supp. 654, 657 (1976). Brief for the government at 20 in *Barnes v. Train*, 13 FEP Cases 123 (D.D.C. 1974) makes the identical argument.

135. *Barnes v. Train*, 13 FEP Cases 123, 124 (D.D.C. 1974).

136. Appellee's Reply Brief, *Corne v. Bausch & Lomb*, at 23.

137. [1968–1973] EEOC Decisions (CCH) ¶ 6087 (1969).

138. 400 U.S. 542 (1971).

139. Brief for Appellee at 20, *Barnes v. Train*, 13 FEP Cases 123 (D.D.C. 1974); Defendant's Brief in Support of the Motion to Dismiss at 5–6, *Williams v. Saxbe*, 413 F. Supp. 654 (D.D.C. 1976).

140. *International Brotherhood of Teamsters v. United States*, 431 U.S. 324 (1977).

141. *Id.*, at 336, n. 15.

142. *Id.*, at 335, n. 15.

143. *Id.*, at 336, n. 15.

144. *General Electric Co. v. Gilbert*, 429 U.S. 125, 140, n. 18 (1977).

145. See the "bisexual defense," *infra*, at 203.

146. As was argued orally by General Electric's attorney concerning pregnancy, reported at 45 U.S.L.W. 3297 (October 19, 1976).

147. [1973] EEOC Decisions (CCH) ¶ 6290 (1971).

148. [1973] EEOC Decisions (CCH) ¶ 6287 (1971).

149. *Tomkins* comes the closest to this approach in suggesting that firing a woman for complaining, while retaining the man without investigation, may be discriminatory. 422 F. Supp. 553, 557 (D.N.J. 1976).

150. As one black scholar has written of women:

Having reduced them to the role of submissive dependents, men then criticized them for being submissively dependent. Having forced them into a position in which they could only achieve their ends by indirection or subterfuge, they were branded by men as false and untrustworthy. Thus her situation is parallel to that of the Negro who, after being deprived of educational advantages, is then called ignorant and unintellectual by the white supremacist. H. R. Hays, *The Dangerous Sex: The Myth of Feminine Evil* (New York: G. P. Putnam's Sons, 1964), at 179.

151. *Skelton v. Balzano*, 424 F. Supp. 1231, 1253 (D.D.C. 1976).

152. *Id.*, at 1235–1236 (emphasis added).

153. *Tomkins v. Public Service Electric & Gas Co.*, 422 F. Supp. 553, 557 (D.N.J. 1976).

154. 424 F. Supp. 1231, at 1235–1236.

155. Although few authorities draw this conclusion so explicitly, it is converged upon and deducible from observations drawn from a plethora of otherwise opposed traditions. See, for example, H. R. Hays, "Fear of female sexuality: it is expressed by both aversion to and idolization of women," *Sexual Behavior* (November 1972), at 13–16; Eleanor Zuckerman, "Masculinity and the Changing Woman," in Zuckerman, ed., *Women and Men: Roles, Attitudes and Power Relationships* (New York: Radcliffe Club of New York, ca. 1975), at 65; Irene de Castillejo, *Knowing Woman: A Feminine Psychology* (New York: G. P. Putnam's Sons, 1973), at 105; Phyllis Chesler, *Women and Madness* (Garden City, N.Y.: Doubleday, 1972), at 241; Katharine M. Rogers, *The Troublesome Helpmate: The History of Misogyny in Literature* (Seattle: University of Washington Press, 1966); Andrea Dworkin, *Our Blood: Prophesies and Discourses on Sexual Politics* (New York: Harper and Row, 1976), at 107; Andrea Dworkin, *WomanHating* (New York: E. P. Dutton & Co., Inc., 1974); Hans Dieter Schmidt *et al.*, *Frauenfeindlichkeit, Sozialpsychologische Aspekte der Misogynie* (Munich: Juventa Verlag, 1973); Wolfgang Lederer, *The Fear of Woman* (New York: Grune & Stratton, Inc., 1968). Lederer proposes that male sexuality, as an expression of a "basic approaching instinct [of] aggression, . . . is essentially an inhibited aggression." "Our language almost says as much: provocative behavior on the part of a man provokes a fight; provocative behavior on the part of a woman arouses a sexual response. If the sexual response is in its turn frustrated, as when the woman is only teasing, then the original aggression against her is likely to re-emerge" (at 224). (When women are "only teasing" is often in the eye of the beholder.) Karen Horney, "The Dread of Women," *International Journal of Psychoanalysis*, vol. 13 (1932), at 348–360. Horney, working within Freudian theory, observes a connection between men's sexual assertiveness, dread of women, and the male definition of self-respect (*e.g.*, at 356). Mary Wollstonecraft observed that men often expressed contempt for women through demonstrations of affection. Mary Wollstonecraft, *A Vindication of the Rights of Women*, Carol H. Poston, ed., (New York: W. W. Norton & Co., 1975), at 9, 27, 126.

156. *Ochoa v. Monsanto Co.*, 335 F. Supp. 53 (S.D. Tex. 1971), *aff'd*, 473 F.2d 318 (5th Cir. 1973), and here, only if intentional discrimination is *alleged*.

157. *Griggs v. Duke Power*, 401 U.S. 424 (1971); *Kober v. Westinghouse Electric Corp.*, 480 F.2d 240 (3d Cir. 1973); *Spurlock v. United Airlines, Inc.*, 475 F.2d

216 (10th Cir. 1972); *Sprogis v. United Airlines, Inc.*, 444 F.2d 1194 (7th Cir.), *cert. denied*, 404 U.S. 991 (1971), *on remand*, 56 F.R.D. 420 (N.D. Ill. 1972); *Robinson v. P. Lorillard Corp.*, 444 F.2d 791 (4th Cir.), *cert. dismissed*, 404 U.S. 1006 (1971); *U.S. v. Local 638 Enterprise Assn. of Steam, Etc.*, 360 F. Supp. 979 (S.D. N.Y. 1973); *Henderson v. First National Bank of Montgomery*, 360 F. Supp. 531 (M.D. Ala. 1973); *Sims v. Sheet Metal Workers Int'l. Assn. Local Union No. 65*, 353 F. Supp. 22 (N.D. Ohio 1972); *U.S. v. Local 638, Enterprise Ass'n., Etc.*, 347 F. Supp. 169 (S.D. N.Y. 1972); *Johnson v. Pike Corp. of America*, 332 F. Supp. 490 (C.D. Cal. 1971); *Clark v. American Marine Corp.*, 304 F. Supp. 603 (E.D. La. 1969); *Boles v. Union Camp Corp.*, 57 F.R.D. 46 (S.D. Ga. 1972); *Fowler v. Schwarzenwalder*, 348 F. Supp. 844 (D. Minn. 1972).

158. *Bradinton v. IBM*, 360 F. Supp. 845 (D. Md. 1973); *U.S. v. Central Motor Lines, Inc.*, 338 F. Supp. 532 (W.D.N.C. 1971), 352 F. Supp. 1253 (W.D.N.C. 1972) (supplemental opinion).

159. 429 U.S. 125, 136 (1976), *vacated and remanded sub nom. Equal Employment Op. Com'n. v. Detroit Edison Co.*, 515 F.2d 301 (6th Cir. 1975) (but affirming the substantial disproportion finding, at 313); *vacated and remanded*, 431 U.S. 951 (1977) (for further consideration in light of *Teamsters v. U.S.*).

160. Magruder, *supra*, note 78, at 383. Perhaps his "circumstances" that "alter cases" would include employment circumstances, in which cases there may be harm in demanding.

161. [1973] EEOC Decisions (CCH) ¶ 6130 (1970). See also Comment, 51 *New York U.L. Rev.* 148, 164–65 (1976) and citations therein.

162. 422 F. Supp. 553, 556 (D.N.J. 1976).

163. 390 F. Supp., at 161.

164. 400 F.2d 385 (5th Cir. 1971).

165. 365 F. Supp. 87 (E.D. Mich. 1973).

166. *Id.*, at 109–110.

167. See *Tomkins v. Public Service Electric & Gas Co.*, 422 F. Supp. 553 (1976) ("The gender lines might as easily have been reversed, or even not crossed at all. . . . the gender of each is incidental to the claim of abuse," *id.* at 556); *Corne v. Bausch & Lomb*, 390 F. Supp. 161 (1975) ("It would be ludicrous to hold that the sort of activity involved here was contemplated by the Act because to do so would mean that if the conduct complained of was directed equally to males there would be no basis for suit," *id.* at 163.)

168. This view was adopted in *Barnes* at 561 F.2d 983, 989, n. 49 and 990, n. 55 and in *Williams* at 413 F. Supp. 654, 659, n. 6.

169. In employment generally, see *Morton v. Macy*, 417 F.2d 1161 (D.C. Cir. 1969); *Scott v. Macy* (II), 402 F.2d 644 (D.C. Cir. 1968); *Gayer v. Laird*, 332 F. Supp. 169 (D.D.C. 1971); *Dew v. Halaby*, 317 F.2d 582 (D.C. Cir. 1963); *Morrison v. State Board of Education*, 1 Cal. 3d 214, 92 Cal. Rptr. 175, 461 P.2d 375 (1969); *McConnell v. Anderson*, 451 F.2d 193 (8th Cir. 1971); *Acanfora v.*

Board of Education of Montgomery County, 491 F.2d 498 (4th Cir. 1974); *Application of Kimball*, 33 N.Y. 2d 586, 247 N.Y.S. 2d 453, 301 N.E.2d 436 (1973). See also G. Cooper, Harriet Rabb, Howard Rubin, *Fair Employment Litigation* (West Publishing, 1975), at 277–278. Recent regression on legal rights of gays, even under the First Amendment, is reflected in *Gay Lib. v. University of Missouri*, 416 F. Supp. 1350 (W.D. Mo. 1976) and 2 Empl. Prac. Guide (CCH) ¶ 6493 (1976).

170. As a matter of fact, it may well not be. Substantial differences have been found between lesbian and gay male sexuality in prison populations. For men, homosexuality in prison is often "a vehicle for the expression of control," while for women it arises out of a need for emotional support and intimacy. "There is no evidence that any of these [lesbian] relationships are coercive in the way that young male prisoners are sometimes pressured into intimacy." Alan J. Davis, "Sexual Assaults in the Philadelphia Prison System," in John H. Gagnon and William Simon, eds., *The Sexual Scene* (Chicago: Aldine Publishing Company, 1970), at 16, 126.

171. 2 Empl. Prac. Guide (CCH) ¶ 6493 (1976).

172. *Smith v. Liberty Mutual Insurance Co.*, 395 F. Supp. 1098 (N.D. Ga. 1975).

173. *Griggs v. Duke Power*, 401 U.S. 424 (1971).

174. Title IX provides the most obvious possibility. It has been thought that two separate standards for making out a prima facie case of "disparate impact" may possibly exist under Title VII and the Equal Protection Clause. After *Geduldig*, there was doubt that a majority of the Court would prohibit a "disparate impact" on one sex as the result of a legislative classification—for example, if a statute concerning some aspect of sexuality were to have a disparate impact. *Dothard v. Rawlinson* seems to have resolved this at least as to the impact on women's access to employment opportunities of legislative classifications such as height and weight. 433 U.S. 321 (1977). As to Title VII, cases have followed up the *Gilbert* suggestion that the plaintiff did not attempt to demonstrate discriminatory effect, with divergent results.

175. *Aros v. McDonnell Douglas Corp.*, 348 F. Supp. 661, 665 (C.D. Cal. 1972). A similar approach was taken in *McDonald:* "Santa Fe [the defendant], while conceding that 'across-the-board discrimination' in favor of minorities could never be condoned consistent with Title VII, contends nevertheless that 'such discrimination . . . in isolated cases which cannot reasonably be said to burden whites as a class unduly' such as is alleged here, 'may be acceptable' [cite omitted]. We cannot agree. There is *no* exception in the terms of the Act for isolated cases; on the contrary, 'Title VII tolerates no racial discrimination, subtle or otherwise.' *McDonnell Douglas Corp. v. Green*, 411 U.S. 792, 801 (emphasis added)." *McDonald v. Santa Fe Trail Transportation Co.*, 427 U.S. 273, 280–281, n. 8 (1976). See also *Vuyanich v. Republic National Bank of Dallas*, 409 F. Supp. 1083, 1089 (N.D. Tex. 1976); *McCreesh v. Berude*, 385 F. Supp. 1365,

1368 (E.D. Pa. 1974); *Barnes v. Costle,* 561 F.2d 983, 993–994 (D.C. Cir. 1977) and citations therein.

176. 42 U.S.C. §2000(e). Under Title IX of the Education Amendments of 1972, 20 U.S.C. §1681, the same argument would apply to sexual harassment in education between teachers and students and between lower ranking faculty and higher ranking faculty and administrators. An analysis of the educational hierarchy, where men also have things women need, would be analogous to the analysis of the employment hierarchy, with variations. Title IX also poses particular legal problems, such as the ambiguous status of the private right of action. See *Alexander et al. v. Yale University,* 459 F. Supp. 1 (D. Conn. 1977). The position of Title IX on employer liability is less clear than under Title VII. Title VII directs its prohibitions to the employer ("It shall be an unlawful employment practice for an employer (1) to ... ") while Title IX directly protects the potential victim ("No person ... shall ... be ... subjected to discrimination ... "). Title VII also explicitly includes "any agent" of the employer under its definition of "employer." The Department of Health, Education and Welfare's regulations under Title IX are more detailed on the question of what interpersonal behavior is sex-based than are the EEOC regulations under Title VII. The HEW regulations provide that a

recipient of federal financial assistance for an educational program or activity may not, on the basis of sex: (1) treat one person differently from another in determining whether such person satisfies any requirement or condition for the provision of ... an aid, benefit or service; (2) provide different aid benefits or services or provide aid, benefits, or services in a different manner; (3) deny any person such aid, benefit, or service; (4) subject any person to separate or different rules of behavior, sanctions, or other treatment; ... (8) otherwise limit any person in the enjoyment of any right, privilege, advantage, or opportunity. § 86.31 (b).

See also Alexandra Polyzoides Buek, "Sexual Harassment: Fact of Life or Violation of Law? University Liability Under Title IX" (unpublished manuscript, prepared for the National Council on Women's Educational Programs, July 1, 1978). She argues "if a professor or staff member of a recipient educational institution imposes or attempts to impose himself sexually upon a female student and conditions that student's academic success upon her acquiescence in his demands, the incident constitutes discrimination on the basis of sex under Title IX" (*id.,* at 3); see also "Sexual Harassment: A Hidden Issue," Project on the Status and Education of Women, Association of American Colleges, 1818 R. Street, N.W., Washington, D.C. 20009. The latter is an excellent and well-informed review and analysis of the cases and the issues; Maura Dolan, "They skip class to avoid sex ... UC women claim 'sexual coercion'," *San Francisco Examiner,* July 21, 1977; Joan White, "Sexual bribery at U.C. alleged," *Oakland Tribune,* May 18, 1978; "Profs pushing may get a surprise," *The Inde-*

pendent and Gazette (Berkeley, California), May 18, 1978; "Strong Charges at U.C. Forum on Sex-for-Grades," *San Francisco Chronicle,* May 19, 1978; "When the professor makes sexual advances," *San Francisco Examiner,* May 18, 1978; Barbara Franklin, "What can be done? Sexual harassment at U.C.," *Daily Californian,* May 18, 1978. The Berkeley situation attracted international notice, "Sexuelle Belastigung von Studentinnen," *Berliner Frauenzeitung Courage* #7 (July 1978), at 14. There are some indications that individual professors are countersuing when faced with these charges. See "MSU Prof Claims 'Defamation' in Grades-for-Sex Accusations," *Missoulian,* March 29, 1978; *The Chronicle of Higher Education,* January 23, 1978. See also Ira Michael Heyman, "Women Students at Berkeley: Views and Data on Possible Sex Discrimination in Academic Programs" (Berkeley: University of California, June 1977), at 63, 73, 77, 86, 121, and Donna J. Benson, "The Sexualization of Student-Teacher Relationships," (University of California, Berkeley: unpublished manuscript, 1977); American Sociological Association, "The Status of Women in Sociology" (Washington, D.C., 1973), at 26–28. Alice Rossi, "Looking Ahead: Summary and Prospects," in Alice Rossi and Ann Calderwood, eds., *Academic Women on the Move* (New York: Russell Sage Foundation, 1973), chap. 21; Adrienne Rich, "Toward a Woman-Centered University" in Florence Howe, ed., *Women and the Power to Change* (New York: McGraw-Hill, 1975), at 28–29.

177. This language is from *Bujel v. Borman Food Stores,* 384 F. Supp. 141 (E.D. Mich. 1974).

178. Comment, 51 *New York U.L. Rev.* 148, 152 (1976). The EEOC has argued that sexual harassment is sex discrimination under Title VII. Brief for the EEOC as *amicus curiae, Corne v. Bausch & Lomb, Inc.,* 562 F.2d 55 (9th Cir. 1977).

179. This test is taken from an adjudication under the Pennsylvania Human Relations Act, Pa. Stat. Ann. tit.43 §955 on the term *sex discrimination, Leechburg Area School District v. Human Rights Commission,* 19 Pa. Commw. Ct. 614, 339 A.2d 850 (1975), which held that a policy which limited maternity leave to married teachers, although facially differentiating only between married and unmarried female teachers, had the effect of creating a condition precedent to the eligibility of an employee for disability leave which must be met only by female (and no male) teachers.

180. Comment, *supra,* note 161, at 164, n. 76. In *Alexander v. Yale,* the plaintiff whose situation survived the motion to dismiss complained of a single incident. 459 F. Supp. 1 (D. Conn. 1977).

181. Susan Brownmiller, "Speaking Out on Prostitution," from a paper delivered to the New York State Legislature, in Anne Koedt, Ellen Levine, Anita Rapone, eds., *Radical Feminism* (New York: Quadrangle Books, 1973), at 76. One example of such a case did not find sex discrimination. The plaintiff alleged she was fired as a cocktail waitress because she was too flat-

chested and refused to pad her breasts so that they would be partially exposed. She complained to the New York State Human Rights Commission that the shapely bust requirement was arbitrary in relation to her duties as a waitress and reflected stereotyped roles and demands of women to appear as sex symbols. The unsuccessfully asserted discrimination was requiring the women to conform to a standard of "sex appeal." *State Division on Human Rights v. Indian Valley Realty Corporation,* No. CS 21209-70 (State Human Rights Appeal Board), *determination confirmed,* 38 App. Div. 2d 890, 330 N.Y.S. 2d 320 (1972).

182. [1973] EEOC Decisions (CCH) ¶ 6321 (1971); [1973] EEOC Decisions (CCH) ¶ 6346 (1972).

183. [1973] EEOC Decisions (CCH) ¶ 6145 (1970).

184. [1973] EEOC Decisions (CCH) ¶ 6160 (1970).

185. *Id.*

186. [1973] EEOC Decisions (CCH) ¶ 6324 (1971).

187. [1973] EEOC Decisions (CCH) ¶ 6100 (1970). Similarly, where whites have been harassed in the same way as blacks, no matter how oppressive the conduct, it is not considered discrimination on the basis of race. In assigning extra work, see [1973] EEOC Decisions (CCH) ¶ 6045 (1969).

188. 454 F.2d 234 (5th Cir. 1971), *cert. denied,* 406 U.S. 957 (1972). The court denied a motion by the plaintiffs asking to limit the investigative scope of the EEOC on the ground the Commission was seeking evidence of an employment practice, verbal abuse, not proscribed by Title VII. The complainant, allegedly discriminated against "because of my natural origin Spanish surnamed American," alleged verbal abuse by the seven "Caucasian females" with whom she worked and firing due to the friction. Characterizing the cause of action, Judge Goldberg said: "Time was when employment discrimination tended to be viewed as a series of isolated and distinguishable events, manifesting itself, for example, in an employer's practices of hiring, firing and promoting. But today employment discrimination is a far more complex and pervasive phenomenon, as the nuances and subtleties of discriminatory employment practices are no longer confined to bread and butter issues." *Id.,* at 238.

189. *Id.*

190. [1973] EEOC Decisions (CCH) ¶ 6354 (1972).

191. [1973] EEOC Decisions (CCH) ¶ 6376 (1972).

192. [1973] EEOC Decisions (CCH) ¶ 6289 (1971). In this case, whites were also verbally harassed, but the black worker was called a "civil rightser" and a "troublemaker" for filing a complaint with the EEOC, told she was "becoming militant" and should "count her blessings."

193. [1973] EEOC Decisions (CCH) ¶ 6346 (1972).

194. [1973] EEOC Decisions (CCH) ¶ 6290 (1971).

195. Rosabeth M. Kanter, *Men and Women of the Corporation* (New York: Basic Books, 1977).

196. [1973] EEOC Decisions (CCH) ¶ 6315 (1971).

CHAPTER 7

1. Quoted in Studs Terkel, *Working* (New York: Avon, 1974), at 58, 59, 61.

2. Susan Griffin, "Rape: The All-American Crime," in Mary Vetterling-Braggin, Frederick A. Elliston, and Jane English, eds., *Feminism and Philosophy* (Totowa, New Jersey: Littlefield, Adams & Co., 1977), at 331.

3. Susan Brownmiller, *Against Our Will: Men, Women and Rape* (New York: Bantam Books, Inc., 1976).

4. Lorenne M. G. Clark and Debra J. Lewis, *Rape: The Price of Coercive Sexuality* (Toronto, Canada: The Women's Press, 1977), at 167.

5. Carolyn M. Shafer and Marilyn Frye, "Rape and Respect," in Vetterling-Braggin, *supra*, note 2, at 340.

6. Susan Rae Peterson, "Coercion and Rape: The State as a Male Protection Racket," in Vetterling-Braggin, *supra*, note 2, at 364.

7. This is especially apparent throughout Brownmiller, *supra*, note 3; see, for example, 283 and 436.

8. This position presumes that the standard definition of consent is meaningful. Brownmiller is particularly illustrative. Never is it asked whether, under conditions of male supremacy, the notion of consent has any real meaning for women. At most, Brownmiller refers to factors of "authority" that disable a woman from withholding consent (as in "dating rape," *supra*, note 2, at 284). Consent is not scrutinized to see whether it is a structural fiction to legitimize the real coercion built into the normal social definitions of heterosexual intercourse. Since rape is ultimately *unwanted* intercourse—this is what the presence of physical force is there to prove—is this not the whole issue? Without it, the presumed split between rape and normal sexual behavior supports the very system of existing law and ideology that the book purports to challenge. If consent is not normally given but taken, it makes no sense to define rape as different in kind. To do so sets women up to fail in accusations of rape when they cannot prove that this situation appears different from most heterosexual encounters. Brownmiller's posture on this crucial issue may, in addition, account for the acceptance of *Against Our Will*. It allows the reader to be suitably horrified at rape—in this the book makes a major contribution—without ever questioning his own potential complicity. Rape is defined in terms far removed from the everyday experience of most readers. They need never confront whether women have a chance, structurally speaking and as a normal matter, even to consider whether they want to have sex or not.

9. The discussion of this point is especially clear in Clark and Lewis, *supra*, note 4, at 144 and 150.

10. Clark and Lewis, *supra*, note 4, at 94.

11. Psychodynamic parallels between victims of incest, of sexual harassment, and rape suggest that intimate violation of women by men should be considered a unified set of events, especially where women's collaboration in their own sexual violation is coerced by other forms of social power wielded by men. "Having been frequently obliged to exchange sexual services for protection and care," one clinical study of incest concludes, "women are in a position to understand the harmful effects of introducing sex into a relationship where there is a vast inequality of power." Judith Herman and Lisa Hirschman, "Father-Daughter Incest," *Signs: Journal of Women in Culture and Society*, vol. 2, no. 4 (Summer 1977), at 735–756. In incest, as in sexual harassment, the overwhelming predominance of instances involve a male perpetrator and female victim, *id.*, at 736. Behavior ranges in coerciveness from "the affectionate through the seductive to the overtly sexual," *id.*, at 742. Secrecy is used in both to coerce a sense of complicity, producing guilt at the thought of exposure. Beating and rape often accompany refusal to participate. Characteristics are constant across classes. Victims tend to "tune out" the whole thing or pretend that nothing is happening, *id.*, at 474, and identify with the aggressor. Professionals deny the existence of the phenomenon, blaming the victim for seductiveness. Perpetrator, doctor, psychotherapist, and judge alike deny that any real harm has been done to the victim. Given these striking similarities, the differences also bear comment. Incest is often in the context of a caring relationship; it is the sexual aspect that is forced. It is unclear if the sex would be experienced as a form of love were it not thought of as wrong. In rape, by contrast, the sex would be considered all right were it not for the force. Sexual harassment at work may be thought of as a kind of cross between the two. The sex itself is not strictly prohibited as between these parties; often there is a caring relation, at least a bond of a sort; but the sex is not wanted, is often forced, although often the *consent* is forced, as in incest. Also like incest, sexual harassment may for a time give the woman a sense of her value or a recognition as a person that the relationship otherwise lacks, even as she feels used and degraded.

12. Some other writers' work can be read as tending in this direction. See Diana E. H. Russell, *The Politics of Rape* (New York: Stein & Day, 1975); Andrea Medea and Kathleen Thompson, *Against Rape* (New York: Farrar, Straus & Giroux, 1974), and, to some extent, Pamela Foa, "What's Wrong with Rape," in Vetterling-Braggin, *supra*, note 2, at 347–359.

13. Shafer and Frye reveal more than they realize (or pursue) when they observe, "rape is a man's act, whether it is a male or a female man and whether it is a man relatively permanently or relatively temporarily; and

being raped is a woman's experience, whether it is a female or a male woman and whether it is a woman relatively permanently or relatively temporarily . . . " *supra,* note 5, at 334. This is the social gender argument in pure form. Given the ways sex roles have defined sexuality and distributed control over material life, sexual harassment could be argued, within the inequality perspective, to be an act of the male gender, whether done by a biological male or female. Being sexually subjected could be argued to be a woman's experience, whether the victim is a woman or a man.

APPENDIX A

1. EEOC Decision 76-67.

2. Sections 703 (a) (1) and (2) of Title VII, 42 U.S.C. § 2000e-2 (a)(1) and (2).

3. *Krause v. Sacramento Inn,* 479 F.2d 988 (9th Cir. 1973).

4. *Planchet v. New Hampshire Hospital,* 115 N.H. 361, 341 A.2d 267 (N.H. 1975).

5. *Singer v. Mahoning County Board of Mental Retardation,* 379 F. Supp. 986 (N.D. Ohio 1974).

6. 29 C.F.R. §1604.4(a); EEOC Decision No. 71-2678; *Gillin v. Federal Paper Board Co. Inc.,* 479 F.2d 97 (2d Cir. 1973); *Sprogis v. United Air Lines, Inc.,* 444 F.2d 1194, 1197–1198 (7th Cir.), *cert. denied,* 404 U.S. 991 (1971).

7. *Willingham v. Macon Tel. Pub. Co.,* 507 F.2d 1084 (5th Cir. 1975).

8. *Schattman v.·Texas Employment Commission,* 330 F. Supp. 328 (W.D. Tex. 1971), *rev'd. on other grounds,* 459 F.2d 32 (5th Cir. 1972), *cert. denied,* 409 U.S. 1107, *rehearing denied,* 410 U.S. 959 (1973).

9. *Wells v. Frontier Air Lines,* 381 F. Supp. 818 (N.D. Tex. 1974).

10. 400 U.S. 542 (1971); *Sprogis v. United Air Lines,* 444 F.2d 1194 (7th Cir. 1971), *cert. denied,* 404 U.S. 991 (1971), held that it was sex discrimination to require stewardesses, and not require male employees, to be unmarried. But *cf. Cooper v. Delta Air Lines, Inc.,* 274 F. Supp. 781 (E.D. La. 1967) and the unemployment case applying it, *Cooper v. Doyal,* 205 So.2d 59 (La., 1967). On a non-Title VII ground, *Cirino v. Walsh,* 66 Misc.2d 450, 321 N.Y.S. 2d 493 (Sup. Ct. 1971) held motherhood of an illegitimate child a sex discriminatory reason for an employment deprivation.

11. *Weinberger v. Weisenfeld,* 420 U.S. 636 (1975); *Califano v. Goldfarb,* 430 U.S. 199 (1977).

12. 42 U.S.C. § 2000e-2 provides, at subsection (a)(2)(e), "Notwithstanding any other provision of this subchapter (1) it shall not be an unlawful employment practice for an employer to hire and employ employees . . . on the basis of his . . . sex . . . in those certain instances where . . . sex . . . is a bona fide occupational qualification reasonably necessary to the normal operation of

that particular business or enterprise...." 29 C.F.R. § 1604.2 (a)(1) and (2) interprets the BFOQ. For a typical judicial interpretation of "necessary to safe and efficient operation," see *Robinson v. P. Lorillard Corp.*, 444 F.2d 791, 798 (4th Cir.), *cert. dismissed*, 404 U.S. 1006 (1971).

13. Pages 229–31, *infra*, discuss this question.

14. *Donohue v. Shoe Corporation of America*, 337 F. Supp. 1357 (C.D. Cal. 1972); *Aros v. McDonnell Douglas Corp.*, 348 F. Supp. 661 (C.D. Cal. 1972); *Roberts v. General Mills, Inc.*, 337 F. Supp. 1055 (N.D. Ohio 1971); *Willingham v. Macon Telegraph Pub. Co.*, 482 F.2d 535 (5th Cir. 1973), are examples.

15. *Fagan v. National Cash Register*, 481 F.2d 1115 (D.C. Cir. 1973); *Wells v. Aetna Casualty & Surety Co.*, 6 F.E.P. Cases 826 (D.D.C. 1973); *Dodge v. Grant Food, Inc.*, 488 F.2d 1333 (D.C. Cir. 1973); *Baker v. California Land Title Co.*, 507 F.2d 895 (9th Cir. 1974), *cert. denied*, 422 U.S. 1046 (1975); *Thomas v. Firestone Tire & Rubber Co.*, 392 F. Supp. 373 (N.D. Tex. 1975); *Wamsganz v. Missouri Pacific Railroad Co.*, 391 F. Supp. 306 (E.D. Mo. 1975); *Bujel v. Borman Food Stores, Inc.*, 384 F. Supp. 141 (E.D. Mich. 1974), are examples.

16. This is a phrase of the court in *Willingham v. Macon Telegraph*, 507 F.2d 1084 (5th Cir. 1975). (This citation is on rehearing, subsequent to the result cited *supra*, at note 14, for the opposite formulation of the same issue.) The phrase was adopted in *McConnell v. Mercantile National Bank at Dallas*, 389 F. Supp. 594, 596 (N.D. Tex. 1975).

17. *Rafford v. Randle Eastern Ambulance Service, Inc.*, 348 F. Supp. 316, 320 (S.D. Fla. 1972).

18. *Id.*

19. This includes the Court of Appeals in *Gilbert v. General Electric Co.*, 375 F. Supp. 367 (E.D. Va. 1974), *aff'd*, 519 F.2d 661 (4th Cir. 1975) and *Wetzel v. Liberty Mutual*, 511 F.2d 199 (3d Cir. 1975), argued at the same time as *Gilbert*.

20. Examples include: *Holthaus v. Compton and Sons, Inc.*, 514 F.2d 651 (8th Cir. 1975); *Liss v. School District of City of Ladue*, 396 F. Supp. 1035 (E.D. Mo. 1975) (for disability following birth of child); *Zichy v. City of Philadelphia*, 392 F. Supp. 338 (E.D. Pa. 1975); *Sale v. Waverly-Shell Rock Board of Education*, 390 F. Supp. 784 (N.D. Iowa 1975); *Singer v. Mahoning County Board of Mental Retardation*, 379 F. Supp. 986 (N.D. Ohio 1974) (compulsory maternity leave violates Title VII); *Communication Workers of America AFL-CIO v. American Tel. & Tel. Co. Long Lines Department*, 379 F. Supp. 679 (S.D.N.Y. 1974) (where pleaded under Title VII and equal protection, subsequent to *Geduldig* allowed leave to replead). This is also the position of the EEOC Guidelines, which provide not only that pregnancy is not a valid ground for discharge or for refusal to hire, but also that pregnancy-related disabilities must be treated like any other temporary disability for all job-related purposes, including sick leave, sick pay, medical and health insurance, and any disability income protection plan. 29 C.F.R. Section 1604.10.

21. 416 F.2d 1257, 1259 (5th Cir. 1969). A similar view, quoting the referenced language, was adopted in *Cohen v. Chesterfield,* first in Judge Haynesworth's dissent, then in his opinion for the majority on rehearing *en banc.* 4
FEP Cases 1237 (4th Cir. 1972), *rev'd,* 474 F.2d 395 (4th Cir. 1973), *rev'd,* 414
U.S. 632 (1974). That *Cohen* arose under 42 U.S.C. Section 1983 does not
change its relevance for the argument being made here. Judge Haynesworth
argued: "We are not accustomed to thinking, as sex classifications, of statutes
making it a crime for a man forcefully to ravish a woman or, without force,
carnally to know a female child under a certain age. Military regulations
requiring all personnel to be clean shaven may be suspect on other grounds,
but not because they have no application to females. Prohibition or licensing
of prostitution is a patent regulation of sexual activity, the burden of which
falls solely on females, but it has not been thought an invidious sex classification. What of regulations requiring adult women sunning themselves on a
public beach to keep their breasts covered? Is that an invidious discrimination
based upon sex, a denial of equal protection because the flat and hairy chest
of a male lawfully may be exposed?" 4 FEP Cases, at 1241.

To the extent they impose a detriment upon one sex, many of these
classifications have increasingly become questioned as unlawfully sex-based.
The passage of state equal rights amendments has been seen to make necessary the sex-neutral rewriting of rape and sexual assault laws, a fact which
would suggest that a rape law allowing only a male perpetrator and a female
victim were not so obviously not a "sex classification" in the minds of many
state legislators. Regulations about beards, in and out of the military, and
about hair length in the military for women as well as for men, have been the
subject of extensive litigation, raising race discrimination (wearing Afro hair
styles) as well as sex discrimination issues. The argument is exactly that, with
regard to hair, the standards are different on the basis of race or sex, to the
detriment of one group. Prostitution laws which penalize the seller (female)
but let the buyer (male) go free have come under successful attack as sex
discriminatory in effect. *Divoky et al. v. Scott et al.* (San Francisco Superior
Court, unreported, 1976, prostitution law is sex discriminatory); *Reimer v.
Jensen* (Alameda County Superior Court No. 445371-9, male customers must
be arrested and jailed with female prostitutes or sex discrimination results,
unreported, 1976). In a recent case in California the ACLU is contesting on
the very grounds suggested the local prosecution of two women for sunning
their breasts. *People v. St. James and Johnston,* Los Angeles Municipal Court
(unreported) (1977).

22. *Cerra v. East Stroudsburg Area School District,* 450 Pa. 207, 213, 299 A.2d
277, 280 (1973) (under the Pennsylvania Human Rights Act) (disallowing
dismissal of public school teacher for her failure to resign after fifth month of
pregnancy as required by school board regulations). See also *Hanson v. Hutt,*

83 Wash.2d 195, 517 P.2d 599 (1974) (sex discrimination, Equal Protection, because "only women become pregnant" and "it is equally clear that only women must remain barren to be eligible for . . . unemployment compensation," *id.*, at 198, under a statutory exclusion of pregnancy-related unemployment from compensation); *Cleveland Board of Education v. Lafleur*, 414 U.S. 632 (1974), (brought under 42 U.S.C. §1983, held mandatory leave for pregnant teachers violates the due process clause of the Fourteenth Amendment before Title VII covered schoolteachers).

23. *Newmon v. Delta Air Lines, Inc.*, 374 F. Supp. 238 (N.D. Ga. 1973).

24. *Godwin v. Patterson*, 363 F. Supp. 238, 240 (M.D. Ala. 1973).

25. 4 FEP Cases 1237, 1240, (4th Cir. 1972), *rev'd*, 474 F.2d 395 (4th Cir. 1973).

26. 429 U.S. 125, 146 (1976).

27. *Id.*, at 130, n. 9, 139, n. 17.

28. *E.g.*, *Geduldig v. Aiello*, 419 U.S. 484 (1974).

29. *Supra*, note 12.

30. Brown, Emerson, Falk, and Freedman, "The Equal Rights Amendment: A Constitutional Basis for Equal Rights for Women," 80 *Yale Law Journal* 871, 893–896 (1971), and discussion at 114–16, *supra*.

31. *Reed v. Reed*, 404 U.S. 71 (1971).

32. Although the "job-relatedness" test is common in race cases, where the BFOQ is not available, it seems to be less used in sex cases, where the explicit standard has more often been that a sex-based differentiation must be either a BFOQ or discriminatory. An implicit argument of job-relatedness *short of* asserting a BFOQ, however, is revealed in cases such as *Sprogis v. United Air Lines*, 444 F.2d 1194 (7th Cir.), *cert. denied*, 404 U.S. 991 (1971), where the court, rejecting a hiring standard that required stewardesses, but not stewards, to be unmarried, held that marriage had nothing legitimately to do with the duties of the job, so to have a different standard for women and men, each married, was sex-based discrimination. This appears to allow for the possibility that a criterion which discriminated by sex might be justified if it were proven job-related, although falling short of a BFOQ standard.

33. The Equal Employment Opportunity Commission's "Guidelines on Discrimination because of Sex" at 29 C.F.R. Section 1604.2 (a)(1)(ii) state that the BFOQ exception will not apply to "the refusal to hire an individual based on stereotyped characterizations of the sexes. . . . The principle of nondiscrimination requires that individuals be considered on the basis of individual capacities and not on the basis of any characteristics generally attributed to the group." The leading case is *Weeks v. Southern Bell Telephone and Telegraph Company*, 408 F.2d 228, 235–236 (5th Cir. 1969); see also *Bowe v. Colgate-Palmolive Company*, 416 F.2d 711, 717–718 (7th Cir. 1969), and *Cheatwood v.*

South Central Bell Telephone and Telegraph Company, 303 F. Supp. 754 (M.D. Ala. 1969).

34. Brown *et al., supra,* note 30.

35. *Weeks v. Southern Bell Telephone,* 408 F.2d 228, (5th Cir. 1969).

36. 442 F.2d 385, 389 (emphasis in original).

37. *Id.,* at 388, "We begin with the proposition that the use of the word 'necessary' in Section 703(e) requires that we apply a business *necessity* not a business *convenience* test." For a treatment of "business necessity" in the context of job qualifications (here, seniority) created by prior employer discrimination in a racial context, see *Local 189, United Papermakers and Paperworkers, AFL-CIO, CLC v. United States, (Mitchell)* 416 F.2d 980 (5th Cir. 1969), *cert. denied,* 397 U.S. 919 (1970).

38. This issue has been litigated most often in the context of state statutes which prohibit, on their face, women from lifting certain weights, working certain hours, and so on. Such statutes have been widely held to be sex stereotypes and not to create BFOQ exceptions. *LeBlanc v. Southern Bell Telephone and Telegraph Company,* 333 F. Supp. 602 (E.D. La. 1971), *aff'd,* 460 F.2d 1228 (5th Cir.), *cert. denied,* 409 U.S. 990 (1972): "tread-worn [*sic*] assertions of the state that 'there are differences between the sexes . . . sociological, physiological and biological . . . which justify rational generic classification,' (brief at 5), and that a prohibition of women working in excess of 8 hours a day or 48 hours a week is such a rational classification. We join with the courts across the nation in condemning such a 'stereotyped classification' " as failing to constitute a BFOQ and as an unlawful employment practice. 333 F. Supp. 608. See also 29 C.F.R. § 1604.2(b); *Rosenfeld v. Southern Pacific Company,* 293 F. Supp. 1219 (C.D. Cal. 1968); *Richards v. Griffith Rubber Mills,* 300 F. Supp. 338 (D. Or. 1969); *Caterpillar Tractor Co. v. Grabiec,* 317 F. Supp. 1304 (S.D. Ill. 1970); *Local 246, Utility Workers Union of America, AFL-CIO v. Southern California Edison Co.,* 320 F. Supp. 1262 (C.D. Cal. 1970) and a leading case, *Ridinger v. General Motors Corp.,* 325 F. Supp. 1089 (S.D. Ohio 1971). In *Dothard v. Rawlinson,* however, male sex was a BFOQ for prison guard jobs where a height and weight standard was set by statute, on the grounds that women are likely to be sexually attacked by prisoners, disrupting prison discipline. 433 U.S. 321 (1977).

39. *Manhart,* at the district court level, noted the intent of the section to strike at an "entire spectrum of disparate treatment of individual men and women resulting from sex stereotypes," finding it sex discrimination to require females to contribute more to a retirement plan, although actuarial tables show women as a class live longer than men. *Manhart v. City of Los Angeles Department of Water and Power,* 387 F. Supp. 980, 984 (C.D. Cal. 1975). See also *Sprogis v. United Air Lines, Inc.,* 444 F.2d at 1198 and, implicitly, the approach in *Pond v. Braniff Airways,* 500 F.2d 161 (5th Cir. 1974).

Index